THEY KNEW THEY WERE PILGRIMS

THEY KNEW THEY WERE PILGRIMS

Plymouth Colony and the Contest for American Liberty

JOHN G. TURNER

Yale

UNIVERSITY PRESS

New Haven and London

Published with assistance from the Ronald and Betty Miller Turner
Publication Fund, and from the foundation established in memory of
Amasa Stone Mather of the Class of 1907, Yale College.

Yale University Press books may be purchased in quantity for
educational, business, or promotional use. For information,
please e-mail sales.press@yale.edu (U.S. office) or sales@yaleup.co.uk
(U.K. office).

Set in Janson type by Integrated Publishing Solutions.
Printed in the United States of America.

Library of Congress Control Number: 2019948863
ISBN 978-0-300-22550-1 (hardcover : alk. paper)

A catalogue record for this book is available from the British Library.

This paper meets the requirements of ANSI/NISO Z39.48-1992
(Permanence of Paper).

10 9 8 7 6 5 4 3 2 1

Contents

Acknowledgments

Even when a book bears a single name, scholarship is by its nature a collaborative enterprise, building on the work of women and men from the distant past and relying on the help of archivists, librarians, and colleagues. Over the course of this project, many institutions made their documents and photographs available to me. I am especially grateful to Carolle Morini of the Boston Athenæum; Jay Moschella of the Boston Public Library; Lisa Lucassen of the Leiden Regional Archives; Marjory O'Toole of the Little Compton Historical Society; Elaine Heavey, Anna Clutterbuck-Cook, and Daniel Hinchen of the Massachusetts Historical Society; Mark Proknik of the New Bedford Whaling Museum; Donna Curtin of Pilgrim Hall; John R. Buckley of the Plymouth County Registry of Deeds; Douglas Mayo of the Rockefeller Library at Colonial Williamsburg; and Danielle Kovacs of the University of Massachusetts (Amherst) Special Collections.

Many individuals gamely read drafts or partial drafts of this book: Sue Allan, Jim Baker, Jeremy Dupertuis Bangs, Alex Beam, Margaret Bendroth, Charlotte Carrington-Farmer, David Hall, Mack Holt, David Lupher, John McWilliams, Lincoln Mullen, Michael Paulick, Paula Peters, Adrian Weimer, and Michael Winship. Other people who provided invaluable advice and assistance include Francis Bremer, Jeff Cooper, John Craig, Jaap Jacobs, Thomas Kidd, Merja Kytö, Andrew Lipman, Jo Loosemore, Vicki Oman, Richard Pickering, Jenny Pulsipher, Anne Reilly, David Silverman, Baird Tipson, and Walter Powell. Andrew C. Smith patiently worked through many iterations of the maps with me.

One of the best parts of researching any subject is the chance to meet knowledgeable and fascinating people, both in person and remotely. One particular pleasure in working on this book was the opportunity to interact with Jeremy Bangs, the director of the Leiden American Pilgrim Museum and the foremost expert on the Pilgrims and the colony they founded. This project was made easier by Jeremy's many publications, including his transcriptions of Plymouth Colony records. Also, Jeremy patiently fielded queries, deciphered difficult handwriting, and was willing to push back against some of my interpretive judgments. I also enjoyed a delightful tour of Scrooby, Gainsborough, and other locations with Sue Allan, who generously shared advice, documents, and transcriptions. Michael Paulick likewise shared many transcriptions and documents pertaining to Robert Cushman's years in Canterbury.

The British Association of American Studies and the Eccles Centre for American Studies provided me with a fellowship that enabled a month's research at the British Library and other London repositories. I am also grateful for a grant received from George Mason University's College of Humanities and Social Sciences. The completion of this book in time for the four-hundredth anniversary of the *Mayflower* crossing was made possible by a Public Scholar fellowship from the National Endowment of the Humanities. Any views, findings, conclusions, or recommendations expressed in this book do not necessarily reflect those of the National Endowment of the Humanities.

Two individuals supported this project at an early stage: my agent, Giles Anderson; and my editor, Jennifer Banks. I am thankful to both of them.

John Robinson, the Leiden pastor to the Pilgrims, once suggested that "wiving and thriving" go hand in hand. He was correct. For her patience with this project, and for our lives together, I am grateful to my wife, Elissa, the best of wives and the best of readers.

Notes on the Text

TWO PARTLY ANACHRONISTIC TERMS feature prominently in this book. The *Mayflower* passengers and the other early English settlers of Plymouth Colony did not understand themselves as *the* Pilgrims. That label emerged around the turn of the nineteenth century. The colonists, however, did think of themselves as "pilgrims." For them, as for many other Protestants, all Christians were "strangers and pilgrims on the earth" (Hebrews 11:13), a phrase that appears in the colony's first promotional tract. With these qualifications in mind, for reasons of familiarity I refer to the early English settlers of Plymouth Colony as the Pilgrims.

Seventeenth-century sources most typically use place-specific names such as Pokanoket, Nauset, and Patuxet for the Native communities and peoples of present-day southeastern Massachusetts. Although variations of the term *Wampanoag* appear in some sources, only later did Wampanoag become the most common designation for these communities and those on the islands to the south of Cape Cod. Again, for reasons of familiarity, I use Wampanoag as a way to discuss the Native communities that found themselves within Plymouth Colony's patent.

For English names, as in the cases of John Myles and Myles Standish, I have spelled names as individuals signed them (or signed them most frequently) or as they appear most commonly in seventeenth-century documents. Few seventeenth-century Native men and women left behind signatures. English records render their names many different ways. I have selected a consistent spelling.

In March 1621, Pilgrim governor John Carver and his Po-kanoket counterpart formed an alliance. The Pilgrims called the Pokanoket sachem by his title *Massasoit*, the Native word for "great leader." The sachem's Native name at the time is unknown, but he later adopted the name Ousamequin, meaning Yellow Feather. I refer to him as Massasoit when discussing Plymouth Colony's first decade, then introduce the name Ousamequin in the 1630s. Ousamequin's sons Wamsutta and Metacom took on the names Alexander and Philip, respectively, shortly after their father's death. Most English documents use Philip; some deeds identify the sachem as Philip alias Metacom. For reasons of familiarity and clarity, I refer to him as Philip. While names matter, I am confident that Philip alias Meta-com cared far more about English encroachment on his land and authority than about what the English called him.

During the seventeenth century, English people used the "Old Style" Julian calendar in which the new year began on March 25. At the time, the Julian calendar was also ten days behind the "New Style" or Gregorian calendar. The Pilgrims first came ashore at the site of their settlement on December 11, according to the Julian cal-endar. Since the late eighteenth century, groups in Plymouth have commemorated the event with an annual Forefathers' Day celebra-tion. For the first such celebration in 1769, the Old Colony Club did not adjust the date correctly and held its event on December 22. When the Pilgrim Society began its own commemoration in 1820, its organizers calculated the date to December 21. The error gives individuals two chances to celebrate rather than one. In order to avoid less fortuitous confusion, I have adjusted the year for dates between January 1 and March 24, while I leave the day unchanged in the text. In the notes, I give both years separated by a slash.

Quotations from the Bible are from the Geneva translation un-less otherwise indicated.

I have modernized the spelling and punctuation in quotations and have expanded abbreviations.

THEY KNEW THEY WERE PILGRIMS

Introduction

AMERICANS LEARN ABOUT THE Pilgrims when they are children. In elementary schools across the country, late November has been a time for Pilgrim hats and Indian headdresses. Along the way, Americans absorb elements of the Pilgrim myth: a ship, a compact, a rock, a winter of death and disease, a harvest, and a Thanksgiving turkey meal. It is a heartwarming story about two peoples feasting together instead of fighting each other.

There is also an alternative, more dispiriting history, a story of betrayal and theft. The Pilgrims made a treaty and alliance with the Indians, then took their land and killed or enslaved those who resisted. Those Native communities that survived found themselves reduced to small, impoverished enclaves. In this line of thought, the ongoing American adulation of the *Mayflower* passengers is offensive. Late November is a time for mourning, not a time for giving thanks.

They Knew They Were Pilgrims includes aspects of the above stories but also introduces other narratives. This is a history of the peoples who lived in Plymouth Colony (alternatively New Plymouth, later known within Massachusetts as the Old Colony) from the English and Dutch events that led to its 1620 founding until its 1691 incorporation into a larger Province of Massachusetts Bay.[1] In its pages, readers will encounter famous men such as Governor William Bradford and Massasoit Ousamequin but also meet less familiar

I

individuals: Awashonks, a female sachem who preserved a Native community for two decades amid dispossession and war; William Vassall, who established a second church within a single town and contended for religious liberty before colonial and English courts; and James Cudworth, a Plymouth Colony magistrate who lost his position when he defended persecuted Quakers. In his own history, Bradford promised to proceed "in a plain style, with singular regard unto the simple truth in all things."[2] Plymouth Colony's history, though, is not plain, singular, or simple.

During the early years of the American republic, ministers, politicians, and historians lionized the Pilgrims. Timothy Dwight, John Quincy Adams, and George Bancroft drew straight lines from the Mayflower Compact to the Declaration of Independence and the Constitutional Convention, making the Pilgrims the heroic progenitors of democracy and republicanism. Then, in the mid- to late nineteenth century, Americans came to associate the Pilgrims with an annual observance of a late-November Thanksgiving Day. The holiday further enhanced interest in the *Mayflower* passengers, now the most famous colonists in the history of what became the United States.

Despite the ongoing popular appeal of the Pilgrims, academic historians have largely ignored Plymouth Colony. When the mid-twentieth-century historian Perry Miller resuscitated an interest in New England puritanism, he concentrated on the more numerous, literary, and wealthy settlers of Massachusetts Bay. Plymouth makes no appearance at all in Miller's magisterial *New England Mind*. Apparently there were no Old Colony minds worth mentioning. In particular, Miller convinced generations of historians that the Pilgrim church exerted no influence on the broader development of New England Congregationalism. For example, historian of puritanism Theodore Dwight Bozeman dismissed Plymouth's congregation as "pathetically unimportant." If Plymouth Colony didn't matter for the development of New England religion, it obviously carried little weight in terms of politics or commerce. Samuel Eliot Morison, Perry Miller's colleague at Harvard, admired the Pilgrims and edited a popular edition of Bradford's history, but he conceded Plymouth's insignificance. "By any quantitative standard," he wrote, "[Plymouth] was one of the smallest, weakest, and least important of the English colonies." For the most part, therefore, historians set Plymouth aside once John Winthrop and his puritan flotilla reach Massachusetts Bay. Boston is the city on a hill, Plymouth a moribund backwater.[3]

Besides their place within American mythology and genealogy, then, do the Pilgrims and their colony matter? The *Mayflower* passengers and the other English settlers of Plymouth Colony had genuine accomplishments. The separatists among the *Mayflower* passengers transplanted a church in which laymen elected their officers and exercised discipline over each other. When they formed a government and made laws, Pilgrim leaders could not envision—and would not have favored—democracy as later Americans would understand it. Nevertheless, they established a political framework with a significant degree of participation and one that endured for nearly seventy years.

Plymouth Colony also matters in a very different respect. A few months after their 1620 landing, the Pilgrims established a mutual defense treaty with Massasoit. While this alliance initially benefited both English settlers and Wampanoags, the Pilgrims took steps to establish themselves as the foremost military power in the region. By the time of Massasoit's 1660 death, Plymouth's magistrates treated and mistreated the Wampanoags as their subjects. Settlers acquired Wampanoag land through purchase, pressure, and swindle. Eventually, sachems in the western portion of New Plymouth chose armed resistance over further dispossession and humiliation. The resulting King Philip's War (1675–78) shattered Native and English communities across New England.

Still, the merit of unearthing and narrating New Plymouth's history does not hinge only on the colony's grand significance or lack thereof. Rather, *They Knew They Were Pilgrims* uses Plymouth Colony as a fresh lens for examining the contested meaning of liberty in early New England. The English settlers who came to New Plymouth over the span of its seven-decade history shared a fierce commitment to liberty, but they understood it in a variety of often contradictory ways.

Prominent among these meanings were the many varieties of Christian liberty articulated by the colony's Protestant Christians. The majority of the Pilgrims were separatists, men and women who had entirely rejected the Church of England. They did so to reclaim what they understood as "the liberty of the gospel," their freedom to form their own churches and choose their own officers. These Pilgrim separatists embarked for North America because they wanted to preserve their liberty to worship God in accordance with their understanding of the Bible. "They knew they were pilgrims," wrote William Bradford. Even before John Bunyan further popularized the motif through *The Pilgrim's Progress*, many English Protestants understood their lives as spiritual pilgrimages, beset with temptations and afflictions but with the promise of eventual glory. Plymouth Colony's settlers disagreed among themselves, however, about the prescribed earthly course for this pilgrimage, in particular about what constituted the pure worship of God.[4]

Many settlers also favored "liberty of conscience," but this was another slippery phrase. Liberty of conscience sometimes simply meant that religious dissenters could opt out of established forms of worship, but it also could imply a fuller toleration of religious pluralism. Throughout most of Plymouth Colony's seventy-year history, magistrates did not force individuals to attend worship, join churches, or have their children baptized. In these significant respects, settlers enjoyed a certain amount of liberty of conscience. At the same time, dissenters did not possess the freedom to air their opinions or gather with like-minded men and women for their own religious exercises. Also, once Plymouth's government mandated that towns tax inhabitants to build Congregational churches and pay Congregational ministers, it did not exempt dissenters from these obligations. Quakers and some Baptists contended for a more complete religious toleration. They eventually gained the liberty to worship according to their own principles, but their struggle against church taxes continued long after New Plymouth's demise.

Some of the Pilgrims suffered persecution for their religious beliefs and practices in England. Once in charge of their own colony, however, they persecuted others. Plymouth's leaders banished a number of dissenters, and they whipped, imprisoned, and fined scores of Quakers. As the historian Alexandra Walsham observes of seventeenth-century Europeans more generally, "This apparent double standard was not rank hypocrisy." Like most of their contemporaries, Pilgrim leaders desired religious uniformity and understood Christian liberty as mandating very specific forms of worship, church government, and discipline. Until late in the seventeenth century, the main argument among European Christians was not whether there should be only one religious option, but what that option should be and how governments should penalize those who did not conform to it.[5]

Debates about liberty were as much about politics as religion. Building upon the ideals of the Mayflower Compact, Plymouth's settlers declared that "according to the free liberties" of England, they would not suffer any law or tax to be imposed on them except by their own consent. They also regarded annual elections and the right to a jury trial as fundamental liberties. Both in New England and old England, there was disagreement about who possessed these liberties and exactly what constituted consent, but there was a common vigilance against the arbitrary exercise of political power.[6] Towns resisted when New Plymouth's General Court ordered them to build meetinghouses or levy church taxes, and settlers protested when a crown-appointed governor imposed taxes on them without their consent.

Finally, there were English men and women who simply wanted the liberty to live as they pleased. These individuals wanted nothing to do with New England's churches or governments. If they criticized those institutions, or in other ways made themselves conspicuous, they suffered reprisals. Especially on the margins of the colony, though, settlers found the space to follow their own principles and pursuits.

When seventeenth-century Englishmen felt deprived of their liberties, they complained that they were being made slaves. It was a powerful argument because the English were well acquainted with slavery and servitude. As was the case in other colonies, Plymouth's settlers reduced people to various forms of bondage. Many English and some Irish men, women, and children came to the colony as indentured servants, and courts sometimes sentenced offenders to periods of servitude.

Even before the Pilgrims anchored off Cape Cod, moreover, Europeans had captured and enslaved dozens of Native people in the region. One of those victims, Tisquantum (or Squanto), was from the site of the Pilgrim settlement. While Plymouth's early leaders criticized the men who had mistreated Squanto, their descendants enslaved large numbers of Native men, women, and children, sometimes for a set number of years, but in many cases for life. Hundreds of Native slaves were exported, ending up in the Caribbean or across the Atlantic Ocean. By this time, Plymouth's English households also owned a small but significant number of African slaves. As in the rest of the transatlantic English world, liberty and bondage developed in tandem.

Over the course of the seventeenth century, New Plymouth's English settlers—and at times, the Native peoples and African Americans within its bounds—came to speak shared languages of liberty, but conflicts about the nature and extent of those liberties remained unresolved. They still are. Present-day Americans cherish liberty but disagree vehemently about its meaning. One person's religious liberty is, from another vantage point, a license to discriminate, and Americans have bitter arguments about who is entitled to the rights enshrined in the founding documents of the United States. Four centuries after the *Mayflower*, the history of the Pilgrims and Plymouth Colony points us back to earlier chapters in this contest for liberty.

CHAPTER ONE

The Lord's Free People

"LORD HAVE MERCY UPON US." *Kyrie eleison.* Since the early centuries of Christianity, worshippers have spoken and sung these Greek words in their liturgies. Familiar from their repetition in the Church of England's Book of Common Prayer, the words assumed a very different meaning when Robert Cushman tacked them on a church door.

Cushman was baptized in 1578 in the Kentish village of Rolvenden, about thirty miles southwest of Canterbury. Cushman's father was a farmer who left each of his sons ten pounds upon his 1586 death. His mother remarried the next year, buried her second husband two years later, and married for the third time in 1593.[1]

When he came of age, Cushman moved to Canterbury. In 1597, he became an apprentice to a grocer named George Masters. For several centuries, grocers had belonged to guilds, which protected their right to sell spices, confections, and sometimes medicines and tobacco. Cushman's inheritance provided the premium that persuaded Masters to engage him. In Canterbury, Masters had the exclusive right to make and sell tallow candles. "It is a nauseous greasy business," cautioned a mid-eighteenth-century manual on apprenticeships. Still, at least in Canterbury, completing an apprenticeship meant an opportunity to become a "freeman," someone with the right to practice a trade and participate in a community's civic life. Cushman could look forward to a future as a respectable tradesman.[2]

Outside of Cushman's christening, the deaths of his parents (his mother died in 1601), and the start of his apprenticeship, nothing is known about Cushman's life to this point. Men like Cushman usually appear in the historical record only if they got into trouble. Cushman did so in the fall of 1603, when he and several other young men wrote and posted "libels" on the doors of Canterbury churches. Their message was simple: "Lord have mercy upon us." The implication was that God needed to save his people from a corrupt church. A few years later, Cushman concluded that the Church of England was beyond rescue. The church-door libels were the first step that took Cushman to the Dutch Republic and then to Plymouth Colony.

Robert Cushman wasn't alone. In 1620, most of the adult passengers on the *Mayflower*—at least, those who were not servants—were separatists, men and women who had rejected the Church of England. Their stories began with small acts of puritan protest that eventually led them out of church and country.

Almost a century before the *Mayflower*, the English Reformation had begun with a messy double divorce: that of a king from his wife, and of a church from Rome. King Henry VIII wanted his marriage to Catherine of Aragon annulled. She had failed to bear him a son, and he was in love with another woman. Pope Clement VII rebuffed the king's request. With the support of English courts and lawmakers, Henry cast off Catherine and married Anne Boleyn. In 1534, Parliament declared Henry "the only supreme head on earth of the Church of England."

The long reign of Elizabeth, who became queen in 1558 after the death of her Catholic half sister Mary, gradually made England a resolutely Protestant country. At the same time, there were large numbers of Protestants unsatisfied with the extent of reform. With more than a hint of self-righteousness, these individuals often referred to themselves as the "godly." Their opponents derided them as "precisians" or "puritans." "The hotter sort of Protestants are called puritans," explained Percival Wiburn, himself a rather fiery minister. While puritans were hot about many different things, most rejected vestments (the robe, white linen surplice, and other priestly garments), the sign of the cross, and saints' days.[3] They associated such practices with the Catholic Church and contended that the Bible did not authorize them. Puritans were leery of prayer books altogether, believing that ministers should instead preach and pray according to their learning and the promptings of God's Spirit. Many puritans, finally, favored what became known as Presbyterianism. They wanted to replace England's bishops and church courts with an ecclesiastical government more akin to that of Geneva or Scotland, in which consistories and synods—comprised of ministers and elders—exercised discipline.

Around the turn of the seventeenth century, *puritan* became a common epithet in England. "A puritan," went one of many insults, "is such a one as loves God with all his soul, but hates his neighbor with all his heart." Neighbors who wanted to enjoy church fairs or a Sunday afternoon at a tavern resented godly attempts to do away with traditional forms of merriment. Playwrights such as Ben Jonson mercilessly skewered puritans as both busybodies and hypocrites. On the page and on the stage, puritans said grace until their food was ice cold, indulged until they became fat and flatulent, and used their conventicles as cover for orgies.[4]

Despite their differences, nearly all Protestants remained loyal to a single national church to which all men and women belonged and whose ministers baptized all children. Puritans insisted that they had no intention of abandoning the church that had nurtured their own faith. Even if they found certain ceremonies and practices abhorrent, even as they formed their own networks of preachers and clandestine gatherings, most of the godly waited and worked for the further reformation of England's church.

A small number of puritans, however, gave up. If other zealous reformers were the hotter sort of Protestant, separatists were the hottest. They wanted to tear down the Church of England and start from scratch. And they would not wait. Their Christian liberty hinged on their willingness to make an immediate separation.

Rooted in the writings of the Apostle Paul, the idea of liberty was central to the thought of the Protestant reformers. For Paul, Christians were freed from sin, Satan, and death not through obedience to the law but by their faith in God's gracious gift of salvation through Jesus Christ. When certain church leaders insisted that non-Jewish men who converted to Christianity be circumcised, Paul objected. "Stand fast therefore," he wrote, "in the liberty wherewith Christ hath made us free" (Galatians 5:1). In a very different context, Martin Luther argued that "a Christian is a perfectly free lord of all, subject to none." Luther maintained that a Christian needed "no works to make him righteous and save him." Christians could not earn their salvation through scrupulous fidelity to the law or any other ecclesiastical requirements. It was God's gift, received through faith. John Calvin fully agreed with his Wittenberg counterpart that Christian freedom was "a thing of prime necessity," a foundation of the Protestant insistence that God justified human beings on the basis of their faith in Christ.[5]

For Luther and Calvin, as for Paul, Christian liberty was not an individual freedom to do what one wished. Rather, liberty undergirded the cohesion of the community. "Use not your liberty as an occasion unto the flesh," Paul warned, "but by love serve one another" (Galatians 5:13). Luther emphasized that Christians were freed precisely so that they could follow the law that had previously condemned them. "A Christian," he wrote, "is a perfectly dutiful servant of all, subject to all." Freedom and subjection went hand in hand. Nor was Christian liberty the license to follow one's personal convictions when it came to religious belief and practice. Instead, the conscience should remain—in Luther's words—"captive to the Word of God." Formerly bound to Satan, individuals whom God had liberated were now bound to Christ, and to the teachings of their church. As the historian Steven Ozment explains, Protestants had only "the right to dissent from Rome and to agree with Wittenberg," or with Geneva if they followed Calvin.[6]

All puritans contended that the work of liberating England's church from the yoke of Antichrist remained very incomplete. While English separatists echoed other puritans on most matters of doctrine and ceremony, they articulated some distinctive ideas about Christian liberty and they advanced them with urgency. For separatists, the idea of an inclusive, national church was a scandal. Bishops and monarchs had herded the wicked and the righteous alike into an impure institution. Separatists taught that church membership should be a voluntary act by which Christians covenanted with each other to follow the dictates of the Bible. Furthermore, once they formed their own congregations, Christians possessed the free-dom to elect their own officers and to exercise church discipline. Without these liberties, Christians remained in bondage, whether to monarchs, magistrates, bishops, or synods. The Pilgrims would take this particular version of Christian liberty to New England.

Separatists had advanced these arguments for decades and had lit-tle to show for it except a stable of martyrs.[7] In or around 1581, the ministers Robert Browne and Robert Harrison concluded that the Church of England was beyond reformation and formed their own independent and illegal congregation in Norwich. While Browne took pains to stress that he fully supported the queen's civil power, he denied that she or any other political leaders held authority over the church. "To compel religion," Browne insisted, "to plant churches by power, and to force a submission to ecclesiastical government by laws and penalties belongeth not to them." Christ was the church's only king and head. As far as the queen and her bishops were con-cerned, this was a simple case of sedition. Browne and Harrison wisely moved with their followers to Middelburg in the Nether-lands, but before their emigration, Browne had preached to groups of like-minded men and women in the Suffolk market town of Bury St. Edmunds. On the basis of a June 1583 royal proclamation, the authorities burned books written by Browne and Harrison and hanged two Bury men—a tailor and a shoemaker—who defended the condemned writings. Although Browne later returned to En-gland and its national church, English separatists became known as "Brownists."[8]

A few years later, the authorities raided a separatist congrega-tion in London and arrested twenty-one men and women. More than a dozen separatist prisoners died in jail, but the ministers John Greenwood and Henry Barrow lived long enough to write lengthy defenses of their principles. For Greenwood and Barrow, the Bible identified the true church as "the city, house, temple, and mountain of the eternal God." It was an enclosed vineyard or garden, an "or-chard of pomegranates," the bride of Christ, the society with which God covenanted to give his peace, love, salvation, presence, power, and protection. A properly organized congregation was something "ravishing" for Christians to behold. There was a spiritual fire at the heart of separatism, coupled with a belief that men and women could find assurance of their salvation within true churches.[9]

Like other separatists before them, Barrow and Greenwood taught that godly men and women should withdraw from England's false, Antichristian church and form their own congregations in which they had the right to govern themselves. Christ's apostles had established churches based on this principle, but the people had "neglected their duty, and gave up their Christian liberty," first to groups of elders and then to bishops. "Christ hath given full power and liberty to all and every one of his servants," insisted Barrow. The laity should not, indeed lawfully could not, surrender that liberty to anyone. The admission of members, the election of officers, and the exercise of discipline rested with the congregation as a whole, or at least with its adult male members.[10]

In April 1593, authorities hanged Barrow and Greenwood, convicted for publishing seditious writings. Two days after Barrow and Greenwood went to the gallows, Parliament passed a statute against attendance at "any unlawful assemblies, conventicles, or meetings under color or pretense of any exercise of religion, contrary to her Majesty's said laws and statutes." The penalty was imprisonment until offenders "shall conform and yield themselves to come to some church, chapel, or usual place of common prayer, and hear divine service." Obstinate nonconformists risked banishment. While the law could apply to a variety of dissidents, its framers intended to use it to stamp out Brownism.[11] Under the leadership of new pastor Francis Johnson, the remainder of the London separatist congregation took refuge in Amsterdam. After other groups of English separatists came to the city, members of Johnson's congregation referred to themselves as the "Ancient Church" to distinguish themselves from more recent arrivals.

Puritans were a much-lampooned minority in late Elizabethan England, but they were a large minority with majority aspirations. By contrast, separatists were a tiny remnant, despised by conformists and puritans alike. As far as many church and government officials were concerned, separatists sought not liberty but license, a throwing off of all restraints. Even radical puritans were unstinting in their criticism of those who chose to leave the church, partly because antagonistic bishops tarred puritans with the brush of Brownism and partly because separatists accused everyone else of being in bed with Antichrist. For Catholics, separatists were the predictable fruit of Protestant schism. No one liked them. "I had as lief [rather] be a Brownist as a politician," quips Sir Andrew in Shakespeare's *Twelfth Night*.

Nonetheless, fierce persecution and nearly universal condemnation could never quite extinguish separatism. There was, after all, a thin line between the more radical expressions of puritanism and outright separatism. Those who preached against the corruption of the Church of England almost inevitably convinced a few in their midst—and sometimes themselves—that they had no choice but to separate from it.

In March 1603, Queen Elizabeth died after reigning for nearly half a century. When James VI of Scotland assumed England's throne, puritans hurried to recruit the new king to the cause of further reformation. James, who understood his kingdoms as bastions of Reformed Protestantism, told church leaders to improve the quality of parish preaching, and he authorized what became the most influential English translation of the Bible. At the same time, the king was entirely unsympathetic to puritanism, because he associated both it and Scottish Presbyterianism with limits on royal prerogatives. Like his predecessors, James placed a supreme value on his own supremacy.

James invited several puritan ministers—moderate reformers, not radicals—to Hampton Court and promptly dismissed most of their concerns as both petty and seditious. The king bristled at any proposals that would weaken the authority of bishops, which James connected to his own power. "No bishop, no king," he maintained. At the end of the conference's second day, the exasperated monarch had heard enough. "If this be all . . . they have to say," he warned, "I shall make them conform themselves, or I will harry them out of the land, or else do worse." James was tickled with his performance. "I have peppered them . . . soundly," he wrote a member of his Privy Council. Those who refused "the airy sign of the cross after baptism," the king added, "should no longer have their purses stuffed."[12]

Scores of ministers soon had lighter purses. In the spring of 1604, Richard Bancroft, the bishop of London, prepared a new set of canons, or church laws. Ministers would have to subscribe, to declare their heartfelt acceptance of England's ecclesiastical government and ceremonies. The canons required them to affirm the king's supreme spiritual authority, the Book of Common Prayer, the sign of the cross, and the surplice. A sizeable faction of the House of Commons understood Bancroft's canons as one of several royal affronts to parliamentary liberties. While disclaiming any sort of "Puritan or Brownist spirit," a parliamentary committee denied the king's "absolute power" to make laws concerning the Church of England. James ratified the new canons anyway. Bancroft became archbishop of Canterbury. Ministers who refused to subscribe lost their positions, and the ecclesiastical campaign nudged a few radical puritans right out of the church. Pockets of separatism reemerged.[13]

One of those pockets was in Canterbury. Ecclesiastical officials regarded the church-door libels as a serious offense and sought advice from Lambeth Palace. A letter signed by Richard Bancroft instructed them to find the "lewd [wicked] seditious persons": the makers, publishers, and "dealers" of the libels. The Court of the High Commission should imprison those responsible. If they refused to provide testimony under oath, the commissioners should jail them until their tongues loosened.[14]

Robert Cushman, the apprentice grocer, talked, though he avoided saying a great deal. His master's son said more. Peter Masters testified that he had seen Cushman write one of the libels and that Cushman had given him several of them. He, Peter, had then given them to someone else to be put on the church doors. George Masters told the court that he regarded Cushman as a "lewd fellow" for getting his son involved. The court confined Cushman in the city's Westgate prison for a night. George Masters paid a fine of twenty pounds.[15]

At the same time, the churchwardens of St. Andrew's parish in Canterbury cited Cushman and another servant named Thomas Hunt for refusing to come to services. They claimed that they stayed away because they could not be "edified" in their church. Presumably their parish minister did not preach sermons, or at least he did not meet their standards. Cushman refused repeated summons from the archdeaconry court, which then excommunicated him in January 1604. He received absolution but did not perform the required public penance, and was excommunicated again later that year. In June 1605, he again asked for and received absolution. He still refused to publicly acknowledge his guilt, and the court eventually dismissed the matter.[16]

Cushman had received a large portion of mercy. His punishments had been light, and while George Masters must not have been pleased about the twenty-pound fine, the affair did not interrupt Cushman's apprenticeship. He became a freeman in 1605. Cushman then married Sara Reader, a sister of two of his fellow libelers. The next year, the couple had their first child baptized in their parish church. Despite their discontents with the Church of England, the Cushmans had not yet broken from it. They grudgingly conformed.

Robert Cushman soon put his respectable future in doubt once more, this time through his association with a theologically adventurous weaver named Gilbert Gore. In 1606, Canterbury church officials accused Gore of heresy. According to the records of the case, Gore denied "the true and comfortable article of justification by faith in Christ Jesus . . . suggesting that a true and lively faith doth help no more in the justifying of elect sinners than, hope, love and obedience do." Gore's accusers charged that the weaver "set up a false Christ which should be a justifier of unbelievers while they are unbelievers." Under considerable pressure, Gore confessed and recanted.[17]

Why did Gilbert Gore take issue with justification by faith, a core tenet of Protestantism? Gore wanted to emphasize that humans in no way earned their salvation. Whether Lutheran or Reformed, Protestant theologians shared this concern and described faith itself as God's gracious gift. "The condition of man after the fall of Adam is such," the Church of England's Thirty-Nine Articles maintained, "that he cannot turn and prepare himself by his own natural strength and good works, to faith." Gore was unusual, though, in fully severing faith from justification. For most Protestant theologians, faith was something fundamentally different than hope, love, and obedience. Faith was the instrument by which God saved his elect. Gore disagreed. He contended that God saved the elect purely on the basis of Christ's righteousness, which God imputed to those he had elected to save.[18]

In the decades ahead, a number of radical Protestants—often

termed "antinomians" by historians—espoused views similar to those of Gilbert Gore. For example, in 1631 authorities in Ipswich accused several men of teaching "that all the elect were justified and made the sons of God by the work of Christ, before they have any faith to believe it." According to historian David Como, the notion was "common currency" among London antinomians. Church officials reacted sharply against such teachings, believing that they took away any incentive for men and women to inculcate faith and righteousness. Whether they were hot or only warm Protestants, English ministers understood their task as convicting men and women of their sinfulness, thus laying the groundwork for them to come to faith in Christ's gracious sacrifice on their behalf. What Gore taught threatened this entire system.[19]

Gore caused further alarm because he won others to his point of view in Canterbury and surrounding villages. His circle included a shoemaker, a blacksmith, a mercer, a hemp dresser, a tailor, several women, and Robert Cushman, who was identified to church officials by his new brother-in-law Thomas Reader. Several of those sympathetic to Gore had been involved in the 1603 libels case.[20]

Gore, meanwhile, promised to confess his errors in church, but when the minister began to read the liturgy, he turned his back "in the most contemptuous manner and went out of the church." At one point, Gore fled Canterbury, then returned. He was excommunicated in 1607.[21]

Thomas Wilson, rector of Canterbury's St. George the Martyr church, led the ecclesiastical response against Gore. Wilson was not an anti-puritan like Richard Bancroft. Cushman later described him as a "lover of goodness and good men," but Wilson did not count Gore among the latter. According to Cushman's account, Wilson caused Gore to be imprisoned for a year, threatened to burn him at the stake, and finally banished him from the city, "and all for a trivial controversy." Wilson did not consider the matter trivial. In fact, he wrote a long dialogue on the subject of justification in which one character (Philautus, meaning a lover of himself, from 2 Timothy 3:2) articulates Gilbert Gore's alleged heresy. For Wilson, Gore was among those "libertines and carnal gospellers, which turn the grace of God into wantonness, and think they may sin more freely the more grace doth abound." In other words, the weaver's doctrines encouraged licentiousness.[22]

Robert and Sara Cushman soon left both Canterbury and the Church of England. It is unclear exactly what pushed them from discontent into outright separatism, but it seems that Wilson's treatment of Gilbert Gore contributed to the decision. Cushman became convinced that "it is a sequestration, and not a reformation that will heal us, help us, and give us a right church estate for to join unto." Unable to openly pursue that "sequestration" in England, the Cushmans went to Holland.[23]

Other men and women from Kent followed a similar path. Around the year 1600, a Canterbury tailor named James Chilton moved his rapidly growing family to the port town of Sandwich. Nine years later, Mrs. Chilton (forename unknown) and several other Sandwich residents attended the private, nonchurch burial of a child. Church officials stated that the child was "strongly suspected not to [have] died an ordinary death," but it is most likely that Mrs. Chilton and the others simply objected to Church of England burial customs.[24]

Many puritans criticized the way that the Church of England conducted baptisms, marriages, and burials. They objected to the sign of the cross at baptisms, the use of rings at weddings, and the "heathenish pomp and customs" that accompanied burials. The separatist Henry Barrow did not think burials should involve clergy or any religious ceremony at all. There should be no "pulpit orations" or the placing of linen crosses on the corpse. No "earth to earth, ashes to ashes," words that came from the Book of Common Prayer rather than from the Bible. Church burials, Barrow alleged, were unheard of "until popery began." Likewise, the Sandwich dissenters denounced church burials as "popish ceremonies." Some puritan ministers agreed and omitted liturgy and other rituals from burials, but very few of even the most radical lay puritans would go so far as to bury corpses on their own. Church officials severely punished those who did so. Mrs. Chilton was excommunicated in June 1609.[25]

Moses Fletcher also was excommunicated for attending the private burial. Fletcher was a poor man whom the church and town helped in several ways. The church gave the Fletcher family relief money and made him a sexton; the town appointed him its beadle of vagrants. Despite the assistance, Fletcher rejected the church. He must have been quickly absolved, because he was excommunicated again a few months later, this time for burying his own daughter privately during "sermon time." Shortly thereafter, Fletcher was excommunicated for a third and final time.[26]

By the end of the decade, there were an estimated thirty separatists in Sandwich, under the leadership of "professed Brownist" Richard Masterson. In Sandwich, Canterbury, and other pockets of Kent, women and men refused to attend parish services. Some left their children unbaptized. A few would not marry or bury as church and state required. Moreover, there were individuals in Kent who, like Gilbert Gore and Robert Cushman, dabbled in ideas the authorities deemed heretical. Especially in coastal ports such as Sandwich, it was easy for religious dissidents to move back and forth between England and the Low Countries. The Fletchers, the Chiltons, and Richard Masterson all moved to Leiden, joined by families from other parts of England.

Joan Ashmore was a young servant to a young gentleman. She worked as a housekeeper at Broxtowe Hall, the home of Thomas Helwys. Edmund Helwys, Thomas's father, was a minor member of the Nottinghamshire gentry. He owned some land on which the family and its tenants raised crops and sheep, and he obtained a lease for Broxtowe Hall. When Edmund Helwys died in 1590, Thomas inherited the bulk of the estate, including the lease to Broxtowe. The younger Helwys trained as a lawyer at Gray's Inn in London, then returned home.[27]

From this point forward, Thomas Helwys lurched from one controversy to another. In 1593, Helwys agreed to sell his interest in Broxtowe Hall and at least some of his farmland to Robert Beresford and Ralph Waddington. According to Beresford, the deal included his sheep and crops as well. The sale soon ran aground. Beresford alleged that Helwys had overstated the number of years remaining on his lease, that some of the land actually belonged to the parish, and that Helwys refused to honor the agreement regarding the sheep and crops. Beresford and Waddington sued. They had given Helwys an advance payment and had sold other properties in order to have the funds on hand to complete the purchase.

Beresford made additional allegations that raised eyebrows. He asserted that Helwys had deeded his property to his housekeeper Joan Ashmore, whose "evil counsel and persuasions" seduced the young gentleman. Whether Helwys was duped or duplicitous or both, Beresford amended his suit to include Joan Ashmore as well. The resolution of the case is unknown.[28]

At roughly the same time, Thomas Helwys faced a complaint from his own sister. Edmund Helwys had left his daughter Anne her mother's jewels and clothes, a horse, a treasured psalm book, some furniture, and his "best cheese." The bequest amounted to more than sixty pounds. Anne Helwys, now Anne Green, asserted that her brother had refused to either give her the items or pay her for them. Perhaps he and Joan had eaten the cheese.[29]

Regardless of whether he had conspired with her to shield his property, Thomas Helwys decided that he wanted Joan Ashmore as more than his housekeeper. In May 1596, churchwardens reported the couple on suspicion of fornication. The evidence was obvious. Joan was pregnant. She gave birth to a son in September.[30]

The truth was rather less scandalous than the accusation suggested. Thomas and Joan had married in the parish church of Bilborough. Why, then, were they accused of fornication? The most likely explanation relates to the date of their wedding. The Church of England, like the pre-Reformation church, forbade marriage at certain times of the year. One hundred and forty-four days were off-limits, to be precise. Thomas and Joan Helwys married during Advent, on December 3. "Advent marriage doth deny," reminded a popular verse, "But Hilary [January 13] gives thee liberty." It was not that one could not wed during Advent. One could, but one needed to purchase a license from one's bishop. Many puritans objected to the marriage date restrictions and regarded the sale of licenses as ecclesiastical extortion.[31]

Because the Helwyses chose not to be extorted, ecclesiastical busybodies harassed them for years. In 1598, the churchwardens presented them again, this time "for living together, as man and wife, who are not known . . . to be married." Fifteen years later, church officials were still searching for their marriage license. By that point, Thomas and Joan Helwys had long since left the Church of England.[32]

In the village of Scrooby, only forty miles to the north of Broxtowe Hall, a group of men and women engaged in other types of puritan nonconformity. Their leader was William Brewster, who lived in a manor house owned by the archbishop of York. Brewster had inherited his father's position as postmaster and with it his residence in the archbishop's house. The Great North Road, carrying mail and travelers between London and Scotland, intersected Scrooby and ran right by the manor house.[33]

Not content to watch the world pass through Scrooby, Brewster went out into it. After studying for a year or so at Cambridge, he became secretary to William Davison, sent by the crown to the Low Countries to negotiate English support for the Dutch Protestant fight against Spanish Catholic rule. Brewster accompanied Davison to cities such as The Hague, Flushing, and Leiden. When Davison returned from abroad, he joined the Privy Council and played a role in the transmission of the warrant that ordered the death of Mary, Queen of Scots. Elizabeth wanted to avoid responsibility for her cousin's execution and settled on Davison as a scapegoat. He escaped serious punishment, but his career was over.[34]

Brewster came back to Scrooby with a great deal of knowledge about everything from foreign relations to court intrigues. Once home, though, Brewster settled down. He married. William and Mary Brewster named their children Patience, Fear, Love, and Wrestling. The names advertised the family's puritan piety.

In 1598, the Brewsters, along with a dozen or so other adults, were reported by their parish churchwarden for "resorting to other churches in service and sermon time." Brewster defended himself before the archdeacon's court by saying that Scrooby shared a preacher with another parish, which he visited on alternate Sundays. It was a polite way of excusing the offense. In all likelihood, Brewster traveled more widely to listen to godly preaching. Brewster also was accused of "repeating sermons publicly in the [Scrooby] church without authority." In Canterbury, Robert Cushman was excommunicated after suggesting that he could not receive edification in his own parish, but the Scrooby dissidents avoided severe punishment. Brewster continued to live in the archbishop's manor house. "Gadding" about to hear sermons was a characteristically puritan habit, but it was not an especially serious act of nonconformity.[35]

The formation of new separatist congregations occurred when several deposed ministers intersected with these lay dissenters. John Smyth studied at Cambridge, was ordained as a minister, and then held a fellowship at Christ's College until his 1598 marriage.[36] Thereafter, Smyth gained employment in Lincoln as a lecturer, a sort of preacher-at-large for the city. Smyth was contentious, however, and he lost his position for what his opponents described vaguely as "enormous [irregular] doctrine and undue teaching of matters of religion." Several years later, Smyth published a tract in which he expressed wariness about the use of set prayers in worship. After his dismissal in Lincoln, Smyth returned to his native Nottinghamshire village of Sturton-le-Steeple and preached irregularly there and elsewhere. A churchwarden in the nearby village of North Clifton described him in July 1603 as "a painful [painstaking] preacher of God's word." Perhaps too painful. With an eye to Smyth's prior indiscretions, John Whitgift, archbishop of Canterbury, revoked his preaching license. Smyth moved to Gainsborough, across the River Trent in Lincolnshire. The silenced minister felt the need to dispel rumors of Brownism. "I am far from the opinion of them which separate from our church," he wrote in a 1605 tract. Not that far, it turned out.[37]

John Robinson was also from Sturton-le-Steeple.[38] From 1598 until 1604, he was a fellow at Cambridge's Corpus Christi College, and he preached in Norwich, including at St. Giles's Hospital. In 1604, Robinson married Bridget White. Although details on this period of Robinson's life are sparse, it seems that his puritan leanings prevented him from obtaining a parish. Like John Smyth, Robinson moved back to Nottinghamshire. As a shepherd without a flock, the restive minister stirred up trouble. That June, seventeen men and women were reported for skipping their own parish services to hear Robinson preach at Sturton.[39]

In 1605, as church authorities increased pressure on puritan ministers to conform, two other Nottinghamshire ministers lost their positions. Richard Clyfton, who had refused to wear the surplice for around fifteen years, was deposed from his position in Babworth after a hearing before the archbishop of York, Matthew Hutton. That same month, Richard Bernard was suspended as vicar at nearby Worksop.[40]

In 1606, Bernard, Smyth, and Thomas Helwys—and possibly John Robinson—traveled to the Coventry home of Isabel Bowes, a wealthy patroness of puritanism. Others who came to the conference included the puritan luminaries John Dod and Arthur Hildersham. Those in attendance discussed how they should respond to the fact that King James had not reformed the church in accordance with their ideals. Was the Church of England still a true church? If not, should Christians leave it and form their own churches? Most of those in attendance rejected separation, which they believed would encourage their ecclesiastical opponents and give comfort to Catholics.[41]

Bernard, however, was done with moderation and patience. He gathered around a hundred women and men from Worksop and surrounding parishes. They covenanted with each other and celebrated the Lord's Supper. According to John Robinson, Bernard and his followers promised to live righteously and to keep away from "wicked or dumb [nonpreaching] ministers."[42]

Smyth vacillated. He later wrote that he "doubted nine months" whether to embrace "the separation." Perhaps because of his inner turmoil, Smyth became gravely ill. During his sickness, he stayed with Thomas and Joan Helwys, who nursed him back to health at their own expense. By then, Smyth was ready to separate, as were the Helwyses.[43]

At this time, William Bradford was a young man living in Austerfield, a few miles north of Scrooby. Bradford's parents had died when he was a child. From the age of around seven, he lived with two of his uncles. The Bradfords were farmers. William probably had little formal schooling, but he was precocious and keenly interested in religious matters from an early age. Richard Clyfton befriended the orphan, and as Bradford approached adulthood he met with Brewster and the other dissidents at Scrooby.

In his history, Bradford wrote that "as the Lord's free people," the separatists "joined themselves (by a covenant of the Lord) into a church estate." They promised that they would "walk in all [God's] ways, made known, or to be made known unto them . . . whatsoever it should cost them." In this covenant, church members declared themselves both free and bound: free from ecclesiastical tyranny and human corruptions of true worship, bound to each other. With this step, they recovered their Christian liberty.

The separatists formed "two distinct bodies or churches," partly because of the ten miles between Scrooby and Gainsborough. Smyth led the Gainsborough group. Clyfton led those who met with William Brewster at the Scrooby manor house. Thus, the Scrooby separatists used a residence owned by the archbishop of York to plot the Church of England's demise. Robinson continued to itinerate without a license, visiting parish churches and private homes at the invitation of like-minded ministers and laypeople.[44]

As the Scrooby and Gainsborough separatists worked to attract others to their principles, the authorities took notice. Tobie Matthew, who became archbishop of York in April 1606, was sympathetic to puritan nonconformists but not to separatists. Matthew convinced Richard Bernard to repent of separatism and restored him to his position at Worksop. Soon after he moved back into the vicarage, Bernard wrote *The Separatists Schisme*, a sharp attack on his former friends. A disgusted John Smyth responded that Bernard was "as changeable as the moon."[45] Smyth and Robinson considered Bernard an apostate, akin to Robert Browne.

In September 1607, Matthew stopped in the village of Bawtry (between Brewster's Scrooby and Bradford's Austerfield) and preached a sermon, "Contra Brownists." The Brownists in question apparently took this as a signal to leave. They would follow the example of other religious dissidents and go to the Low Countries where, as Bradford put it, "they heard was freedom of religion for all men." One sizeable group went to the Lincolnshire town of Boston, on the River Witham, where they planned to board a ship that would take them into exile.[46]

It was illegal to leave the country without permission, even if enforcement was often loose. While many individuals moved back and forth between England and Holland, the flight of a large number of people was risky. In this case, the shipmaster betrayed them. Customs officers seized their belongings, and the authorities imprisoned a number of the men, including William Brewster. Also, officials charged fifteen men—including Brewster, Clyfton, Gervase Nevyle, and Thomas Helwys—with avoiding parish services and attending "unlawful assemblies [and] conventicles." The charges alleged that the men were "malicious" and in "contempt" of the king. Still, the hand of the law was light. Bradford recalled that the magistrates "used them courteously, and shewed them what favor they could."[47]

Bradford's assertion that he and his fellow separatists left England because they "were hunted and persecuted on every side" and "watched night and day" is an exaggeration. Unlike the separatists inspired by Robert Browne, John Greenwood, and Henry Barrow, the Scrooby and Gainsborough separatists did not suffer severe persecution. Archbishop Matthew did not imprison Robinson, Smyth, or Clyfton. Robinson was still preaching in churches as late as March 1608.[48]

Still, the screws slowly tightened. Two months after his arrest in Boston, Gervase Nevyle—a Nottinghamshire gentleman—was brought before the archbishop's High Commission. The court required individuals to swear an ex officio oath, agreeing to answer any questions, even if those answers amounted to self-incrimination. Moreover, the court was not obliged to inform individuals what crimes they were suspected of having committed. The separatist Henry Barrow had denounced the Court of High Commission as "the very throne of the beast, utterly commingling, confounding, and subverting . . . the whole liberty of Christians." It symbolized the tyranny of bishops over true churches and true Christians. A number of legal thinkers also argued against the legality of the High Commission, asserting that Parliament had never empowered it to imprison defendants and that the ex officio oath trampled on the traditional English liberties enshrined in Magna Carta.[49]

In the presence of Archbishop Matthew, the court arraigned Nevyle as "one of the sects of Barrowists, or Brownists." Nevyle refused to take the oath, and he enjoyed needling his interrogators. He would answer—without an oath—questions from the other commissioners, but he refused to talk with Matthew at all, "protesting very presumptuously and insolently in the presence of God against his authority (and as he termed it) his ANTICHRISTIAN HIERARCHY."

The archbishop remanded him to the prison at York Castle. Nevyle was probably fortunate that his words did not cost him more dearly.[50]

The archbishop's pursuivant next pursued Brewster, who twice failed to appear in court as required. Each time, he incurred a fine of twenty pounds. Thomas and Joan Helwys also felt the archbishop's legal pincers. In March 1608, Joan Helwys and two men were arrested, refused to take the oath, and joined Nevyle in York Castle. Joan was released, only to be reported in April—along with her husband—for having skipped church and Communion for half a year.[51]

The crackdown showed no sign of abating. Brewster was not wealthy enough to pay a twenty-pound fine every few months. As Bradford stated, "They could not long continue in any peaceable condition." It was time for a second attempt to flee England.[52]

"It was Mr. [Thomas] Helwys," John Robinson wrote a few years later, "who above all . . . furthered this passage . . . if any brought oars, he brought sails." Robinson spoke metaphorically, but Helwys actually did bring oars and sails. This time, the departure point was a secluded location on the south bank of the Humber Estuary. Helwys hired a keel, a flat-bottom barge with a sail. He told its master, Henry Spencer, that he needed to transport some goods belonging to his wealthy uncle, Sir Gervase Helwys. If Spencer didn't know it from the start, he soon figured out that his cargo would consist of men, women, and children. Helwys had him sail the keel up the River Trent to Gainsborough, where fifteen individuals— mostly women and children—climbed aboard. The keel made other stops, and soon carried around eighty persons. Spencer then steered his vessel back toward Hull, where the muddy and shallow Humber collides with tidal waters that rush in from the North Sea.[53]

The group spent the night of May 11 and the next morning huddled in a "sheepcote" near the small harbor of Stallingborough, where a stream emptied into the Humber. The marshy shoreline, with its many quiet inlets, was a good place to hide. Other men and women, including Thomas and Joan Helwys, traveled by land to join the group at Stallingborough.

In the mid-afternoon of May 12, a Dutch hoy arrived. The keel had become mired near the creek, so around fifteen of the men clambered into a "cockboat," and two oarsmen rowed them to the hoy. Before the rowboat could bring a second group, a party of armed men appeared in the hills. "Sacramente," the Dutch captain swore. His crew pulled anchor and put out the sails.[54]

Having been desperate to leave, the men aboard the hoy now longed to return to their wives and children. "It drew tears from their eyes," wrote Bradford, "and anything they had they would have given to have been ashore again."

Instead, they remained at sea for two weeks, blown to the coast of Norway and nearly sunk by a violent storm. Like the Apostle Paul aboard a ship bound for Rome, Bradford and his companions went days without seeing the sun, moon, or stars. In Bradford's account, the sailors gave up, while the faithful men aboard the hoy pleaded with God to spare them. "Lord thou canst save," they cried out as the seawater lashed their faces. "Upon which the ship did not only recover," Bradford wrote, "but shortly after the violence of the storm began to abate." The god of early seventeenth-century England was often fearsome. He punished the land with plagues. He unleashed mighty storms against the godly and ungodly. At the same time, Bradford believed that God listened to the cries of his faithful. He did not always end their afflictions, but when the storms relented, the separatists attributed it to God's mercy.[55]

Of those left behind at Stallingborough, some men fled, and the troops rounded up the women and children. Helwys refused to talk. Henry Spencer and his servant testified about what they had done, but they had nothing to say about the motivation behind the undertaking. The authorities let them go. The Helwyses ignored summonses from the High Commission that summer. Gervase Nevyle and his two fellow prisoners languished in York Castle for another year. The Privy Council then banished them.[56]

As individuals and families gathered the means, they found passage out of England. In the Low Countries, they restored kinship and congregational ties. Others, from places such as Canterbury and Sandwich, joined them. It was the first step in the transplantation of churches that would eventually reach across the Atlantic.

CHAPTER TWO

Leiden

T HE DUTCH REPUBLIC WAS in the early years of what later generations would call its "Golden Age." In the coming decades, a young nation would grow wealthy through textiles, trade, and banking, produce artists such as Rembrandt and Vermeer, and acquire an empire that stretched from Brazil and the Hudson River to present-day Indonesia. When the new wave of English separatists arrived, however, Dutch Protestants were still seeking to secure their independence. In 1609, half a century after the northern provinces of the Netherlands had revolted against Philip II, the Dutch Republic (or United Provinces) signed a twelve-year truce with Spain.[1]

The 1579 Union of Utrecht, which had formed the United Provinces, declared that "each individual enjoys freedom of religion and no one is persecuted or questioned about his religion." At the same time, the republic maintained a single "public church." Magistrates gave Reformed (Calvinist) congregations the exclusive use of church buildings, paid their ministers' salaries, and exercised some oversight of church affairs. Consistories, comprised of a city's ministers and elders, meted out church discipline, and magistrates enforced public morality. Obtaining and maintaining church membership hinged on an individual's acceptance of this system of discipline. Much to the consternation of the Calvinists, only a small minority of Dutch men and women actually belonged to the Reformed

27

churches. In the early years of the republic, there were as many Catholics as Calvinists, and there were sizeable Lutheran, Mennonite, and Jewish minorities as well.[2]

Dutch Calvinists were deeply committed to their "liberty" but, like English Protestants, they disagreed about its meaning. All cherished liberty from idolatry and superstition—Catholicism, in other words—and they stressed God's sovereignty in saving his elect. There were many fault lines, however. Reformed ministers and many other Calvinists expected government support but opposed government interference, especially when it came to the selection of church officers. At the same time, "freethinkers" and "libertines" favored open church membership without consistorial discipline. For them, liberty meant freedom from any sort of ecclesiastical control, be that the papacy or the consistory.[3]

Despite the Union of Utrecht's declaration of religious freedom, the situation for religious minorities and dissenters was uneven and uncertain. Most Dutch politicians and ministers defended "liberty of conscience," but by that they meant private belief and practice, not public worship or dissent. Catholics thus could not hold processions and public celebrations, and many cities forbade the construction of non-Reformed church buildings and synagogues. Especially after the demise of Robert Harrison's congregation, Dutch Reformed leaders in Middelburg and Amsterdam made plain their disapproval of Brownism. Even Lutherans sometimes found their liberties under assault. In other places, by contrast, officials tacitly permitted religious minorities to gather for worship, which they sometimes did in large private homes and buildings that functioned as churches without advertising themselves as such. It was toleration by connivance.[4]

Dutch toleration was good enough for most English exiles, but it did not satisfy those separatists who became the *Mayflower* Pilgrims. For them, the Dutch Republic's liberty was both too fragile and too expansive. The Spanish might regain control of the northern Low Countries, or Dutch magistrates might restrict their liberties. In the meantime, they could worship according to their principles, but they feared that pluralism, libertinism, and licentiousness would corrode their church and lead their children astray. Leaving unwanted types of liberty behind, they decided to chart their own, more perilous course.

The Scrooby and Gainsborough separatists first took refuge in Amsterdam. James Howell, who visited the city a decade later as an agent for a London glassworks, marveled that a rapid and "monstrous increase of commerce and navigation" had turned the low-lying city into "one of the greatest marts of Europe." Churches proliferated nearly as quickly as merchant houses. After lodging with a Brownist who lived near a Jewish synagogue, Howell joked that "there's no place so disunited" as the United Provinces.[5]

English separatists were disunity specialists. Even before all of the Scrooby and Gainsborough congregants reached Amsterdam, John Smyth and the leaders of Francis Johnson's Ancient Church were at odds. Smyth's initial complaint centered on the use of the Bible during worship. Like most puritans, Smyth objected to the Book of Common Prayer's liturgy. Unlike them, he also wanted to banish written texts from psalm singing and teaching. "In neither of them the Spirit is at liberty," he argued. The primitive Christians, Smyth believed, prayed, taught, and sang "merely out of their hearts" and in so doing allowed God's Spirit to move their affections. Adam in Eden had worshipped God this way, and so would Christians in heaven. Outside of worship, Smyth and his followers used the Bible to edify themselves and to settle questions of doctrine, but when it was time to pray, sing, and preach, they "shut the book." Any use of the Bible in worship was idolatry.[6]

The leaders of the Ancient Church found Smyth's objections absurd. Most English Protestants cherished psalm singing. It was the one part of worship guaranteed to keep congregants awake, and it was precious to separatists who had discarded other liturgy. Henry Ainsworth, the Ancient Church's teacher (a second minister alongside Francis Johnson), was a skilled Hebraist whom William Bradford later praised as "a man of a thousand." Ainsworth made his own translation of much of the Old Testament, including a metrical psalter set to a number of tunes. The separatists who settled Plymouth Colony brought copies of Ainsworth's psalter with them.[7]

There was a second point of contention as well. The Ancient Church vested disciplinary authority in its elders. Ainsworth defended the practice. "If the multitude govern," he asked, "then who shall be governed?" Ainsworth argued that "Christian liberty (which all have) is one thing, the reins of government (which some have) is another thing." Smyth insisted that the people held these reins. Drawing on classical republican models of mixed government, he understood Christ alone as the church's king, the elders as an elected aristocracy, and the remaining members as "a democracy or popular government." Smyth insisted that "the negative voice is in the body of the church, not in the elders." Otherwise, the people surrendered their liberty to the arbitrary rule of their officers.[8]

As English Protestants had rejected Rome, and as the separatists had withdrawn from the Church of England, Smyth fled idolatry once more. Rather than joining his followers to Johnson's church, he formed a "second English Church" in Amsterdam. Smyth next concluded that only baptisms received through true churches were valid. Thus, he considered himself unbaptized despite his infant baptism in the Church of England. So he baptized himself. Smyth's critics mocked him as a "Se-Baptist," or self-baptizer. Smyth then baptized Thomas Helwys and his other followers.

Smyth regretted his self-baptism after becoming acquainted with an Amsterdam congregation of Mennonites, descendants of the sixteenth-century reformer Menno Simons. Other Protestants referred to the Mennonites and like-minded churches as Anabaptists (meaning those who rebaptize) because of their rejection of infant baptism. Smyth concluded that because the Mennonites belonged to a true church, he should have asked them to baptize him. Smyth died before his followers completed their process of uniting themselves with the Mennonites. For most English Protestants, these events confirmed their suspicion that separatism was a byway to Anabaptism.[9]

Thomas and Joan Helwys followed Smyth in rejecting infant baptism, but they then returned to England instead of uniting with the Mennonites. In London, Thomas Helwys helped organize a church on Baptist principles. He also became a bold if impolitic defender of religious liberty, arguing in his *A Short Declaration of the Mistery of Iniquity* (1612) that the king had no "power to command men's consciences." Rulers should not punish heretics, Jews, Turks, or even Catholics. "Men's religion to God, is betwixt God and themselves," he wrote. On the inside cover of a copy of his book, Helwys inscribed an incendiary note addressed to King James: "The king is a mortal man, and not God, therefore hath no power over the immortal souls of his subjects." King James disagreed. "Kings are not only God's lieutenants upon earth," he explained to Parliament, "and sit upon God's throne, but even by God himself they are called gods." Helwys died in prison.[10]

Back in Amsterdam, the Ancient Church endured a schism. George Johnson, the pastor's brother, had complained for years about the haughty attitude and stylish, revealing fashions of his brother's wife, Thomasine. The church finally excommunicated George Johnson and the brothers' father, who had made a futile attempt to reconcile them. Several congregants then accused Elder Daniel Studley of beating his wife, seducing his stepdaughter, and committing adultery with a married woman. The less colorful issue of church government also caused a rift. Francis Johnson favored greater authority for the church's elders than did Ainsworth. Eventually, Ainsworth's faction gained control of the Ancient Church's building, and Johnson took his followers to Emden in Friesland. Nottinghamshire separatist Richard Clyfton went with Johnson as his assistant. The Ancient Church members who remained in Amsterdam chose Ainsworth as their pastor.[11]

Richard Clyfton, John Smyth, and Thomas Helwys. All three were key leaders in the development of separatism in and around Scrooby and Gainsborough, and now all three had gone separate ways.

John Robinson went his own way as well. He requested permission to bring one hundred men and women to Leiden, twenty-five miles to the southwest of Amsterdam. In a letter, Robinson informed Leiden's magistrates only that they were "members of the Christian Reformed religion." Ralph Winwood, the English agent at The Hague who recently had helped finalize the truce between Spain and the United Provinces, complained to Leiden's city leaders. Why were they granting shelter to a group of sectarians that England's government considered seditious? In response, a city official told Winwood that he had not known that Robinson's congregants were "Brownists" but that all honest and law-abiding individuals were welcome in Leiden. In the spring of 1609, Robinson and his flock moved to what William Bradford later described as a "fair and beautiful city."[12]

In 1573–74, Leiden had withstood two Spanish sieges. Half of the city's twelve thousand residents perished, but Leiden itself recovered quickly. William of Orange established a university in Leiden for the purpose of training Reformed ministers; the institution lent the city intellectual and political prominence. Protestant refugees from the still-Spanish southern Netherlands flooded into Leiden. Flemish migrants in particular revived and remade the city's textile industry, and Leiden became Europe's foremost producer of "new draperies," lighter types of woolen cloth such as serge. The growth was staggering. By 1620, Leiden's population stood at nearly forty-five thousand.[13]

There are hundreds of references to the separatists in the Leiden archives: marriages, births, deaths, and property transactions. Such documents are terse, though. There are no diaries, no autobiographies, and precious few letters. Thus, we know that a couple married, but nothing about their marriage. We know that dozens of men, women, and children worked in the textile industry, and we know that their labor was difficult, but we do not know how individuals experienced it.

At least eleven of the English separatists worked as "drapers," who produced the finished cloth and had workers underneath them. More were weavers and wool combers, who typically worked at home, which meant that their wives and older children spun yarn and knitted alongside them. Everyone worked who could work. Sons were typically apprenticed around the age of twelve, sometimes for terms as long as twelve years.[14]

William Bradford was around twenty years of age when he came to Leiden. Bradford at first worked for a French silk weaver. Then he sold his land in England and started his own enterprise weaving fustian, a cloth made from linen and wool. Although Bradford apparently encountered some setbacks and exhausted much of his inheritance, he soon had his own house. In 1613, he married Dorothy May, whose parents had lived in Amsterdam the past five years. She gave birth to a son a few years later.[15]

Robert Cushman, the Canterbury grocer, became a wool comber in Leiden. He purchased a house in 1611, albeit a residence worth one-third that of the more prosperous Bradford. In 1616, Sara Cushman died while giving birth to the couple's second child, who per-

Isaac van Swanenburg, The Removal of the Wool from the Skins and the Combing, *ca. 1595. (Collection Museum De Lakenhal.)*

ished two weeks after its mother. The next summer, Cushman remarried, to Mary Shingleton, the widow of a Sandwich shoemaker.[16]

The task of earning a living in drastically changed circumstances consumed much of their time and energy, but the separatists could gather together without the fear of arrest or imprisonment. At least for most of the 1610s, the congregation met in or near John Robinson's home, a property in the shadows of Leiden's imposing Pieterskerk. They chose their own officers: Robinson as pastor; William Brewster as ruling elder, assisting with everything except the sacraments; and Samuel Fuller and John Carver as deacons.

Morning worship consisted of extemporaneous prayers by Robinson and Brewster, psalm singing, the reading of several chapters of scripture, a "preached" rather than "read" sermon, the Lord's Supper, and a collection for the minister's salary and the poor. When families such as the Bradfords and Cushmans had children, John Robinson baptized them without the sign of the cross or the liturgy of the Book of Common Prayer. When necessary, Sunday services included the censure or excommunication of members who had failed to walk in the ways of God as required by the church covenant.[17]

Families then ate their dinner before returning for prophesying in the afternoon. In this context, to "prophesy" did not mean to make predictions about the future. Rather, prophesying was the spiritual gift of expositing scripture's meaning. During these afternoon gatherings, select laypeople as well as church officers could speak. "Ye men and brethren," instructed the New Testament, "if ye have any word of exhortation for the people, say on" (Acts 13:15). While some puritans supported lay prophesying, others objected to this hallmark of separatist worship. Why would congregants want to listen to weavers or wool combers? Robinson countered that "the people's liberty" included the "exercise of prophesy." Teaching was not the sole privilege of ministers and lay elders. Robinson even defended the right of women to prophesy, at least under the unusual inspiration of the Spirit. That separatists debated this point among themselves suggests that some women claimed this gift.[18]

Despite their removal to Leiden, the separatists—and John Robinson in particular—remained engaged within the broader world of English Protestantism. In 1610, Robinson came to know William Ames, a renowned puritan minister who had recently fled England. The two men respected each other's learning but disagreed about separation. At the time, Robinson's position was that true Christians could not have "visible communion" with individuals who remained within the Church of England. They could not pray together, for instance. As far as Ames was concerned, Robinson's stance was narrow and bitter. "Are you more holy than Christ?" an exasperated Ames asked.[19]

Robinson soon changed his mind. In 1614, he published a book in which he made a distinction between public church communion and private fellowship. He now allowed that regardless of church membership, Christians could meet privately and pray together, sing psalms together, and read the Bible together. Ames urged Robinson to discard public separation as well. Robinson would not go so far, but he soon allowed his congregants to hear sermons in Church of England parishes. The latter question arose whenever the separatists visited England.

For most separatists, attendance at Church of England services was tantamount to apostasy. Protestants would not go near a Roman Catholic mass. How could true Christians listen to sermons delivered in Antichristian English churches? The Ancient Church in Amsterdam customarily excommunicated individuals who went to hear Church of England preaching. "Our liberty is to them as rat's bane [poison]," Robert Cushman commented, "and their rigor as bad to us as the Spanish Inquisition." Even within the Leiden congregation, Robinson's stance remained controversial.[20]

Robinson softened his rhetoric as the years proceeded, but he never repented of his separation. The Church of England, Robinson wrote, was a false church because it made every man a member, "will he, nill he, fit, or unfit, as with iron bonds." Rather than a house of God, it was "more like a common inn, whose door stands wide open to all that pass by the high way." The separatists would not accept all women and men, but they also forced no one to join them. Robinson drew a stark contrast between the ecclesiastical tyranny of the Church of England and his congregation's liberty. Male church members—"women by their sex are debarred of the use of authority in the church"—elected their officers, admitted members, and excommunicated gross offenders. Robinson was quick to add that the church's government was mixed rather than democratic. Christ was their king, and they deferred to the leadership of their chosen officers. Still, Robinson conceded that their church state was "after a sort popular, and democratic." The people governed themselves and worshipped as the Bible instructed. They exercised their liberty.[21]

Critics of separatism, Robinson insisted, would change their minds if they could observe the "heavenly harmony, and comely order" of his congregation. "Never people upon earth lived more lovingly together," wrote Edward Winslow, a printer's apprentice who moved from London to Leiden. Other English exiles joined them, as did some Dutch and Walloon Reformed Protestants. The congregation numbered several hundred by the end of the decade. Especially in comparison to the schisms in the Ancient Church and among John Smyth's followers, the Leiden separatist church enjoyed an unusual period of growth, stability, and concord. The true church was "heaven on earth," Robinson enthused.[22]

If they had heaven on earth in Leiden, why did the Pilgrims leave? Some church members concluded that in order for their congregation to persist, they needed more than Christian liberty. When worship ended, there was heavy labor and, for many congregants, grinding poverty. In retrospective accounts, William Bradford and Edward Winslow stressed the hardships of their Dutch exile, which drained their wealth and wore out their bodies. Their economic dislocation discouraged English separatists (and puritans contemplating separation), who chose "bondage" in England rather than the "liberty of the gospel" in the Netherlands. More would join them if they coupled Christian liberty with greater prosperity.[23]

There were other considerations as well. While the separatists rejoiced in their Christian liberty, the Dutch Republic did not fit their model of a properly ordered Christian society. The Dutch were not strict in their Sabbath observance and, from the perspective of the separatists, they allowed heresy and libertinism to flourish. The separatists worried about the future of their children. Bradford reported that some children of the church became soldiers and sailors, professions associated with dissolute and ungodly living. Would they even remain English? "How like we were to lose our language, and our name of English," Winslow wrote. Their children would become Dutch and perhaps lose their inheritance rights to property back in England. Some church members began contemplating emigration across the Atlantic.[24]

Other congregants countered that they would rather be Dutch than dead. Founding a colony was just about the most foolish thing a congregation or any other group of Europeans could do. French Huguenots (Calvinists) had colonized sites in Brazil and Florida, but Portuguese and Spanish troops, respectively, massacred them in the mid-1560s. (More successfully, Huguenots moved to Dutch and British North American colonies later in the seventeenth century.) As the Leideners contemplated emigration, other English separatists did so as well. Shortly after Francis Johnson's 1618 death, members of his church sailed for Virginia. "Packed together like herrings" on an overcrowded ship with insufficient fresh water, scores died during a voyage prolonged by unfavorable winds and navigational confusion. Some members of the Leiden congregation worried that even if they made it to their destination alive, Natives would flay their skin and eat their flesh.[25]

While the congregation remained divided about the idea of "removal," a majority of male members voted to at least explore options. In the fall of 1617 they dispatched Robert Cushman and John Carver to meet with members of the Virginia Company.

By this time, an ecclesiastical and political crisis had engulfed the Dutch Republic, a signal that the political tranquility the separatists had enjoyed in Leiden might come to an end. Everyone from the king of England to John Robinson waded into the controversy.[26]

It began as a theological argument between the Leiden professors Jacobus Arminius and Franciscus Gomarus. The two agreed that the human will was depraved and that God had decreed the salvation and damnation of all humans prior to his creation of the world. Arminius, though, carved out a small place for meaningful human choice and cooperation within this divine economy. God foresaw who would believe, elected to save them, and then created a world in which they would respond with faith to his grace. Perhaps these were minor distinctions, but to Arminius, they made clear that God was not the author of human sin. For Gomarus, God's decrees were simply absolute and inscrutable. God gave faith to those he had elected and withheld it from everyone else. If God seemed to be the author of evil, that was only because humans could not understand God's ways. The disagreement between Arminius and Gomarus festered for years and created deep fissures not only within Leiden's university but within its churches as well.[27]

Arminius's 1609 death did not put an end to the controversy. The next year, his supporters sent a remonstrance to the States of Holland, the provincial assembly. The petition repeated Arminius's teachings on predestination, but it also called on the provincial government to resolve the disagreement and urged it to permit more theological latitude within the church. The Remonstrants had an ally in Johan van Oldenbarnevelt, the land's advocate for the States of Holland and the most powerful politician within the United Provinces. Oldenbarnevelt favored greater state authority over the public church but also substantial freedom for dissenters and religious minorities. The Gomarists prepared a counter-remonstrance, which they presented at a disputation before the States. They were aghast at the idea of more state control over ministerial appointments, and they wanted less rather than more toleration.

The crisis took on international proportions when King James intervened on the side of the Counter-Remonstrants. Although James discouraged his own ministers from speculating on the finer points of predestination, he agreed with Gomarus on the matter. Moreover, the king associated dissent and calls for toleration with sedition and instability. When it came to the inner workings of Dutch politics, James favored the princely ambitions of the *stadholder* (governor-general) Maurits of Nassau against the parliamentary authority of Oldenbarnevelt. James made it clear that he wanted Remonstrant literature suppressed and Remonstrant leaders themselves imprisoned or banished, if not executed. The English king treated the United Provinces like a mistress he would cast aside if she no longer pleased him. If the Dutch did not do his bidding, he would marry his son Charles to a Spanish Habsburg princess.[28]

John Robinson and William Brewster were also partisans in the controversy, ironically on the same side as the king whose bishops and officials had once persecuted them. When Robinson came to Leiden, he moved into a house only fifty yards away from Arminius's residence. Robinson attended lectures at the university, sampling the opinions of both factions. According to Bradford, Robinson was "terrible to the Arminians" because he disagreed with their understanding of predestination. He took part in a disputation with Simon Episcopius, an Arminian professor at the university. Although Episcopius probably assessed the outcome differently, Bradford trumpeted his pastor's "famous victory." Brewster, meanwhile, published an abridgment of William Ames's rebuttal of a Remonstrant author. As English exiles in the Netherlands, it was risky for Robinson and Brewster to insert themselves into the crisis.[29]

Leiden remained at the epicenter of the national controversy. The city's ministers and university faculty were divided, but the Counter-Remonstrants had more supporters among the populace. By 1617, it had come to a de facto schism. The two factions worshipped separately. Mobs attacked Remonstrant services, and all attempts by the magistrates to suppress rioting only fanned the flames of violence. In October, the magistrates hired new guards and ordered the construction of barricades to protect the town hall from the Counter-Remonstrant mobs.[30]

One of those mobs attacked James Chilton, who with his wife

The Arminian Redoubt at Leiden, *ca. 1617–18.*
(Courtesy of Prentenkabinet, University of Leiden.)

and family had moved from Sandwich to Leiden. After he and his daughter Ingle came home from church one Sunday, a crowd gathered outside of their house. About twenty boys and young men shouted that the Chiltons were allowing "Arminians" to meet in their home. James Chilton opened his door and confronted the mob. No, there had not been an Arminian at his house, he said. Nor had he hosted any other meeting. Go home, he told the toughs. Most of them began to disperse, but one boy picked up a cobblestone and hurled it at Chilton's head. It struck him just above his left eye. Chilton collapsed to the ground, unconscious. The sixty-three-year-old tailor was lucky to survive.[31]

Given the mounting political and ecclesiastical chaos in the Dutch Republic, it was only prudent that the English separatists surveyed other options for their future. As Bradford noted, the twelve-year truce between the United Provinces and Spain would expire in 1621. Especially given the unpredictability of English policy, war might return. "The Spaniard might prove as cruel as the savages of America," Bradford reasoned. As Leiden's magistrates barricaded the city's town hall, Cushman and Carver went to London.[32]

The congregation's representatives met with Sir Edwin Sandys, a principal director of the Virginia Company. A longtime power in the House of Commons, Sandys had shaped the 1593 legislation against conventicles. Twenty-five years later, Sandys still did not like Brownists, but he was desperate for anyone willing to work in Virginia's tobacco fields. Even so, the Pilgrims knew that their reputation for schism and dissent was a problem, especially when it came to securing legal protection for a colony. Therefore, congregational leaders began a long and never fully successful campaign of obfuscation, of portraying themselves as something other than the separatists they were.[33]

In a list of seven articles sent with Cushman and Carver, Robinson and Brewster stated that they assented to the Church of England's "confession of faith" and that they kept "spiritual communion" with those true Christians within the national church. The pair also professed their loyalty to the king and acknowledged that it was lawful for him to appoint bishops to "oversee the churches and govern them civilly." Robinson and Brewster left unsaid that they understood the Church of England as a false church and did not accept the spiritual authority of its bishops. It was good enough for the Virginia Company, but some members of the Privy Council wanted more information before they lent their support to a bunch of schismatics.[34]

Robinson and Brewster sent clarifications to Sir John Wolstenholme, a member of the Virginia Company council. English Protestants sympathized with persecuted Huguenots in France, so Robinson and Brewster stated that their system of church government and administration of the sacraments conformed in nearly all ways to those of the French Reformed churches. It was a way for the Pilgrims to showcase their Reformed bona fides while again remaining silent on their rejection of England's church. In their most blatant attempt to mollify the king, Robinson and Brewster expressed a willingness to take the oath of supremacy, which declared that James was the "supreme governor of the realm," including in "all spiritual or ecclesiastical things." This was yet another dodge. Robinson and Brewster meant only that James was the supreme governor of a church they had rejected. Finally, Robinson and Brewster provided some details about their congregation's practices of baptism and discipline. Wolstenholme was wise to the situation and realized that to share the additional material would "spoil all." He kept it to himself.[35]

By now it was February 1618. The Virginia Company arranged for Sir Robert Naunton, who had just become secretary of state, to present the plan to the king. James was no fool when it came to English puritans in exile. He may have known about Brewster's fines from a decade earlier, and it would have been easy to learn about John Robinson. The king did not mind shipping religious dissidents to colonies, however. The Leiden congregants told the king that they intended to make profits in Virginia by fishing. According to Edward Winslow's later secondhand report, the king loved the idea. "So God have my soul," the king laughed, "'tis an honest trade, 'twas the apostles' own calling." Separatists who thought they had reconstructed the primitive church would follow the occupation of Jesus's first disciples! Still, while James said he would "not molest them," he also would not give the group his public blessing. Negotiations with the Virginia Company stalled.[36]

While Carver and Cushman were in England, a political earthquake shook the Netherlands. Maurits of Nassau, the stadholder of Holland and most of the republic's other provinces, became Prince of Orange after his brother's death in 1618. The accession increased Maurits's power and stoked his monarchical aspirations. Egged on by King James, Maurits arrested Oldenbarnevelt and other leading Remonstrants, neutered the power of local magistrates, and called a national Reformed synod. The next spring, after a show trial, Oldenbarnevelt was beheaded.

It was a political coup with significant implications for Dutch religious affairs and the country's relations with Spain and England. The resulting Synod of Dordrecht (Dort) declared that God chose without any conditions certain individuals for salvation and others for damnation. Jesus had died only for those predestined for salvation. The English delegation at the synod encouraged stern measures to extinguish the alleged heresy of the Remonstrants. Arminian ministers could submit to the synod's precepts or face deposition and banishment. So much for what Bradford termed "freedom of religion for all men."

Although John Robinson wrote a book defending the Synod of

Dort, the recent developments threatened his own congregation. The States-General outlawed private religious gatherings, and lawmakers also required that printers send copies of their books to state officials. Robinson's congregants realized that they might enjoy less liberty going forward.

As the political crisis crested, the publishing activities of William Brewster and Thomas Brewer attracted the attention of English officials. Brewer was a gentleman and a prosperous merchant, dubbed by Amsterdam English puritan John Paget as the "special patron" of the English separatists abroad. After he moved to Leiden, he enrolled at the university and bought a house next door to John Robinson's. Brewster and Brewer sought to advance the cause of true Christianity by publishing books that were then smuggled back into England. For the separatist printers, books were weapons. In his *Acts and Monuments,* John Foxe had described how brave reformers would fight "not with sword and tergate [shield]" but with "printing, writing, and reading." Printing was "the secret operation of God" that would subdue Antichrist's kingdom. Brewer poured his wealth into that operation.[37]

The separatist pair acquired type but did not own their own printing press, relying instead on several Leiden printers to bring out their titles. They published separatist works by John Robinson, Francis Johnson, and Robert Harrison, but also books by puritan luminaries such as William Ames. Two of their titles in particular attracted the ire of the English government. They printed David Calderwood's anonymous broadside against King James's plan to impose the episcopal hierarchy of the Church of England on the Scottish Kirk. Brewster and Brewer also published Calderwood's anonymous *Perth Assembly,* which similarly criticized a meeting of the Kirk called by James in 1618. Calderwood accused the king of ecclesiastical and political tyranny. Not surprisingly, the king deemed the books seditious.

In his long campaign against the Remonstrants, James and his officials had made it clear that they would pursue their opponents in the Netherlands. Hunting for the publisher of Calderwood's books, English ambassador Dudley Carleton came to Leiden in July 1619 and learned that Brewster and Brewer had printed them. Carleton reported to Robert Naunton—who had supported the separatists'

interest in moving to Virginia—that "their practice was to print pro-
hibited books to be vended underhand in his majesty's kingdoms."
For months, James's officials pressured Dutch officials to capture
and extradite the printers. English exiles in the Low Countries could
not feel assured of their safety.[38]

As it turned out, the separatists reaped the benefits of their leaders' friendship with Leiden's faculty and magistrates. City officials
moved as deliberately as they could without needlessly antagonizing
Carleton. They let Brewster get away but arrested Brewer and kept
him in the university's prison. The authorities seized type, books,
and papers from Brewer's house. Because Brewer was a member of
the university, its officials refused to simply turn him over to the
English. Political negotiations eventually sent Brewer to London
with the promise that he would not be arrested. While Brewer and
Brewster avoided serious consequences, the long arm of the English
crown had suppressed separatist publishing efforts. Brewster was
lucky to escape with his life.

The congregation briefly explored leaving under Dutch auspices.
After Henry Hudson sailed up the river that would receive his name,
Dutch fur traders had established a fort near present-day Albany. In
early 1620, officials of the New Netherland Company petitioned
the States-General to bring "a certain English minister . . . living at
Leiden" and four hundred families to what would later become New
Amsterdam and later still New York. The company also asked for
"two ships of war" to protect Dutch interests in the region. The
company's proposal gained no traction. Recruiting English colonists
was probably not the best means of securing Dutch interests in the
region, and the Prince of Orange did not want to antagonize King
James by lending assistance to Brownists. Maurits said no.[39]

At this point, an English merchant and smuggler named Thomas
Weston came to Leiden and offered to raise financing for the frustrated separatists. Over the past several years, Weston had shipped
English textiles to France and the Netherlands. In 1618, he was reported for violating a crown-granted monopoly on the export of un-
dyed, unfinished white woolens to the Netherlands. Now he gathered
a group of investors (known as "Adventurers" for their willingness
to venture their capital) to back the planned colony. Weston did not

Adam Willaerts, The Departure of the Pilgrims, *1620.*
(Private collection, courtesy of Jeremy D. Bangs.)

care either way about separatism. His previous enterprises had brought him indebtedness rather than riches. Colonies were very risky propositions, but Weston and his partners envisioned high rewards.[40]

Cushman and Carver went back to London to finalize arrangements. John Peirce, one of Weston's prospective investors, obtained a patent from the Virginia Company on behalf of the separatists. Those involved in the planning also had word that a new group (known as the Council for New England) led by Sir Ferdinando Gorges would soon receive English jurisdiction over a vast swath of land from present-day Philadelphia to nearly the mouth of the St. Laurence River. The colonists might need to get a new patent after they crossed the Atlantic. Meanwhile, the congregation remained divided and unsettled about its future. Most families either did not want to go or had no means to do so. Since the majority would at least for a time stay in Leiden, they prevailed upon Robinson to remain with them. Elder Brewster would go.

In July 1620, the colonists took their leave. The congregation held what Bradford termed a "day of solemn humiliation." They fasted. Robinson preached. They feasted. They sang psalms, which Edward

Robert W. Weir, Embarkation of the Pilgrims, *1843.*
(Courtesy of the Architect of the Capitol.)

Winslow called "the sweetest melody that ever mine ears heard."[41]
They wept.

A quarter-century later, Winslow recalled his pastor's parting
message. Robinson expressed confidence that "the Lord had more
truth and light yet to break forth out of his holy Word" and urged
the colonists to be receptive to what God revealed to them. He criticized other Protestants for stopping short of the more thoroughgoing reformation he and his congregants had accomplished. Robinson's words were not a plea for toleration or open-mindedness.
Christians should test any idea against the firm rule of scripture. At
the same time, he warned his departing congregants against self-
satisfaction and complacency. Even true churches, those that resembled heaven on earth, fell short of the purity and perfection revealed
in the Bible.[42]

Those who were staying accompanied the departing to the port
of Delfshaven. Friends from Amsterdam came as well. According to
Bradford, John Robinson and the others fell to their knees, prayed,
and wept again. On or around July 22, the *Speedwell*'s crew hoisted
its sails.

Bradford explained that despite their sorrow at leaving, "they knew they were pilgrims, and looked not much on those things, but lift[ed] up their eyes to the heavens, their dearest country, and quieted their spirits."[43] The words alluded to the eleventh chapter of the New Testament epistle to the Hebrews, which lauds exemplars of faith as "strangers and pilgrims on the earth." Among them is Abraham, who in obedience to God's call "went out, not knowing whither he went" and reached "the land of promise." These Pilgrims also did not know their precise destination, nor did they have any assurance of earthly success. They went by faith, secure in the knowledge that even should their earthly pilgrimage end in prisons or wildernesses, they would reach their eternal home.

CHAPTER THREE

Mayflower

IN THE SEVERAL DECADES before 1620, growing numbers of
English fishermen, colonists, and pirates sailed back and forth
across the Atlantic. West Country fishermen went to Newfoundland, caught and dried cod, and sold it back in Europe.
Church-prescribed fasts guaranteed a massive demand for fish. English colonizers established fragile settlements at Jamestown and
on the Somers Isles (Bermuda), and English sea dogs preyed on
Spanish vessels. Alongside the Dutch, England was an ascendant
power in the Atlantic, but ocean travel remained risky in the best of
circumstances.

Those the Pilgrims faced were far from the best. The trouble
had begun before the departure from Delfshaven. The congregation's leaders had reached an agreement with Thomas Weston about
the financial terms of the venture. The basic arrangement was that
the "Adventurers" (investors) and the "Planters" (settlers) would
form a joint-stock company, a partnership that would last for seven
years. Individuals received shares on the basis of their investment or,
in the case of the passengers, for undertaking the work of planting a
colony. The point was to ship furs and other commodities back to
England, and at the end of seven years all shareholders would divvy
up the profits. Over the course of those seven years, the settlers
would have two days a week to work for themselves, and they would
own any houses they built.

When Weston returned to London and met with his investors, they demanded two changes. Even the houses and gardens, or rather their value, would be included in the company's pool of assets, and, apart from the Sabbath, the settlers would work every single day for the company. Weston agreed, and Robert Cushman assented to the altered terms.

Back in Leiden, John Robinson and others were livid at the new terms, which they deemed "conditions fitter for thieves and bond-slaves than honest men." In a letter to John Carver, Robinson lamented "that you and your likes must serve a new apprenticeship of seven years, and not a day's freedom from task." Yes, the Adventurers would hazard their money, but the settlers would risk their lives. In return, the Adventurers were reducing them to servitude. Robinson concluded they had depended too much on Weston.[1]

Robinson and the most prominent congregants—Samuel Fuller, Edward Winslow, William Bradford, and Isaac Allerton—were upset with Weston, but they were furious at Robert Cushman. Angry letters went between Leiden and London. Robinson denounced Cushman as "most unfit to deal for other men." Cushman was piqued at the criticism. He had done his best for them. Did they think he had "no brains?" Fuller and the others answered that they wished he had used them.[2]

Under this torrent of criticism, Carver and Cushman turned on each other. Carver insisted that it was Cushman's fault alone. Cushman countered that Carver too had consented to the changes.

In a letter to his disgruntled coreligionists in Leiden, Cushman explained that when the Adventurers had seen the initial agreement, they had refused to accept it. Two leading investors had promptly withdrawn five hundred pounds. He had to give way or scuttle the entire plan. "If we will not go," the former grocer explained, "they are content to keep their moneys." Cushman maintained that the alterations were insignificant. Any houses they built would be worth very little, and any profits that accrued would benefit themselves as well as the Adventurers. They would not be like slaves. The whole point was to found a prosperous colony that would attract more settlers. If the congregation no longer trusted him or if they wanted him to stay behind, they could cast him off the way Jonah had been thrown overboard to avert God's wrath. Cushman's explanation never reached Leiden. According to Bradford, Carver "stayed [withheld]" it "for giving offence." The bad feelings festered throughout the summer.[3]

The Pilgrims found a second development troubling as well. Weston had arranged for a group of "strangers" (that is, not members of the congregation) to join the colony. Some of these men invested money in the venture, and given that most of the congregants had remained in Leiden, the planned colony needed the boost in numbers. The additional bodies, however, further corroded the group's cohesion. Christopher Martin, on behalf of the strangers, became a third agent alongside Carver and Cushman. The separatist agents quickly took a dislike to their new partner. Against Cushman's counsel, Martin went to Kent and began purchasing provisions for the voyage, prompting Cushman to accuse him of acting like a "king [rather] than a consort." It was already a "flat schism," Cushman lamented.[4]

Preparations continued despite the rancor. Weston chartered a second, much larger vessel named the *Mayflower*, which sailed from London to Southampton to meet the group coming from Leiden. For the voyage and their first winter, the colonists needed beef, hard biscuits (Shakespeare once called a fool's brain as "dry as the remainder biscuit after a voyage"), peas, barley, fish, butter, cheese, and oatmeal. They needed beer, partly to get down the biscuit, but mainly because it provided more nutrients and spoiled less readily than water. They needed tools to build houses. They needed seeds to plant crops. They needed armor and weapons—matchlock muskets and cannons—to defend themselves against Natives and rival Europeans.

When the Pilgrims on the *Speedwell* arrived at Southampton, their leaders informed Weston that they would not accept the changes to the agreement. Because they would not agree to the new terms, Weston told them "to stand on their own legs." Those legs were weak.[5] The Pilgrims did not have enough money to purchase the provisions they needed for the coming winter. They sold some extra butter, but they were still short on other necessities.

The venture hung by a thread, but it did not collapse. The Pilgrims had determined to go and had no intention of slinking back to Leiden. The Adventurers, for their part, wanted to recoup what

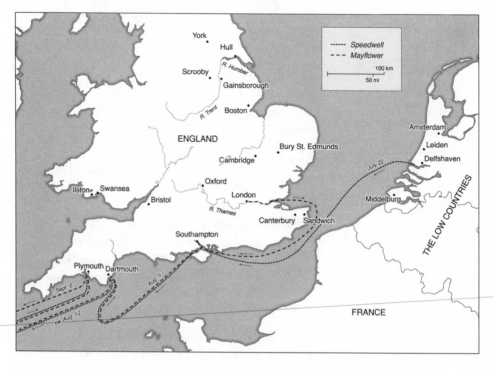

Tracks of the Speedwell *and the* Mayflower, *1620.*
(Map by Andrew C. Smith.)

they had already invested. The basic arrangement was clear, in any event. The Adventurers anticipated profits from what the settlers shipped back to England, and the Pilgrims expected that their investors would send more colonists and supply them with provisions and trading goods. At the same time, the ongoing disputes were troubling. If the two sides could not reach terms while in England, there was little reason to think they could cooperate when separated by an ocean.

In early August the Pilgrims sailed from Southampton aboard the *Mayflower* and the *Speedwell*. Their fates now rested in the seaworthiness of the two vessels and the skill and trustworthiness of their crews. They did not get very far. When the *Speedwell* started to leak badly, the two ships put into Dartmouth, a small Devonshire port.

By this point, Cushman was beside himself. "Our victuals will be half eaten up . . . before we go from the coast of England," he lamented in a letter to a friend. They would have nothing to eat when they reached their destination. Meanwhile, Martin's contempt for the separatists ate away at Cushman's morale. The former grocer and wool comber was suffering from a malady he suspected would prove fatal. He and fellow passenger William Ring wondered "who shall be meat first for the fishes." Cushman reckoned it would take a miracle for them to plant a colony under these circumstances.[6]

A week later, they set forth again, sailing a few hundred miles into the waters of the Atlantic before the *Speedwell*'s leaks worsened. They reversed course for Plymouth, where the *Speedwell*'s master declared his vessel unseaworthy. It is likely that after the *Speedwell*'s crew refitted her for the Atlantic crossing, her masts and rig were too tall and large for her hull, opening her seams under the pressure of ocean winds. Bradford blamed the ship's master, suggesting that he and his crew wanted to free themselves from the risks of the journey and noting that the *Speedwell* soon returned to service.[7]

Whether or not the *Speedwell*'s master had intentionally created the leaks, the passengers were down to a single ship, and the *Mayflower* could not take everyone and everything. Cushman now bowed out. The criticism he had received from his pastor and fellow congregants had broken his spirit. According to Bradford, Cushman's "heart and courage was gone." William Ring also chose to remain behind, and several families with young children were pleased to escape "the brunt of this hard adventure." Bradford compared the Pilgrims to Gideon's army. Before Gideon led his soldiers into battle, God told him to send away those who were afraid. God continued whittling down the army until only a tiny fraction remained. Likewise, the remaining Pilgrims were only a fraction of the Leiden congregation. Bradford took heart from the fact that Gideon's few valorous men had scattered the enemies of Israel.[8]

When the *Mayflower* once again set sail, it was already September 6. Most of the passengers had been living aboard the ships for at least a month, just the beginning of what Bradford later termed their "long imprisonment . . . at sea."[9] The lateness of the season, the shortfall in provisions, and the constant bickering all augured poorly for the success of their venture.

According to William Bradford's list, 102 men, women, and children were passengers on the *Mayflower*. The crew, headed by shipmaster Christopher Jones, probably numbered around 30 men. Two dogs were aboard, a mastiff and a small spaniel.

A majority of the free adult men—those who were not servants to other passengers—were members of the Leiden congregation or closely connected to its members. Among them were stalwarts such as Elder William Brewster; deacons John Carver and Samuel Fuller; and respected men such as William Bradford, Edward Winslow, and Isaac Allerton. The oldest passenger was James Chilton, recovered from the April 1619 assault that had nearly killed him.

Many historians have presumed that Myles and Rose Standish numbered among the "strangers."[10] Myles Standish had served with a company of English soldiers in the Dutch Republic. He survived the Siege of Ostend, which ended in 1604 and left around seventy-five thousand soldiers dead. Standish's company was probably garrisoned in Leiden, and at some point he became well acquainted with John Robinson. The Pilgrims' pastor once directed a message to "your captain, whom I love." Standish in turn bequeathed a small inheritance to Robinson's granddaughter Mercy. Standish's library in New Plymouth included several puritan titles and one tract by the Ancient Church's Francis Johnson. If Standish did not belong to the Leiden congregation, he was at the very least sympathetic to its principles.[11]

Jamestown began as an exclusively male settlement, but more than a quarter of the *Mayflower* passengers were women or girls. Many families had made difficult decisions that summer. William and Dorothy Bradford, for instance, left their son John in Leiden. Samuel Fuller's wife and child remained behind as well. Other couples, however, preferred to risk death together than to part. Among the nonseparatists, William White, John Billington, and William Mullins all brought wives and children. Three women were in the final trimester of pregnancy when the *Mayflower* left Plymouth.

Other than some members of the ship's crew, Stephen Hopkins was the only individual aboard who previously had crossed the Atlantic. In 1609, Hopkins had left his family behind and headed for Jamestown as a minister's clerk. Hopkins's duties included reading psalms and other passages of scripture during services. After seven weeks on the Atlantic, the *Sea Venture* sailed into a hurricane. Massive waves and wind buffeted the ship. The sky "like an hell of darkness turned black upon us," wrote passenger William Strachey. As the storm finally abated, the battered vessel foundered just off the Bermuda islands.

Having cheated death, and now gorging on fish, fowl, wild boars, turtle, and berries, some of the men wanted to stay in their new-found paradise rather than proceed to Virginia. Hopkins was among the rebels. He argued that the shipwreck on Bermuda had made them free. If they reached Jamestown, however, the investors of the Virginia Company might detain them even after their terms of service expired. They would live as slaves. Thomas Gates, on his way to Jamestown as Virginia's new governor, did not think the rebels deserved to live at all. Hopkins was manacled, found guilty of mutiny, and sentenced to death. Hopkins now made clear his preference for servitude over execution. He "made so much moan" about the "ruin" his demise would cause his family back in England that Gates issued a pardon.[12]

Hopkins eventually survived a few years in Jamestown and then returned to England. He found that his wife had died, but he was reunited with their three children. Undeterred by his near death at sea and the hardships in Virginia, he chose to return across the Atlantic on the *Mayflower.* He brought his second wife and three children, and during the crossing Elizabeth Hopkins gave birth to a son, whom they named Oceanus.[13]

Roughly one in five passengers came as a servant, apprentice, or ward; some were attached to Leiden congregants and some to Weston's recruits.[14] Four children became *Mayflower* passengers in scandalous circumstances. They were the "spurious brood" of one Samuel More. In order to consolidate and preserve his family's property, More's father had arranged a marriage between the seventeen-year-old Samuel and a relative six years his senior. Two sons and two daughters arrived at a rapid clip between 1612 and 1616, but by then, Samuel More realized that another man had been fathering them. The cuckolded More in short order disinherited his children, sued his wife's lover, and annulled his marriage.

More next acted to get rid of the children. He later wrote that he decided to free them from the "blots and blemishes" of bastardy, but he chose a callous if effective way of freeing himself from them. The first ship sailing for Virginia happened to be the *Mayflower*. More invested money on behalf of each child, and a servant handed the children over to Cushman and Weston. The Carvers and Winslows each took one child; William and Mary Brewster added the remaining two to their household. In the span of a few years, the "spurious brood" had lost their parents, property, and homeland.[15]

Out of all of the passengers, perhaps only Stephen Hopkins was prepared for what lay ahead. "Being in a ship is being in a jail," the eighteenth-century literary giant Samuel Johnson commented, "with the chance of being drowned." Johnson added that an inmate had "more room, better food, and commonly better company." Sea travel was a nightmare one endured and hoped to survive. A typical Atlantic crossing took about eight weeks. For much of that time, passengers huddled below deck, crammed into dim, foul quarters.[16]

The Pilgrims comforted each other during these months, but otherwise they agreed with Johnson's observation about the "company." Some of the nonseparatists probably leaned puritan, but if they were like nearly everyone else in England, they disdained Brownists. The Pilgrims for their part loathed Christopher Martin. Worst of all were the sailors, whom the self-styled godly regarded as a godless rabble.

The weather soon became even worse than the company. Fierce storms pounded the ship, which sprang leaks. At times, gales forced the crew to furl the ship's sails and lie at hull. The passengers probably felt much as John Donne did when he endured a ferocious tempest off the Azores in 1597. "Some coffin'd in their cabins lie," wrote the poet, "equally / Griev'd that they are not dead, and yet must die." Brave passengers crept from their quarters like "sin-burden'd souls" raised on the last day, expecting to receive the worst of news. Storms at sea and shipwrecks were recurring motifs in the Bible; theologians, philosophers, and poets returned to the subject again and again. The 95th Psalm declared that the sea belonged to God; tempests displayed his power and wrath. In the calm that followed, relieved travelers glimpsed God's mercy.[17]

One storm caused "one of the main beams in the midships" to buckle and crack. At that point, Jones and the crew contemplated turning around and limping back to Plymouth. From the Low Countries, however, the passengers had brought a "great iron screw," a jack used to raise heavy objects during the construction of a home. It allowed the beam to be raised back into place, and the carpenter then secured it with a post. Jones pronounced the ship "strong and firm underwater." They caulked leaks and continued.[18]

In his history, Bradford recounted two stories that illustrate how the Pilgrims made sense of the events of the crossing. Aboard the *Mayflower* was a sailor who "would always be condemning the poor people in their sickness, and cursing them daily with grievous execrations." This seasoned sailor looked down on the seasick landlubbers around him and looked forward to taking their belongings once he had tossed their corpses into the deep. Then, not yet halfway across the Atlantic, God chose to "smite this young man with a grievous disease." Even his fellow sailors agreed it was "the just hand of God upon him." They tossed him into the sea.[19]

Conversely, Bradford asserted that God saved John Howland, a servant of John Carver. Howland unwisely came above deck during a fierce storm and fell into the sea. Just as God had chosen to slay the profane seaman, so it "pleased God" to save a godly servant. Howland caught hold of a rope. The sailors pulled him out of the water and used a boat hook to bring him back aboard.[20]

English Protestants had complex and contradictory notions about God's providence. God punished sin and rewarded righteousness, at least at times. At other times, God's will was simply inscrutable. The ungodly sometimes prospered and the godly often suffered. In the months that followed, sailors and passengers, strangers and separatists, servants and masters, would die in roughly equal numbers. As the Apostle Paul wrote, there was no respect of persons with God. Still, separatists, like other pious Protestants, interpreted such outcomes not as mere fate or fortune, but as expressions of God's will.[21]

After more than two months at sea, the crew sighted what they recognized as the eastern coast of Cape Cod. Still aiming for somewhere in the vicinity of the Hudson River, the passengers persuaded Christopher Jones to sail south. Past the Cape's southeastern corner, dangerous shoals forced them to turn back. After rounding the Cape's tip, the crew dropped anchor on November 11 in what is now Provincetown Harbor.

When he recounted these events in his history, William Bradford felt the need to "make a pause." He urged his readers to remember the passengers' piety, their poverty, and the goodness of
God. "They fell upon their knees and blessed the God of heaven,"
he wrote, "who had brought them over the vast and furious ocean
. . . again to set their feet on the firm and stable earth." The Pilgrims
were not yet ashore, but one can imagine them aboard the ship, on
their knees in prayers of thanksgiving.

Bradford recalled that "they had now no friends to welcome
them, nor inns to entertain or refresh their weather-beaten bodies."
Men on Malta had helped the Apostle Paul's shipwrecked company,
but the Pilgrims had no one to succor them, only a wilderness "full
of wild beasts and wild men." They were like the Israelites after the
exodus from Egypt, with only the spirit of God to sustain them.
Bradford closed the scene with a paraphrase of the 107th Psalm,
which he adapted from the Geneva Bible, the translation the Pilgrims
brought to New England. "Let them therefore praise the Lord," he
began, "because he is good." Their souls were overwhelmed by the
forbidding landscape and the adversities they knew they would soon
encounter. Nevertheless, an annotation to the psalm reminded them
that "there is none affliction so grievous, out of the which God will
not deliver his." Like the ancient Israelites, the Pilgrims understood
themselves as God's people, and he had already calmed the storms
and stilled the waves.[22]

Despite the strife and delays of the summer, the crossing had gone
well. Except for two men, everyone had survived. In addition to the
one crew member, passenger William Butten—a young servant of
Samuel Fuller—died shortly before the *Mayflower* reached land.
Now, though, the Pilgrims had to reckon with the enormous mistake they had made in leaving England so late. There was no time to
prepare for a winter that had already begun.

According to Bradford's history, "some of the strangers" also
wanted to be rid of the separatists and had made "mutinous speeches"
against them during the crossing. Once ashore, they intended to
"use their own liberty." In a 1622 promotional tract for the colony,
Bradford and Edward Winslow stated that when they first reached
land, some passengers were "not well affected to unity and concord,

Jean Leon Gerome Ferris, The Mayflower Compact, *1620, 1899.*
(Courtesy of Library of Congress.)

but gave some appearance of faction." The situation resembled that faced by Stephen Hopkins and the other men who had wrecked on Bermuda. The Pilgrims had no patent that empowered them to form a government on Cape Cod. Thus, nothing restrained any individuals or groups from going their own way. For the colony to have any chance, the passengers needed to establish the concord and cooperation that had eluded them for months, and they needed to do so right away.[23]

To that end, the passengers formed what Bradford variously termed a "combination," "agreement," or "association," which later became known as the Mayflower Compact.[24] It was short and to the point. First, the Pilgrims declared themselves the "loyal subjects" of King James, whom they recognized as the "Defender of the Faith." Next, they noted that they had sailed for "the northern parts of Virginia" in order to glorify God, advance Christianity, and honor their king and country. In order to further those goals, and presumably to survive and prosper, they chose to "covenant, and combine ourselves together into a civil body politic, for our better ordering and preservation, and furtherance of the ends aforesaid; and by virtue hereof to enact, constitute, and frame such just and equal laws, ordinances, acts, constitutions, offices from time to time, as shall be thought most meet and convenient for the general good of the colony." The forty-one men who signed the document promised to render "all due submission and obedience" to those chosen officers and laws.[25]

That was it. The Mayflower Compact did not resemble a constitution or a bill of rights. The document said nothing about voting rights, requirements for holding office, or liberties such as the right to a trial by jury. In keeping with other colonial charters, there was no discussion of how the colony would relate to Native peoples other than a vague nod to their conversion. The colonists had been confined on a ship together for months with nothing to do, but they apparently drafted the agreement only right before going ashore. Given the urgency of establishing a settlement, there was no time to devise anything other than the sparsest framework for self-government.

The language of covenant would have resonated with many English Protestants, but there was a particular congruence with separatism.[26] As "the Lord's free people," William Bradford and William Brewster had once covenanted to form a church and to walk in God's ways. The compact, however, made the "civil body politic" broader than the body of Christ. Whether out of choice or necessity, political participation did not hinge on church membership or any test of religious orthodoxy. There is also a decided lack of religious content in the Mayflower Compact. When colonists in Bermuda signed their names to a set of six articles in 1612, they promised to worship God, defend the Church of England, observe the Sabbath, and to live righteously. The Pilgrims made no such promises. Their compact was a bare-bones political agreement.[27]

The Mayflower Compact was in keeping with the instructions of the Virginia Company. Shortly after the company assigned the Pilgrims a patent, its council voted that the leaders of "particular plantations . . . shall have liberty till a form of government be here settled for them, associating unto them divers of the gravest and discreetest of their companies, to make orders, ordinances and constitutions." The Pilgrims, though, did not consider the compact a temporary expedient. Instead, it was fundamental to their political order. When the settlers later revised and published their laws, they included the compact's text, pointing to it as the act that had created an enduring body politic, a little commonwealth within a larger imperial order.[28]

Shortly after the American Revolution, figures such as John Quincy Adams and Daniel Webster began to identify the Mayflower Compact as the starting point of American democracy and republicanism.[29] In recent decades, historians have poured ice-cold water on such notions. George F. Willison, an influential mid-twentieth-century chronicler of the Pilgrims, concluded that rather than "the very cornerstone of American democracy," the compact "was conceived as an instrument to maintain the status quo on the *Mayflower*, to show inferiors in general and servants in particular their place and keep them . . . under the thumbs of their masters." Mutinous and factious men promised to obey the leaders and laws chosen by the group.[30]

Nathaniel Philbrick takes this one step further by declaring it "deeply ironic that the document many consider to mark the beginning of what would one day be called the United States came from a people who had more in common with a cult than democratic society." As Philbrick notes, there were parallels between the separatist church covenant and the civil covenant of the Mayflower Compact. In both instances the people possessed the liberty to choose their own officers. Philbrick, though, claims that once chosen, Robinson was "more a benevolent dictator than a democratically elected official." Likewise, the Mayflower Compact enabled the separatists on the ship—a "bare majority" according to Philbrick, and in the minority according to Willison—to take control. The compact, thus, was a separatist power grab.[31]

The Mayflower Compact was not a republican document, as illustrated by its professions of loyalty to King James. Nor did it seek to establish democracy. In early Stuart England, *democracy* remained a dirty and dangerous word. Indeed, rumors soon reached England that the Pilgrims had overturned the social and political order. "You are mistaken," Bradford responded, "if you think we admit women and children [to participate in decisions of government]." Only men above the age of twenty-one might qualify themselves, and Bradford added that the colony's leaders consulted them only "in some weighty matters" at their discretion.[32]

Still, if John Quincy Adams and Daniel Webster misunderstood the compact and overstated its significance, recent reappraisals go too far in the other direction. For starters, the separatists certainly were not cultists. While the Leiden congregants revered Robinson, the separatist insistence on the liberties of the people weakened the authority of ministers. The congregation, not John Robinson, admitted members, exercised discipline, and elected officers. Before the Pilgrims had left Southampton, moreover, Robinson had reminded his congregants that because of the strangers who had joined them, their "body politic" would not be coextensive with their membership in the body of Christ. Unlike the Massachusetts Bay Colony, moreover, New Plymouth never made church membership a requirement for the franchise. The Pilgrims were neither democrats nor theocrats.

Furthermore, despite Bradford's suggestion that elected officers governed without undue interference, the Mayflower Compact incorporated significant elements of consent and participation. The Pilgrim men chose their officers "by common consent."[33] Those elected officers then expected obedience and deference, but the compact also promised its signers at least some ongoing role in framing the "just and equal laws, ordinances, acts, constitutions, [and] offices" that would shape their lives. From the start, the Pilgrims held annual elections. If a leader made himself obnoxious, the colonists could choose someone else the next year.

The inclusion of at least nearly all adult men within the "civil body politic," moreover, departed from English conventions. In his influential *De Republica Anglorum*, the politician and diplomat Thomas Smith defined a commonwealth as "a multitude of free men collected together and united by common accord and covenants among themselves." The Pilgrims had done just that, but by Smith's standards, very few of them were "free men." For Thomas Smith, servants and men without property did not possess the liberties enjoyed by landed elites. They had no say, and in some cases they were very nearly the chattel of their superiors, little better than "bondmen" and "slaves." In the early seventeenth century, for instance, the authorities in London sometimes rounded up indigent persons and shipped them off as servants to Virginia and the Caribbean.[34]

The Mayflower Compact, by contrast, gave farmers, common laborers, and even servants a place within a body politic. John Carver signed the compact, but so did his servant John Howland. At the very least, nearly all adult male passengers added their names to the agreement. It was pragmatic for Pilgrim leaders to ask disgruntled men to "promise all due submission and obedience," but their decision to include nearly every male body within their body politic is still striking. Voluntarily subscribed compacts were hardly the only possible means of quashing mutiny and faction.

Bradford writes that after signing the compact, the Pilgrims elected John Carver as their governor "for that year." Now they were ready to go ashore.[35]

CHAPTER FOUR

Thanksgiving

A
T THE START OF the seventeenth century, Europeans who explored Cape Cod and nearby coastlines described thickly settled Native villages and verdant fields. They rhapsodized about the region's natural bounty and suggested ways that it could make them rich. The Pilgrims did so as well, but they encountered a place already transformed by contact with Europeans. The fish and fowl remained abundant, but many of the region's human inhabitants had vanished.

Contemporary scholars use the term *Wampanoag* to designate the communities of southeastern Massachusetts. Some seventeenth-century sources used versions of the term as well, but Natives and Europeans generally employed more particular names: Paomet and Nauset on the eastern cape, Manomet and Patuxet along the western shore of Cape Cod Bay. Farther to the west, in present-day Bristol, Rhode Island, the Pokanokets—whose sachem the Pilgrims called by his title Massasoit—exercised a fragile hegemony over these communities. Massasoit was not a king but a paramount sachem, a sachem over other Wampanoag sachems. Along with those living on the islands to Cape Cod's south, the above-mentioned peoples were bound together through kinship, a particular dialect of Algonquian, ritual practices and a shared cosmology, and a rough acceptance of Massasoit's leadership. The Wampanoags were among the many Algonquian peoples of the region, and they were surrounded by peoples who were both rivals and trading partners: the Narragansetts and Pequots to the west, the Massachusetts to their north, and beyond them the Abenaki.[1]

These coastal communities thrived because of the region's abundance of seafood. Shellfish included clams, mussels, and oysters. Whales were abundant, if hard to catch. Easy to catch were eels, present near Patuxet in tremendous numbers. Europeans expressed astonishment at the diversity and quantity of fish: cod, striped bass, sturgeon, and many other species. Wampanoag and other regional communities supplemented their diets with corn, the cultivation of which had spread gradually from present-day Mexico and the American Southwest into the eastern woodlands of North America.[2]

In 1602, the English explorer and colonizer Bartholomew Gosnold sailed to present-day southern Maine, then continued to what he named "Cape Cod" for its "great store of cod-fish." Gosnold rounded the Cape, proceeding nearly as far as Narragansett Bay. Gosnold's men and the peoples they encountered had a few moments of tension, but there was bartering and feasting rather than violence. A published account of the venture boosted English interest in what was then called Norumbega or northern Virginia, a place teeming with seafood, waterfowl, and deer, a landscape rich in sassafras (used as a treatment for syphilis) and copper.[3]

Subsequent English-Native encounters were less peaceful. The peoples of the region quickly learned that the English did not fish only for cod. They were also fishers of men. In 1605, George Waymouth abducted five Abenaki men while trading along the Maine coast. The English sailors enticed a few men to come aboard their ship by offering them food and "trifles." They also used brute force. Waymouth's men subdued two other "strong" and mostly "naked" men by grabbing them by their long hair. Presumably, Waymouth intended to groom the men as translators and navigators, a long-established European tactic.[4]

Upon reaching England, Waymouth handed over three of his captives to Sir Ferdinando Gorges, commander of the fort at Plymouth. The Abenaki men fired Gorges's imagination with their talk of navigable rivers and safe harbors. "This accident," he later wrote, "must be acknowledged the means under God of putting on foot and giving life to all our plantations." Gorges never set foot on North

American soil, but he helped secure charters for the London and Plymouth companies, with the latter obtaining the privilege of settling northern Virginia. On the first of many expeditions he backed over the next several decades, Gorges sent Waymouth's captives as guides and translators for a short-lived colony at the mouth of the Kennebec River.[5]

Other kidnappings followed. In 1611, ship captain Edward Harlow abducted five Natives. Among them was Epenow, from an island known as Capawack or Noepe, which Gosnold had named Martha's Vineyard. In London, Harlow exhibited Epenow to paying crowds. "When they will not give a doit to relieve a lame beggar," quipped a character in Shakespeare's *The Tempest*, "they will lay out ten to see a dead Indian." A living Indian was even better. But when Londoners tired of Epenow, Harlow turned him over to Gorges, who described him as "of a goodly stature, strong and well proportioned." Gorges was more impressed with Epenow's body than with his brains. He joked that the captive knew only enough English "to bid those that wondered at him, welcome, welcome."[6]

Gorges badly underestimated his captive, who was a quick study of the English language and of English greed. Epenow spun tales about gold mines on Martha's Vineyard, and in 1614 Gorges sent him back across the Atlantic to show Captain Nicholas Hobson where to find them. According to Gorges, when Hobson reached Martha's Vineyard, Epenow's "brothers" and "cousins" came aboard and "were kindly entertained." When they departed, they promised to come back the next day to trade. Hobson sensed trouble. He did not want to lose his Native guide. Three men guarded Epenow, and they dressed him in "long garments, fitly to be laid hold on, if occasion should require." Occasion required. When his people returned the next day, Epenow jumped overboard, wriggled out of the baggy clothing, and swam to freedom while his cousins and brothers sent a "shower of arrows" at the English ship. A wounded Hobson returned to England without any gold and without his captive. He reported that Epenow was among those Natives his men had slain in the fight.[7]

While Hobson's disaster unfolded, John Smith mapped the coastline from the Bay of Fundy to Cape Cod and christened the region "New England." Five years earlier, Smith had played a pivotal but

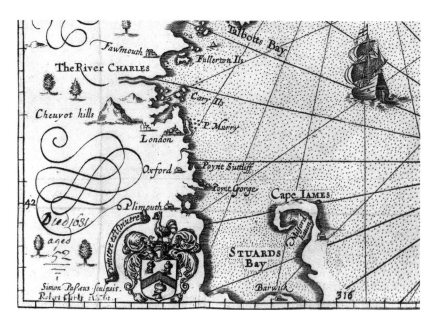

Detail of map of New England drawn by Simon van de Passe, 1616, from notes made by John Smith. The Pilgrims named their settlement Plimouth on the basis of this map. (Courtesy of the John Carter Brown Library.)

contentious role in the early years of the Jamestown colony. He had watched its settlers search in vain for precious metals, leaving themselves vulnerable to starvation and attack. Smith now maintained that colonists and traders should turn their attention to New England, which offered less exotic but more readily attainable riches. If fish "seeme[d] a mean and a base commodity" compared to gold or even copper, Smith promised that the sea's bounty was a living, inexhaustible mine that would reward English industry. The region's human resources were also promising. He described villages along Massachusetts Bay at peace with one another, "planted with gardens and corn fields," and eager to trade. Ignoring his experiences in Virginia, Smith imagined that English conquistadors could quickly intimidate and subdue New England's Native peoples, who would then deliver valuable fish and furs to them. Smith sailed back to England in August 1614. Despite receiving a commission as the "Admiral of New England," Smith never returned to the region.[8]

One member of Smith's expedition tried a more crooked path to profits. Thomas Hunt, captain of a second vessel under Smith's command, used his own initiative to kidnap around twenty Indians at Patuxet, a community Smith marked as "Plimouth" on his map. A man named Tisquantum, or Squanto, was among the captives. Following the example of Waymouth and others, Hunt lured them aboard through overtures of friendship and trade, then seized them. Hunt also captured some Nauset men on the eastern cape. Unlike Waymouth and Harlow, Hunt brought his captives to the slave markets of Spain. According to Gorges, after Hunt had sold several, "the friars of those parts took the rest from them and kept them to be instructed in the Christian faith." Squanto somehow ended up in England, living with John Slany, an official of the Newfoundland Company, under whose auspices he sailed back across the Atlantic.[9]

John Smith condemned Thomas Hunt's actions, writing that his "treachery among the savages" taught Natives to hate the English. The abductions imperiled English crews and disrupted commerce. Ferdinando Gorges also denounced Hunt's duplicity and rapacity, noting that "the poor innocent creatures . . . in confidence of his honesty had put themselves into his hands." Gorges interpreted Waymouth's human captives as a gift from God, and Smith raised no objections to the earlier kidnappings. Why did they single out Hunt for denunciation? In their minds, the other abductions were temporary. Gorges intended to transform captives into loyal servants and send them home as cultural mediators between their people and the English. Both Gorges and Smith stressed that Hunt, by contrast, "sought to sell them *for slaves*." Gorges and Smith distinguished between Spanish slavery and impressment into English service, a distinction that captives such as Epenow did not accept.[10]

Meanwhile, in Newfoundland, Squanto met Thomas Dermer, another agent of Ferdinando Gorges. Dermer and Squanto both wanted to go to New England, though for very different reasons. Dermer wanted to fish and trade there; Squanto simply wanted to go home. The pair went to England to confer with Gorges, then returned to Newfoundland in 1619 and headed southwest along the coast toward Cape Cod. Gorges probably had no delusions of gold this time around, and Dermer's account suggests that he and Gorges secured Squanto's cooperation by promising him a reunion with his people. Still, the gist of the plan was to use a man the English had kidnapped to repair trading relationships damaged by the abductions.

When Squanto went to Patuxet, all of his people were gone. Those who were not dead had fled. Dermer and other Europeans described the culprit as the "plague" because the results resembled those of the Black Death's worst outbreaks in Europe. The bubonic plague probably could not have survived the ocean crossing. Historians and epidemiologists have proposed many different explanations, including smallpox, typhoid fever, and—more recently— leptospirosis (a bacteria spread primarily through rodent urine). The precise malady remains uncertain, but it was a disease brought by Europeans for which Natives lacked immunity.[11]

Squanto helped Dermer establish peaceful contact with several Native communities, including the Pokanokets to Patuxet's west. At the Pokanoket village of Sowams, Dermer met "two kings," one of whom was Massasoit. It turned out that there were European captives in the region; Dermer gained the release of two Frenchmen who had survived a shipwreck. After Squanto left to search for Patuxet survivors, though, Dermer fared poorly on his own. When his vessel ran aground off the east coast of Cape Cod, his crew freed it by tossing most of their provisions overboard. Then the Nausets at the southeastern tip of Cape Cod took Dermer prisoner until his men purchased his freedom with several hatchets.

Dermer then went to Martha's Vineyard. He met Epenow, who, it turned out, had not perished during the fight between his people and Hobson's crew. Epenow now "laughed at his own escape, and reported the story of it." The former captive also sensed an opportunity for revenge. Dermer planned to sail to Virginia and then return to New England. Epenow encouraged him to stop again at Martha's Vineyard when he did. When Dermer came back to the region the following summer, he first went to Sowams and found that the previously friendly Pokanokets now bore "an inveterate malice to the English." The change might have given Dermer pause about visiting other communities, but he pushed ahead. Again in the company of Squanto, Dermer and his crew went back to Martha's Vineyard, where they were attacked. Most of Dermer's men were slain. He was wounded, barely escaped with his life, and headed for Jamestown. Squanto's role in the attack, and his whereabouts in the aftermath, are unknown.[12]

Unwittingly, the Pilgrims had come to a place of death and captivity.

The *Mayflower* passengers confined their explorations to the tip of Cape Cod while the ship's crew repaired a shallop they had brought from England that had been damaged during the crossing. Men waded ashore to gather firewood, women washed clothes in frigid water, and the Pilgrims surveyed their immediate surroundings. If there had been snow, the Pilgrims would have mentioned it, so it was a drab autumnal landscape. From the boat they saw no people, but they commented on the sandy hills and wide variety of trees: oaks, pines, sassafras, birch, holly, ash, walnut, and juniper, the latter of which they collected and used as a source of firewood.

Myles Standish led an expedition on November 15, joined by Stephen Hopkins, William Bradford, and around a dozen other men. They wore armor and carried muskets and swords. Almost immediately they spotted a small group of Natives, who when they saw the armed Pilgrims disappeared into the woods. Eager to make contact— too eager—the Pilgrims gave chase for about ten miles, slept the night, and then gave up the trail after they plunged into some tough undergrowth. The English pursuit probably convinced the fleeing Indians that the men chasing them were a new group of kidnappers or marauders. The hungry and thirsty explorers restored their strength at springs of fresh water. "[We] sat us down," Pilgrim leaders wrote, "and drunk our first New England water with as much delight as ever we drunk drink in all our lives."[13]

The Pilgrim men found old cornfields and other land "fit for the plow," and they discovered graves. Of the latter, the Pilgrims excavated some and examined their contents, but they covered the objects back up because they "thought it would be odious unto them [the Indians] to ransack their sepulchers." Inspired by the Spanish extraction of gold from Inca tombs in Peru, the English had with great excitement opened graves from Baffin Island to Roanoke. Such efforts yielded no gold, and at Jamestown, grave opening and grave looting prompted Powhatan reprisals. The Pilgrims were right to hesitate.[14]

The explorers also unearthed a substantial cache of corn and a large European-made ship's kettle. They hesitated again, but they decided to take all they could carry. Bradford compared their bounty to a cluster of grapes that Israelite spies had found on a scouting mission into the promised land. Likewise, the corn was a special providence of God, who thereby preserved the Pilgrims from starvation. They filled the kettle with corn and stuffed their pockets, intending to return the kettle and "satisfy" the Indians for the corn when they could. The Pilgrims were pleased to see other promising sources of food, including caches of nuts and strawberries as well as abundant geese, ducks, and deer. They even found an artfully constructed deer trap, which snagged William Bradford by the leg when he stumbled into it.

Ten days later, after the carpenter had completed the shallop repairs, a larger party set forth. By this time it was snowing, windy, and bitterly cold. After one night ashore, they sailed down as far as the first expedition had reached. They took more corn, and beans as well. After following a few paths, the Pilgrims came upon a larger grave than they had found on their earlier venture. In it, they uncovered a series of objects buried between mats, including a bow, bowls, trays, and other "trinkets." Eventually, they came to "two bundles," one large and one small.

The large bundle contained the bones and skull of a man covered with a red powder the Pilgrims presumed was a type of embalmment. The skull had "fine yellow hair still on it," and some of the flesh remained "unconsumed." With the corpse were a few objects, including a knife and a large needle. The smaller bundle contained the corpse of a "little child," strings and bracelets, a little bow, and "some other odd knacks."

The larger corpse in particular intrigued them. Was it an "Indian lord and king?" The yellow hair suggested it was instead "a Christian." Had the Indians honored this individual who had died in their midst? Or had they killed him and buried him as a sign of "triumph"? The Pilgrims took "sundry of the prettiest things" and covered up the corpses again.

During the second expedition, after disturbing and looting the above-mentioned gravesite, the Pilgrims entered homes that they could tell had been recently used. Pilgrim writers offered an admiring description of Wampanoag *wetus* (houses). They were made from "young sapling trees," bent, stuck into the ground, and tied together to create a dome or arbor. The Wampanoags covered the exterior and interior with mats that kept out rain and kept in heat. The door was only a yard high, but the Pilgrims were impressed that adult men could stand upright within the homes. In the middle, there were stakes, and sticks laid between the stakes held cooking pots. The roof had a hole at the center to let out smoke, though the Pilgrims noted that the opening could be covered in the event of rain. Other colonists praised wetus as better insulated than English houses.[15]

Within the houses, they found a freshly killed deer head, along with some antlers, eagle claws, pieces of fish, and baskets of acorns. The explorers took "some of the best things," probably some seeds, baskets, and other household belongings. They intended to bring beads as payment and as a "sign of peace." The Pilgrims must have made a very poor impression on the Natives of Cape Cod. It is hardly surprising that people who faced possible starvation took food when they found it, but the taking of other objects demonstrates that the Pilgrims had very little respect for the people who had made them.

As the weeks passed, the Pilgrims grew desperate to select a place for their settlement. Some of the passengers had been living on the ship for four months. Their supplies of food were dwindling, and they were running low on beer. They needed to build houses, survive the winter, and plant crops in the spring. They had not found a location they considered suitable on the Cape, but they also did not want to range too far to the north. One of the ship's pilots, Robert Coppin, recalled "a great navigable river and good harbor" on the other side of the bay. On December 6, around twenty men set out to find it or another place that would meet their needs.

It was now so cold that water froze on their clothes and made them "like coats of iron." Sailing around fifteen miles to the south, they stopped and made camp after seeing a group of Indians "busy about a black thing," which the Pilgrims called a "grampus." It was probably a pilot whale. The next day, they scouted out the area and found it no better than the Cape's tip. They hunkered down for a second night at a stream now called the Herring River. As they breakfasted at early dawn, they suddenly found themselves under attack. The Pilgrims emerged unscathed from a brief skirmish, and the Nauset attackers apparently suffered no casualties either. The Indians probably intended to warn rather than kill the English interlopers.

Soon they were underway again. Coppin guided the shallop along the southern rim of the bay and then headed north into a biting mixture of rain, snow, and wind. The vessel's rudder broke, and they had to steer with oars. Next the gale split their mast into three pieces. Finally, they saw the harbor, and the storm blew their vessel into it. Coppin steered the shallop toward a sandy shore. It turned out to be a small island, which the Pilgrims named for John Clarke, another member of the *Mayflower*'s crew and the first to step ashore.[16] With difficulty, the cold and wet Pilgrims made a fire. They spent a day recovering from their ordeal while they observed the Sabbath.

On Monday, December 11, they explored the harbor.[17] "We marched also into the land," Pilgrim leaders wrote, "and found divers cornfields, and little running brooks, a place very good for situation." On Tuesday, the men excitedly returned to the *Mayflower.*

Bad news greeted them. Dorothy Bradford had died on December 7, the day after her husband and the others had departed on the shallop. William Bradford did not mention her death in his narrative history. In 1650, when Bradford listed the deaths of *Mayflower* passengers, he simply noted that his wife "died soon after their arrival." Historians continue to regurgitate the notion that she committed suicide. The idea stems from an 1869 short story, in which a brokenhearted Dorothy Bradford kills herself because her husband loves another woman. The tale has no more historical value than Henry Wadsworth Longfellow's *The Courtship of Miles Standish*, which narrates a love triangle involving Standish, John Alden, and Priscilla Mullins. How, then, did Dorothy Bradford die? In his 1702 history of New England, Boston minister Cotton Mather stated that she "accidentally" fell overboard and "drowned in the harbor." One imagines that like others who succumbed during these months, she was weakened by malnutrition and disease.[18]

Dorothy Bradford's was not the only death. Jasper More, one of the four bastard children taken in by the Pilgrims, died in early De-

cember, as did a servant of John Carver. James Chilton, the oldest
passenger on the *Mayflower*, was also dead. No sources specify the
cause of their deaths. There was also one addition. Still aboard the
Mayflower, Susanna White gave birth to a son she and her husband
named Peregrine.[19]

On Friday, December 15, the *Mayflower* weighed anchor for the
place that the explorers had found. Winds forced them back until
the following day, but the ship reached the harbor late on Saturday.
Again, the Pilgrims observed the Sabbath, likely with William Brewster delivering a sermon and with respected members of the congregation prophesying in the afternoon. On Monday, December 18, they
came ashore and looked at potential places for a settlement. Some
proposed Clark's Island, which would have been easy to defend but
had limited potential for farming or fresh water. They instead chose
an area on the mainland, bisected "by a very sweet brook," with cornfields already cleared and a hill on which they could mount their
cannon and look far out into the sea. It was Patuxet, Squanto's old
village. They realized that this was the place John Smith had christened "Plimouth," and so the Pilgrims called their colony "Plimoth
Plantation" (Bradford's spelling) or "New Plymouth."

Each year, a million people go to Plymouth to see the rock on which
the Pilgrims came ashore, undeterred by the fact that the Pilgrims
themselves wrote nothing about clambering out of their boat onto a
boulder. Regardless of where they took their first steps, the Pilgrims
walked into a disaster. The poor nutrition during the crossing left
their health fragile, and they lacked sufficient food for the months
ahead. Exposure to bitter-cold weather and wading in water did
not help matters. Bradford did not describe the illnesses in detail,
simply stating that they were "infected with the scurvy and other
diseases." Scurvy develops after a protracted period of vitamin C
deficiency, beginning with weakness and irritated skin, progressing
to blackened and swollen gums, and ending with fevers, hemorrhag-
ing, and death. Many ship crews in the sixteenth and early seventeenth century suffered from the ailment, as did English colonists
on Newfoundland.[20]

During the first months at Plymouth, many of the Pilgrims remained aboard the *Mayflower* in cramped quarters. According to Bradford, the few who remained healthy "did all the homely and necessary offices for them which dainty and queasy stomachs cannot endure to hear named." They washed "loathsome clothes" and diseased bodies. They cleaned chamber pots, beds, and the ship's deck of vomit and diarrhea.[21]

Bradford contrasted the Christian charity of the settlers with the selfishness of the seamen. The sailors wanted to keep the dwindling supply of beer for themselves and would not give even a small amount to a sick passenger who requested it. Then the sailors also fell ill and "began now to desert one another." The Pilgrims, though, extended their love to those who had mocked and mistreated them. "You, I now see," commented a sick crew member, "show your love like Christians indeed one to another, but we let one another lie and die like dogs." Master Jones relented and sent some beer ashore for the sick Pilgrims there. Not all members of the crew were antagonistic toward the settlers. In February, Giles Heale, the ship's surgeon, received a book from Isaac Allerton. It was a copy of Henry Ainsworth's psalter. Presumably Allerton made the gift because of Heale's care for the settlers, including Allerton's own ailing wife. Heale carried the volume back to England.[22]

Deaths mounted as the winter months progressed: eight in January, among them Rose Standish; seventeen in February, including Mary Allerton; Elizabeth Winslow and a dozen others in March. By then, barely half of the passengers remained alive. "The living were scarce able to bury the dead," Bradford wrote the next fall. Some entire households died, including Christopher Martin, his wife, and two servants, as well as John Turner and his two sons (Turner's daughter, who had stayed in Europe, later came to New England). Sisters Ellen and Mary More died within months of their brother Jasper; only Richard More survived the winter. Priscilla Mullins was the sole member of her family to survive the winter. She soon married John Alden, a cooper hired by the Pilgrims at Southampton.[23]

What the *Mayflower* passengers endured was grim but not exceptional. As had been the case since Christopher Columbus left a group of men behind on Hispaniola in 1492, Europeans who founded new colonies endured initial months or even years of misery. For instance, about two-thirds of the Jamestown settlers died during that colony's first year.[24]

None of Plymouth's settlers wrote letters or journals that reveal much about their emotional state during these months. They were too busy trying to survive, too sick to write. Promotional tracts written by Bradford, Winslow, and Robert Cushman advertised New England's bounty and glossed over the settlers' initial challenges. Many years later, though, Bradford reflected on the hardships of the first winter when he eulogized William Brewster in his history. Like the Apostle Paul, Bradford wrote, the Pilgrims had endured "perils among the heathen" and "perils in the wilderness"; they had known pain, hunger, thirst, and cold. How had they persevered? "It was God's visitation that preserved their spirits," Bradford asserted. He added that God often preserved his saints "not by good and dainty fare" but through "fears, and many afflictions." This was standard puritan discourse. What we do not know is how the men, women, and children among the Pilgrims interpreted these afflictions as they unfolded.[25]

In early Jamestown, settlers recorded stories of despair, madness, and even cannibalism. For instance, a malnourished man named Hugh Pryse came into the "marketplace blaspheming and crying out that there was no God, alleging that if there were a God, he would not suffer his creatures whom he had made and framed to endure those miseries and to perish for want of food." George Percy, governor of Jamestown at the time, noted that God used the "savages" to smite Pryse. Wolves then ripped apart his corpse. Another man murdered his pregnant wife, ripped their child out of her uterus, threw it in the river, and then "chopped the mother in pieces and salted her for his food." Percy described Jamestown's sick and starving settlers as "so lean" that they looked like last year's unpicked and now withered fruit. They cried out. They stumbled around. They lost their marbles and their morals.[26]

Things were just as wretched in Plymouth, and men and women in such circumstances could not have always acted like saints. Phinehas Pratt, who joined the colony a few years later, wrote that during their first winter, the Pilgrims propped ailing men against trees and leaned muskets against them. Fearing the Indians would take advantage of their weakness, they risked the lives of their sick in a false show of strength. Pratt's secondhand report may or may not be accurate, but disease and death must have shaken and perplexed the Pilgrims. Did they wonder why God in his providence willed that so many of their family and friends should die? Did they conclude that God was chastising them for their sinfulness?[27]

Yet the Plymouth settlers did not fall out with each other. There were quarrels, but there was no mutiny or blasphemy, let alone murder and cannibalism. Apparently no one begged to return to England on the *Mayflower.* In order to survive beyond that first winter, however, the settlers needed to do more than take care of each other. They needed help.

During their first weeks at Plymouth, the Pilgrims saw many abandoned houses and some fires in the distances, but no "savages." Then in mid-February, a settler hid in fear when he stumbled upon a group of twelve Indians. Also, two settlers reported that Natives had stolen some tools left behind in the woods.

In response to the apparent theft, the settlers prepared to defend themselves. They chose as their military captain Myles Standish, who had been acting the part since the *Mayflower* first anchored off Cape Cod. A few days later, the sailors helped the men drag their cannons up the hill. For the next month, the settlers maintained a heightened state of military preparedness. No attack came.

Then in mid-March, an Indian man strolled into the settlement. He headed straight for the Pilgrims' common house, but they cut him off before he went inside. "He saluted us in English," they wrote, "and bade us welcome." The English understood his name as Samoset. The unexpected visitor was tall, straight; despite the cold weather, he wore only a narrow fringe around his waist. He told them that he was an Abenaki "sagamore," a minor sachem from the north. He had learned English from fishermen. It is unclear how he had ended up among the Wampanoags; perhaps he had become their captive. Given past English-Native encounters up and down the New England coast, Samoset had probably worked hard to muster courage for his errand. Probably relieved that the Pilgrims had neither killed nor kidnapped him, he now asked them for beer. They had none, but they gave him "strong water" (some type of spirits), biscuit, butter, cheese, pudding, and a piece of mallard duck.[28]

From their guest, they learned about the Native communities that surrounded them, including the Pokanokets and their great sachem—Massasoit—to the west. Samoset told them about the kidnappings by Thomas Hunt, which helped explain why the Nausets on Cape Cod had attacked them. Finally, the settlers learned why they had encountered so many graves and abandoned houses. Samoset informed them that "an extraordinary plague" had killed the people who had lived here. Everyone had died. "There is none to hinder our possession," the Pilgrims concluded, "or to lay claim unto it." Many English writers made the same argument, that New England was a depopulated wilderness, a *vacuum domicilium* (empty dwelling). The Pilgrims interpreted the epidemics as God's providential preparation for English settlers.[29]

The settlers talked with Samoset all afternoon. They were nervous. Was he a spy, sent to gather information about their numbers and defenses? The settlers wanted to send Samoset away at nightfall, but he did not want to leave. Then they tried to take him to the *Mayflower* for the night, but the wind was too strong. So they put him up with Stephen Hopkins and kept a close eye on him. When he left the next morning, the settlers gave him a knife, a bracelet, and a ring. They told him they wanted to trade. Samoset said he would return with some of Massasoit's people.

The next day, Samoset was back, with five companions. The Indians brought a few beaver skins, but it was the Sabbath, so the Pilgrims rushed the visitors away as quickly as possible, asking them to come back with more pelts. On March 22, the Plymouth settlers met Squanto, and Samoset told the settlers that Massasoit was nearby. After some negotiations, the Pokanoket sachem came to the settlement, accompanied by his brother Quadequina and around twenty other men. The Pilgrims did their best to impress him. Captain Standish and six armed men greeted Massasoit at the brook. They brought him to a partly built house, in which they placed a green rug and several cushions. Governor Carver entered the building, with a drummer and trumpeter following him, along with several other armed men.

Cyrus E. Dallin, Massasoit, *1920, on Cole's Hill in Plymouth.*
(Photograph courtesy of Library of Congress.)

The Pilgrims described Massasoit as a "very lusty [strong] man, in his best years, an able body, grave of countenance, and spare of speech." His face was painted a deep mulberry red, and "he looked greasily" because of oil applied to his head and face. Massasoit wore "a great chain of white bone beads" around his neck. On his back, he kept a small bag of tobacco, which he shared with the Pilgrims. Several years later, a visitor to Plymouth described Massasoit as wearing only "a black wolf skin" upon his shoulder and a five-inch belt of "beads about his middle." When he first met the Pilgrims, however, Massasoit and his men wore long pants and used deerskins to keep themselves warm.[30]

Carver and Massasoit quickly formed an alliance. In the treaty recorded by the Pilgrims, there were several provisions, but the one that mattered the most was simple: the Plymouth settlers and Massasoit's warriors would aid each other in case of attack. Both sides also promised to leave their weapons "behind them" when they visited each other. An exception to this general reciprocity was a stipulation that Massasoit allow the English to punish any Indians who "did hurt to any of ours." At least in their record of the agreement, the English made no like promise to turn over any settlers who harmed the Indians. They assured Massasoit that if he kept to the treaty's terms, King James would consider him a friend and ally.[31]

The Pilgrims' reasons for concluding the alliance are obvious. They needed security in the midst of their weakness, and they needed food and other help in order to survive. Massasoit for his part needed new allies and wanted trade. The epidemics had devastated Massasoit's people but had left their Narragansett enemies largely unscathed. For Massasoit, moreover, there was no apparent downside. His village of Sowams lay around forty miles to the west, far from Patuxet. He had no reason to expect that the English newcomers would encroach on his land or authority. Nor did he care about what the Pilgrims wrote down on paper. For Massasoit and his people, friendship and alliances rested on the reciprocal exchange of gifts and expressions of hospitality.

The successful negotiations were the turning point for the fledgling colony. By the time the *Mayflower* sailed for England in early April, the season of death had loosened its grip. Squanto in particular proved invaluable to the Pilgrims as their principal interpreter and navigator. He caught passels of eels for them and guided them to the best fishing spots. Squanto also showed them how to plant maize and instructed them to fertilize it with fish, which—in addition to creating what must have been a massive stench—produced a fine crop of corn, some English wheat, and meager quantities of English barley and peas. Over the course of the summer, the Pilgrims, like other Europeans who came to southern New England in the seventeenth century, were astonished at what seemed to be the limitless supply of fish, eels, lobsters, deer, turkeys, ducks, berries, grapes, and plums. For a stretch of months, the settlers ate well. They could see what looked like endless sources of timber and firewood. "A better place cannot be in the world," wrote one settler in a letter back to England.[32]

If the Plymouth colonists were now dying at a slower rate, the challenges that lay before them remained daunting. With the exception of their new allies, whom they did not trust, they were alone on unfamiliar ground. If they were to survive another year, the settlers needed supplies of food that would last them through the next winter. If the colony was to succeed, they needed commodities that would translate into English profits and attract additional settlers. The *Mayflower*, however, returned back across the Atlantic without the fish and furs the Pilgrims' financial backers eagerly anticipated.

John Carver died in April, followed by his wife a few weeks later. As their next governor, the settlers chose William Bradford. Isaac Allerton became his assistant. Despite the winter's mortality, the colony's leadership was safely in the hands of the separatist majority, with Bradford and Allerton as magistrates, Standish as military captain, and Brewster as the church's elder.

Plymouth's first marriage took place in May, when Edward Winslow married Susanna White. Her first husband, William, had died in February, but her two sons had survived the winter. In keeping with separatist teaching, the wedding was strictly a civil affair. Likewise, burials were simple, with no ceremonies or eulogies. Worship services moved from the ship to the shore to a common house. Elder Brewster preached most Sundays, but other male congregants delivered sermons on occasion, and the church's leading men prophesied during afternoon worship. With their minister John Robinson still in Leiden, though, church members did not celebrate the Lord's Supper or present their children for baptism.

In June, Edward Winslow and Stephen Hopkins traveled the forty miles to Massasoit's village of Sowams, stopping in other Wampanoag communities along the way. The two were among the very few Europeans who had left the coastal waterways and rivers of New England and followed Native paths through its interior. They saw unburied "skulls and bones" in now empty places of habitation, and they saw tall weeds that had overtaken cleared fields. When they reached the Pokanokets, they slept on a mat in close quarters with the sachem, his wife, and two of his chief men. Between the "bad lodging, the savages' barbarous singing . . . lice and fleas within doors, and mosquitoes without," they were eager to return to Plymouth. Fear, curiosity, and even wonder had characterized the Pilgrims' emotions during their first interactions with the Indians. Winslow now chronicled extreme discomfort, even revulsion.[33]

Even so, the visit cemented the alliance. Winslow and Hopkins presented Massasoit with "a horseman's coat of red cotton," which he gladly donned, "not a little proud to behold himself." By this point, the Pilgrims had become annoyed by the constant stream of Wampanoag families who came to Patuxet to enjoy the hospitality of their new allies. Massasoit agreed that his people "should no more pester" them. The sachem then gathered his men and "made a great speech"; he and those present affirmed his authority over some thirty Wampanoag communities. They smoked tobacco and talked about England. According to Winslow, Massasoit declared that "it was King James his country, and he also was King James his man." If Squanto's translation and Winslow's record are accurate, what did Massasoit mean by such statements? Did he assert that his people and the settlers were on equal terms with the English king's subjects? Or was he simply professing his friendship with the English? Regardless of Massasoit's intentions, the Pilgrims interpreted such statements as their ally's acceptance of English sovereignty.[34]

Later in the summer, Winslow—and probably Hopkins—went on a second errand. John Billington, a boy of around sixteen, had become lost and wandered into Manomet, a Wampanoag village to Plymouth's south. The sachem there sent Billington east to the Nauset sachem Aspinet, whose people remained aggrieved over the Hunt kidnappings. While going to retrieve Billington, Winslow's party stopped at a community named Cummaquid, where an elderly woman came before them "weeping and crying excessively." When the English asked her the reason for her tears, she explained that Hunt had tricked her sons into coming aboard his ship and had then "carried them captives into Spain." The Pilgrims told her and her people that "Hunt was a bad man." They would not act like him. It helped their cause that they had with them Squanto, another of Hunt's victims. When the party finally reached Nauset, the English retrieved Billington and arranged to make restitution for the corn they had stolen the previous fall. They also learned that the Nausets could have easily wiped them out. Even after the epidemics, Aspinet had a hundred men. By releasing Billington, Aspinet demonstrated that he too was nothing like Thomas Hunt.[35]

Aspinet also conveyed some troubling news. The Narragansetts had seized Massasoit. The alarmed Pilgrims hurried back to Plymouth, where they learned that their ally was free but had been driven from his village. Even worse, a sachem named Corbitant—at Mattapoiset, not far from Sowams, in present-day Swansea—had rebelled against Massasoit because he disliked the Pokanoket sachem's newfound friendship with the English. At Nemasket, Corbitant had confronted Squanto and Hobomok, a trusted counselor of Massasoit's who had moved with his family to Plymouth. Hobomok escaped and reported that Corbitant had taken and possibly murdered Squanto.

Myles Standish now sprang into action, leading fourteen men to Nemasket. Hobomok guided them to a house, which the settlers surrounded. The plan was simple. They would let no one out. If Squanto was dead, they would behead Corbitant. They planned to spare the women and children, which implies that they intended to kill all of Corbitant's men. Standish charged into the house and learned that while Corbitant and Squanto were not there, their friend was alive. The Pilgrims still had their translator. Corbitant soon renewed his fidelity to Massasoit.

After the fall harvest, Governor Bradford decided that the settlers "might after a more special manner rejoice together." Like other puritans, the Plymouth separatists disliked many forms of entertainment and mirth, especially church fairs, maypole dances, and the theater. But they were not complete killjoys, and they happily celebrated their improved fortunes. Bradford sent men to shoot a prodigious amount of fowl, which may well have included the "wild turkeys" his history mentions. There was probably also duck, eel, and fish. "Among other recreations," wrote Winslow, "we exercised our arms." Massasoit and ninety of his men came, probably because they heard the Pilgrims firing their guns. The Wampanoags killed five deer, which added to the bounty. It was not the formal meal of nineteenth-century paintings, not least because the Pilgrims probably had no forks and did not eat around a large table.[36]

The Pilgrims did not understand these festivities as a "thanksgiving." In England and its colonies, days of thanksgiving were

Jennie A. Brownscombe, The First Thanksgiving at Plymouth, *1914.*
(Pilgrim Hall Museum, Plymouth, Massachusetts.)

church- and government-appointed assemblies of prayer and worship. These were solemn affairs, though they might involve a communal feast and recreations after the sermons and prayers were over. The 1588 English victory over the Spanish Armada prompted days of thanksgiving across England and then a national thanksgiving in late November. Other European peoples—Catholic and Protestants alike—also engaged in similar religious rituals. In the sixteenth century, Spanish and French colonists in what are now parts of the United States had observed days of thanksgiving.[37]

It is entirely possible that the Pilgrims observed a formal day of thanksgiving after their first harvest, but no records document such an occasion. Rather, the 1621 celebration was more akin to an English harvest festival. Agrarian communities in England and other parts of Europe took part in feasts and recreations after they had brought in the harvest. In England, such festivities were typically parish affairs, often held at or in front of churches. Contrary to the description of some historians, devout English Protestants would not have understood the celebration as "secular," and there is no reason to doubt that the Pilgrims were unusually thankful for their recent bounty. "By the goodness of God," Winslow wrote, "we are so far from want." The festivities were also a "diplomatic event," a cementing of the alliance Massasoit and John Carver had formed the previous spring.[38]

The Pilgrims assigned no historical significance to the celebration. Bradford does not mention the occasion in his history, and the single description appears in a letter written by Edward Winslow. The notion of a Pilgrim "First Thanksgiving" did not become widespread until nineteenth-century magazines and novelists popularized the image. The Pilgrims would have objected to the way that later Americans appropriated them for an annual holiday. Like other puritans, the Pilgrims loathed recurrent holidays, especially when imbued with a sacred significance for which they found no warrant in scripture.[39]

The celebration, however, does not lose its significance when stripped of its mythology. The early history of English colonization in North America was grim, for Native communities but also for English explorers and settlers. Nevertheless, despite the gulfs of language and culture that separated peoples, and despite fears and suspicions, there were moments of concord and mutual enjoyment, often around shared meals. At Roanoke, Natives had refreshed the hungry and weary English settlers with venison, fish, and maize. Bartholomew Gosnold's men and Natives had likewise feasted together. The Plymouth settlers and the Wampanoags did not always enjoy each other's company, but on this occasion they did. "We entertain them familiarly in our houses," Winslow wrote, "and they are friendly bestowing their venison on us." Such moments serve as reminders that conflict between Europeans and Natives was not inevitable.[40]

The separatists among the Pilgrims still enjoyed the "liberty of the gospel" dear to them, and they now had some reason to hope that their colony might flourish and entice other godly settlers to join them. Massasoit and his people had found a new ally to help them cast off their subjection to the Narragansetts. Once a captive bound for a Spanish slave market, Squanto was now an invaluable bridge between two cultures. In freeing themselves from starvation, subjection, and captivity, the Pilgrims and the Wampanoags had bound themselves in new ways. They had pledged to defend each other from outside attack. At least in English minds, Massasoit had proclaimed himself "King James his man." Squanto professed loyalty both to Massasoit and to the English. It would not be long before the strength of these new bonds was tested.

CHAPTER FIVE

Good News

I N NOVEMBER 1621, THE Pilgrims were surprised to see a ship
sail into Plymouth Harbor. Sent by Thomas Weston and the
colony's investors, the *Fortune* carried thirty-five settlers, mostly
"lusty [strong] young men, and many of them wild enough."
When the newcomers first saw the "naked and barren" landscape of
Cape Cod, they begged the captain to take them home. He promised them that if the *Mayflower* planters were dead or vanished, he
would transport them to Virginia. According to William Bradford,
the fact that the surviving Pilgrims had supplies of food convinced
the *Fortune* passengers to remain. In order to feed the newcomers,
Bradford put everyone on half rations for the rest of the winter.[1]

The *Fortune* brought no trading goods or provisions, other than
a few cheap suits of clothing. More valuable was a patent from the
recently chartered Council for New England made out to John
Peirce, one of the Adventurers. The Peirce Patent put the colony on
legal footing for the next seven years, though it did not demarcate
any specific boundaries for New Plymouth. The Mayflower Compact asserted that the settlers would elect their own officers and give
consent to their own laws. By contrast, the Peirce Patent granted
the right to make laws and elect officers not only to the Plymouth
settlers, but also to the London-based Adventurers. At this time,
however, the Adventurers concerned themselves only with the colony's commodities, not its local self-government.

Also arriving on the *Fortune* was Robert Cushman, the Leiden congregant who had fallen out with other Pilgrim leaders and then had stayed behind in England. Cushman had come not as a settler but as an agent for Thomas Weston. He handed Governor Bradford a letter from Weston that excoriated the Pilgrims for having sent the *Mayflower* back to England without a valuable cargo. "That you sent no lading in the ship is wonderful [astonishing]," Weston scolded them. "I know your weakness was the cause of it, and I believe more weakness of judgment than weakness of hands." Other visitors to New England claimed that the region's trade could yield a thousand skins per year. Why had the Pilgrims accomplished nothing?[2]

Weston now made several demands. He wanted an accounting of "how our moneys were laid out." He also wanted the Pilgrims to finally agree to the terms as they had been modified by the investors. And they had better not send the *Fortune* back empty. "The life of the business depends on the lading of this ship," he warned.[3]

Bradford seethed when he read the letter. Perhaps the Adventurers had lost some money, but half of the *Mayflower* passengers were buried in New England soil. "Of the one there may be hope of recovery," he answered, "but the other no recompense can make good." Cushman told Bradford to trust Weston, and John Robinson and others in Leiden sent letters that urged the governor to accept the Adventurers' terms. With matters settled, Weston would send the Pilgrims a "speedy supply." Pilgrim leaders finally capitulated and agreed to the deal.[4]

The Pilgrims loaded the *Fortune* with pelts of beaver and otter as well as clapboards for barrel making. A party led by Edward Winslow and Squanto had gone to Massachusetts Bay and traded for skins. Some came right off the backs of Massachusetts women, who then "tied boughs about them[selves]" to safeguard their modesty. Getting sight of what the English later called Boston Harbor, Winslow's party wished that "they had been there seated." They would not move their settlement, but they grasped that expeditions to the north might bring them the furs that would settle the colony's debts and secure its prosperity. In a tract extolling the colony's potential, Winslow advertised New Plymouth as a rare place "where religion and profit jump together."[5]

Winslow's boast was premature. The Pilgrims wanted their colony to prosper and in the process to attract more godly settlers, but they were not free to seek after riches for themselves. They were bound by their agreement with their investors. Those who belonged to the church were bound to each other through its covenant and through their membership in the body of Christ. The settlers had no land of their own and grew food that went into a common store. Except for those men who ventured forth on trading expeditions, most settlers remained confined to a tiny outpost surrounded by what seemed a harsh and terrifying wilderness.

In December, Robert Cushman preached a sermon, which he published once he returned to England. As his text, he took a verse from First Corinthians: "Let no man seek his own, but every man another's wealth" (10:24). Two decades later, the English Presbyterian William Rathband used this sermon "by a comber of wool" as evidence that New England Congregationalists disregarded the necessity of an educated, ordained ministry. The Pilgrims cherished John Robinson's learned sermons, but they believed that some "private persons" had the gift of preaching and prophesying.[6]

Cushman urged the Pilgrims to guard against the "disease of self-love" that had turned the Virginia colonists into "mere worldlings." The cure for this disease was Christian love and friendship: "And as you are a body together, so hang not together by skins and gymocks [joints], but labor to be jointed together and knit by flesh and sinews; away with envy at the good of others, and rejoice in his good, and sorry for his evil, let his joy be thy joy, and his sorrow thy sorrow: let his sickness be thy sickness: his hunger thy hunger: his poverty thy poverty: and if you profess friendship, be friends in adversities: for then a friend is known, and tried, and not before." Cushman's message was blunt. God might soon "visit you with death," he warned, "as he hath done many of your associates." How would they be found when death came? Would they be "in murmurings, discontents, and jars [discord]"? Or would they be "in brotherly love, and peace"? If the latter, they would be "translated [taken] from this wandering wilderness, unto that joyful and heavenly Canaan." If they loved only themselves, Cushman implied, they would make themselves the objects of God's wrath.

For the Pilgrims, the question was not whether they should bear each other's burdens. Had they not done so the previous winter? Nor was it a question of how hard they would work. Rather, it was for whom they would work. According to the arrangement with the Adventurers, the Pilgrims did not even own the homes they built. The value of those homes, along with any profits generated by trade, would be divided among company shareholders when the seven years were up. Yes, the *Mayflower* passengers and other settlers who bought into the company would get a portion of those profits, but the Adventurers held the greatest number of shares in the company and would profit the most. The agreement that Cushman had persuaded the Pilgrims to sign required them to seek the wealth of those more wealthy than themselves.

Cushman argued that these arrangements were not only reasonable but also biblical. He reminded the settlers that the first Christians had lived as one and that "Israel was seven years in Canaan, before the land was divided unto tribes, much longer, before it was divided into families." Cushman also urged the Pilgrims to remember their economic and Christian obligation to their investors. "We also have been very chargeable to many of our loving friends," he preached, "that before we think of gathering riches, we must even in conscience think of requiting their charge." The Pilgrims should cheerfully labor to pay off their debts. That Cushman felt the need to argue these points suggests discontent among the settlers. Cushman criticized those who "dig hard whilst their own garden is in planting, but is it so as the profit must go wholly or partly to others, their hands wax feeble, their hearts wax faint." Clearly, many settlers wanted to work for themselves.[7]

A few days later, Cushman boarded the *Fortune*. He left behind his thirteen-year-old son Thomas in the care of William Bradford. As the historian Michael McGiffert comments, the former grocer and wool comber "was one who loved himself too well to stay and practice what he preached." His ship turned out to be inaptly named. A French vessel seized the *Fortune* and took it to the Île d'Yeu, off the coast of western France, where the island's governor impounded the *Fortune*'s cargo, read its mail, and imprisoned its crew on an unpleasant diet of "lights [lungs], livers, and entrails." After two weeks, he let them go. For the second time, a mostly empty ship disappointed the indebted and demoralized Thomas Weston.[8]

Many of the *Fortune* passengers were single men, whom Bradford and Isaac Allerton distributed among Plymouth's households. Only two women—both married and with their families—were among the new arrivals. One of them, Martha Ford, gave birth to a girl the very night she and her husband landed. In a few instances, the *Fortune* reunited families separated by the *Mayflower* crossing. The Brewsters welcomed their eldest son Jonathan, and Edward Winslow greeted his brother John.

A majority of the *Fortune* passengers were not separatists from Leiden.[9] On December 25, according to Bradford, most of the "new company excused themselves and said it went against their consciences to work on that day." Like other puritans, separatists did not think the Bible authorized the holiday and associated it with unseemly revelry, but Bradford told the newcomers that they could take the day off "till they were better informed." When he and the other colonists returned from the day's tasks at noon, they discovered the observers of Christmas pitching bars (to see who could throw a piece of wood or metal the farthest) and playing stool-ball. The governor impounded the bars and ball and told them "that was against his conscience, that they should play and others work." If they wanted to keep Christmas, they could do so privately. In this instance, Bradford termed it a conflict "rather of mirth than of weight." Still, with satisfaction he noted that since then there had been no repeat outbreaks of Christmas merriment.[10]

A less mirthful challenge arrived that winter. A messenger from the Narragansett sachem Canonicus brought Squanto a bundle of arrows tied with a rattlesnake skin. Both Squanto and a Narragansett man then at Plymouth interpreted the arrows as a sign of hostility, so Bradford sent the snakeskin back stuffed with powder and shot. "The message was clear enough," observes historian Jeffrey Glover, "whatever your intentions toward us, our weapons are better than yours." Edward Winslow reported that the bundle eventually made its way back to Plymouth, which to him signified that the Pilgrims' response "was no small terror to this savage king."[11]

The terror in the settlement was not small either. Alarmed by Canonicus's apparent expression of enmity, the Pilgrims palisaded their town, including the hill on which they had placed their cannons. They built gates that they kept locked at night. After the Pilgrims received word the next summer that the Powhatans had killed hundreds of English settlers in Virginia, they built a fort on top of the hill. Their actions were incongruous with the way their promotional tracts described New England. Bradford wrote that no one hindered the Pilgrims from taking possession of Patuxet. Likewise, Robert Cushman observed that the land around them was "empty . . . spacious and void." But for all of their talk of empty land free for the taking, the Pilgrims occupied a mere speck of the New England coastline. They looked fearfully into the woods that lay beyond their fields.[12]

As their second winter came to an end, the Pilgrims prepared to send Standish, Winslow, and nine other men back to the Massachusetts on another trading expedition.[13] Hobomok, who had been living at Plymouth with his family for around a year, warned them against the trip. He informed them that the Massachusetts and Narragansetts had agreed to join forces to eradicate Plymouth and had recruited none other than Squanto to their cause. Bradford, Allerton, Standish, and the other leading men of the colony conferred. They were not sure whom to trust, but given their nearly empty stores of food, they felt they had no choice but to risk the trip and to send both interpreters with Standish.

Just as the shallop left Plymouth Bay, a man with a bloody face stumbled into the town, leading its settlers to believe he was being chased. He belonged to Squanto's family. The man told them that the Narragansetts, the Pocasset sachem Corbitant (whom Standish had planned to behead the previous summer), and their ally Massasoit intended to attack the town while the shallop was away. Bradford ordered that the cannons be fired. Those on the boat heard the discharge and sailed back to Plymouth. Hobomok sent his wife to confer with Massasoit, who sent word that he remained their ally and that Squanto's deception was gravely offensive.

Pilgrim leaders concluded that Squanto "sought his own ends and played his own game," as Bradford later put it. He used his friendship with the Pilgrims to increase his own status, telling other

Wampanoags that he could shape English policy toward their communities. He even claimed that the English could send the "plague" wherever they wanted, and presumably wherever he directed. The recent subterfuge was to have been his masterstroke. He had intended to provoke the settlers to attack Massasoit, in the process elevating himself in the eyes of other sachems and the English. Governor Bradford reprimanded Squanto but did not send him away or otherwise punish him. Standish and the others set out again, still accompanied by the two translators. It must have made for an awkward trip.

When the traders returned to Plymouth, a livid Massasoit was waiting for them. He left after expressing his displeasure, then sent a messenger demanding Squanto's execution. The Pilgrims demurred. Bradford asked if they might keep their favored interpreter despite his offense. Without Squanto, the governor explained, the Pilgrims would not be able to understand Massasoit or anyone else. More men came from Sowams, reminding the Pilgrims that according to the terms of their alliance they could not shelter Squanto. The Pokanokets and the Pilgrims had pledged to defend each other from enemies. The messengers brought a knife. They offered Bradford beaver skins in return for Squanto's head and hands. Bradford now tried to claim the high ground. He stated that it "was not the manner of the English to sell men's lives at a price." Principles aside, Squanto remained useful to the Pilgrims. Because Massasoit wanted him dead, Squanto had no choice but to cleave to the English. At the same time, because the Pilgrims did not trust any Indians, it was useful to have Squanto as a second source of information alongside Hobomok. Massasoit's messengers would not budge, though, and Bradford prepared to yield to their demands in order to preserve the peace.

Squanto was saved, however, when an English shallop sighted in the bay provided a distraction. It carried a small number of new colonists, dispatched from a fishing vessel sent to New England by Thomas Weston. By this point, the Pilgrims' erstwhile supporter had broken with the other Adventurers. Over the course of the summer, ships arrived with fifty or sixty men Weston had recruited to form his own colony. The ships unloaded the men at Plymouth while the venture's leaders searched for a site for their plantation.

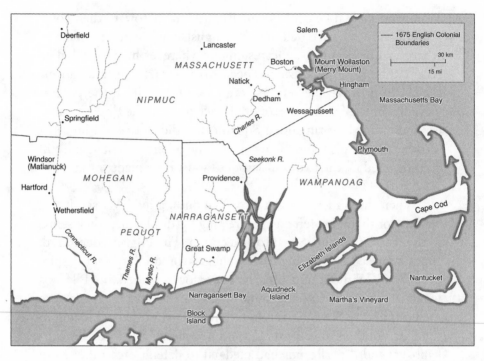

Colonial boundaries of New England, ca. 1675. (Map by Andrew C. Smith.)

The Pilgrims were dismayed. They wanted Weston to feed them, and instead Weston had sent them dozens of men to feed. According to Winslow, the visitors were rude and duplicitous. They stole immature corn. They made clear their distaste for the separatists. When they finally departed for a place called Wessagusset on Massachusetts Bay, they left behind their sick for the Pilgrims to nurse back to health. Perhaps worst of all, their presence at Wessagusset threatened to disrupt the trading relationships the Pilgrims had established with the Massachusetts.

Despite the ill will on both sides, the Pilgrims and Weston's men chose to work together. They both needed food to survive the next winter. In November, men from Plymouth and Wessagusset set off together on the *Swan*, one of Weston's ships. As Standish was ill, Governor Bradford himself led the mission, with Squanto as pilot. (After Weston's colonists arrived, Massasoit's men had dropped their insistence that the Pilgrims execute their interpreter.) The *Swan* rounded the Cape's tip, then headed south. Squanto navigated through the shoals that had forced the *Mayflower's* shipmaster to turn back. Reaching a harbor in present-day Chatham, the English traders obtained corn and beans.

The traders intended to continue around the Cape, but Squanto developed a fever and died. Bradford recorded that as Squanto approached death, he asked the governor "to pray for him, that he might go to the Englishmen's God in heaven." He bequeathed his few belongings to his friends among the Pilgrims. Bradford's recollection probably reveals more about Squanto's social isolation than his spiritual state. Squanto had received Christian instruction from Spanish friars; it is possible that he had been baptized as a Catholic. Still, it is hard to believe that he wanted to spend eternity with the English and their God rather than with his own Patuxet kin. Edward Winslow did not include Squanto's request in his contemporary account of the trading mission, even though it would have bolstered his suggestion that the Pilgrims would share the Christian gospel with New England's Indians. Against all odds, Squanto had survived kidnapping, a slave market, ocean crossings, and Massasoit's call for his execution. Now he died in the company of English settlers who did not trust him.

Even in death, though, the Pilgrims regarded Squanto as indispensable. Without him, they abandoned their plan to round the Cape. They instead turned back, traded with the Massachusetts, and then visited several Wampanoag communities. Bradford and his fellow traders obtained enough food for the Pilgrims to stave off catastrophe. With Squanto dead, Hobomok now became the colonists' most valuable mediator.

In Wessagusset, meanwhile, things quickly became desperate. According to Bradford and Winslow, the hungry settlers debased themselves by becoming servants to the Indians, doing the most menial of work for morsels of food and trading away their coats and bedcovers. Some of the Wessagusset colonists then stole corn. Obtakiest, a Massachusett sachem whose people lived nearby, demanded that Wessagusset leaders execute those responsible. The colonists responded that they had already whipped a man for the theft, but they refused to kill him. "All sachems do justice by their own men," Obtakiest replied. "If not we say they are all agreed and then we fight, and now I say you all steal my corn." According to several sources, the English eventually hanged the man, but their plight only worsened. Men were starving and dying, and Obtakiest did not rescue them the way that Massasoit had saved the Pilgrims.[14]

In March 1623, as the situation at Wessagusset deteriorated, the Pilgrims received word that Massasoit was sick and near death. By this point, Plymouth's leaders knew that when a sachem neared death, those loyal to him came to visit, even from long distances. Upholding this etiquette, Bradford dispatched Edward Winslow to Sowams. Winslow traveled in the company of Hobomok and John Hamden, a visitor from England.[15]

When Winslow's party reached its destination, he received a glimpse of Wampanoag religious culture and rituals of healing. Massasoit's house was jammed with people, and several women were busy rubbing the ailing sachem's limbs to warm him. "They [were] in the midst of their charms for him," Winslow wrote. Winslow later explained that when an individual fell sick, a *powah* would invoke a deity named Hobomok, which Winslow correlated with the devil. Neither Winslow nor any of the other Pilgrims drew a connection between the deity's name and that of their translator. "The powah," Winslow continued, "is eager and free in speech, fierce in countenance, and joineth many antic [bizarre] and laborious gestures with the same over the party diseased." Powahs were shamans who harnessed spiritual power, or *manitou*, to bring about desired outcomes such as healing. Other men and women joined in prayers, dances, and the application of balms and other remedies.[16]

When Massasoit was informed of Winslow's arrival, he called the Englishman to his side. Winslow took his knife, put some "confection of many comfortable conserves" on it, and then pushed a bit through Massasoit's teeth. The sachem swallowed the sweet preserve, evidently the first thing he had gotten down in two days. Winslow next examined Massasoit's "furred" mouth and swollen tongue, which had prevented him from eating and drinking. He washed his mouth, scraped his tongue, and cleaned away pus. He gave Massasoit more of the confection. Massasoit drank, then made a stool. The next morning, Winslow prepared a broth from strawberry leaves, sassafras root, and cornmeal. Massasoit drank some more, and three more stools followed. At Massasoit's request, Winslow then attended to other men and women, washing out their mouths and giving them broth. He found the task unpleasant. The mouths reeked. That evening, Massasoit overindulged on fatty duck, then spent four hours vomiting and bleeding from his nose. However, he stabilized and went to sleep. When the sachem awoke, Winslow washed Massasoit's face, beard, and nose.[17]

Winslow rejoiced that he had succeeded where the powah had failed. He mocked Wampanoag healing rituals because their "hellish noise . . . distempered us that were well, and therefore unlike to ease him that was sick." After one of Massasoit's bowel movements, by contrast, Winslow thanked God for effecting a cure through his own "raw and ignorant means." It was not quite Elijah besting the priests of Ba'al, but for Winslow, God's message was plain. As the Wampanoags came to grasp the impotence of their powahs, they would reject their deities and embrace the Christian God.

Massasoit's people fed Winslow and Hamden well, then the sachem announced that he wished to do them a more special kindness. He revealed that the Massachusetts intended to attack the English. They had recruited as allies several Wampanoag sachems and *pnieses*—high-status individuals who had proven themselves through spiritual ordeals and in battle—and they planned to strike both Wessagusset and Plymouth. In all likelihood, Plymouth could defend itself against an attack. Could the men at Wessagusset? And was Massasoit telling the truth? The Pilgrims had angered him when they had refused to punish Squanto. Was a now grateful Massasoit upholding his end of the alliance, or was he feeding the Pilgrims false information to serve his own purposes?

Winslow headed back to Plymouth. On his way home, he spent the night with the sachem Corbitant at Mattapoisett. Despite Corbitant's prior rebellion against Massasoit, Winslow liked his host, who was "full of merry jests and squibs, and never better pleased than when the like are returned again upon him." Winslow had restored the gravely ill Massasoit to health. If Corbitant fell sick and sent word to Patuxet, he asked, would Winslow attend him? Yes, Winslow promised.

Corbitant wondered why Winslow was bold enough to travel with only one English companion. "My heart was so upright towards them," replied Winslow, "that for mine own part I was fearless to come amongst them." Corbitant recognized that Winslow's answer was not fully true. "If your love be such," the sachem probed, "and it bring forth such fruits, how cometh it to pass, that when we come to Patuxet, you stand upon your guard, with the mouths of your pieces presented towards us?" Winslow parried the question by claiming that pointing guns at visitors was an English sign of respect. Corbitant countered "that he liked not such salutations." Both he and Winslow knew that the English used their guns to impress and intimidate their Wampanoag allies.

As the men ate together, the questions kept coming. Corbitant asked why the English prayed before and after their meals. Winslow answered that they believed that any good thing came from God, so they thanked God for their food, then afterward thanked him again for their "refreshing." Winslow also introduced the Ten Commandments. Corbitant objected to the seventh's stricture "that a man should be tied to one woman."

After his first year in New England, Winslow had written that the Indians had "no religion." "Therein I erred," he now corrected himself. He described many Wampanoag beliefs and practices as congruent with Christianity. While they believed in "many divine powers," Winslow explained, they identified a deity named Kiehtan as "the principal and maker of all the rest . . . [he] created the heavens, earth, sea, and all creatures contained therein." Kiehtan, Winslow continued, had created one man and one woman, from whom all humans descended. Winslow suggested that the Wampanoag conception of life after death resembled Christian beliefs. Good men would dwell with Kiehtan in the west, while bad men would be refused entrance. According to Winslow, Wampanoag communities gathered together to "sing, dance, feast, give thanks, and hang up garlands and other things" in Kiehtan's honor. Winslow apparently did not talk with Corbitant about Jesus Christ, nor did Plymouth's emissary offer his understanding of how God saved human beings. Instead, he sought points of connection between the two cultures.

At the same time, Winslow thoroughly disapproved of some Native practices and beliefs. He reported that Wampanoags and neighboring peoples would not only sacrifice their possessions to appease the devil Hobomok, but that they also "in some cases kill children." No evidence corroborates the assertion. He also asserted that the Narragansetts "offer almost all the riches they have to their gods," their priests tossing their belongings into a great fire. The Narra-gansetts were not so profligate. Altogether, though, Winslow was more curious than condemnatory. Winslow relished his nightlong discussion with Corbitant and wrote that he had "never had better entertainment amongst any of them." It was how he and his fellow Pilgrims wished their relations with the Indians might proceed. The next morning, Winslow and his companions returned to Plymouth.[18]

On March 23 (just before the Julian calendar advanced to 1623), the colony held what had become its annual General Court. Men with voting rights reelected Bradford as governor and Isaac Allerton as his assistant. The main topic of discussion was how the Pilgrims should respond to the rumors of a Massachusett plot. Winslow commented that the colony's leaders could not "undertake war without the consent of the body of the company."[19]

Winslow's intelligence from Massasoit had coincided with other warnings. Myles Standish had just returned from Manomet, to the south of Plymouth, where he had encountered the Massachusetts pniese Wituwamat. According to Standish, Wituwamat made a speech in which he threatened to "ruinate" Weston's colony and "overthrow" Plymouth. How should the Pilgrims respond? The settlers both feared being attacked and the moral hazard of striking first. Plymouth's voting men deputized Bradford, Allerton, and Standish to make the decision, and they settled on a preemptive attack.[20]

Standish knew that it would be futile for armed and armored Englishmen to simply march into Massachusett territory. Their enemies would vanish into the woods or ambush them. So the Pilgrims opted for treachery and trickery. Standish and his men would pretend to be on a trading mission and look for a chance to assassinate Wituwamat, whom they regarded as the chief instigator of the hostility against them.

Before Standish's party left Plymouth, a refugee from Wessagusset—Phinehas Pratt—staggered into the settlement. Pratt's report was grim. The men at Wessagusset were starving to the point that they had sold their clothes to the Massachusetts for corn. One man had even left the settlement and "turned savage." The Indians constantly harassed and threatened the colonists, many of whom had

left the town and gathered in small dispersed companies. Furthermore, Pratt confirmed that the Massachusetts intended to strike at
both Wessagusset and Plymouth, "to kill all English people in one
day when the snow was gone." Pratt had fled Wessagusset, running
through snow and streams like a deer chased by wolves.[21]

Standish and his company, accompanied by Hobomok, left on
their mission. Reaching Massachusetts Bay, they first encountered a
small group of Englishmen on the shore gathering groundnuts.
"They feared not the Indians," Winslow wrote, "but lived and suffered them to lodge with them." A horrified Standish went to Wessagusset, found the colony's leaders, and told them what he and his
men intended.[22]

The tension soon rose. Wituwamat and his fellow Massachusetts
pniese Pecksuot showed up and informed Hobomok that despite
Standish's pretensions to trade, they knew that the Pilgrim captain
wanted to kill them. Wituwamat brandished a knife and bragged
about having previously killed both French and English.[23] Pecksuot
insulted Standish, calling him "a little man." Standish must have
been terribly short, as many seventeenth-century writers commented
on his small stature. William Hubbard, the Ipswich, Massachusetts,
minister and historian, connected Standish's impulsiveness to his
diminutiveness. "A little chimney is soon fired," Hubbard explained.
For the time being, though, Standish patiently bore the insults.[24]

The next day, Standish was in a house with both Wituwamat and
Pecksuot. The Pilgrim captain gave a signal, and his men shut the
door. Standish grabbed Pecksuot's knife and stabbed him again and
again. Hobomok, who watched the murders, observed that the dimin-
utive Standish was "big enough to lay him [Pecksuot] on the ground."
The other Plymouth men slew Wituwamat and another Indian man
who was present, and they hanged Wituwamat's eighteen-year-old
brother. The Pilgrims cut off Wituwamat's head and took it with
them. They then dispatched a fourth Indian at a nearby location,
and another Plymouth detachment killed two more.

Standish was looking for more Indians to kill when the Pilgrims
encountered the sachem Obtakiest and a group of men. A fierce
battle ensued. Hobomok, Standish, and the other Pilgrims occupied
a small hill, while the Massachusetts unleashed a barrage of arrows
toward them. Hobomok bravely led a charge that prompted the

Massachusetts to retreat into a swamp. Standish "dared the sachem to come out and fight like a man," declaring that the sachem had been "base and woman-like . . . in tonguing [talking]." Obtakiest and his men wisely slipped away. In retaliation for the murders, the Massachusetts killed three captive Wessagusset colonists.[25]

Standish and his company sailed their shallop back to Plymouth, where the settlers placed Wituwamat's head on top of their fort. William Bradford explained that the head served "for a terror unto others." The decapitation and display were conventional English punishments for traitors, vile criminals, and military enemies. Within a culture of violent punishment, what the Pilgrims did was brutal but in many respects unexceptional.[26]

At the same time, Pilgrim leaders knew that when reports of the violence reached England, they would face criticism, at least from Weston's men. Prospective settlers might think twice about joining them. Therefore, when Winslow sailed to England in September 1623 to meet with the colony's investors, he published an account of the above events. Most promoters of North American settlement wrote books that painted an unrealistically rosy picture of their colonies. Winslow, by contrast, narrated intrigues, rumors, confusion, and bloodshed, closing with unconvincing paeans to New England's natural resources and potential for trade. In Winslow's book, the only *Good News from New England* was in his title.

Winslow defended Standish's campaign against the Massachusetts. He documented the multiple reports of the alleged conspiracy against the English. Winslow did not hide the fact that the Pilgrims had chosen to decoy their enemies into a trap and then murder them, but he insisted that their actions were prudent. In a second edition of his book, Winslow added a brief mention of Virginia's "bloody slaughter," the March 1622 deaths of hundreds of English settlers at the hands of the Powhatans. Winslow stressed that the Pilgrims had received word of the massacre prior to their move against the Massachusetts. Comparatively tiny Plymouth could have been wiped out, he implied. The Pilgrims were right not to wait to be attacked.[27]

Winslow's account raises many questions. Why did some of the Wessagusset settlers live without any fear of the Indians? If Wituwamat and Pecksuot suspected Standish's intentions and themselves planned to attack the English, why did the Massachusett pnieses act like doves rather than serpents and allow themselves to be taken by surprise? Along those lines, was there really a conspiracy against Wessagusset and Plymouth? Massasoit could have been using the Pilgrims to strike a blow against the Massachusetts and against those Wampanoag sachems who had rebelled against his authority.

For their part, the Pilgrims might have welcomed the chance to display their military strength. The operation also led to the dispersal of the Wessagusset colony, a welcome development for Plymouth. Winslow complained that after Weston's men had established their plantation, "the trade both for furs and corn was overthrown in that place" because the new settlers overpaid for food. In the wake of the murders, the Wessagusset colonists had no choice but to hightail it for Maine or England. It would have been unsafe for them to stay. Thus, in killing Wituwamat and Pecksuot, the Pilgrims indirectly eliminated a rival English colony.[28]

Winslow was correct to anticipate objections. From Leiden, John Robinson wrote to Bradford about what he deemed un-Christian bloodlust. "How happy a thing had it been," the minister chided the settlers, "if you had converted some, before you had killed any." Even if a reprisal was necessary, could they not have killed only one or two men? Being a "terror to poor barbarous people" was glorious "in men's eyes" but not "pleasing in God's." Robinson questioned the judgment of Standish in particular and wondered if he lacked "that tenderness of the life of man (made after God's image)."[29]

A decade or so later, Thomas Morton wrote a much more acerbic denunciation of what the Pilgrims had done. Morton came to New England in the mid-1620s, became Plymouth's rival in trade, and then became the separatists' political antagonist back in England. He termed the assassination and other killings a "massacre," making careful note of the way Standish had tricked his victims by setting a feast before them prior to slaying them. Morton also questioned why the Pilgrims had not done anything to secure the release of the three English settlers the Massachusetts had killed in retaliation. Morton added that after the massacre, the Massachusetts took to calling the English "*Wotawquenange*, which in their language signifieth stabbers or cutthroats." Winslow complained that the Wessagusset settlers had made "Christ and Christianity stink in the nostrils of the poor infidels." Morton believed that it was the Pilgrims who had made Christianity odious. On the other hand, Morton stated that Obtakiest did plan to attack the Pilgrims, whom he accused of having desecrated the grave of the sachem's mother. Thus, if there was a Massachusetts conspiracy against them, the Pilgrims had only themselves to blame for their plight.[30]

Some historians have savaged the Pilgrims for their preemptive violence and for placing their economic interests above the lives of both the Massachusetts and the Wessagusset settlers. In portraying Plymouth as one of many fronts in the English "invasion of America," Francis Jennings alleges that Winslow "falsified events sufficiently to implicate the Indians as conspirators against Plymouth and to conceal the premeditation of the massacre."[31] Such criticism ignores contrary evidence. Winslow did not conceal Plymouth's premeditated treachery. He wrote about it quite openly, and Bradford transcribed Robinson's stinging rebuke into his history. Nor does it seem that the Pilgrims simply made up their fears. Had Winslow and Bradford been in the business of outright fabrication, they surely would have placed Phinehas Pratt's arrival and evidence before Plymouth's decision to assassinate and decapitate Wituwamat. At the same time, Plymouth's campaign against the Massachusetts met with such little resistance that it suggests there was no Native conspiracy against the English.

The Pilgrims themselves had a very limited grasp of the communities that surrounded them. They poorly understood the relationship between their ally Massasoit and other Wampanoag sachems. Even those Pilgrims who became familiar with Algonquian dialects and culture relied on translators and mediators. The Pilgrims saw the world beyond their settlement as if through a dark glass. Historians attempting to interpret the Wessagusset massacre on the basis of a few documents—all written by English settlers— see that world even more dimly.

The Wessagusset massacre ushered New Plymouth into a new era. The Pilgrims had served notice of their strength. In the coming months, when the settlers heard that other allegedly hostile sachems had forsaken their homes and then died from disease, they understood it as the just judgments of an angry God. "How few, weak, and raw were we at our first beginning," Winslow reminded his readers, "and there settling, and in the midst of barbarous enemies?" Yet God had delivered them. For the Pilgrims, the conclusion was obvious. "I cannot but think," he reasoned, "that God hath a purpose to give that land as an inheritance to our nation." It was a divine transfer of land from heathen Indians to faithful English.[32]

That summer, Plymouth's leaders jettisoned what Bradford termed the "common course." Until this point, the settlers had put crops into a storehouse for the use of the entire community, but men had not wanted to work to support other men's families. Now the colony's leaders assigned each household a plot of land and asked them to grow corn for themselves, with a portion reserved for the colony's traders, fishermen, magistrates, and poor. Everyone worked harder. Plymouth's women even "took their little ones with them to set corn," not unlike their Wampanoag counterparts.[33]

In his 1621 sermon, Robert Cushman had reminded the Pilgrims that the first Christians had lived as one. Nothing "more resembles hellish horror," Cushman had preached, "than for every man to shift for himself . . . to affect particulars, *mine* and *thine*." A quarter-century later, Bradford reflected on the shift in policy. Bradford now associated the "common course" with the "vanity of that conceit of Plato's and other ancients . . . that the taking of property and bringing in community into a commonwealth would make them happy and flourishing, as if they were wiser than God." In Bradford's history, the pooling of resources became the idea of non-Christian philosophers (Protestants often termed them "heathen" as well), not part and parcel of the primitive Christianity that the separatists aspired to emulate. Bradford allowed that the new policy was in some way a concession to human sinfulness. "I answer," he wrote, "seeing all men have this corruption in them, God in His wisdom saw another course fitter for them." What Cushman labeled "self-love" was no longer a problem, but a badly needed spur to industry.[34]

Hard work, however, was no match for a stubborn drought that afflicted the colony that summer. It hardly rained from late May until mid-July. Corn and beans withered. Bradford appointed a day of fasting and prayer, and the Pilgrims assembled in the morning to confess their sins before God and promise to walk more faithfully. Sermons and prayers stretched into the afternoon, when clouds gathered and rain began to fall. Their crops revived, though storms damaged those of nearby Wampanoag communities. According to Winslow, it was like the case of Massasoit's restoration to health. The events had shown "the difference between their conjuration, and our invocation on the name of God for rain." When the Pilgrims brought in a large harvest that fall, Bradford appointed a formal day of thanksgiving, the first such observance recorded in Plymouth Colony. The threat of starvation finally faded.[35]

Also in July 1623, two shiploads of settlers and supplies arrived. Emmanuel Altham, one of the Adventurers, visited the colony in which he had invested. In glowing letters back to England, he described New Plymouth as a well-situated plantation with about twenty houses on either side of a "great street." He also recorded a rather modest six goats, about fifty hogs, and many chickens. At the top of the hillside was "a strong fort . . . with six pieces of reasonable good artillery," at which the Pilgrims maintained a "continual watch." Altham predicted that they would spot any Indian who approached the palisaded town.[36]

Many of the new arrivals had come on what Bradford referred to as "their particular," meaning that they had paid for their own passage and were not bound by the Pilgrims' agreement with their investors. Nor did they have a vote in the colony's government. New Plymouth now had two classes of settlers, which bred uncertainty and discontent. Bradford and the Particulars quickly reached an accommodation. The Particulars would receive land, swear to obey the colony's laws, pay an annual tax into the common store of corn, and promise not to trade with the Indians. The latter point was critical. In order to fulfill their obligations to the Adventurers, the Pilgrims needed all the furs they could get at the most reasonable price. They did not want competitors.[37]

Among the more welcome newcomers was the widow Alice Southworth, who married William Bradford in August. The wedding celebration was a reprise of the 1621 harvest festivities. Massasoit came with one of his wives, accompanied by four sachems and more than a hundred other men. Plymouth's men greeted them with musketry and military maneuvers, displaying the settlement's power and adding to the festive atmosphere. The Wampanoag guests danced for their hosts. Massasoit presented Bradford with venison and turkey; everyone had a full portion of meat and good cheer. Over the last two years, the Pokanokets and the Pilgrims had made each other stronger. In the years ahead, it would prove more difficult for the fortunes of both peoples to rise in tandem.

CHAPTER SIX

Sacraments

OR THE PILGRIMS, A true church was a congregation formed when Christians covenanted with each other to walk in the ways of God. The covenant was, John Robinson taught, "the true essential property of the visible church." The formation of a covenant was the reclamation of Christian liberty, the free act of the Lord's free people. From it stemmed the "spiritual power, and liberty . . . to communicate, and partake in the visible promises, and ordinances."[1] Separatists also taught that true churches practiced proper government and discipline, and like other Reformed Protestants, they understood godly preaching and the biblical administration of the sacraments to be marks of true churches. By the standards of the Pilgrims, the Church of England remained a false church, an institution in which bishops tyrannized true Christians and denied them the liberty to worship God according to the dictates of the Bible.

At the same time, most other English Protestants would have regarded Plymouth's congregation not as a church but as a lay conventicle. The colonists listened to sermons from a ruling elder—William Brewster—and other laymen. Because Robinson had remained behind in Leiden, the Pilgrims had no minister with them. No minister, no sacraments. New Plymouth's children, such as *Mayflower* babies Oceanus Hopkins and Peregrine White, remained unbaptized. The colony's men and women never celebrated the Lord's

Supper. Key components of ordinary church life, thus, were absent in Plymouth.

Even so, the nature of Plymouth's church was not a flashpoint of controversy at first. Whatever their religious inclinations, the settlers focused on their survival, and there is no evidence that anyone took issue with the colony's religious services. Moreover, even some settlers with no connection to the Leiden congregation expressed satisfaction with Plymouth's church. For instance, William Hilton came to Plymouth in 1621 and wrote a glowing report of the colony's prospects to a cousin in England. He was not a separatist, but he appreciated "the word of God taught us every Sabbath." The fact that Brewster kept his sermons and prayers short by seventeenth-century standards probably endeared him to some settlers. "I know not anything a contented mind can here want," Hilton maintained. In the long run, though, the irregular and stunted nature of Plymouth's church was bound to cause problems.[2]

These problems arrived soon after the Wessagusset murders, when a string of English visitors and newcomers highlighted New Plymouth's political fragility. Some newly arrived settlers, along with some of the Adventurers back in England, found it repugnant that Brownists governed the colony. A few settlers began worshipping according to the Book of Common Prayer. For the separatists among the Pilgrims, criticism from England and religious dissent at Plymouth were both alarming. They had left England to preserve their Christian liberty, and they worshipped according to their understanding of the Bible. The Pilgrim separatists knew that if other Englishmen wrested control of the colony away from them, they stood to lose that liberty.

In the spring of 1623, Thomas Weston sailed into Plymouth's harbor. Once the Pilgrims' benefactor, Weston was now a fugitive, on the run from his debts and from criminal charges. In a desperate bid to restore his finances, Weston had contracted to transport some cannons across the Atlantic, then turned around and sold them to an unknown buyer. According to Bradford, Weston made his way to New England, was forced to abandon his shallop during a storm, had his belongings and clothing stolen by Indians, borrowed some clothes in Piscataqua, and then showed up in Plymouth. Out of pity and gratitude for Weston's past assistance, Bradford staked him with a hundred beaver skins.[3]

In September, Robert Gorges, son of Ferdinando Gorges, visited Plymouth. Over the past fifteen years, Ferdinando Gorges had financed a series of expeditions to New England. None had planted a colony or established a successful trade, but Gorges never fully abandoned his ambitions to make a fortune across the Atlantic. After establishing the Council for New England, Gorges sought new ways to promote colonies and commerce. For a while, the council planned to ask magistrates and judges to indenture pauper children and send them to New England, but the idea never gained traction.[4]

Gorges reckoned that investors would more readily fund colonies if they received allocations of land as their fiefdoms. He accordingly took a map of New England and divided it into some twenty portions. In June 1623, he invited prospective proprietors to Greenwich, where King James watched them draw lots for the portions. The king himself drew for several men who were absent. Sir Samuel Argall and Barnabe Gooch drew portions that together roughly comprised the subsequent boundaries of New Plymouth. Argall had spent the better part of a decade in Virginia; he is most remembered for his 1613 abduction of Pocahontas. Gooch was the longtime master of Cambridge's Magdalene College; as of 1623 he also held a seat in Parliament. Neither man had any serious intention of setting foot on the New England lands assigned to them, but the council's deliberations indicated New Plymouth's insignificance and vulnerability.[5]

In the meantime, the council commissioned Robert Gorges as New England's governor-general and asked him to establish a model plantation. Back in 1613, the younger Gorges had fatally stabbed a man in Exeter. Ferdinando Gorges obtained a pardon for his son, who then spent the next eight years as a mercenary soldier on the continent. When he returned to England, he worked alongside his father at Plymouth's fort. None of these experiences had equipped Robert Gorges to plant a colony and govern New England.

The governor-general was also asked to apprehend Thomas Weston. After reaching Massachusetts Bay, Robert Gorges started up the coast to look for Weston, but a storm blew him off course. Gorges took shelter at Plymouth, and Weston had the misfortune to arrive for a visit at the same time. Bradford pled with Gorges to treat

Detail, from William Alexander, An Encouragement to Colonies *(1624).*
The names on the map are those of the patentees of the Council for
New England, reflecting the lots drawn at Greenwich in June 1623.
(Courtesy of Library of Congress.)

Weston with leniency. The indecisive Gorges arrested Weston, then changed his mind and released him. Weston made his way to Virginia, where he briefly held a seat in the House of Burgesses before moving on again, first to Maryland and then finally back to England, where he died in the mid-1640s.

When he came to New England, Robert Gorges brought several gentlemen, two Church of England ministers, and a number of families. Inauspiciously, they chose to settle at the site of the failed Wessagusset colony. The younger Gorges did not like the looks of his realm and sailed for home the next spring. Most of the colonists followed suit or went to Virginia, while a few scattered around Massachusetts Bay. Once more, Ferdinando Gorges's ambitions had come to naught. It was much easier to draw lots and maps than it was to actually plant colonies.

When William Morrell, one of Robert Gorges's ministers, visited Plymouth, he told its settlers that the Council for New England had granted him "power and authority of superintendency" over the region's churches. Surely this raised some eyebrows among the Pilgrims. Morrell was not even a puritan, and the Pilgrims would never have accepted his superintendency. "It should seem he saw it was in vain," Bradford commented. Morrell soon took passage for England.[6]

Much like Gorges and Morrell, some of the New Plymouth "Particulars"—those who had come to the colony at their own expense—decided that New England was not for them. They objected to the quality of the water, fish, and soil, and to the quantity of mosquitoes. On the latter point, Bradford commented that "they are too delicate and unfit to begin new plantations and colonies, that cannot endure the biting of a mosquito." Such timorous souls should stay in England "till at least they be mosquito proof." Bradford relished the fact that other would-be colonists fled from the same hardships the Pilgrims had overcome.

The Particulars also disliked Plymouth's church, and when they reached England, they lodged complaints with the Adventurers. On behalf of the other investors, James Sherley forwarded their allegations to Bradford and demanded a quick response. At the top of the list was "diversity about religion." Bradford denied that there had been any "controversy or opposition" pertaining to Plymouth's church. The returned Particulars, though, expressed concern over the "want of both of the sacraments," baptism and the Lord's Supper. Bradford had a ready answer. "Our pastor is kept from us," he reminded Sherley. Under the leadership of William Brewster, the settlers enjoyed prayers, psalm singing, and sermons, but no John Robinson, no sacraments.[7]

For the Pilgrim separatists, as for other Protestants, the sacraments were not a theological necessity. John Robinson drew a distinction between the "*outward baptism by water,* and an *inward baptism by the spirit.*" The two "ought not to be severed . . . yet many times are." God would save his elect and bring them to faith, baptism or no baptism. Some English separatists had risked persecution by withholding their children from baptism in what they regarded as a false church.[8]

Still, like other Protestants, separatists insisted on the spiritual significance of something Jesus had commanded. "God hath made it [baptism] a most comfortable pledge and seal of his love and help to our faith," taught Henry Barrow, the separatist martyr. Regardless of what their ministers taught, moreover, many English Protestants regarded baptism as a prerequisite for heaven. Until recently, the Church of England had permitted lay baptisms in the event an infant would die before a minister could perform the rite. Therefore, the inability to have their children baptized weighed on the minds of Plymouth Colony parents.[9]

The Leiden separatists had indicated the importance they placed on the Lord's Supper by celebrating it each week. In this they were very unusual. Rural parishes in England celebrated Communion only the few required times each year. John Robinson never wrote a comprehensive statement of his understanding of the Lord's Supper, but most separatists understood it as more than a mere symbol of Christ's sacrifice. They did not believe that the bread and wine became the actual body and blood of Jesus Christ, but they understood the elements as—in Robinson's explanation—"the communion of the body and blood of Christ, that is, effectual pledges of our conjunction, and incorporation with Christ, and one with another . . . all which eat of one bread, or one loaf, are one mystical body." The Lord's Supper furthered the unity of church members with Jesus Christ and with each other. The absence of the ritual each Sunday was a reminder that the ocean—and perhaps the Adventurers—had disrupted that unity.[10]

Given the importance of the sacraments, Elder Brewster in 1623 wrote Robinson to ask if he might baptize and preside over the Lord's Supper until Robinson or another minister arrived. Robinson responded with a polite but firm no.[11] Although the Pilgrims do not seem to have realized it at the time, Robinson's presence (or his authorization of Brewster) would have caused more problems than his absence. Robinson and Brewster would have restricted the Lord's Supper to church members and baptism to their children, and nonseparatists would have been deeply offended.

A few months later, the Pilgrims welcomed a minister, but not the one they wanted. In March 1624, the *Charity* reached the colony, carrying Edward Winslow back from his errand to England, and with him New Plymouth's first cattle (one bull and three cows), a patent for a fishing outpost on Cape Ann, and some badly needed supplies and trading goods. The *Charity* also brought the Reverend John Lyford, accompanied by his wife, Sarah, and several children. "He knows he is no officer amongst you," wrote Robert Cushman, "though perhaps custom and universality may make him forget himself." Cushman and Winslow had told Lyford that he would have no ecclesiastical authority in Plymouth unless church members there elected him as their minister. Separatists insisted that ordinations at the hands of bishops were invalid. Only a particular congregation could ordain a minister, and a minister exercised spiritual authority only within that congregation. At the same time, Cushman and Winslow had consented to the Adventurers' decision to send Lyford. If they could not have John Robinson, Plymouth's church members should at least give Lyford a chance.[12]

Lyford was used to going where he wasn't wanted. In 1613, the Oxford-educated minister had gone to Ireland. England's nearest colony was a dumping ground for nonconformist puritans. English bishops were quite happy to send nettlesome ministers to Irish parishes, where they might convert a few individuals among the Catholic masses. Lyford went to Ulster, which King James had turned into an English plantation in 1609. After about a decade in the parish of Loughgall, Lyford accepted the Adventurers' offer to go to an even less desirable place. Despite what he must have heard about the Pilgrims, Lyford presumed the settlers would be pleased to have him.[13]

Pilgrim leaders greeted Lyford with the respect due a learned minister. They gave him a generous allotment of food and invited him to give counsel on the colony's affairs. Lyford quickly joined the church. "He made a large confession of his faith," Bradford recounted, "and an acknowledgment of his former disorderly walking, and his being entangled with many corruptions, which had been a burden to his conscience." In other words, Lyford regretted his prior ministry within an insufficiently reformed Church of England. He thanked God "for this opportunity of freedom and liberty to enjoy the ordinances of God in purity among his people." In Lyford's confession, the Pilgrims heard an articulation of the Christian liberty they cherished. Apparently, Lyford also told the church that he "held not himself a minister till he had a new calling." Plymouth's congregants were pleased with Lyford's sentiments and invited him to preach.[14]

Despite the promising start, the Pilgrims concluded that Lyford was unfit to be their minister. According to Thomas Morton, who would soon come to New England and become the separatists' bitter antagonist, Plymouth's congregants demanded that Lyford "renounce his calling to the office of the ministry, received in England, as heretical and papistical." Lyford would not go so far, halting at the line between puritan nonconformity and separatism. He maintained that the Church of England was "defective" but nevertheless a "true church." Lyford's stance was unacceptable to the Plymouth separatists. Their pilgrimage from England to Leiden to New England had begun with the decision to separate from a church they deemed beholden to Antichrist. At the same time, the Pilgrims' demands were entirely unacceptable to Lyford, who quickly became disenchanted with the colony's leadership.

Lyford had brought his family across the ocean and failed to obtain the single ministerial position in New England. Unsurprisingly, he resented the separatists who had rejected him. According to both Bradford and Thomas Morton, Lyford formed an attachment to John Oldham, one of the Particulars. Oldham was both disaffected and turbulent—Morton dubbed him a "mad Jack in his mood." Bradford and other Pilgrim leaders learned that Lyford and Oldham were meeting with other malcontents. "It was observed," Bradford chronicled, "that Lyford was long in writing," drafting letters that would besmirch the Pilgrims' reputations back in England.

Lyford wrote quickly because he intended to send his letters on the *Charity's* return trip. When the ship anchored a few miles offshore prior to its departure for England, Bradford, Edward Winslow, and Isaac Allerton rendezvoused with the ship and visited with William Peirce, its captain. The Pilgrims had decided that they needed their own representatives in London to handle business with the

Adventurers. Thus, Winslow was headed back across the ocean, this time accompanied by Allerton. Peirce, meanwhile, had been a friend of the Pilgrims since his first visit to the colony the year before.[15]

Bradford had not come to see Peirce for a friendly chat, however. The governor wanted the correspondence of Lyford and Oldham. Peirce gladly handed over more than twenty of Lyford's letters, along with some written by Oldham. In the midst of their espionage, Bradford, Winslow, and Allerton discovered that their own correspondence was falling into the wrong hands. Within one of Lyford's epistles they found copies of two letters, one addressed to William Brewster and one that Winslow himself had penned the previous winter while awaiting passage from Gravesend on the Thames. Evidently someone had filched them while Winslow was attending to other business. Lyford was sending the copies to a ministerial opponent of the Pilgrims back in England.

According to Bradford, Lyford had penned criticisms of the colony's leaders "tending not only to their prejudice, but to their ruin and utter subversion." In one of the letters, moreover, Bradford learned about a rather unusual conspiracy. "Mr. Oldham and Mr. Lyford," Bradford wrote, "intended a reformation in church and commonwealth; and, as soon as the ship was gone, they intended to join together, and have the sacraments." The rebellious settlers conspired to topple New Plymouth's separatist government—not with guns, but with bread, wine, and water. The Pilgrim snoops made copies of the letters and kept a few originals to prove that Lyford had authored them. After Bradford obtained the letters, he did not tip his hand for several weeks. The governor wanted to see what Lyford and Oldham would do and who would support them.

Things soon came to a head. On the basis of his "episcopal calling [ordination in the Church of England]," Lyford began presiding over his own Sunday meetings, and there were settlers at Plymouth who very much wanted what he offered. William Hilton was among them. After coming to the colony in 1621, Hilton had expressed his satisfaction with Plymouth's church. His wife and two children joined him two years later, and the couple had a third child the next year. When the separatists and Lyford failed to come to terms, the Hiltons asked the spurned minister to baptize their newborn son. As any Church of England minister would have done, Lyford obliged.[16]

Oldham caused different sorts of problems. According to Bradford's account, when Myles Standish confronted Oldham about refusing guard duty, Mad Jack pulled a knife on the captain. The Pilgrims "clapped up [imprisoned]" Oldham. Thomas Morton told a similar story. Plymouth's magistrates asked Oldham to come to the "watch house." When he refused, they gave him a "cracked crown" and "made the blood run down about his ears." Regardless of who had started the fight, Oldham ended up a prisoner.[17]

Bradford decided it was time for action and summoned Plymouth's citizens to a court. He reminded them that they had come to "enjoy the liberty of their conscience and the free use of God's ordinances" and that they had suffered greatly for those ends. By liberty of conscience, Bradford did not mean that individuals could pursue whatever religious convictions they happened to hold but that the separatist Pilgrims could worship God in ways that did not violate their consciences. Likewise, by the "free use of God's ordinances," Bradford did not mean that anyone should have access to the sacraments. Separatists objected to the "mixed multitude" of the Church of England, in which ungodly individuals sullied the Lord's Supper. Bradford and other Pilgrim leaders contended that Lyford and Oldham threatened liberty, properly understood, by introducing corrupt forms of worship and by subverting the authority of Plymouth's elected leaders. As far as Plymouth's governor was concerned, it was a matter of sedition. If Oldham and Lyford had their way, the separatists would no longer govern New Plymouth.

Lyford protested his innocence, whereupon the governor produced the purloined letters and had them read aloud. The gathered settlers heard Lyford's accusations, namely, that they "would have none to live here but themselves." Lyford advised the Adventurers to keep the Leideners, especially John Robinson, away from Plymouth. Instead, the Adventurers should send enough nonseparatists "as might oversway them here." Especially if the Particulars gained the right to vote and hold office, New Plymouth would cease to be a separatist colony. Lyford added that if given a choice, the settlers would eagerly select a replacement military leader, "for this Captain Standish looks like a silly boy, and is in utter contempt." The oft-maligned Standish had to bear more insults about his stature.

The court convicted Lyford and Oldham—the exact charges are

unclear—and banished them. Oldham left for Massachusetts Bay but returned the following spring and was arrested again. This time around, the Pilgrims dispatched him with more ceremony. The court "appointed a guard of musketeers which he was to pass through, and everyone was ordered to give him a thump on the brich [buttocks], with the butt end of his musket." A boat then carried away Oldham's sore bottom and bruised pride. Eventually, Mad Jack had something of a religious conversion, settled in Massachusetts Bay, and made his peace with Plymouth's leaders.

For his part, Lyford made a public confession in church and begged for mercy. After the church's deacon, Samuel Fuller, urged clemency, Plymouth gave him a reprieve from his expulsion, dangling the possibility of a pardon should his contrition prove genuine. It did not. In August 1624, Bradford again finagled one of the minister's letters, addressed to the Adventurers. In it, Lyford criticized the nature of Plymouth's church, which he claimed comprised "the smallest number in the colony." He alleged that the separatists did not believe the church had any responsibility to those outside of its membership, who remained "destitute of the means of salvation." For Lyford, a church encompassed everyone within the bounds of a parish. For the separatist Pilgrims, a church was a covenanted community of the godly.

Knowing that at least some of Lyford's allegations had reached England, Bradford sent the Adventurers yet another defense of Plymouth's church and government. He stated that instead of ignoring the unconverted, Plymouth enforced church attendance. The magistrates appointed several men to "visit suspected places" every Sunday. One surmises that given Bradford's proven ability to locate incriminating letters, the Pilgrims easily tracked down Sabbath breakers. They punished those they found that were "idling and neglect[ing] the hearing of the word." As to the lack of a minister, Bradford observed that their enemies kept their pastor from Plymouth and then unjustly reproached them for his absence. Still, they had Brewster. They preferred his lay leadership to what they considered Lyford's false ordination.

Meanwhile, the Pilgrims carried out Lyford's sentence of banishment. In the spring of 1625, the minister and his family followed Oldham to Nantasket on Massachusetts Bay, as did several other discontented Plymouth settlers. William Hilton and his family were among those who left. Several years later, the Virginia parish of Martin's Hundred called Lyford as its minister. He moved parishes in Virginia at least once, then died in 1630 or shortly thereafter. Sarah Lyford, meanwhile, returned to New England with her children after her husband's death. She settled in Massachusetts Bay and remarried.[18]

Lyford's expulsion and death did not expiate Bradford's wrath. When Plymouth's governor composed this section of his history around two decades later, he wrote at great length about Lyford and included very unflattering information about the rejected and ejected minister. According to Bradford, Sarah Lyford exposed her husband's past immoralities on the eve of their banishment. "She feared to fall into the Indians' hands," Bradford explained, "and to be defiled by them, as he [John Lyford] had defiled other women." A long list of outrageous sins followed. Lyford had fathered a "bastard" prior to his marriage, denied it to Sarah during their courtship, and then brought the son into their home after their nuptials. Even worse, Sarah Lyford could not employ maids without her husband pressing himself upon them. The Pilgrims obtained corroboration of Lyford's immoral behavior. In England, Edward Winslow found two witnesses with knowledge of his indiscretions in Ireland. They testified that the minister had arranged a private conference with a young woman prior to her marriage, then had raped her while taking care to "hinder conception."[19]

Thomas Morton, who probably met Lyford after the latter's banishment from Plymouth, suggests that the separatists had "blemish[ed]" Lyford's character in order to portray him as a "spotted beast, and not to be allowed, where they ordained to have the Passover kept so zealously." In other words, he lacked the separatist purity the Pilgrims demanded. Bradford's accusations against Lyford, however, seem like more than just a smear. Scandal would explain Lyford's departure from Ireland and his willingness to bring his family to a colony with which he had no prior connection. The minister probably had some spots.[20]

In his history of New England's first sixty years of English settlement, Massachusetts Bay minister William Hubbard suggested that "the term of wickedness" with which the Plymouth separatists had branded Lyford and Oldham was "too harsh." For Hubbard, the Lyford-Oldham controversy was a "small tempest" that "hazard[ed] the loss of a weak vessel." For the separatists, however, it mattered precisely because their vessel—their colony—was so weak. Lyford and Oldham did exhibit "antipathy against the way of the separation," but it was the combination of ecclesiastical dissent and political threat that produced the harsh reaction.[21]

The Pilgrims could have faced consequences for banishing a Church of England minister. Lyford and his supporters might have sought redress with the Council for New England, or with crown and ecclesiastical officials. It seems, however, that their complaints went no further than the Adventurers, and Winslow's witnesses forestalled any serious repercussions. Bradford and Winslow had outfoxed their opponents and kept the colony's political leadership in their own hands. "Thus was this matter ended," stated Bradford.[22]

The matter was not ended, however. Coming on the heels of complaints from the Particulars, the fallout from the Lyford controversy prompted many of the Adventurers to withdraw their financial backing. As an investment, Plymouth had been an utter failure. Those who had ventured money had not received it back, let alone reaped profits. James Sherley informed Bradford that "want of money" was the paramount issue, but it was not just about money. Sherley did not mince words. Most of the Adventurers now loathed the Pilgrims, having read letters that denounced them as "Brownists, condemning all other churches, and persons but yourselves and those in your way."[23] The Pilgrims had pretended not to be separatists when they sought partners and patents for their emigration. Lyford had forced them to show their theological cards.

A few of the Adventurers still backed the Pilgrims. Sherley informed Bradford that the colonists and the remaining investors had £1,400 in debts, which the Pilgrims should settle by continuing to ship commodities to England. The price of beaver had risen in recent years, but the debt was imposing and hampered the colony's prospects. In 1625, the Pilgrims loaded two ships with fish and furs. One ship dallied in English ports and did not reach the European market for dried fish until after a price collapse. Barbary pirates captured the second ship after it had already reached the English Channel, seizing its valuable cargo of beaver furs and enslaving its crew. "God's judgments are unsearchable," Bradford lamented.[24]

The year 1625 brought other heavy blows. Robert Cushman, who had never fully restored his friendship with the Pilgrims, died that spring. King James also died and was succeeded by his son Charles. An outbreak of the plague postponed the new king's coronation and eventually killed seventy thousand of his subjects. "This year the great plague raged in all this kingdom," wrote an official in Plymouth (England). The same outbreak killed one-fifth of Leiden's population. The ten thousand dead included members of the English separatist congregation. John Robinson died after a brief illness, though apparently not from the plague. Far removed from the epidemics, Bradford reflected on the fact that his humble pastor and a great prince "left this world" within weeks of each other. "Death makes no difference," he observed. It took the lofty and the lowly.[25]

The Leiden Pilgrims came to the New World to establish a haven and beacon for separatism, not a bastion of religious toleration and freedom. Their goal was to transplant a congregation, found a prosperous colony, and attract puritans wavering on the threshold of separatism to join them. Robinson's death weighed heavy. The Pilgrims would not be reunited with their beloved pastor in this world, and only a small number of additional Leiden congregants emigrated after 1625.

Especially with most of the Leiden separatists remaining in the Dutch Republic, the Pilgrims were faced with questions to which they had given little thought prior to the *Mayflower* crossing. What would the relationship be between New Plymouth's church and its government? How would that government deal with those settlers who kept themselves aloof from its separatist church or who wanted to worship according to their own consciences? By the mid-1620s, the Pilgrims had begun to answer such questions. The Pilgrims did not compel anyone to join their church, and the Mayflower Compact did not make civil distinctions on the basis of religious convictions or church membership. Church attendance, though, was compulsory, and the colony's leaders banished those who began worshipping according to other principles.

Why, James Sherley wondered, were the Pilgrims "contentious, cruel and hard hearted ... towards such as in all points both civil and religious, jump not with you?"[26] Could they not have reached an accommodation with Lyford, or at least have permitted him to baptize the Hiltons' son? In an important sense, however, there was nothing unusual about the way that the Pilgrims had acted. As of 1625, hardly anyone in old England or New England had abandoned the idea of religious uniformity. Most English Protestants, including conformist puritans such as Lyford, did not think that Brownists had the right to form their own churches within English parishes. Likewise, Plymouth's leaders thwarted Lyford's attempt to establish alternative worship services in the colony. The Pilgrims were determined to keep New Plymouth's church and government in their own hands. They preserved their own liberty by denying it to others.

CHAPTER SEVEN

The Lord of Misrule

THOMAS MORTON CAME TO New England in the mid-1620s, founded an outpost he called Ma-re Mount (or Merry Mount), raised a maypole, and made merry with the Natives. After accusing him of selling guns to the Indians, the Pilgrims shipped Morton back to England, and the Massachusetts Bay colonists—who began arriving in 1628—chopped down his maypole and burned his house.

A maypole. A trade war. Dancing and poetry. Guns and Indians. Thomas Morton has provided generations of novelists, poets, and historians with an irresistible counterpoint to the puritans who usually dominate narratives of seventeenth-century New England. In his short story "The May-Pole of Merry Mount," Nathaniel Hawthorne narrates a struggle between "jollity and gloom," and gloom scores a decisive win when Morton's maypole crashes to the ground. William Carlos Williams later praised Morton as a "New World pioneer taking his chances in the wilderness." Long after puritans had lost control of New England's churches and governments, it became easy to see Thomas Morton as an early embodiment of America's future, a man whose free-spirited mirth was crushed by petty puritan despots who would go on to execute Quakers and alleged witches.[1]

Both Thomas Morton and his Pilgrim opponents sought liberty, but of very different sorts. Morton wanted to live where he pleased, trade where he pleased, sell what he pleased, and party as he pleased. Pilgrim leaders understood Morton's liberty as licentiousness and recklessness, a threat to their colony's economic viability and ultimately to their cherished Christian liberty. In the rise and fall of Merry Mount emerged two very different visions for the colonization of New England.

The place and date of Thomas Morton's birth remain unknown, though several scholars have suggested he hailed from Devon. He described himself simply as a "gentleman" and the "son of a soldier."[2] Morton was proud to be of Clifford's Inn, one of the Inns of Chancery, schools at which young men prepared to become lawyers and made the social connections that might make their fortunes. Morton became fluent in both law and rhetoric, both of which he later wielded against his puritan antagonists. He also drank deeply from the wells of irreverence and merriment characteristic of the Inns of Chancery and the Inns of Court, which the playwright Ben Jonson termed "the noblest nurseries of humanity and liberty."[3]

By liberty, Jonson meant something entirely different than the Christian liberty of the Pilgrims. In this context, explains historian Philip Finkelpearl, liberty meant "revelry, rebellion, uninhibited satire, relaxed playfulness, libertine wantonness, licensed fooling, and political freedom." Aspiring lawyers understood their knowledge of the common law as essential not only to securing wealth but also to safeguarding the political liberties that belonged to England's propertied elite. At the same time, many students set aside serious concerns for the future and enjoyed being young in London. They found pleasure in literature, entertainment, and sex. The inns themselves organized revels, over which a "Lord of Liberty" or "Lord of Misrule" might preside. In this spirit, students attended masques, dances, feasts, and plays. They visited brothels. They frequented taverns and rubbed shoulders with barristers and poets.[4]

Morton's career as a London lawyer never amounted to anything, but in the late 1610s he met a wealthy widow who lived in the Berkshire village of Swallowfield. Alice Miller's first husband's will provided her and their many daughters with considerable income from his estate. At the same time, their son George became the master of the house in which his mother still lived. An awkward situation became worse when both Alice Miller and her son decided to marry. As a precaution should Thomas Morton turn out to be interested only in her money, George Miller persuaded his mother to lease her interest in the estate to him. According to Morton, however, the son promised to leave the lease in his mother's hands so that she could destroy it should her second husband prove honorable.

After Alice Miller became Alice Morton in November 1621, family relations quickly descended into a messy pottage of lawsuits. George Miller asserted that just before the wedding, his mother broke into his trunk and destroyed the lease. He further alleged that his mother, stepfather, and several others entered his residence, brandished pistols and warrants, and evicted everyone save Miller's pregnant wife. Morton then returned, broke down the wife's doors, and dragged her "out of her naked bed." On the Sabbath, no less.

Morton countered that George Miller denied his mother and his many sisters their rightful income and marriage portions. Morton also claimed that when George beat his mother in an attempt to shorten her life, he caused her to miscarry the child that she and Morton had conceived.

In June 1623, the chancery judge tasked with enduring the sordid tale ordered mother and son to take possession of separate farms. The judge observed that Thomas Morton "had nothing in the premises but in right of his wife" and added that if Morton chose to live elsewhere, he "should suffer her to enjoy her own estate." Morton had already made that choice. No one had seen or heard of him since February. The judge reported that Morton had sold all of Alice's goods, including her clothing. Alice Morton died a few years later.[5]

Still without a fortune, Morton sought yet another path to riches. He became a minor investor in a venture organized by two erstwhile pirates, Humphrey Rastall and Captain Richard Wollaston. Rastall was a merchant who had spent two decades trafficking in various sorts of human cargoes. He carried African slaves around the Mediterranean and to Spain, and he was convicted of piracy for seizing Turkish ships and their passengers. Wollaston was another sea dog with a dubious past. Back in 1615, he had crossed paths with John Smith while the latter was a prisoner on a French corsair.[6] Two years later, Wollaston joined Walter Raleigh's expedition to Guiana, then deserted to chase French prizes off the coast of Newfoundland. By the early 1620s, the merchant Rastall and ship's captain Wollaston had joined forces to merchandise a different sort of human commodity. They planned to purchase the indentures of servants, sail to New England, trade with the fishing outposts there, and sell the servants in Virginia.

Rastall, Wollaston, Morton, and around thirty servants left England aboard the *Unity* and reached Cape Ann in June 1624. Rastall chartered a smaller ship and transported a number of the servants to Virginia. Wollaston stocked the *Unity* with cod and oil, purchased some provisions at Monhegan Island, and set sail for Virginia, only to encounter winds that forced a return to England. Morton and some servants remained behind under a Lieutenant Fitcher at an outpost that became known as Mount Wollaston, only several miles removed from Thomas Weston's failed Wessagussett colony. Wollaston and Rastall never set foot in New England again; they were both dead by 1627.[7]

According to William Bradford, once Wollaston and Rastall were gone, Morton organized a mutiny. He gave the remaining servants "strong drink" and "junkets," sweetened curds. Then he warned them that they would "also be carried away and sold for slaves" in Virginia. If, however, they thrust out Fitcher, they would be "free from service" and could "live together as equals" and partners in trade. Fitcher left.[8]

Morton rechristened the outpost Ma-re Mount. Because he so relished wordplay, scholars have perceived many possible references in the name: the Virgin Mary, marriage, and even a horse (being mounted). Most obvious, though, remains Charles Francis Adams Jr.'s interpretation of "hill by the sea." The Latin *mare* means "sea," and the outpost enjoyed a commanding and visible position above the bay.[9]

Little is known about the servants whom Wollaston and Rastall had brought to the New World, but Bradford employed the term *slaves* for good reason. In a London teeming with starving migrants from the countryside, constables periodically seized poor children and confined them in Bridewell Prison. In 1619, several hundred of these children were indentured to Virginia Company investors, who transported them to colonial tobacco fields. Many well-to-do men in England praised such schemes. John Donne, the poet turned dean of St. Paul's Cathedral, told the investors of the Virginia Company that colonization would "sweep your streets, and wash your doors, from idle persons, and the children of idle persons." The human cost of this cleansing was high. By 1622, nearly all of the three hundred "servants" shipped to the Chesapeake had died. One succumbed after her master punished her with a reported five hundred blows. Over the course of the century, English authorities shipped thousands of Irish rebels, religious dissidents, criminals, and vagrants to North American and Caribbean colonies. Many of them went as servants for life. Perhaps their children would be free, but in every other respect, they were slaves.[10]

Bradford and other Pilgrim leaders sympathized with servants facing the sale of their labor to Virginia, but they would not sanction the casting aside of indentures. Nor did they think that men should or could live together as equals. Bradford wrote that New England's planters feared that Morton's upsetting of the social order would make it impossible for them to keep any servants. "All the scum of the country, or any discontents, would flock to him [Morton]," Bradford complained. Plymouth's governor added that Morton "inveigl[ed] . . . men's servants away from them." According to Bradford, Merry Mount threatened his colony's already weak social hierarchy.[11]

What Morton more immediately threatened was Plymouth's new-found commercial success. After a half decade of disasters, Plymouth finally managed to ship large quantities of fur to England precisely as the price of beaver skins soared.[12] The furs were not coming to Plymouth; no interior river reached the colony. While the Pilgrims had obtained furs on Massachusetts Bay, the richest trading sites in New England lay farther afield. In 1625, Edward Winslow sailed up the Kennebec River (in present-day Maine), traded Plymouth-grown corn, and returned with around four hundred beaver furs. Winslow's shipment was worth nearly three hundred pounds, and this time it was not lost to shipwreck or piracy.[13]

Shortly after Winslow's Kennebec trip, the Pilgrims put themselves on a firmer financial footing. Plymouth's leaders sent Isaac Allerton to London to work out a new agreement with their remaining backers. A tailor from Suffolk, Allerton, with his pregnant wife and three children, had joined John Robinson's congregation in Leiden and then had become passengers on the *Mayflower*. Shortly after the first passengers explored the future site of Plymouth, Mary Allerton gave birth to a stillborn son aboard the ship. She then died during the company's first months in Plymouth. Four years later, Isaac Allerton married Fear Brewster, William Brewster's daughter. Each spring, male settlers with voting rights reelected Allerton as one of several assistants to Governor Bradford.[14]

In London, Allerton met with the remaining Adventurers, who still hoped to recoup some of their investment and were willing to extend additional capital. The investors set aside any claims on the settlers' houses, land, and livestock, thus extricating the Pilgrims from the conditions Thomas Weston had imposed on them. The settlers then bought out the Adventurers for £1,800, payable in nine annual installments, the last falling due in 1636.

Plymouth's leading settlers—Bradford, Standish, Allerton, Winslow, and several others—took responsibility for making the annual £200 payments and also agreed to repay an additional £600 in debts. Should the colony default, these "Undertakers" would be personally liable. At the same time, the Undertakers reached an agreement with the rest of the male colonists. In return for their assumption of the colony's financial obligations, the Undertakers alone would reap the profits of the beaver trade for the next six years. Using these anticipated profits as collateral, the Pilgrim traders obtained fresh loans from James Sherley and two other backers. The rate of interest was high, but so was the current price of beaver. The Pilgrims used some of the borrowed funds to help some of their fellow congregants in Leiden finally come to Plymouth.[15]

Another development also enhanced the colony's prospects. During the mid- to late 1620s, Pilgrim traders embraced wampum, which increasingly functioned as a regional currency across New England. The Pequots and several other coastal peoples made wampum beads from the shells of clams and whelks. Belts, sashes, necklaces, and other items made of strung beads were symbols of rank and wealth, used for dowry payments and worn by sachems. The beads also possessed a ritual significance, representing access to spiritual power. In the early 1620s, Dutch traders discerned wampum's

Portrait of a Native sachem with wampum headpiece, earrings,
and necklace, ca. 1700. (Courtesy of Rhode Island School of Design.)

value in their interactions with the Pequots. They obtained large
stocks of wampum beads and used them to purchase rich cargoes
of furs from outposts up the Hudson and Connecticut Rivers. As
Thomas Morton commented, "These beads are current [accepted
as currency] in all the parts of New England, from one end of the
coast to the other."[16] Through the beaver-wampum trade, some
coastal peoples, such as the Narragansetts and Pequots, became
wealthier and more powerful.

In 1626, the new secretary of the New Netherland Company,
Isaack de Rasière, complained that the "Brownists of Plymouth
come near our places to get wampum." Plymouth had established a
trading outpost at Aptucxet on Buzzards Bay, giving English traders
ready access to Narragansett Bay, the Connecticut River Valley, and
Long Island without having to sail around Cape Cod and the dangerous shoals to its south. De Rasière wanted to control the access

of English and French traders to wampum, "either by force or by spoiling their trade by outbidding them with duffels [a coarse woolen cloth] or hatchets." Hoping to forestall competition through diplomacy, De Rasière visited the Pilgrims in October 1627.[17]

While in Plymouth, De Rasière watched the colonists prepare for Sunday worship: "They assemble by beat of drum, each with his musket or firelock, in front of the captain's [Myles Standish's] door; they have their cloaks on, and place themselves in order, three abreast, and are led by a sergeant without beat of drum. Behind comes the Governor [Bradford], in a long robe; beside him, on the right hand, comes the preacher [Brewster] with his cloak on, and on the left hand, the captain with his side-arms and cloak on, and with a small cane in his hand; and so they march in good order, and each sets his arms down near him." The settlers processed with military discipline up the hill to the fort that doubled as a meetinghouse. On the ground floor, the congregation sang psalms and listened to Brewster's sermons. Above them, six cannons commanded the surrounding country and bay. De Rasière commented that the Plymouth settlers were "constantly on their guard night and day." While the Pilgrims aimed to impress De Rasière with their preparedness, they were not unusual in carrying firearms to church. Some colonies, such as Virginia, required men to bring guns, swords, and ammunition to worship in order to deter Native attacks.[18]

De Rasière sold Plymouth's settlers some £50 of wampum and encouraged them to take it north to the Kennebec. The Dutch gambit backfired. Although Plymouth at first concentrated its attention on the Kennebec, its traders soon visited wampum-making sites along the southern New England coast and discussed ways to encroach on the Connecticut River fur trade. The Wampanoags also became wampum producers. "It makes the Indians of these parts rich and powerful and also proud," Bradford commented. The Dutch feared English traders and settlers would supplant them. In 1627, the directors of the West Indian Company reported that "the English of New Plymouth threaten to drive away" the Dutch settlers on the Hudson.[19]

The beaver boom also stoked competition among the English traders along Massachusetts Bay and the upper New England coast. After he gained control of Mount Wollaston, Thomas Morton became one of many men seeking the same sources of furs. As far as Plymouth was concerned, Thomas Morton got more than his share. He made money and made merry. In so doing, he made enemies.

"The more I looked," Morton recalled his early impressions of New England, "the more I liked it."[20] One part ethnography, one part a depiction of the land and its resources, one part history, and from start to finish a bawdy anti-puritan polemic, *New English Canaan* stands out among the sermons, sacred histories, and Christian poetry that characterize seventeenth-century New England literature.

When William Bradford described the New England landscape, he stressed its forbidding strangeness. Morton, by contrast, gushed about a lush country ripe for English trade and settlement. New England was "nature's masterpiece." It was a "fair virgin" ready to be "enjoyed" and exploited by English "art and industry." It was a second Canaan, as promising as the land God had given to the ancient Israelites. "If this land be not rich," Morton waxed, "then is the whole world poor." With even more hyperbole than Plymouth's boosters employed, Morton wrote of plentiful fish that practically leapt ashore, trees that bent from the weight of ripe grapes, of boughs and skies thick with birds, and forty-eight-pound turkeys that men could shoot while standing in their doorways. Morton claimed that settlers were immune from colds and coughs and that sick men from Virginia were cured by New England's pure air.[21]

Like his English contemporaries, Morton concluded that God had prepared New England for colonization by sending a plague to "sweep away by heaps the savages." The decimation of the Native population had made New England "so much the more fit, for the English nation to inhabit in, and erect in its temples to the glory of God." Morton, though, had unusually positive things to say about the survivors of the epidemics. They were intelligent and modest. They treated their elders with reverence. Morton praised their "more happy and freer life, being void of care." Unlike most other English writers, Morton compared the Indians positively to those English who had settled near them. "I found two sorts of people," he wrote, "the one Christians, the other infidels, these I found most full of humanity, and more friendly than the other." The Indians were not dangerous; the Plymouth settlers had no need to huddle behind the walls of their fort. Instead, Morton argued that it was the treacherous Pilgrims who posed a danger to English traders and prospective settlers.[22]

The marrow of *New English Canaan* is a sustained satire and critique of New Plymouth and Massachusetts Bay, interwoven with Morton's account of his Merry Mount outpost. Morton wrote in the mid-1630s while working for Englishmen who were trying to topple New England's puritan governments. *New English Canaan*, thus, is not a straightforward contemporary account of Merry Mount's rise and fall, but neither is the account in William Bradford's history. Both men placed the episode in the context of English debates over merriment and revelry, which King Charles and Archbishop Laud favored and the Pilgrims opposed.

In their dueling histories, Morton and Bradford agree on a few essentials. After Wollaston and Rastall left New England, there was a mutiny. Morton and his men erected and danced around a maypole, which Plymouth's separatists denounced as an idol. Meanwhile, the two colonies collided as they competed for beaver pelts. In June 1628, the Pilgrims arrested Morton and banished him from his outpost. Bradford and Morton flesh out this story with colorful but contradictory details.

Morton put revelry at the center of his story. According to *New English Canaan*, the inhabitants of Merry Mount celebrated "after the old English custom." They cut down an eighty-foot pine tree and nailed a pair of buck antlers to it. Native visitors helped Morton's men raise their maypole, which served as the fulcrum of their festivities and a signal for others who might find the way to "mine host of Ma-re Mount," as Morton styled himself. The liquor flowed and merriment ensued. One of the company sang, and the others danced "hand in hand about the maypole." Morton recorded the song: "Drink and be merry, merry, merry boys . . . Lasses in beaver coats come away / Ye shall be welcome to us night and day." All were welcome to join in trade and revelry.[23]

One of the more curious items in *New English Canaan* is Morton's claim to have composed and affixed to the maypole an enigmatically lewd poem intended to confuse his separatist foes. "Rise Oedipus," it begins, "and if thou canst unfold." Overstuffed with allusions to Greek and Roman mythology, Morton's poem describes a rich widow—Scylla—to whom the sea god Neptune has brought "a new paramour," but one lacking in masculine virtue. The poem ends with a new suitor, as Scylla is pointed to Merry Mount, where "the first of May . . . shall be kept holiday."[24]

Morton reported that Plymouth's pious "moles" suspected that the verse "was in memory of a whore." While Morton reveled in erotic wordplay, the maypole poem was about political and economic power rather than sex. The historian Edith Murphy suggests that the "rich widow" is the land of New England itself. The Indians are her late husband, swept away by the plague. The seas have brought the Pilgrims to this land, but they are the unsuitable paramour. Morton presents himself and like-minded gentlemen as fitting replacements for both the departed Indians and the unworthy separatists.[25]

Morton explained that his maypole was a "lamentable spectacle to the precise separatists that lived at New Plymouth." According to him, they understood it as an idol, akin to the golden calf worshipped by the Hebrews after the exodus. Merry Mount's "host" understood his opponents. Bradford explained that:

> Morton became lord of misrule, and maintained (as it were) a school of atheism. . . . They also set up a maypole, drinking and dancing about it many days together, inviting the Indian women, for their consorts, dancing and frisking together (like so many fairies, or furies rather), and worse practices. As if they had anew revived and celebrated the feasts of the Roman goddess Flora, or the beastly practices of the mad Bacchanalians. Morton likewise (to show his poetry) composed sundry rhymes and verses, some tending to lasciviousness, and others to the detraction and scandal of some persons, which he affixed to this idle or idol maypole.

Drunkenness, idolatry, fornication. It was a puritan hell dream, the specter of a sin city on a hill. Three-quarters of a century later, Boston's Cotton Mather dismissed Merry Mount as a "plantation of rude, lewd, mad English people."[26]

The Pilgrims' decision to apprehend Morton, however, had nothing to do with a maypole. When Thomas Weston's colonists reached Damariscove Island (off the coast of present-day Maine) in 1622, they found that fishermen had "newly set up a maypole and were very merry." Plymouth's leaders did not consider organizing an expedition to destroy it. Phinehas Pratt and Samuel Maverick, contemporaries who wrote brief accounts of Merry Mount, did not mention a maypole. Presuming Morton actually erected a maypole, the Pilgrims left it standing. Nor did the Pilgrims care a great deal about poetry that spring rains would have quickly washed away.[27]

Although Bradford denounced Morton's alleged idolatry and immorality, his chief complaint against Morton was the sale of guns and ammunition to the Indians. Plymouth's governor wrote letters to Ferdinando Gorges and his Council for New England in which he asserted that Morton's trade in firearms posed a mortal danger to Plymouth and warned that its settlers might have to "quit the country" or "be beaten with our own arms if we abide." Bradford also obliquely referenced the threat Morton posed to the colony's prosperity, mentioning that because of Morton's willingness to sell weaponry, nothing else was "vendible amongst them." Morton's guns disrupted the market.[28]

Morton does not mention the firearms trade in *New English Canaan*. He simply states that the Plymouth separatists charged him with "criminal things." If Morton did sell guns to the Indians, he was a small part of a New England trade that was beginning to boom. Bradford's letters make it clear that other English traders also sold weapons and ammunition to Natives, and the Dutch did so with even fewer restraints.[29]

Amid his tale of maypoles and merriment, Morton pinpointed what he understood as the real reason for Plymouth's move against him, one that Bradford had tacitly confirmed in his letters to Gorges. Morton stated that the Pilgrims opposed him because they envied Merry Mount's "prosperity," based on its being "in a good way for gain in the beaver trade." Morton bragged that he and his traders had preempted the trade on the Kennebec River. The Pilgrim traders lost out because Morton's "boat had gleaned away all before they came." Regardless of how Morton had outmaneuvered them, Plymouth's Undertakers could not afford the loss. They had to make the annual payment on their debts.[30]

The Pilgrims had checked several threats to their colony, and they felt emboldened to snuff out one more. Bradford—with the support of other traders and settlers scattered around Massachusetts Bay—sent Myles Standish to arrest Morton. According to Bradford, Standish's party found Morton and his men "so steeled with drink" that they could not lift their weapons. The only bloodshed occurred when one drunkard stumbled into a sword and cut his nose. They then found a ship going from the Isle of Shoals and sent Morton to England in the custody of none other than John Oldham, whom New Plymouth had banished several years earlier.[31]

In Morton's more uproarious version of the raid, a party led by "Captain Shrimp" (Standish) surprised "mine host" while his men were away on a trading expedition. After apprehending Morton, his enemies drank themselves into such a stupor that their prize slipped away in the middle of the night. A chagrined Standish then pursued him to his "den." In order to avoid needless bloodshed, Morton agreed to surrender when promised he could retain his goods and his arms. Captain Shrimp agreed, but then stripped Morton of his guns, and the Plymouth men "fell upon him, as if they would have eaten him." After dragging Morton back to Plymouth, the separatists marooned him on an island without weapons or adequate clothing. Morton received food, liquor, and other supplies from Indians. "So full of humanity are these infidels before those Christians," he commented. A ship eventually picked him up and brought him across the Atlantic.[32]

Without "mine host," the maypole did not last long. Shortly after Morton's expulsion, around one hundred puritan colonists led by John Endecott crossed the Atlantic and settled just south of Cape Ann. Endecott's settlers were the vanguard of what became the migration of thousands of English settlers to Massachusetts Bay over the next dozen years. According to Bradford, Endecott ("Captain Littleworth" in *New English Canaan*) promptly visited Morton's colony, cut down the maypole, and chastised Morton's men "for their profaneness."[33]

Meanwhile, when he reached England, Morton received not so much as a rebuke from the Council for New England. Ferdinando Gorges and his allies had far more in common with Morton than

William L. Sheppard, Endicott Cutting Down Morton's Maypole,
ca. 1885, from Walter Montgomery, American Art
and American Art Collections *(1889).*

they did with the Pilgrims, and they were unconcerned about the
possibility that Natives with guns would menace puritan settlers.

In the spring of 1629, Morton crossed the Atlantic again, this
time with Plymouth's own Isaac Allerton. As Plymouth's representa-
tive, Allerton had obtained a patent from the Council for New England, which granted the Pilgrim Undertakers the exclusive right to
trade on the Kennebec River. In order to protect their monopoly
from competitors, the Pilgrims built a trading house at Cushnoc,
about thirty miles up the Kennebec near present-day Augusta. Allerton subsequently obtained another patent, made out to Bradford
and signed by the Earl of Warwick on behalf of the Council for New
England. This document superseded the Peirce Patent. It specified
New Plymouth's boundaries for the first time, and it empowered the

colony's settlers to incorporate themselves and "to frame and make orders, ordinances, and constitutions."[34]

The patent was welcome news, but the other Pilgrims were flabbergasted when Allerton told them that he had hired Morton as his scribe. Perhaps Morton had helped Allerton obtain the patent, or perhaps Allerton thought he could benefit from Morton's trading acumen. In his history, Bradford alleges that Allerton by this point had grown more concerned with his own trading operations and neglected the interests of his fellow Undertakers.[35]

Plymouth's other leaders were angry with Allerton, but they felt dependent on him to manage their London relations. They would not tolerate Morton, however. Bradford was convinced that Morton had come "to nose them," as a spy for the colony's English enemies. The magistrates soon sent him away, and he made his way back to "his old nest." Although Plymouth's leaders and Morton retained their mutual dislike, Endecott and other Massachusetts Bay leaders became Morton's chief antagonists going forward. According to Morton, Endecott deputized a party that went to Merry Mount and stole most of the outpost's corn. Morton wrote that although deprived of his grain, he had no trouble shooting sufficient fowl and venison "in a country so much abounding with plenty of food." If Endecott and his men had any brains, Morton maintained, they could have found a way to feed themselves without resorting to theft.[36]

In the summer of 1630, a much larger group of puritans came to New England under the leadership of John Winthrop, now the governor of the Massachusetts Bay Company. Surrounded by puritans and within the Bay Colony's charter, Merry Mount could not survive. Massachusetts leaders ordered Morton's arrest and pronounced him guilty of having stolen a canoe from the Indians and of having done them many other wrongs "from time to time." The magistrates ordered Morton shackled until he could be sent to England, and they ordered his goods seized and his house "burned down to the ground in the sight of the Indians." It was a rather harsh punishment for canoe theft. Several years later, Morton wrote that the "Brownists of New England" had deprived him of all of his "goods, moneys, and writings."[37]

In his journal, John Winthrop made a vague mention that Morton had committed "other misdemeanors." Several years earlier,

Winthrop had recorded a note about a "Thomas Moreton late of Swallowfield" who had murdered a business partner back in the early 1620s. The charge against Morton may have originated with George Miller, who had good reason to smear his father-in-law and continued to repeat the murder accusation into the 1630s. According to Bradford, Lord Chief Justice Nicholas Hyde sent a warrant for Morton's extradition.[38]

Morton sat in a Boston jail for several months until a ship agreed to transport him. When the time came, "mine host" apparently refused to go aboard. According to Samuel Maverick, an "old comer" who lived near Thomas Weston's failed colony, the puritan authorities "hoisted" Morton aboard "by a tackle" and then sailed him "in sight of his house" while they burned it to ashes. The charges of murder did not stick, however. Once he reached England, Morton was a free man.[39]

"Morton's ultimate offense," writes historian Michael Zuckerman, "was simply to insist upon his own liberty, because in early Massachusetts there was no place for such a man."[40] It was not just that Morton lived as he pleased. Since the early 1620s, there had been individuals who moved beyond the tight-knit communities of puritan New England or who lived at their margins. Morton, though, was not content to remain on the margins. He invited others to join him at Merry Mount, and he thumbed his nose at the Pilgrims and at Bay Colony leaders. By making himself conspicuous, he made himself someone that puritan magistrates would not tolerate.

After his second banishment, Morton stayed away from New England for more than a decade. Plymouth had rid itself of a nimble economic competitor, and Massachusetts Bay had swept aside an unwanted presence within its charter. New England's puritan magistrates soon discovered, however, that Morton posed a greater danger to them in England. By making enemies of men like Morton, Pilgrim and Bay Colony leaders made themselves conspicuous, garnering unwanted attention from English officials and bishops.

CHAPTER EIGHT

Out of Small Beginnings

B Y THE LATE 1620s, the puritan cause in England was entering its nadir. Shortly after his accession, King Charles married Henrietta Maria, a French Catholic princess, and he allowed his wife's chaplain to remain at court. The new king also bestowed his favor upon a faction of bishops determined to extinguish puritanism once and for all. William Laud, newly elevated bishop of London, introduced new forms of ceremonialism into parish worship and punished and defrocked ministers who objected to his innovations. In the past, puritan ministers had met the demands of the hierarchy and then quietly resumed their nonconformity. Especially after he became archbishop of Canterbury in 1633, Laud made such compromises next to impossible.

It wasn't just Laud and the Catholic queen consort, though. Puritan discontent with ecclesiastical policy coincided with political tumult over taxation and the prerogatives of Parliament. Needing money to fund wars against Spain and France, in 1626 Charles demanded what became known as a "forced loan" from his subjects. Charles called it a loan, but it amounted to taxation without parliamentary consent. Large numbers of gentlemen, many of them puritan, found themselves in jail when they failed to love their king enough to give him their money. Such actions raised the related question of whether the king could imprison individuals without showing cause. Pamphleteers alleged that the king, or at least the king's counselors, aimed to deprive the people of their liberties and reduce them to slavery. Parliamentary pushback eventually forced the king to accept a petition (known as the Petition of Right) that declared that no person should be compelled to "contribute to any tax, tallage, aid, or other like charge not set by common consent, in Parliament." Charles resented what he understood as an assault on his own prerogatives. In March 1629, the exasperated king dissolved Parliament and would not call another for eleven years. The controversy advanced a fear of arbitrary government in both old England and New England, a fear present in subsequent political debates on both sides of the Atlantic.[1]

Especially as Laud increased pressure on puritan ministers, many of the godly, with great reluctance, concluded that it was time to leave. "England hath seen her best days," preached Thomas Hooker, the future minister of Hartford, Connecticut, "and now evil days are befalling us: God is packing up his gospel." First in small numbers, but soon by the thousands, English puritans also packed up and left for New England. They were joined by other men and women seeking economic opportunity, reuniting with relatives, or fleeing trouble at home. The first waves of new emigrants settled on the rim of Massachusetts Bay, but they soon formed communities across New England.[2]

Even as Laud harried their ministers out of England, most puritans wanted nothing to do with separatism, still an object of scorn among nearly all English Protestants. Nevertheless, Plymouth's leaders successfully introduced themselves to the new emigrants as kindred spirits rather than seditious Brownists. The Pilgrims and the Massachusetts Bay settlers found that they shared many ideas about Christian liberty. John Cotton, who became Boston's minister in 1633, explained that he and other emigrants had come to New England to "enjoy the liberty, not of some ordinances of god, but of all, and all in purity." Separatists and other puritans wanted worship free of nonbiblical corruptions: no vestments, prayer books, or signs of the cross.[3]

Before they came to New England, very few puritans had embraced the key elements of congregational polity that were part and parcel of separatism: the restriction of church membership to godly Christians, coupled with the restriction of the sacraments to members of particular, covenanted churches; the liberty of the people to elect officers and discipline offenders; and the autonomy of each congregation. The puritan emigrants to Massachusetts Bay adopted precisely this sort of congregationalism, and they did so in large part through the influence of Plymouth's emissaries and example. At least for a moment, the Pilgrims' wildest dreams became reality.

In September 1628, the emigrants under the leadership of John Endecott settled at what the English called Naumkeag (after the Native people of the region). There were already a few settlers there, including Roger Conant, who had come to New Plymouth earlier in the decade but then moved north with a few other families. Conant and Endecott together renamed their settlement Salem, a Hellenized version of *shalom*, the Hebrew word for peace. The new name turned out to be more aspirational than descriptive.

John Endecott was a tempestuous man, the Bay Colony counterpart to Myles Standish. Likely hailing from England's West Country, Endecott moved to London, fathered a child out of wedlock, paid another man to raise him, and enlisted as an English volunteer fighting the Spanish in the Netherlands. The time abroad repaired his reputation. When he returned to England, he married Anne Gower and became one of the patentees of the New England Company. The company (the forerunner of the Massachusetts Bay Company), obtained a patent—soon confirmed by a royal charter—for an area stretching from the Merrimack River to south of the Charles River.[4]

At Salem, disease and malnutrition led to a partial reprise of Plymouth's first winter. Bradford wrote that many of the settlers perished, "some of the scurvy, other[s] of an infectious fever." Endecott sent word to Plymouth asking for help, and the Pilgrims dispatched Samuel Fuller as their emissary. Born in 1581 in a Norfolk village, Fuller worked as a weaver after his 1611 emigration to Leiden. As a deacon in John Robinson's congregation, Fuller oversaw collections, paid the minister's salary, and attended to the needs of the poor. The deacon left his wife, Bridget, behind when he sailed on the *Mayflower*; she joined him three years later. In New Plymouth, Fuller became one of the Undertakers who assumed financial responsibility for the colony's debts. Fuller's accumulation of live-

stock and servants indicates a prosperity he would have been unlikely to enjoy had he remained in England or Leiden.[5]

Fuller proved a welcome visitor at Salem. At some point in the
1620s, the former weaver had become a self-taught physician and
surgeon. By the time of his 1633 death, he owned a number of "physic
[medicinal] books." At Salem, Fuller's ministrations were not very
effective. In 1621, Edward Winslow had urged transatlantic passengers to take lemon juice with them to ward off scurvy. Fuller's primary treatment, however, remained bloodletting, which was at best
a source of hope for those patients who believed in its efficacy. In his
New English Canaan, Thomas Morton castigated Fuller as a "quacksalver" and "Doctor Noddy [that is, a fool]" and alleged that in his
incompetency Fuller cured Endecott "of a disease called a wife."
Anne Endecott died during the colony's first year, but Salem's governor did not blame Fuller. Instead, John Endecott thanked Bradford profusely for Fuller's assistance.[6]

Fuller also treated the negative preconceptions the new settlers
had about separatism and Plymouth. As in medicine, Fuller was self-
taught but well read in theology. In addition to the works of John
Robinson and Henry Ainsworth, Fuller's large library included titles
by Calvin, Theodore Beza, Thomas Cartwright, and John Dod.
Fuller, moreover, shared the relative moderation of Leiden separatists such as Robert Cushman and John Robinson. The fact that
Fuller had favored clemency for John Lyford—the minister whom
Pilgrim leaders had banished in 1624—probably endeared the physician to Bay settlers such as Roger Conant.[7]

John Endecott liked what he heard from the deacon. "I am by
him [Fuller] satisfied," wrote Endecott to Bradford, "touching your
judgments of the outward form of God's worship . . . no other than
is warranted by the evidence of truth." Endecott went so far as to
assert that his people and Plymouth's were "sealed with one and the
same seal, and have for the main, one and the same heart." Fuller
convinced Endecott that the Plymouth colonists were godly Reformed Protestants, not schismatics.[8]

In the summer of 1629, bolstered by several hundred new arrivals, Salem's settlers proceeded to form a church. Thirty men gave
their assent to a confession of faith and entered into a simple covenant with God and each other in which they bound themselves "to

walk together in all his ways, according as he is pleased to reveal himself unto us in his blessed word of truth." The procedure and language closely resembled those used by the separatists in Scrooby and Gainsborough more than two decades earlier, when as "the Lord's free people" they had covenanted to walk in God's ways.[9]

Next the newly covenanted church members elected and ordained their officers. Early New England churches that could afford to do so typically installed two ministers: a pastor and a teacher. The former typically bore more responsibility for church discipline and pastoral care, and the latter exercised more authority when it came to doctrine. Most simply, however, if a congregation secured both a pastor and a teacher, the two men shared a heavy ministerial burden. The 1629 emigrants to Salem included the ministers Samuel Skelton and Francis Higginson, who both held master's degrees from Cambridge. Skelton and Higginson did not claim that their authority rested on their prior ordinations in the Church of England. Instead, the pair acknowledged that ministers needed "an outward calling" from a covenanted people and that all male church members "are to have a free voice in the choice of their officers." Church members voted by secret ballot, selecting Skelton and Higginson as pastor and teacher, respectively. Leading congregants then laid hands on Skelton and Higginson, praying over them and ordaining them into their new offices. The congregation repeated the procedure two weeks later when it chose elders and deacons. Bradford and other emissaries from Plymouth's church came to Salem and gave their counterparts "the right hand of fellowship," signaling their acceptance of the new congregation as a true church. Fuller went so far as to praise John Endecott as a "second Burrow [Henry Barrow]," the separatist martyr. He did so because Salem had so thoroughly embraced Plymouth-style congregationalism.[10]

Just as John Lyford and others objected to Plymouth's church, so too some settlers at Salem expressed discontent. Not everyone who had come to Salem was a puritan, let alone a congregationalist. The brothers John and Samuel Browne were among the New England Company's patentees and had arrived in Salem before the formation of its church. Along with a few other settlers, they now convened their own services, at which they used the Book of Common Prayer. Endecott quickly arranged a confrontation between the brothers and the ministers. The Brownes denounced Skelton and Higginson as "separatists, and would-be Anabaptists." Skelton and Higginson rejected the charge. "They did not separate from the Church of England, nor from the ordinances of God there," they insisted, "but only from the corruptions and disorders there." Puritans had suffered in England from their refusal to use the prayer book and the ceremonies it prescribed. Now "being in a place where they might have their liberty," Skelton and Higginson concluded, "they neither could nor would use them." Salem's ministers celebrated their liberty, which they understood as the pure, biblical worship of God.[11]

Endecott handled the Brownes as William Bradford had treated John Lyford and John Oldham. He purloined the brothers' letters, accused them of promoting mutiny and faction, and informed them that "New England was no place for such as they." The Brownes had no liberty to participate in what Salem's ministers considered the "sinful corruptions in the worship of God." Endecott shipped the brothers back to England, where they lodged bitter complaints about their treatment and about "rash innovations begun and practiced in [Salem's] civil and ecclesiastical government." The Massachusetts Bay Company eventually compensated the brothers for their financial loss.[12]

There was more ecclesiastical drama the next year, when new Massachusetts Bay governor John Winthrop—a wealthy lawyer—led around one thousand passengers to New England. Winthrop's ships reached Salem in June 1630 with the company's royal charter, a legal security the Pilgrims never obtained. Unlike the Brownes, these new arrivals relished the chance to worship without the Book of Common Prayer. They received a surprise, though, when Salem's Samuel Skelton refused to admit them to the Lord's Supper or to baptize children born during the Atlantic crossing. Puritans wanted to exclude known sinners from the sacraments, but why the exclusion of godly men and women, including Governor Winthrop himself?

John Cotton, a leading nonconformist minister back in England whose congregants were among those excluded from the sacraments, was appalled at the news from Salem. "You went hence of another judgment," he lamented, "and I am afraid your change hath sprung from New Plymouth men." Cotton could think of no explanation for Salem's exclusionary policies other than Plymouth's influence. Skelton responded that "no man may be admitted to the sacrament, though a member of the catholic [universal] church, unless he be also a member of some particular Reformed church." Skelton now believed that England's parish churches did not meet that standard.[13]

Skelton made one notable exception, however. He "admitted one of Mr. [John] Lothrop's congregation, not only to the Lord's Supper, but his child unto baptism." This settler belonged to an independent congregation in London founded by Henry Jacob and now pastored by Lothrop (who later emigrated to Plymouth Colony). During the earliest years of his ministry, Jacob was a puritan critic of both ecclesiastical corruption and separatism. By 1610, he was in the Dutch Republic, on friendly terms with both John Robinson and the exiled puritan theologian William Ames. Jacob came to agree with the separatists that a true church was a local, covenanted congregation, but unlike Robinson, he did not denounce the Church of England as false or Antichristian. Instead, he simply returned to London and gathered his own congregation. In 1622, he made plans to emigrate to Virginia, and he apparently died there two years later. Lothrop then succeeded Jacob as the congregation's minister. Skelton considered the Jacob-Lothrop congregation a true church. The other new emigrants did not belong to covenanted churches and therefore had not qualified themselves to receive the sacraments.[14]

Winthrop and most of the 1630 emigrants went south to Charlestown, at the confluence of the Mystic and Charles Rivers. Samuel Fuller spent time there as well, draining the blood of the sick and draining away objections to New Plymouth congregationalism. Once again, Fuller's religious diplomacy proved more effective than his medicine. Sickness ravaged the colonists at Charlestown, prompting Governor Winthrop to set aside a day for fasting and prayer. At the conclusion of the fast, leading male settlers would form a church by covenanting with the Lord. Winthrop asked Plymouth to hold a fast on their behalf on the same day. The Pilgrims obliged.

It is a wonder New Plymouth did not respond to Winthrop's request with a day of thanksgiving. England's transplanted puritans were remaking themselves in Plymouth's image. As the Bay colonists dispersed into towns, each formed its own covenanted church and restricted the Lord's Supper and baptismal privileges to members of particular congregations. Furthermore, just as John Robinson had done, Massachusetts Bay ministers advised their members that it was permissible to hear sermons in English parish churches but that they should not partake of the Lord's Supper.[15]

Since the early 1630s, participants, critics, and many generations of historians have argued about the extent to which the Pilgrims influenced the development of Massachusetts Bay congregationalism. Perry Miller, who still looms large over the historical study of early New England, entirely rejected the idea of Plymouth's influence. "How can we have much respect for the intellectual development of these people [the Bay colonists]," he asked, "when they did not seem to know where they stood or what they wanted, when the determination of their gravest problem lay at the chance mercy of a medical visit from Deacon Fuller?" According to Miller, Skelton, Higginson, and Endecott were influenced not by John Robinson, William Bradford, and "Doctor Noddy," but by "non-separating" congregationalists such as William Ames, one of a small number of puritans prior to 1630 who had embraced congregational polity but had not flat out rejected England's church. As far as Miller was concerned, the Pilgrims were a collection of fringe unsophisticates, while the Bay colonists brought an established theological system to New England.[16]

Miller underestimated the Pilgrims. True, Plymouth's church did not have a minister who could match the erudition or reputation of Thomas Hooker or John Cotton. For most of the colony's first decade, Plymouth had no minister at all, but the Pilgrims had remained engaged with ecclesiastical and theological developments in England. Bradford, Brewster, Fuller, Winslow, and Standish were all well-read laymen quite prepared to make convincing arguments for their church way.

Without Plymouth's example and diplomacy, it is quite possible that Salem's settlers would have covenanted with each other to form a church and elect officers. What is much less likely is that the Salem colonists would have barred even their fellow puritans from the sacraments had they not planted their colony a day's sail from the Pilgrims. Between Fuller's visit, the friendly relations between Winthrop and Bradford, and Cotton's initial response to the policies at Salem, the evidence for Plymouth's influence is strong. Other communities in Massachusetts Bay and Connecticut did not need to use

Plymouth as a model, as they largely replicated the procedures used at Salem.[17]

The Bay Colony influenced Plymouth as well. Whereas the Pilgrims had brought fairly simple standards for church membership to New England (John Robinson required a basic profession of faith and the acceptance of a congregation's covenant), many churches in the Bay Colony began requiring prospective members to publicly describe how God had regenerated their souls. At some point, Plymouth's church adopted the Bay Colony's stricter membership standards. Bradford noted in 1648 that New England's churches—including his own—were "rather more strict and rigid in some proceedings about admission of members" than the Leiden separatists had been. Despite the mutual influence, the church establishments of the two colonies were not identical. Massachusetts Bay linked citizenship to church membership, while Plymouth did not. Also, over the course of the seventeenth century, many Plymouth Colony congregants remained more wary of innovation and intercongregational synods than their counterparts in the Bay Colony.[18]

Regardless of their minor differences, the leaders of both colonies sought to establish communities centered around town churches comprised of godly men and women and their children. Their churches were separated from the Church of England in deed if not in word. Plymouth-style separatism and Bay Colony puritanism converged to create New England Congregationalism, or what John Cotton called the "New England Way."

Once Winthrop's ships reached New England, the population of Massachusetts Bay was much larger than that of New Plymouth. The interests of the two colonies sometimes diverged, and Massachusetts Bay proved a rival as often as it did an ally in the decades to come. Still, as William Bradford looked back on the establishment of the Bay Colony from the vantage point of the mid-1640s, he allowed himself a rare moment of satisfaction. "Thus out of small beginnings," he wrote, "greater things have been produced by his hand that made all things of nothing . . . as one small candle may light a thousand, so the light here kindled hath shone unto many." In coming across the ocean, the Pilgrims hoped that their church would become more attractive to English puritans. They had finally succeeded.[19]

CHAPTER NINE

Soul Liberty

THE PURITAN MIGRATION TO New England that began in the late 1620s brought a modest number of additional settlers to New Plymouth. Thirty-five Leideners came in 1629, followed by a second group of congregants the next year. Compared to the puritan flood washing ashore at Massachusetts Bay, the additions to the Plymouth church amounted to a trickle. For the Pilgrims, though, the newcomers represented a much-needed infusion of congregational vitality and momentum. "We became through the goodness of God pretty numerous and were in the best estate respecting the church that we had as yet been in New England," wrote Nathaniel Morton, who later became the colony's long-time secretary.[1]

The Pilgrims had a larger congregation, but would anyone other than Elder Brewster lead it? After nearly a decade, Plymouth finally secured a minister chosen by one of its own. In 1628, Isaac Allerton brought a Mr. Rogers to the colony. Church leaders were wary after their experience with John Lyford. After a trial period they concluded that Rogers was "crazed in his brain" and paid to send him back. Allerton apparently had no better judgment when it came to ministers than secretaries.[2]

The next ministerial candidate came at less expense. Ralph Smith paid his way to Massachusetts Bay in 1629. When New England Company leaders learned of his separatist principles, they regretted having transported him. From England, they instructed John Endecott that unless Smith proved more tractable, they should "suffer him not to remain within the limits" of the company's charter. Smith moved to an outpost in present-day Hull, Massachusetts, then came to Plymouth. The Pilgrim congregation chose him as its pastor. The resumption of the sacraments was surely welcome news to some men and women who had endured their absence for nearly a decade. Church members could finally partake of the Lord's Supper and have their children baptized. After a few years, however, Plymouth's congregants and Smith grew disenchanted with each other, and Pilgrim leaders explored hiring another minister. By 1636, feeling unappreciated and underpaid, Smith had resigned.[3]

In the early 1630s, Plymouth briefly added a more talented man to its stable of preachers. When he was in his early teens, Roger Williams's intelligence and diligence caught the attention of renowned barrister, judge, and politician Sir Edward Coke. He employed the young Williams as a clerk and then paid for his education. In 1627, Williams graduated from Cambridge at a time when bishops made it more difficult for puritans to obtain parish positions. He continued his studies at Cambridge for a time, then was employed as a chaplain by Sir William Masham, a political ally of Coke and a man who advanced the prospects of many puritan ministers. In addition to providing spiritual counsel to Masham's family and friends, Williams carried messages among the king's parliamentary enemies.[4]

In July 1629, Williams traveled to the Earl of Lincoln's estate in Sempringham in the company of puritan luminaries John Cotton and Thomas Hooker. Williams informed his companions that he disagreed with their willingness to use the Book of Common Prayer. Cotton countered that he "selected the good and best prayers in his use of that book" and that prayer books were not a "fundamental error." Williams would not let his fellow puritans off the hook. The prayer book was an idol. Christians who used it engaged in "false worship." If kings and bishops forced Christians to choose between "peace" and "truth," God commanded them to risk everything for truth. At Sempringham the trio met with John Winthrop and other members of the Massachusetts Bay Company. Williams, Cotton, and Hooker all decided to remain in England for the time being, but they would cross paths again on the other side of the Atlantic.[5]

Williams was as headstrong in romance as he was in theology. That same year, he had the temerity to woo Jane Whalley, the niece of a prominent puritan noblewoman. Lady Jane Barrington informed the young minister that his station was beneath that of his beloved. "I have learned," Williams apologized to Lady Barrington, "to still my soul as a weaned child and give offence to none." Williams was wrong; he could never still his soul, his mouth, or his pen. "We hope to live together in the heavens," he wrote Lady Barrington the next month, "though the Lord has denied that union on earth." The rebuffed Williams soon rebounded by wedding Mary Bernard. Her father was Richard Bernard, the Worksop vicar who after flirting with separatism had written tracts against John Robinson. Given Williams's connections to the king's political enemies, it was not safe for the couple to remain in England. They reached Boston in early 1631.[6]

Once Williams crossed the Atlantic, he became even blunter. He told New England's magistrates and ministers that they fell short of God's mark. Whereas other puritans took great pains to distance themselves from separatism, Williams could find almost nobody he deemed sufficiently separated. He became an arch-separatist, convinced that New England's churches were in the clutches of Antichrist. Cotton Mather later compared Williams to a windmill whipped by such high winds that its millstones started a great conflagration. The firebrand minister sowed controversy wherever he went.[7]

Many New Englanders, though, liked blunt and uncompromising ministers, and Williams had no trouble finding congregations that wanted him. First was the church at Boston. In the fall of 1630, John Winthrop had led a large group of settlers across the river from Charlestown, and they named their new settlement Boston. Williams later recalled that Boston's church unanimously offered him a position but that he had refused to "officiate to an unseparated people." Winthrop explained that Williams would not join with the church because its congregants "would not make a public declaration of their repentance for having communion with the Churches of England while they lived there." For Williams, true separation meant not just a withdrawal from England's church, but a heartfelt apology for having participated in its corrupt ceremonies. During his time in Boston, Williams also raised eyebrows with some of his opinions. According to Winthrop, he asserted that magistrates possessed no authority to enforce the "first table" (the first four) of the Ten Commandments. For example, the court could not punish individuals who did not observe the Sabbath. Williams's stance foreshadowed his subsequent arguments for the strict separation of church and state. By the time Williams left Boston, its leading citizens were glad he had refused their church's offer.[8]

More stridently separatist Salem was Williams's next stop. Francis Higginson, the congregation's teacher, had died the previous summer. The Salem church now called Williams as Higginson's replacement, but the colony's General Court moved to quash Williams's appointment because of the ideas he had expressed in Boston. Although one faction of Salem's church wanted Williams, he did not get the position.

Williams moved again, this time to Plymouth, where he covenanted with the church and acted as an unpaid assistant alongside Ralph Smith. According to Williams's later account, he "spoke on the Lord's days and weekdays" and also "wrought hard at the hoe for my bread." Williams impressed William Bradford as a "godly and zealous" man. Plymouth's governor later expressed his thanks "even for his [Williams's] sharpest admonitions and reproofs." Bradford tolerated the newcomer's zeal more easily than had his Massachusetts Bay counterpart.[9]

The next year, John Winthrop, John Wilson (Boston's minister), and several others from Massachusetts Bay visited Plymouth and lodged at the home of Governor Bradford, whom Winthrop described as a "very discreet and grave man." On Sunday, the visitors worshipped in the morning and the afternoon. The morning services included the Lord's Supper, and the Pilgrims invited the Boston visitors to partake. Winthrop wrote more about the afternoon meeting, which consisted of what puritans termed "prophesying," still a regular practice among the Pilgrims. Williams "propounded a question," and Ralph Smith then "spoke briefly" to it. Williams, Bradford, Brewster, and several others added their judgments. Winthrop and Wilson were invited to give their views as well. At the

close of the service, Samuel Fuller encouraged members to make
their contributions. The congregants "went down to the deacon's
seat, and put it into the box."[10]

According to Cotton Mather's turn-of-the-eighteenth-century
history, the topic discussed at the afternoon meeting was the custom
of calling "any unregenerate man by the name of Goodman." Could
congregants greet those outside the church with the customary ap-
pellation of "Goodman" or "Goodwife"? Mather writes that Williams and Ralph Smith, "leavened so far with the humors of the
rigid separation," deemed it unlawful. Why call wicked men good?
Mather informs that for his part, Winthrop "distinguished between
a theological and a moral goodness" and argued that it "was a pity
now to make a stir about a civil custom, so innocently introduced."
According to Mather, Winthrop's discourse "put a lasting stop to
the little, idle, whimsical conceits, then beginning to grow obstrep-
erous." Winthrop's journal does not identify the topic discussed or
suggest that he settled the question, but even if Mather's tale is
apocryphal, the story captures Williams's contentiousness. Williams
was as keen to separate the sheep and the goats as he was to separate
church and state.[11]

Williams's time in Plymouth soon came to an end. In a letter to
Winthrop, Williams lamented that "to seek the Lord further" was
"a duty not so frequent with Plymouth as formerly." What Williams
meant is that the Pilgrims had stopped short of complete separation
from impure churches and worship. He later wrote that although
Plymouth would not admit "the most godly to communion without
a covenant [that is, without membership in a covenanted church],"
the Pilgrims were "yet communicating with the parishes in Old [En-
gland], by their members repairing on frequent occasions thither."
Plymouth's leaders had continued John Robinson's policy of allowing congregants to hear sermons in parish churches when they visited
England. Like many other separatists, Williams equated attendance
at a Church of England service with apostasy.[12]

Elder Brewster had heard enough. According to Boston minister
John Cotton's later report, Brewster "warned the whole church of
the danger of his [Williams's] spirit." Plymouth's leaders encouraged
Williams to depart. Church covenants were solemn, binding agree-
ments among individuals. In order to join another congregation,

Williams needed a formal dismissal from Plymouth's church. Apparently, some church members wanted to retain Williams in Plymouth, but Brewster persuaded the church to grant Williams's request. Shortly after Mary Williams gave birth to a daughter in August 1633, she and her husband returned to Salem. Plymouth's congregation also dismissed "such as did adhere to [Williams]," who followed him out of the colony.[13]

Before he left Plymouth, Williams had expressed what William Bradford deemed "some strange opinions." He wrote a treatise in which he asserted that English patents were invalid because they were an "unjust usurpation upon others' possessions." Like Plymouth's leaders, Massachusetts ministers and magistrates claimed that they had the right to settle on land that God had made empty for them. Williams considered such claims specious. New England belonged to its Native peoples. Against English arguments that Indians left most of the land unused and unimproved, Williams pointed out that Natives used vast swaths of land for hunting. If Englishmen wanted title to the land on which they had settled, they should buy it from those who already possessed it.[14]

Bradford asked for a copy of Williams's manuscript, and so did John Winthrop. The Massachusetts governor consulted several ministers, who agreed that Williams should be censured at the colony's next General Court. It was not just Williams's contention but the way he had advanced it. According to Winthrop's summary of the treatise, Williams accused the late King James of having committed "blasphemy" for having called Europe "Christendom." As far as Williams was concerned, most Europeans were not Christians. Even worse, Williams applied several choice verses in the Book of Revelation to King Charles, implying that the king of England had "taken up arms with Antichrist against the Lord Jesus" and had "committed fornication with the whore [of Babylon]."[15]

The magistrates in Boston did not take kindly to Williams's stunning lack of discretion. At a time when anti-puritans in England were maneuvering to invalidate the patents held by the New England colonies, the magistrates did not want to invite allegations of sedition by having one of their ministers call the king a blasphemer and a fornicator. Winthrop accused Williams of having "provoked our king against us, and put a sword into his hand to destroy us." In early 1634, Williams apologized and swore an oath of loyalty to the king.[16]

Williams, though, still could not still his mouth. In April 1635, he publicly objected to the colony's requirement that all residents swear an oath of obedience to its government, magistrates, and laws. Oaths were sacred acts of worship. Individuals swore with God as their witness. "So help me God," they said in conclusion. Williams regarded such oath taking as a profane farce in that it forced the "unregenerate" (men who had not experienced God's work of grace) to "take the name of God in vain." It also forced the godly to have "communion with a wicked man in the worship of God." The simplest solution was for governments to dispense with oaths entirely, or at least not to require them.[17]

Precisely as Williams aired these opinions, Salem's congregants again called him as their teacher. When the colony's magistrates and ministers began urging Salem to cast off their newly chosen minister, Williams and his supporters interpreted the pressure as proof positive that the Bay Colony's leaders no longer respected the liberty of Christians to freely choose their own officers. The colony's ministers were acting like England's bishops, repeating the sin of a national church oppressing covenanted Christians. Williams gave his congregants an ultimatum. Either they sundered all communion with other Massachusetts churches because of their "Antichristian pollution," or he could no longer remain in communion with them. The majority of Salem's church members chose obedience to the magistrates over fidelity to their new teacher.[18]

The Bay Colony's leaders would not tolerate the accusation that they had succumbed to Antichrist. In October 1635, the Massachusetts General Court ordered Williams to leave the colony within six weeks. Because he was ill at the time, the court postponed his banishment until the next spring. Williams was not too sick to preach, which he did to men and women who gathered in his house. It was rumored that he intended to take twenty or so followers and form his own colony on Narragansett Bay. The alarmed magistrates decided to send Williams to England on the next ship and ordered Captain John Underhill to arrest him and "carry him aboard." Possibly tipped off by none other than John Winthrop, Williams slipped away and headed south on foot in the dead of winter. Winthrop may have wanted to spare Williams the humiliation and hardships of forced deportation, or he may have welcomed a new English foothold in southern New England.[19]

Williams bought land on the eastern shore of the Seekonk River from the sachem of the Pokanokets. The Pilgrims had called the sachem by his title, Massasoit, but by the early 1630s he had adopted the name Ousamequin, meaning Yellow Feather. New Plymouth claimed that the purchased land fell within its patent, and Edward Winslow—elected governor in one of the rare years that the settlers excused Bradford from the office—told Williams to move to the other side of the river. The Pilgrims "were loath to displease the Bay [Colony leaders]" by allowing the banished minister to settle within their jurisdiction, but Winslow assured Williams that once he moved beyond their bounds, he would be "as free [as] themselves." Like Winthrop, Winslow had a soft spot for the zealous minister. He visited him and "put a piece of gold into the hands" of Mary Williams. Winslow promised Williams that he and the Pilgrims would be "loving neighbors." Williams at times was a valuable ally of both New Plymouth and Massachusetts Bay, but he also remained a thorn in their sides for the next half century.[20]

After crossing the Seekonk, Williams purchased land from the Narragansetts. A number of families from Salem joined him at what he named Providence, for God's provision of a refuge from persecution and hardship. Other Bay Colony dissenters, some of them banished by the same magistrates, soon settled on Aquidneck (Rhode) Island to Providence's south. In 1644, Williams obtained a parliamentary patent for what was then called "Providence Plantations in Narragansett Bay," though the colony became known as Rhode Island.

Williams soon departed from the church order of Massachusetts and Plymouth in another way. As John Smyth and Thomas Helwys had done in Amsterdam, Williams rejected infant baptism. He helped form a Baptist church in Providence, though he soon left it as well. Roger and Mary Williams from that point on were fervent Christians without a church. They prayed with each other. It was the logical endpoint of Williams's separatism.

As Providence developed, its government practiced what Williams had preached in Plymouth and Massachusetts Bay. The Providence settlers signed a compact or agreement in which they promised to obey laws made "by the major consent of the present inhabitants." Unlike the framers of the Mayflower Compact, Williams dispensed with even a passing reference to God.[21] While the Pilgrims wanted to protect true churches from magisterial interference, they expected godly magistrates to support true churches, compel Sabbath observance and church attendance, and punish heresy. Williams disagreed. For him, monarchs and magistrates were not appointed by God as Old Testament judges and kings had been. Thus, civil rulers could neither define nor punish heresy. Accordingly, Providence did not compel anyone to attend worship or to otherwise keep the Sabbath. Settlers possessed liberty of conscience to worship according to their principles, or not to worship at all.

By the 1640s, Williams called this absence of state-controlled religion "soul liberty." Other Protestants, Williams explained, wanted "their own souls only to be free" and to keep other souls in bondage, but Williams insisted that governments should permit Jews, Turks, and even "Antichristians" to live at peace. He favored soul liberty for everyone. Williams argued that for a government to violate an individual's conscience was "a soul or spiritual rape . . . more abominable in God's eye, than to force and ravish the bodies of all the women in the world."[22] Governments should abandon the goal of religious uniformity because it was impossible to achieve without gross violations of conscience.

Williams did not favor protections for dissenters because he liked and respected them. Quite the contrary. Williams believed that nearly all existing churches were full of Antichrist. In a sense, though, Williams's own intolerance and zeal led him to embrace religious liberty. He opposed national churches and church establishments out of his desire to fence off Christ from Antichrist, to protect pure worship from the corruptions of the world. As the years passed, Williams became more and more forceful in his insistence that "forced worship stinks in God's nostrils."[23]

As far as the Congregational settlers of New England were concerned, the stench emanated from Providence and Rhode Island. In 1638, John Winthrop reported that "now men's wives, and children, and servants, claimed liberty . . . to go to all religious meetings."[24] In the eyes of puritan magistrates, "soul liberty" bred social disorder. In fact, very few men and women in the transatlantic English world of the mid-seventeenth century favored religious toleration as broad as Williams established in Rhode Island. Most Protestant advocates for liberty of conscience wanted restrictions on certain groups, such as Catholics or atheists. New Plymouth's William Bradford saw eye to eye with Winthrop on this subject. He found the idea of "soul liberty" repugnant. Nevertheless, some Plymouth Colony settlers agreed with Williams's understanding of baptism and accepted his arguments for soul liberty. As Williams would have predicted, Plymouth's magistrates eventually resorted to persecution in an attempt to maintain religious uniformity.

CHAPTER TEN

Hope

A S OF 1630, THERE were only several hundred English inhabitants in New Plymouth, but the colony was finally poised
for significant growth. Some of the thousands of puritan
emigrants to New England headed south into Plym-
outh's patent. The colony became a string of communities as newcomers arrived and longtime settlers moved away from the original
Pilgrim settlement. Men discontented with Plymouth's religious
and political order had gone their own way since the early 1620s,
but now pillars of the community moved out. By 1632, John Alden
and Myles Standish had taken their families to the northern end of
Plymouth Bay. They were close enough to attend church in Plymouth during the summer and promised to winter in the town to
make church attendance possible when travel became arduous. With
the congregation's reluctant consent, however, those to the north
formed the town and church of Duxbury. Other settlers moved to
what became Scituate, the colony's northernmost town along its bor-
der with Massachusetts Bay.[1]

Some of the "ancient inhabitants," as Plymouth's early settlers
called themselves, opposed the dispersal of the town's population,
and the General Court adopted several measures designed to retard
it. In 1633, the court revoked the land allotments of settlers who had
moved away and reassigned them to "such as do or shall inhabit the
said town of Plymouth." On other occasions, the court granted the

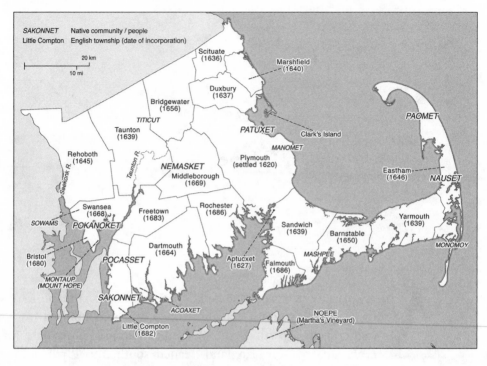

Native communities and Plymouth Colony townships.
(Map by Andrew C. Smith.)

use of land to Plymouth townspeople contingent upon their on-going residence. The court also barred those living outside of the town from coming to its waterways to catch alewives that were used as fertilizer for corn. None of these stratagems succeeded. For instance, the colony granted "good farms to special persons, that would promise to live at Plymouth." The lands in question lay to the north of Duxbury, and the grantees formed their own community, which became the town of Marshfield. Edward Winslow and his family relocated there later in the decade.[2]

Amid the arrival of new emigrants and the formation of townships, Plymouth Colony remained a trading enterprise. After the Undertakers obtained their 1629 patent for the exclusive right to trade on the Kennebec River, they were in a stronger position to compete for the natural riches of New England. For a brief stretch of time, Plymouth became the dominant fur-trading power in the region, but it had too few men, too little firepower, and too many rivals to maintain its position. Although the Dutch gave way in Connecticut, the French threatened Plymouth's outposts in northern New England. The foremost challenge to Plymouth's commercial success, however, came from other English traders and the growing strength of Massachusetts Bay.

The colony's voting men continued to elect Isaac Allerton as one of the assistants to William Bradford each year, but Allerton's relationship with his fellow Undertakers was now fraying badly. As Bradford once had alleged of Squanto, so he now asserted that Allerton "played his own game." He pursued his own trade, borrowing money at high rates of interest and then shipping goods to Massachusetts Bay. Even worse, Allerton was a careless accountant and did not keep his private business dealings separate from those of the Undertakers. Allerton maintained a close relationship with James Sherley, the investor who had facilitated the arrangement with the Undertakers. Working with Allerton, Sherley backed a trading post near the Penobscot River that threatened to undercut Plymouth's Kennebec trade. The Undertakers felt they had no choice but to join in the Penobscot venture, but they replaced Allerton as their agent with Edward Winslow.[3]

Had Allerton's activities produced profits despite his indiscretions, all might have been well. Instead, the Undertakers lost ground. At the start of their arrangement, they had agreed to make nine annual payments of £200 each and had assumed an additional debt of £600. They obtained some fresh loans to finance the Kennebec patent, the transportation of congregants from Leiden, and the outlays needed for their trading operations. Despite cornering a sizeable share of New England's fur trade, and despite making each annual payment, James Sherley informed Bradford in early 1632 that they now owed nearly £6,000. According to Plymouth's governor, Allerton had "hoodwinked" them all and had even "screwed up his poor old father-in-law's [William Brewster] account to above two hundred [pounds]." Allerton's accounts were such a mess that it was impossible to make any sense of his dealings.[4]

For Bradford, Allerton's activities were not merely negligent or duplicitous. They were sinful. He had betrayed his financial partners and broken the covenant that bound together Plymouth's church members. "The love of money is the root of all evil," Bradford quoted 1 Timothy 6:10. It became a matter of church discipline, and "the church called him to account for . . . his gross miscarriages." Allerton "confessed his fault, and promised better walking." While Allerton continued to serve as one of Plymouth's magistrates for several more years, Plymouth's other leaders no longer trusted him. "The truth is," Winslow informed John Winthrop, "he loveth neither you nor us." For a congregation supposedly knit together as the body of Christ, Winslow's was a serious charge.[5]

No sources reveal Allerton's side of the story. Either because of his alienation from his partners, or because he glimpsed richer prospects elsewhere, Allerton left New Plymouth after the 1634 death of his wife. He moved first to Massachusetts Bay, then kept residences for the last two decades of his life in both New Haven and New Amsterdam.

With Allerton sidelined and with their debts mounting, the other Undertakers became more aggressive in their pursuit of furs. They sought to defend their Kennebec and Penobscot outposts from the French and gain a foothold on the Connecticut by outmaneuvering the Dutch. The resulting profits were both heady and deadly.

In June 1632, a French ship sailed into Penobscot Bay. Plymouth's leading men at the outpost had left to collect a supply of trading goods, and only a few servants remained behind. A Scotsman working for the French—perhaps a captive, perhaps a turncoat—told the servants that his vessel was leaking and asked for permission to repair it on shore. The unsuspecting servants welcomed the French visitors. One Frenchman asked to examine a gun on the wall. Soon the French had the Plymouth servants at gunpoint. When they sailed away, they took £300 worth of beaver skins and everything else of value.[6]

While the Pilgrim traders struggled to maintain their northern outposts, they also turned their attention to the Connecticut River Valley. The rich furs that Native traders brought down the river stoked competition among several peoples. With the Mohegans to their west and the Narragansetts to their east, the Pequots under their sachem Tatobem exercised fragile authority over a number of river valley communities. In the summer of 1633, the Dutch purchased a plot of land up the river at present-day Hartford and built a fort they named the House of Good Hope. The Dutch wanted to

trade not only with the Pequots but with their tributaries and enemies as well. When the Pequots killed several Natives heading toward the fort, the Dutch responded by kidnapping and murdering
Tatobem, whose successor Sassacus proved less adept at retaining
the allegiance of nearby communities.

The Pilgrims laid plans to wrest the Connecticut fur trade away
from the Dutch. In the early 1630s, Plymouth began sending its
traders west. Just as Edward Winslow had sailed up the Kennebec
to open up Plymouth's trade in that region, so he quietly made con-
tacts with the Native communities along the Connecticut. Then in
July 1633, Winslow and William Bradford visited Boston and conferred with John Winthrop about "joining in a trade to Connecticut." The plan was to establish an English trading outpost on the
river. Winthrop declined, telling Bradford that the "warlike Indians" in the valley made "the place not fit for plantation."[7]

Rebuffed by Winthrop, the Pilgrims proceeded on their own.
They purchased land from Natawante, an enemy of the Pequots
grateful for new allies who talked about restoring him as "the right
sachem of this place." In September 1633, Plymouth sent William
Holmes (lieutenant to Myles Standish) up the river with a "small
frame of a house" and clapboards in his vessel. As Holmes and his
men approached the House of Good Hope, the outraged Dutch
trained their cannons on the English bark and threatened to fire if
the English proceeded. Holmes did not stop, the Dutch held their
fire, and the English hastily palisaded an outpost at a place called
Matianuck.[8]

The Dutch sent word to New Amsterdam, whose leaders dis-
patched a force of seventy men to eject the English interlopers. The
Pilgrims made clear their readiness to defend their outpost, and the
Dutch force backed down, not wanting to risk war. For the moment,
Plymouth had cornered an incredibly rich source of furs. Back in
Boston, John Winthrop estimated that 10,000 skins had been com-
ing down the Connecticut to Dutch traders. Bradford reported that
Plymouth shipped 3,366 pounds of beaver fur and 346 otter skins to
England that year. At fourteen or fifteen shillings a pound, the bea-
ver fetched more than £2,000.[9]

The Dutch next countered by sending a small party farther up
the Connecticut. The Pilgrim traders did not obstruct their passage,

but the Dutch effort failed when an epidemic killed the Indians with whom they had settled. The starving traders sought relief at the Pilgrim outpost. In the spring of 1634, the smallpox ravaged the Indians at Matianuck. Bradford recorded that the Indians died "like rotten sheep," their skin cleaving to the mats on which they lay and then flaying off of their bodies when they turned. Natawante was among those who perished. According to Bradford, the Pilgrim traders ministered to the sick and buried the dead.[10]

The Pilgrims "did the Dutch no wrong," asserted Bradford, "for they took not a foot of any land they bought, but went to the place above them." When it came to Plymouth's Kennebec monopoly, however, Bradford had an entirely different perspective on such tactics. In April 1634, John Hocking sailed up the Kennebec, intending to jump the Pilgrims just as Plymouth's men had jumped the Dutch. Hocking was a fur trader at a small English plantation at Piscataway, in the employ of Lord Saye (William Fiennes) and Lord Brooke (Robert Greville).[11]

Plymouth magistrates John Howland and John Alden were at the Kennebec outpost when Hocking approached. Howland warned him not to "infringe their liberties, which had cost them so dear." The Pilgrims had bought the exclusive right to the Kennebec River trade. No one else was at liberty to purchase furs there. Just as Holmes had done on the Connecticut, Hocking kept going and anchored upstream. Unlike the Dutch, Howland was not bluffing. He pursued Hocking, planning to send him back downstream. Hocking threatened to shoot anyone who cut his cables, but three Plymouth men took a canoe, piloted it to Hocking's bark, and severed a cable. Hocking repeated his warning, and he too was not bluffing. When Plymouth's Moses Talbot steered the canoe to cut the next cable, Hocking shot him. One of Plymouth's men then shot Hocking. Both men died instantly.[12]

John Alden stopped in Boston on his way back to Plymouth. The Piscataway men came as well. They alleged that the Pilgrim magistrates had been too quick to use violence to defend their claim. In this telling, when Howland and Alden sent the canoe to cut the cables, they had ordered their men to stand "in their own pinnace with their pieces charged and ready to shoot." Massachusetts leaders concluded that Plymouth's magistrates were culpable in Hocking's death. They had Alden arrested until they could learn whether or not Plymouth intended to "do justice in the cause." Myles Standish rushed to Boston and convinced Bay Colony leaders to let Alden go. At the same time, Standish had to post a bond for his own appearance before a Massachusetts court and provide a further explanation of what had transpired on the Kennebec. The Pilgrims, meanwhile, were livid that Bay Colony leaders presumed to exercise authority beyond their charter's jurisdiction.[13]

Hocking's death remained a point of contention between the colonies for several months. In Boston, John Winthrop fretted that the Pilgrim traders "had brought us all, and the gospel under a common reproach of cutting one another's throats for beaver." Winthrop feared that once the news reached England, it would redound to the political harm of both colonies by giving "occasion to the king to send a general governor over." Winthrop wrote a letter to an influential friend of Lords Saye and Brooke. He lamented that Plymouth had occupied all of the best trading spots in New England, which Winthrop knew was a sore point with the lords. Massachusetts leaders signaled their disapproval of Plymouth's use of violence in other ways. "We refuse to hold communion with them," Winthrop informed the lords. He added that he hoped to get Pilgrim leaders to "see their sin and repent of it."[14]

In July 1634, Plymouth's leaders traveled to Boston and met with the Bay Colony's magistrates and the ministers John Cotton and John Wilson. By this point, both sides were more conciliatory. Massachusetts leaders agreed that Plymouth had the right to hinder others from trading on the Kennebec. Not only did they have the patent, but the land had been vacant and no Natives had disputed the claim. By initiative and providence, moreover, Edward Winslow had carried "wampum thither." At the same time, the joint leaders concluded that in acting precipitously, the Plymouth men had disregarded the Sixth Commandment ("Thou shalt not kill"). They should have preserved their claim by another means at another time. In other words, they should not have killed for beaver. The Pilgrims sent Winslow to London to mollify Lords Saye and Brooke, who let the matter drop.[15]

The Pilgrims' audacity had paid off. By 1634, the Plymouth Undertakers had become the most successful fur traders in New

England. Winthrop complained that Plymouth had "engrossed all the chief places of trade": the Kennebec and Penobscot Rivers, the Narragansett country, and the Connecticut River Valley. Plymouth had trading houses at each location. Winslow shipped nearly four thousand pounds of beaver pelts that year, most of which the Pilgrims had purchased with wampum. The shipments did not entirely erase the Undertakers' obligations, but if their success continued, they could look forward to the profits that long had eluded them.[16]

When Winslow sailed to London in the wake of John Hocking's death, it turned out that Lords Saye and Brooke were the least of his concerns. Plymouth's agent arrived precisely as several men joined together in an effort to reorganize New England into a royal colony with a crown-appointed governor.

Chief among those antagonists were Sir Ferdinando Gorges and Archbishop of Canterbury William Laud, whose objectives overlapped but were not identical. England's wars with Spain and France had occupied the commander of Plymouth Fort in the late 1620s and had prevented him from pursuing his interests in North America. By the time Gorges could resume his efforts, the Massachusetts Bay Company had obtained a royal charter. Gorges complained that the Bay colonists had "made themselves a free people," governing themselves without oversight by Gorges's Council for New England. Sir Ferdinando wanted to reestablish the council's political authority over New England and retain portions of it as proprietary colonies for himself and other gentlemen.[17]

For his part, Archbishop Laud wanted to bring his anti-puritan campaign to England's overseas possessions. Whereas previous monarchs and bishops understood colonies as ideal dumping grounds for religious dissidents, it did not sit well with Laud that nonconformists could escape punishment by taking their sedition to New England.

Joining with Gorges and Laud were several men who had clashed with New England's magistrates. One such individual was Christopher Gardiner, who came to Massachusetts Bay in the spring of 1630 and introduced himself as a European knight of an uncertain order. He brought with him a few servants and a "comely young woman," whom he passed off as his cousin. The ruse did not fool the colony's suspicious magistrates. Isaac Allerton and William Peirce arrived with the news that, back in London, they had spoken with two women who both claimed to be Gardiner's wife. The first wanted him back; the second wanted his ruin. The magistrates decided to send the alleged bigamist back to England, but Gardiner fled, got lost in the woods, and wandered into New Plymouth's jurisdiction. William Bradford paid Natives to capture him. Once the prey was caught, Bradford obtained a "little notebook" that documented Gardiner's conversion to Catholicism. He turned his prisoner and the notebook over to Winthrop. Meanwhile, the Bay Colony governor got his hands on a packet of Gardiner's letters, which contained correspondence with Thomas Morton—the erstwhile "host" of Merry Mount—and Gorges. The Massachusetts magistrates now proceeded more gingerly, realizing that Gardiner could do them political harm. The errant knight went back to England of his own accord, where he joined forces with Gorges and Morton.[18]

At the end of April 1634, the Privy Council made Archbishop Laud head of the new Commission for Regulating Plantations. When the text of Laud's commission crossed the Atlantic, Bradford filled two pages of his history with it. Laud and the commissioners could promulgate laws and constitutions governing colonial land, trade, and churches. Those who violated such laws hazarded their liberty and their lives. The commissioners could "displace the governors or rulers of those colonies" and appoint replacements. They could collect tithes to support Church of England ministers.[19]

At least on paper, the commission posed a severe threat to the religious and political liberties the Pilgrims had claimed at New Plymouth. If Laud and Gorges had their way, the Pilgrims would no longer be able to elect their own rulers and enact their own laws, as they had agreed to do in the Mayflower Compact. Laud in particular might extinguish their "liberty of the gospel," the ability of covenanted church members to choose their officers and worship according to their understanding of the Bible.

Gorges and his allies had the archbishop's ear and laid plans to have the king revoke the Massachusetts Bay charter. New Plymouth would have been a sideshow to the conflict. Its settlers were too small in number to disrupt Gorges's grander plans for New England colonization, and Laud's opprobrium centered on the ministers and colonists he had harried out of England himself. Still, when Edward

Winslow turned up in London a few months after the creation of the new commission, he attracted the attention of the commissioners by petitioning them for a "special warrant" for New Plymouth and Massachusetts to defend themselves against the Dutch and the French. No one in England questioned the right of settlers to fight off incursions from rival powers. Winslow sought to use the Dutch and French threats to gain some sort of official sanction from the commission, a reflection of Plymouth's political fragility. The Pilgrims still only had the patent from the Council for New England, now even less meaningful given the creation of the new commission. What Plymouth needed was a more secure patent or charter, preferably with the sort of direct royal approval the Bay Colony had obtained. Winslow's petition was a misstep, however. There was no way William Laud was going to help Plymouth.[20]

For Gorges, though, Winslow's petition was an opportunity. He stated that the Pilgrims had become alarmed when King Charles had learned of "their disaffections both to his Majesty's government and the state ecclesiastical." Fearing that English officials would punish their sedition, they had conspired with the Dutch. It was nonsense, but Gorges argued that it was "more than time these people [of New Plymouth] should be looked unto."[21]

Laud was happy to look into the matter. Using information received from Thomas Morton, the archbishop asked Winslow a series of awkward questions. Was it true that Winslow had preached in church even though he was not a minister? Was it true that Winslow had married couples civilly, based on his authority as a magistrate? What was the nature of Plymouth's church? What did the Pilgrims assert about England's church?

Winslow had backed himself into a corner. He drafted an answer to Laud's queries. He allowed that he had preached and contracted marriages but only because the Pilgrims had lacked a minister for so many years. Winslow did not add that New Plymouth magistrates continued to marry couples civilly even after they had procured a minister. He conceded that the Pilgrims had left England because they "disliked many things in practice here in respect of church ceremony," but he stressed their unflinching loyalty to the king. Winslow denounced Morton and Gardiner as a "delinquent" and a "Jesuited [Catholic] gentleman," respectively. Finally, he suggested if the commissioners stripped New Englanders of their "liberty of conscience" and "freedom of government," it would only assist the Dutch and the French by weakening the English hold on the region.

By liberty of conscience, Winslow did not mean that individuals in New Plymouth exercised freedom of religion but that the Pilgrims had obtained tacit permission to worship and govern their church according to their principles. As for freedom of government, nothing in the Council for New England's own charter empowered it to make such grants. For the Pilgrims, though, religious liberty and political self-government were inseparable. If the commission and the king sent a governor to New Plymouth, he would invariably "impose the same things upon us we went thither to avoid." The end result would be a resumption of the persecution William Brewster and others had endured a quarter-century before.[22]

Laud had no objection to the renewed persecution of Brownists. The archbishop sent Winslow to the Fleet Prison, where the separatist martyrs Henry Barrow and John Greenwood had spent several years prior to their executions. After four months in the Fleet, Winslow—who had some well-connected friends—successfully petitioned for his release and returned to New England late in 1635.

Gorges moved ahead with his plans. The members of the Council for New England decided to resign their patent in order to enable the political reorganization of the region. In 1637, the Privy Council appointed Ferdinando Gorges general governor of New England. At the time of his political triumph, however, Gorges was bankrupt. He sent his cousin Thomas to New England as his deputy in 1640, but Thomas Gorges soon realized he was in no position to direct affairs there and returned home. The elder Gorges died in 1647, never having set foot on the lands that had captivated his imagination for nearly half a century. Sir Ferdinando obtained charters and drew lines on maps while traders, fishermen, and puritans settled New England and exploited its resources.

The Privy Council also ordered Bay Colony leaders to return their charter, threatening that a refusal to do so would lead the king to assume direct royal control of the colony. For several years, Massachusetts Bay had strengthened its defenses for precisely this eventuality, but neither the king nor his council forced the issue. By 1638,

Charles, Laud, and their officials were distracted with a rebellion against their attempts to impose a version of the Book of Common Prayer on the Church of Scotland. New Plymouth and Massachusetts Bay retained their governments, but the stage was set for future confrontations.

Shared apprehension about developments in England prompted the magistrates of New Plymouth and Massachusetts Bay to settle their differences about the Hocking case, but the two puritan colonies were rivals as much as allies. In 1635, events in both northern New England and on the Connecticut River brought Plymouth Colony's newfound trading success to an abrupt end.

That August, the French returned to the Penobscot, this time intending to take more than its furs and goods. Thomas Willett, who had moved from Leiden to Plymouth around 1630, was in charge of the Pilgrim outpost. The French captain, Charles de Menou d'Aulnay, persuaded some of the Plymouth men to board his shallop and pilot him into the harbor. By his own account and Bradford's, d'Aulnay with impeccable politeness told Willett and his men to take what they could carry with them and leave. Retreating to Boston, the Plymouth traders had the additional misfortune of losing the goods and their boat in a hurricane that pummeled the New England coast.

Plymouth made an attempt to recapture the outpost, but this was not an instance in which Myles Standish could recruit a few men, march in, behead someone, and declare victory. Instead, Standish went to Boston and hired a "ship of force" whose captain squandered his powder at a great distance from the outpost and apparently had no intention of engaging the enemy. Standish returned to Boston and begged its magistrates for assistance, but they had no desire to risk war with the French in order to defend a rival colony's trade. Even worse, rumors soon reached Plymouth that English traders from Massachusetts Bay were doing business with the French usurpers.[23]

In an even bigger setback for the Pilgrim Undertakers, Massachusetts Bay traders outflanked them on the Connecticut River. John Winthrop had declined Plymouth's July 1633 offer to form a joint Connecticut venture, but only because Bay Colony leaders wanted all of the expected profits for themselves. Later that summer, the Massachusetts leaders sent John Oldham on an overland trading expedition to the Connecticut River. Nearly a decade after his expulsion from Plymouth, Mad Jack had become a respectable citizen and church member in the Massachusetts Bay town of Watertown. Following Native paths, Oldham reached an area of the Connecticut River Valley well to the north of Plymouth's fort at Matianuck. He brought back beaver pelts, hemp, and what Winthrop described as "black lead," possibly graphite.[24]

In 1635, a group of Bay Colony traders settled on a portion of the land Plymouth's traders had purchased two years earlier. Jonathan Brewster, son of Elder William Brewster, informed Plymouth's leaders that "the Massachusetts men are coming almost daily." The newcomers were unimpressed by Plymouth's claim to have bought the land, arguing that it was "the Lord's waste, and for the present altogether void of inhabitants." Just as the Dutch had allowed William Holmes to sail past them, Plymouth's men now grudgingly gave way. As at Penobscot, the Plymouth traders lacked the numbers and firepower they would have needed to defend their claim. In an agreement reached with the Massachusetts settlers, Plymouth retained only one-sixteenth of the land it had purchased. The usurpers provided compensation for the rest. "Thus was the controversy ended," Bradford commented, "but the unkindness not so soon forgotten." The Pilgrims had been "little better than thrust out" by their English rivals. The land around Matianuck became the English town of Windsor.[25]

More English settlers flooded into the region. In late 1635, John Winthrop's namesake son sent parties to build a fort at the mouth of the Connecticut, named Saybrook for Lord Saye and Lord Brooke, who had obtained a patent for the entire region. The next spring, Thomas Hooker, a minister at Newtown (soon renamed Cambridge), led most of his congregation to Connecticut and founded what became Hartford.

The Pilgrims still maintained their Matianuck fort, but their bid to dominate the river's fur trade had failed. In fact, Plymouth's days as a regional trading power were over. The French had taken the Penobscot outpost, and the Pilgrims were now a marginal presence in Connecticut. The Undertakers also gave up on their Kennebec outpost and turned the trade over to the colony as a whole; Plymouth's magistrates finally sold the claim in 1661. Since 1620, New Plymouth had been a colony, a congregation, and a trading venture. Because of the rapidly growing strength of the Bay Colony, that venture had failed.

The Dutch and English moves up the Connecticut River Valley destabilized the entire region. Relations between the Pequots and Narragansetts were particularly unsettled, as more communities that had paid tribute to Tatobem now switched their allegiance to the Narragansetts. In response to their growing isolation, the Pequots made some unsuccessful overtures toward the Bay Colony's magistrates. Meanwhile, the devastation from the August 1635 hurricane left many English communities in both Connecticut and Massachusetts hungry and desperate.[26]

As relations between English settlers and the Pequots frayed, an English trader found John Oldham's mutilated corpse off the northern tip of Block Island. Bradford identified Mad Jack's gruesome death as "one ground of the Pequot War." It was a strange catalyst, because the Niantics on Block Island were tributaries not of the Pequots but of the Narragansetts. At the same time, Massachusetts leaders belatedly decided to hold the Pequots responsible for the death of John Stone, a provocative trader killed in 1633 after he kidnapped two Indians and forced them to guide him up the Connecticut River.[27]

In August 1637, Bay Colony leaders sent John Endecott to move against both the Block Islanders and the Pequots. Endecott's orders were to kill the Niantic men and take women and children captive, but the Niantics scattered when the English arrived. The Massachusetts men chopped down the island's cornfields and proceeded to the second part of their mission. Joined by men from English settlements in Connecticut, Endecott sailed up the Pequot River (later renamed the Thames River). He demanded that Pequot sachems hand over those men responsible for Stone's death and pay a thousand fathoms of wampum. Endecott also asked for some children as hostages to secure the Pequots' good behavior. The Pequots hedged and stalled, and Massachusetts Bay soon had the war that its magistrates seem to have wanted.

Over the next year, groups of Pequots raided and besieged English settlements along the Connecticut, while Bay Colony leaders secured alliances with the Narragansetts and Mohegans in preparations for an offensive. In the spring of 1637, then Massachusetts Bay governor Henry Vane asked Plymouth to join in the fight. Still smarting from their setbacks in Maine and Connecticut, Plymouth's magistrates hesitated. They sent Edward Winslow to Boston with a list of complaints—mostly about Plymouth's loss of its Kennebec outpost—and demands. At the very least, Plymouth wanted what amounted to a mutual defense pact. Plymouth would help its Massachusetts counterparts if they promised to help Plymouth in a similar crisis.

John Winthrop, just voted back into office as the Bay Colony's governor, sent a polite but firm response. He would not limit his people's "liberty" and "freedom" to use their "reason" to assess any future Plymouth plea for assistance. He allowed that Massachusetts Bay could not "wholly excuse [its] failing" pertaining to Plymouth's conflicts with the French, but he insisted that his government had not authorized any interference with Plymouth's Kennebec trade. Winthrop also contended that all of the English had a shared Christian interest in the campaign's success. If the Pequots succeeded, it would embolden them and other Native peoples to "the rooting out of the whole [English]." The Massachusetts governor warned Plymouth's leaders that if they did not help now, they could not expect the Bay Colony's assistance in the future. The Plymouth magistrates remained reluctant; Bradford was sure Winthrop was lying about the Kennebec trade. They planned to bring the possibility of joining the war before a general court scheduled for June 7, and the colony's leaders did not see fit to call an earlier session.[28]

Before the court met, word came that English forces had slaughtered the inhabitants of a fortified Pequot village situated on a hill overlooking the Mystic River. Led by a much larger number of Native (mostly Mohegan) allies, ninety English soldiers had crept toward the village undetected, divided their forces, and pushed through the fort's two gates at daybreak. Some of the awakened Pequots fought back fiercely, while others retreated into their homes. Frustrated by his men's inability to engage their foes, Connecticut captain John Mason grabbed a firebrand and declared, "We must burn

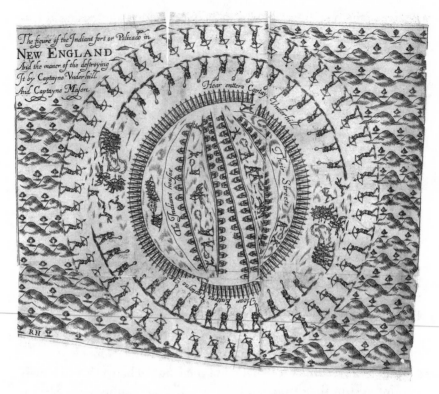

The May 1637 attack on the Pequot fort on the Mystic River,
from John Underhill's Newes from America *(1638).*
(Courtesy of the John Carter Brown Library.)

them." Mason began setting wigwams ablaze. Other English soldiers
followed his lead, and the village was soon in flames. The attackers
shot or hewed down those who attempted to flee. Hundreds of men,
women, and children died in what Mason termed "a fiery oven" and
what Cotton Mather later likened to a barbecue of human flesh.[29]

William Bradford had no qualms about the inferno. "It was a
fearful sight," he wrote in his history, "to see them thus frying in
the fire, and the streams of blood quenching the same." The stench
was "horrible" but redemptive. Alluding to the Bible's description of
burnt offerings as a "sweet savor," Bradford implied that the "sacrifice" had pleased God, who had used the English as a tool to punish
the Pequots.[30]

After the decisive massacre, Plymouth finally voted to assist the

Bay Colony and the Connecticut settlers "in revenge of the innocent blood of the English." Plymouth organized an expedition of
thirty men led by William Holmes. Winslow informed Winthrop
that Plymouth's men would be ready sooner if Massachusetts helped
outfit them. The Bay Colony agreed, but "when they were ready to
march . . . they had word to stay; for the enemy was as good as vanquished." Massachusetts Bay wanted the blessing of its neighbors,
but it did not need their help.[31]

With the Pequots vanquished, the Narragansetts and Mohegans
became southern New England's most powerful Native peoples. The
English, however, treated them as vassals and potential enemies.
Much to the detriment of Dutch interests in the region, English
migration led to the creation of the colonies of Connecticut, New
Haven, and Saybrook, the latter of which merged with Connecticut
in 1644.

The Pequot War introduced a practice central to any discussion of
liberty in seventeenth-century New England: the enslavement of
Natives.[32] Motivated by a combination of vengeance and greed, English officers rounded up more than three hundred Pequots—mostly
noncombatants—as the spoils of war. For example, militia captain
Israel Stoughton sent about fifty Pequot women and children to
Boston. He asked to have the "fairest and largest" woman for himself. Bay Colony magistrates distributed or sold the rest. When some
Pequots taken to Boston escaped, Native allies of the English recaptured them. Massachusetts officials then branded the runaways on
the shoulder. Some captives ended up thousands of miles from their
homes. Ship captain William Peirce, the old friend of the Pilgrims,
headed to Bermuda with fifteen Pequot boys and two women. When
Peirce's vessel sailed past Bermuda by mistake, he took his human
cargo to Providence Island, where the governor referred to the Pequots as "cannibal Negroes from New England."[33]

In 1569, the Star Chamber had declared that England possessed
"too pure an air for slaves to breathe in." That was not quite true.
Merchants and other Englishmen often retained African slaves as
their property after keeping them in England for many years, and
kidnapped Native men and women also breathed England's air.
Nevertheless, especially when criticizing rival powers such as Spain,

Russia, or the Ottomans, the English prided themselves on the absence of slavery in England. At the same time, the English understood human bondage elsewhere as uncontroversial in large part
because of its near universality. Whether they traveled to Russia or
to Java, English explorers and merchants saw enslaved people. As
they developed colonies in Virginia and the Caribbean, English
planters did not hesitate to acquire African slaves.[34]

The Bible offered clear sanction for the enslavement of defeated
peoples, as did a host of philosophers and legal theorists stretching
from Aristotle to Grotius. In a just war, or at least in a properly declared war, it was permissible to enslave one's opponents, which was
at any rate more merciful than killing them. Accordingly, European
powers enslaved prisoners during wartime. The Scottish minister
John Knox, for example, ended up as a slave on a French galley for
a year and a half. Even so, victors generally did not enslave noncombatants en masse at the conclusion of intra-European wars. The
English regarded other peoples as more fit for servitude and slavery,
however. In the wake of rebellions against its rule in Ireland, England shipped thousands of men, women, and children to its Caribbean and North American colonies. English settlers also deemed
slavery a fitting punishment for Native peoples who fought against
them. For instance, after the 1622 massacre in Virginia, settlers
there called for reducing the Powhatan to slavery and transporting
at least some Indian slaves to Bermuda. Settlers also understood the
economic value of Native captives, both as laborers and as commodities who could be sold in the marketplace or exported to the
Caribbean.[35]

None of the New England colonies had any laws about slavery
at the time of the Pequot War. A few years later, the Bay Colony
codified the enslavement of wartime captives. "There shall never
be," it declared, "any bond-slavery, villeinage and captivity amongst
us; unless it be lawful captives, taken in just wars, and such strangers
as willingly sell themselves, or are sold to us." According to the law,
it was perfectly legal for colonists to enslave and then sell captives
such as the Pequots. The language also suggested that settlers might
buy and sell previously enslaved Africans. It was the first codifica-
tion of slavery in any English colony in North America. New Plymouth did not pass any laws regulating the treatment of Native cap-

tives for several more decades, and although some Plymouth settlers acquired African slaves, the colony's statutes remained silent on the matter.[36]

Both Roger Williams and the Native allies of the English objected to the enslavement of Pequot captives. The Algonquian peoples of southern New England frequently took captives in war, in part to replenish diminished populations. Captives usually performed menial sorts of labor, but they and especially their children assimilated into their new communities. Natives generally did not understand captives as commodities to be bought and sold. Williams advised Bay Colony leaders that "it would be very grateful to our neighbors, that such Pequots as fall to them be not enslaved . . . but (as they say is their general custom) be used kindly, have houses and goods and fields given them." Williams agreed that it was lawful according to the Bible for a victor to deprive an enemy of wives and children, but he urged the Massachusetts magistrates not to subject Pequot captives to "perpetual slavery." Would it not be better, he asked, to set them free after a period of service?[37]

Despite his criticisms, Williams himself found one captive irresistible. After a pinnace carrying a group of Pequots stopped at Providence, Williams asked Winthrop for "the keeping and bringing up of one of the children" and specifically requested the "little one with the red about his neck." The boy's mother and two of his siblings were also among the captives. Winthrop agreed, and Williams sent someone to fetch the boy. Did he see the boy as an adopted child? A servant? (A year later, Williams referred to a Native "servant" named Will.) An object for evangelism? Did Williams ask for the boy in order to spare him from export to the Caribbean? It is impossible to know. Because he sometimes criticized the way that other English colonists treated Indians, historians sometimes attribute benevolent intentions to Williams in the absence of evidence.[38]

A few Pequot captives ended up in New Plymouth. Nicholas Simpkins, formerly the captain of the Bay Colony's Castle Island fort, brought his family and an Indian servant to the new Cape Cod town of Yarmouth after the war. Edward Winslow also obtained a servant named Hope, probably a Pequot War captive.

Captive Indians became "servants" of a different sort, with dimmer prospects for eventual freedom unless they escaped and without the legal protections afforded to English servants. Some Indian captives endured terrible mistreatment, as in the case of a woman who fled the household of Boston innkeeper Samuel Cole and sought refuge among the Narragansetts. After her recapture, she told Roger Williams that "she of all the Natives in Boston is used worst, is beaten with firesticks and especially by some of the servants." According to Williams, a Boston official had "burned [branded]" her "because a fellow lay with her." The woman reported that she had "refused" the man's advances. In other words, she had been punished after a man had raped her.[39]

In 1640, a servant named John Hatch accused Yarmouth's Nicholas Simpkins of "attempting to lie with an Indian woman," likely the captive he had received after the war. Plymouth's General Court dismissed the charge, but it fined Simpkins forty pounds for not having brought his "Indian maid servant" to court. Presumably the court wished to hear her testimony, though it remitted the fine when Simpkins explained that she "neither had shoes nor was in health to come." What was the nature of their sexual relationship? And why did the court not order Simpkins to properly attire his servant (or slave—it is hard to know which word is most appropriate), as it might have done in the case of an English girl?[40]

In other cases, English masters educated and evangelized their Pequot captives. Several Pequots gained prominence as Native converts to Christianity and played key roles in the English missions that began in the 1640s. Some served as interpreters and carried messages between the communities of southern New England. Others escaped from their English masters and helped reconstitute Pequot communities.

What about Hope? As of 1647, he was a servant or slave of Edward Winslow. In the late 1630s, the Winslows had moved from Plymouth to what became the town of Marshfield, where they built Careswell, an estate on the site of a former Wampanoag village. It was a large household: the couple's two children, Susanna's two from her first marriage, and an unknown number of servants.

In January 1648, a ship's captain named John Mainfort came to Boston to purchase "provision for the belly" for Barbadian planters. Because the profits in sugar were "infinite," the planters preferred to obtain their food from New England or elsewhere and not waste

Edward Winslow, 1651. (Pilgrim Hall Museum, Plymouth, Massachusetts.)

their labor on its local production. While in Boston, Mainfort purchased Hope. John Winthrop handled the transaction by the "order and consent" of Susanna Winslow, whose husband was once more in England as an agent for Plymouth and Massachusetts Bay. According to the agreement, Hope would serve Mainfort "according to the orders and customs of English servants in the same Island [Barbados], both for maintenance and other recompense, for and during the full term of ten years." The language suggested that he would be treated like an unfortunate English or Irish servant sent to Barbados.[41]

Edward Winslow did not own his English servants. He owned their labor for a set amount of time, and he was obliged to feed and clothe them. Winslow sometimes assigned their labor to other men, but unless one of them committed a serious crime, it would have been unthinkable for Winslow to sell the labor of his English servants to John Mainfort or a Barbadian planter. Yet for an unspecified amount of money (the bill of sale mentions only "good and valuable consideration"), the Winslows sold Hope.

The Winslows are among the best-documented individuals in seventeenth-century New England. Archives and museums preserve scores of Winslow letters, deeds, publications, and other objects. Hope, by contrast, appears in the historical record only at the moment of his sale from Susanna Winslow to Mainfort. When was he separated from his mother and siblings? Or were they dead as well? The bill of sale identifies him as a "man." Had he been a boy at the time of the Pequot War? What sort of life did he have at Careswell? Did the English servants abuse him? Edward and Susanna Winslow knew what it meant to send a servant or slave to Barbados. Most men and women did not last ten years on the sugar plantations. Who decided to sell Hope, and why?

When he became Mainfort's property, it was probably not the last time Hope was sold. Mainfort would have sold him to an English planter on Barbados. If Hope survived the ten years of his indenture, his master might have sold him again or have found a way to extend his service. Hope almost certainly died on Barbados.

CHAPTER ELEVEN

Freemen and Freedom

F REEDOM IN NEW PLYMOUTH — AS in the rest of the transatlantic English world—was a complex and contested matter. Since the decline of slavery in Norman England, Englishmen had been "free" if they were not bound in service
and if they were not villeins, peasants tied to a particular lord or
manor. More particularly, though, a "freeman" had the liberty to
live and practice a trade in a given town. Depending on local circumstances, a freeman might have the privilege or even the obligation to
participate in a community's civic and political life. A man could
possess this sort of freedom by birth or obtain it through marriage,
an apprenticeship, or a particular honor. For instance, Robert Cushman had become a freeman in Canterbury after his apprenticeship
as a grocer. He paid a fee and swore an oath to obey Canterbury's
mayor, do his part in taxes and watches, and inform the authorities
if he knew of any seditious activity in the city.[1]

It was not a given that servants and apprentices would achieve
this status. Moreover, there was still a massive gulf between the liberties of a landless "freeman" such as Cushman and those of the
aristocrats and landed gentry. For instance, Magna Carta and the
1628 Petition of Right were about making sure the king did not im-
pinge on the rights of the landed elites. What about the liberties of
less exalted Englishmen? By the mid- to late 1640s, more radical
voices made themselves heard. The Levellers, political reformers

whose ideas gained both support and notoriety during the English Civil War, began speaking about the rights of all Englishmen. They supported broad religious freedom, favored near-universal adult male suffrage, and opposed economic monopolies benefiting men of great means.[2]

The Pilgrims were not Levellers. Plymouth's leaders intended to establish a godly society according to the dictates of scripture and English traditions. They wanted each town to have one Congregational church and no other religious meetings. They had no objection to monopoly, at least not if the privilege was theirs. Pilgrim leaders expected to govern with minimal interference. At the same time, a high percentage of adult men could vote in elections and give or withhold their consent to proposed laws. Individuals accused of serious crimes received jury trials. In several important respects, then, Plymouth's settlers enacted political reforms and safeguards against arbitrary rule that remained scarcely imaginable in England.[3]

In October 1636, Plymouth's General Court voted to review, revise, and compile the colony's laws, a task accomplished by a committee over the span of several weeks. The freemen met again the next month. They listened to the Mayflower Compact and declared that "as freeborn subjects of the state of England we hither came endowed with all . . . singular privileges belonging to such." Those privileges included the necessity of their consent for laws and taxes. Building on the principles of the Mayflower Compact, they insisted that "no imposition, law, or ordinance be made or imposed upon us . . . but such as shall be made [or] imposed by consent according to the free liberties [of the] state and kingdom of England." In England, such humble and common people had no such liberties.[4]

The revised laws maintained the simple, participatory government that the Pilgrims had established through the Mayflower Compact and their first years at Plymouth. The colony's freemen attended an annual court of election at which they chose a governor and six or seven assistants. Participation was mandatory for freemen, who faced fines if they skipped sessions of the General Court, and those elected to office were fined if they declined to serve. While the General Court typically convened several other times each year, the elected magistrates also held what were known as courts of assistants, acting as an executive and judiciary but without the authority to enact any statutes or levy taxes.

In neighboring Massachusetts Bay, early settlers endured a series of contests over the relative authority of freemen and elected magistrates. Before he left England, John Winthrop had observed that other plantations had failed in part because "they used unfit instruments, viz., a multitude of rude and misgoverned persons, the very scum of the land . . . they did not establish a right form of government." Winthrop wanted the elected magistrates to govern. At the very least, Winthrop contended that elected magistrates should wield a veto against laws enacted by the freemen or their deputies. Otherwise, he warned, "our government would be a mere democracy." Other men, and the governments of several towns, pushed back against Winthrop's understanding of governance. By the mid-1640s, political decisions in Massachusetts Bay required the consent of both magistrates and deputies.[5]

By Winthrop's standards, New Plymouth was a "mere democracy," in which only a unicameral legislature—the General Court—could pass laws or raise taxes. Plymouth's 1636 framework of government left all statutory authority in the hands of the colony's freemen, who comprised the General Court. That same framework gave the governor a "double voice," meaningful in courts of the assistants but of no great consequence at meetings of the General Court. Plymouth's magistrates and governors did not have the authority to veto decisions made by the colony's freemen. The power of the Undertakers over the colony's trade and grants of land was an anomaly within this system, but in 1639 the General Court bought out the Undertakers and returned "all the residue of the lands" to "the whole body of the freemen." The decision cut against the idea of an aristocratic or magisterial elite.[6]

Plymouth's declarations about liberty and self-governance did not apply to all of the colony's male settlers, however. Under the terms negotiated between the Adventurers and the Pilgrims, only shareholders of the resulting joint-stock company participated in its government. Those shareholders included the free male passengers on the *Mayflower* and other early arrivals who accepted the arrangement with the Adventurers. Those men who came on their own "particular" had no right to vote. The dissolution of the company and the modest growth in the colony's population made new arrangements necessary. In 1636, the court clarified that only "the freemen of the corporation and no other" could make laws and elect officers. Not all adult men, not even all adult men free from service, were "freemen." In 1633, the colony's magistrates made a list of sixty-eight freemen. Francis Billington, whose father was hanged for murder in 1630, was not on the list, nor were several other men present in the colony since the mid-1620s. In all, more than half of adult male taxpayers received freeman status, but that left many adult men without the right to vote.[7]

Why and how did Plymouth's magistrates and citizens choose to exclude certain men from the body politic? And what standards of admission did they use? The sparse records provide few clues. In 1631, the magistrates of Massachusetts Bay restricted freeman status to church members and granted that status to around one hundred men. The Bay Colony's action might have prompted Plymouth's magistrates to examine the question, but the Pilgrims did not simply follow the example of their neighbors. Probably because the Mayflower Compact had already made the body politic broader than the body of Christ, Plymouth did not create any sort of formal religious test for freeman status until the late 1650s. Nor did the colony codify a property threshold until 1669. It seems that the General Court at first admitted men who had established themselves as heads of household and who had not otherwise disqualified themselves.

The percentage of men who were freemen declined as the years passed and the colony's population grew. By the early 1640s, only around a quarter of adult men were freemen. Some of those who did not have the colony-wide franchise at that time became freemen at a later point in their lives, but growing numbers of men never attained this status. It is likely that most men did not ask to become freemen, in part to avoid the expense and inconvenience of traveling to the town of Plymouth, or perhaps because they sensed that the General Court would not admit them. Coupled with the fact that there was no corresponding category of freewoman, only a small percentage of adult settlers elected the colony's leaders and gave their consent to laws and taxes. In some respects, New Plymouth functioned as an oligarchy, as men like William Bradford, Edward

Winslow, Myles Standish, and Thomas Prence filled key offices year after year.

Despite these limitations, political participation in New Plymouth remained unusually broad by English standards. Even for those who were not freemen, there were other forms of political engagement. After the dispersal of settlers into a number of towns, settlers elected deputies who attended sessions of the General Court as their representatives. Also, a larger percentage of adult men participated in town affairs. For example, until 1650 all male householders could attend the town of Plymouth's meetings and vote on proposed laws. Thereafter, Plymouth's householders elected seven selectmen each year who handled most town business on their behalf. At both the colony-wide and local levels, political liberties were much less constrained by property and rank than they were in England.[8]

For some individuals, Plymouth's political order and the availability of land in the colony enabled liberty and prosperity they would have been very unlikely to attain in England. Edward Winslow came from a well-to-do family in Worcestershire, but he would never have acquired the extent of land or political prominence in England that he did in New Plymouth. A number of servants and common laborers also advanced themselves. John Alden, the cooper on the *Mayflower*, became one of the Undertakers who assumed financial responsibility for the colony's debts. Alden also became an assistant, annually elected for decades on end, and he acquired substantial land in Duxbury. John Howland, who came as a servant to John Carver, was another Undertaker. While he did not match Alden's prosperity or prominence, he also accumulated property and was chosen as a deputy to the General Court for many years.

Social and economic advancement was not confined to the initial passengers. When the partnership between the Adventurers and the Pilgrims was dissolved in 1627, each head of household and non-indentured single man received twenty acres of tillable land. These men had the right to subsequent divisions of common land as well. In the early 1630s, moreover, the General Court declared that servants would receive land in Scituate at the end of their indentures.

Not all of the *Mayflower* servants and wards became pillars of the community.[9] Unruly servants were a persistent source of tension in the colony. Edward Doty, who came as a servant to Stephen Hopkins and signed the Mayflower Compact, was constantly in trouble. In June 1621, Doty and his fellow servant Edward Leister were convicted of dueling with sword and dagger. The "whole company" sentenced the pair to be tied together for twenty-four hours by their heads and feet, and without anything to eat or drink. After an hour, Doty and Leister convinced Governor Bradford that the first sixty minutes—and the wounds they had inflicted on each other in the duel—were sufficient punishment.[10]

Doty soon received his liberty from service and began obtaining property. In 1623, Pilgrim leaders assigned him one acre of land. A few years later, he received a share in the colony's stock of cattle and goats and another twenty acres of land. In 1635, Doty married fifteen-year-old Faith Clarke, his second marriage. Doty kept adding to his landholdings, and in 1637 he sold several lots for £150.

All the while, Doty was constantly in physical and legal scrapes. He spent a good portion of his time suing and being sued. He appeared regularly before the court, accused of cheating other settlers and allowing his cattle to damage their crops. Doty still liked to brawl, and he got the upper hand more often than not. In 1634, the court convicted Doty and another man of fighting but fined Doty more because he had drawn blood. Twice in 1637, George Clarke—possibly a relation by marriage—sued Doty for damages pertaining to a land transaction. Doty was also fined twenty shillings for having assaulted Clarke. Many other court actions followed, but despite his transgressions, Doty was a freeman. He could vote, and the colony granted him land on several occasions. When he died, he left an estate valued at nearly £140, including considerable land and livestock. The irascible Doty was an upwardly mobile troublemaker.[11]

Doty's years in service to Stephen Hopkins did not make him sympathetic toward his own servants. In 1634, Doty was sued by an apprentice named John Smith, who alleged that Doty had failed to provide for him. Doty left his servant poorly clad and fed. Citing Doty's neglect of his duties, the General Court cut the duration of Smith's indenture in half and reminded Doty of his obligation to provide his servant with two suits of clothing upon his freedom. The case demonstrates that despite their lack of political privileges, servants could take action against masters who failed to fulfill their legal responsibilities.[12]

Not all servants were so fortunate, as demonstrated by the short life and brutish death of John Walker. Nothing is known about Walker's background. His master was Marshfield's Robert Latham; his mistress was Susanna Winslow Latham, daughter of John Winslow (Edward Winslow's brother) and *Mayflower* passenger Mary Chilton. In 1655, at the age of fourteen, Walker died under suspicious circumstances.

The Lathams had neglected and abused their young servant for some time. They did not give John enough food or proper clothing, and they overworked him. They forced him to carry a log "beyond his strength." It fell on him, and they then whipped him for his weakness. John lived in abject misery. Possibly because of the emotional distress he endured, he wet his bed at night and then lay in clothes that froze about him. Had Walker's parents been alive and in New England, they probably would have gotten wind of his mistreatment. If neighbors observed the abuse, they did not intervene until it was too late.

After Walker's death, a grand jury examined the boy's body. It was full of wounds and bruises. His back was raw from the whippings. His extremities were frozen. There were holes in his buttocks. When his corpse bled at the nose during a second examination, moreover, it was taken as a sign of homicide. Seventeenth-century New England settlers believed that corpses would bleed in the presence of their murderers or at their touch. In one Plymouth Colony instance, a jury asked a mother and several other family members to touch the corpse of a dead girl as a way of assessing their possible guilt.[13] In the case of John Walker, a grand jury determined that "of cruelty and hard usage he died." It indicted Robert Latham for "felonious cruelty" and later expanded the indictment to include Susanna Latham.

Robert Latham was convicted of "manslaughter by chance medley"—unpremeditated homicide. Despite the overwhelming evidence of abuse, the jury may have concluded that there was no evidence that he intended to kill his servant. Alternatively, the jury may have decided to give Latham a way to avoid execution. "Willful murder" was a capital crime in Plymouth, but the colony's 1636 laws did not offer any guidance on manslaughter. In England, however, there was a well-established mechanism by which individuals guilty of certain felonies could save their lives. Prior to sentencing, a convicted offender would read the first verse of Psalm 51: "Have mercy upon me, O God, according to thy loving-kindness: according to the multitude of thy compassions put away mine iniquities." Manslaughter, but not murder, was a crime for which one could escape death by reciting the "neck psalm."[14]

Robert Latham accordingly saved his neck from the gallows by requesting "the benefit of law [clergy] . . . a psalm of mercy." Latham's case is the only known application of the custom in New England prior to 1686. (After the 1770 Boston Massacre, two British soldiers convicted of manslaughter received benefit of clergy.) The court spared Latham's life, branded him on the hand, and confiscated his goods. The General Court eventually dropped the case against Susanna Latham because no witnesses came forward to testify against her. In the years after his conviction and punishment, Robert Latham achieved a measure of respectability. He swore the oath of fidelity to the colony, which enabled him to participate in Marshfield's town affairs. He eventually moved to Bridgewater, where he obtained land.[15]

There are fewer court records involving female servants in New Plymouth, which suggests it was more difficult for them to take legal action against their masters and mistresses. Masters sometimes placed obstacles in the way of their female servants who wished to marry, as both marriage and pregnancies reduced their productivity as laborers. It was enough of a problem that the General Court passed a law empowering magistrates to resolve cases in which masters denied a motion of marriage "through any sinister end or covetous desire."[16]

Dorothy Temple did not have the chance to marry the father of her child. Temple was a servant of *Mayflower* passenger Stephen Hopkins, and she became pregnant by another servant named Arthur Peach. After living in Massachusetts Bay for several years, Peach had served in the war against the Pequots and then indentured himself to Edward Winslow. No records reveal anything at all about Dorothy Temple's background.

In the summer of 1638, Peach ran away. He did so because both he and Temple knew that she was pregnant. The consequences for both Peach and Temple would have been a whipping and possibly a marriage. Not wanting to be whipped or married, Peach fled.

Three other servants joined Peach: Thomas Jackson, Richard Stinnings, and Daniel Cross. Presumably they simply wanted to get away.[17] Their intended destination was New Netherland, where they could work for themselves. Back in the 1620s, Plymouth's leaders had grown concerned that Thomas Morton's Merry Mount outpost would entice servants to cast off their indentures. Especially as English settlements proliferated in the 1630s, masters worried that their servants would run off to places where they would be impossible to retrieve. The flight of the four Plymouth servants suggests that many individuals chafed against the bonds that restricted their freedom.

Few Englishmen without Native guides risked overland travel, and Peach and his fellow runaways quickly became lost in what early Bay Colony settler William Wood described as a "strange labyrinth of unbeaten bushy ways in the woody wilderness." The Plymouth servants wandered to the north and west, toward Massachusetts Bay and then toward Narragansett Bay. They crossed paths with a Nipmuc man named Penowayanquis, on his way to the Bay Colony with some beaver skins and beads. Like the Plymouth men, Penowayanquis was also a servant. The Nipmucs inhabited what is today central Massachusetts. As of the mid-1630s, their communities were tributaries of their more powerful neighbors, including the Narragansetts, on whose behalf Penowayanquis engaged in trade.[18]

The next day, the four servants spotted Penowayanquis again. On his way back to Narragansett country, Penowayanquis now had five fathom of wampum and three coats. Peach persuaded his more reluctant companions that they should kill the trader. The wampum and coats might get the servants to New Netherland, and they may have had other motivations as well. According to Bradford's information, Peach alleged that Penowayanquis "had killed many of them" during the Pequot War.[19]

Peach called to the trader to come and smoke tobacco with them. As Penowayanquis reached for the pipe, Peach grabbed a rapier and stabbed his victim through the leg and belly. The English attackers could not finish him off, however, and Penowayanquis escaped them, disappearing into the swampy woods. Peach and the others took the coats and the wampum. When he got word of the assault, Roger Williams went to see the wounded man and brought him to Providence, where a physician tried in vain to save his life. It was now murder.[20]

English settlers on Aquidneck Island, alerted to the crime, apprehended the runaways. The attack was committed at a place called Misquamsqueece, in present-day Seekonk, Massachusetts. No group of English exercised jurisdiction over the area at the time, though both Massachusetts Bay and Plymouth would later claim it. So who should try the men?

The family and friends of Penowayanquis informed Williams that should the murder go unpunished, they intended to kill an Englishman in retaliation. Therefore, Massachusetts Bay governor John Winthrop maintained that despite a lack of clear jurisdiction, Plymouth should judge its own men. If Plymouth took no action, Winthrop advised Williams to hand at least Peach over to the dead man's friends so that they might avenge his death. In the meantime, Daniel Cross escaped from Aquidneck Island and managed to reach Pascataqua in present-day Maine. The other three men were taken to Plymouth. According to Bradford, "Some of the rude and ignorant sort murmured that any English should be put to death for the Indians." Thomas Prence—chosen as New Plymouth's governor the previous March—worried that the men would appeal their case to England, bringing about unwanted scrutiny of New England's governments.[21]

After some dithering, the Pilgrim magistrates impaneled a jury. The three men confessed to the assault, but there was some question about whether or not Peach's thrust had indeed killed Penowayanquis. Upon the testimony of Roger Williams, the physician, and two Indian witnesses, the jury convicted the three men of murder. Peach, Stinnings, and Jackson were immediately taken to the place of execution and hanged in the presence of what was probably a large assembly of English and Native onlookers. As far as Plymouth and Massachusetts leaders were concerned, the executions brought the case to a satisfactory end. The punishment stayed Nipmuc calls for revenge, kept the levers of justice in English hands, and avoided an appeal to England.

Plymouth's magistrates were not quite done with the consequences of Arthur Peach's actions, though. After Dorothy Temple gave birth to a son in early 1639, her master Stephen Hopkins refused to provide for his servant and her infant. For many years, Hopkins had been an assistant to Plymouth's governor. By the late 1630s, however, he had lost the respect of the colony's other leading citizens. Hopkins kept a shop and tavern in Plymouth, and the court convicted him of encouraging drunkenness and permitting gambling. Hopkins also was repeatedly presented to the court for overcharging customers. Hopkins's beer was so bad that it was not worth half what he charged, and he overpriced his wine so much that it contributed "to the oppressing and impoverishing of the colony." In another instance, Hopkins reportedly sold a mirror for sixteen pennies when a similar object cost only nine pennies in the Bay Colony. The churches and courts of puritan New England restrained merchants from extracting from their customers what the market would bear. By their standards, Hopkins cheated his customers, and the magistrates now accused him of cheating his wayward servant and her child.[22]

Dorothy Temple had two years of service remaining. The court held that Hopkins and Temple were bound to each other. Even if pregnancy and childbirth had interrupted her work, Hopkins had to provide food and clothing for her and the child. If he would not do so, the colony would provide for her and fine Hopkins the amount expended. Hopkins refused. The court imprisoned him for contempt. A few days later, Hopkins paid John Holmes three pounds to support Temple and her child during her last two years of service. At the time, Stephen Hopkins was nearly sixty years of age. He died in 1644, predeceased by his wife, Elizabeth.[23]

In a colonial society built upon hierarchical relationships, both the Nipmuc friends of Penowayanquis and Dorothy Temple approached English courts from a position of weakness. The Nipmucs at least had the threat of revenging themselves upon an English settler. Dorothy Temple, a female indentured servant who bore a bastard child of a murderer, had no such leverage. Yet the court did not permit Stephen Hopkins to cast her off. Like the other puritan colonies, New Plymouth privileged the welfare and stability of the community. In this case, communal obligations ensured that Temple and her infant would be fed and clothed.

It was justice, though, not mercy. A few months later, about one year after Arthur Peach had abandoned her and run away from Edward Winslow, the court ordered that Temple be whipped twice for her "uncleanness and bringing forth a male bastard." Most fornication cases involved couples who had conceived a child prior to their marriage. Time in the stocks or a single whipping were the most common punishments. Dorothy Temple received a double penalty. When she fainted during her first whipping, the court remitted the second.[24]

Most men and women lived out their indentures, obtained their freedom, and married. Webb Adey's life did not follow these expectations, and his experiences illustrate the precariousness of freedom in New Plymouth. Adey's parentage and place of English origin are unknown. He might have come to New England as a servant, and he might have stopped in Massachusetts Bay before coming south to New Plymouth. It is also unclear how Adey scratched out a living. Perhaps he hired himself out or attached himself to a family. Robert Charles Anderson terms Adey "the best-recorded antisocial pauper in Plymouth Colony." Present in the colony since at least the early 1630s, Adey at a certain point in his young adult life stopped fitting into the social order the Pilgrims had established.[25]

Adey first appears in colonial records on New Year's Day (March 25) 1633, when he was assessed nine shillings in taxes—the lowest possible amount. Three years later, the magistrates assigned Adey three acres of land, with the stipulation that he and other grantees could not sell the land "from their houses." In the same allocation of land, most men received six acres. Adey received only three, probably because he was single rather than the head of a household.[26]

Shortly afterward, Webb Adey began to get into trouble. That October, Adey and four other men were presented to the court "for disorderly living" and required to "give an account how they live." The next year, Adey was cited on successive weeks for working in his garden on the Sabbath. One of his two accusers was Ralph Smith, now Plymouth's former minister. The court convicted Adey of "disorderly living in idleness and nastiness." Apparently Adey made a point of working on Sunday but was indolent the rest of the week. In June 1638, the court ordered Adey to sell or rent his property so that he could properly clothe himself and to find a master who would take him into service.[27]

The punishment was severe. Those who broke the Sabbath, even repeatedly, usually faced fines or, at worst, whippings. Adey lost his property and his freedom. What was the nature of his disorderly living? Had Adey been prone to drunkenness, the court would have fined or whipped him for that infraction. A few scholars have suggested that Adey's "disorderly living" might have included sexual relations with other men, especially because same-sex attraction would explain why he apparently did not marry. Given the frequency of his legal troubles, however, he would have been charged with sodomy if that were the case. In August 1637, Plymouth's magistrates convicted John Alexander and Thomas Roberts of "lewd behavior and unclean carriage one with another, by often spending their seed one upon another." Sodomy was a capital crime according to the colony's 1636 laws, but New Plymouth never executed anyone for the offense. The court punished Alexander severely for being a repeat offender and for "seeking to allure others." He was whipped, branded on the shoulder with a hot iron, and banished forever. Roberts was whipped and banned from obtaining land unless he reformed his behavior. Adey's first presentment for disorderly living came only two months after the convictions of Alexander and Roberts. If someone had accused him of the same crime, the court surely would have taken it very seriously.[28]

What, then, was the nature of Adey's "disorderly living"? The limited record suggests that the root of the problem was Adey's decision to live by himself or in the company of other men. The entire structure of New England towns rested upon a set of hierarchical and interlocking relationships, those of parents and children, husbands and wives, masters and servants, magistrates and citizens. While the relationships were unequal, they bound individuals and families together in a web of mutual obligations. The religious thought of the Pilgrims, like that of other puritans, emphasized the sacred nature of those bonds. Robert Cushman had urged the settlers to be "jointed together and knit by flesh and sinews," not to live in isolation.

Thus, when men and women reached adulthood, they were expected to marry. If they did not do so, they faced pressure to attach themselves to other households as servants or laborers. When single men came to Plymouth in the early 1620s, for instance, the Pilgrims assigned them to existing households.

In both New Plymouth and Massachusetts Bay, magistrates fretted about "extravagant" men who moved between the two colonies. In this context, an "extravagant" man was a vagrant, someone who wandered or roamed and often settled in a community without permission. According to Bradford, Plymouth's leaders warned settlers not to receive any "servants, or other dwellers," in part to make certain that individuals were not fleeing indentures. If vagrants were not already bound in service elsewhere, courts sometimes assigned them to masters. In 1634, Plymouth's General Court bound Thomas Higgens—who had "lived an extravagant life"—as an apprentice to John Jenny for eight years. It was a long indenture, but at its conclusion Jenny would give Higgens two sets of apparel, twelve bushels of corn, and twenty acres of land.[29]

Plymouth had no law against a man choosing to live alone, but doing so was aberrant and attracted scrutiny and suspicion. And Webb Adey did more than simply live by himself. Given the reference to apparel, perhaps he did not clothe himself properly. At least for stretches of his life, he did not attend church. In certain parts of Europe, these sorts of antisocial behaviors made individuals— especially women—vulnerable to charges of witchcraft. Plymouth made witchcraft a capital crime in 1636. Only one individual was indicted for witchcraft in the colony's seven-decade history, Mary Ingham of Scituate, who was cleared by a jury. In Webb Adey, the magistrates saw not witchcraft but dissipation, the sort of social disorder and moral rot they perceived at Wessagusset and Merry Mount.[30]

In July 1638, the court arranged for Adey to become the servant of Thomas Prence, governor in one of the rare years in which Plymouth's citizens elected someone other than William Bradford. Prence was wary of Adey. The court stated that if Prence "shall dislike him [Adey] upon trial," the governor could cast him off and the court would find him another master. On the court's order, Adey sold his land and house for seventeen pounds.[31]

A stint of service did not change Webb Adey's ways. By 1642, he was a free man again, but that year the court convicted him of "licentious and disorderly" living and ordered him imprisoned. Eventually, despite his poverty and social isolation, Adey became a landowner again. He bought six acres of land in 1645, later sold a house for four pounds, and owned an extremely modest home at the time of his 1652 death. Perhaps even more surprisingly, at the end of his life Adey had an attachment to Plymouth's church, for he bequeathed thirty shillings—a fifth of his meager estate—to its then minister John Reyner.[32]

Webb Adey occupied a nebulous place between freedom and servitude. The colony never admitted him as a freeman. He probably did not ask it to do so, as it is hard to imagine Adey choosing to attend general courts. Thus, a body politic in which Adey did not participate reduced him to servitude and stripped him of his property. In New England's puritan colonies, as in old England, liberty did not mean license to live where or how one saw fit. Instead, liberty was always circumscribed by law and social conventions. Landownership did not release Adey from these expectations. Webb Adey was an unusual case, but Plymouth had its share of malcontents, social misfits, and cultural rebels, men and women who would not reform their ways.

CHAPTER TWELVE

Salamanders

I N THE EARLY TO mid-1640s, William Vassall tried to overturn the religious and political order of both New Plymouth and Massachusetts Bay. Vassall first brought his family to Salem in 1630, but the Vassalls sailed back home before the year was up. Five years later, they returned to New England, stopping in Roxbury but then moving south to the rapidly growing Plymouth Colony town of Scituate. When the Vassalls made their second emigration, they did so with a full awareness of New England's Congregational orthodoxy. William Vassall joined Scituate's church, swore an oath of fidelity to the colony, and became a freeman.[1]

Vassall had much in common with one of New Plymouth's leading citizens, Edward Winslow. Vassall and Winslow were among the colony's most cosmopolitan men, well attuned to moneymaking opportunities around the Atlantic world. They were also restless, quick to cross the ocean on political errands and in search of profits. In the end, both men went back to England, then ended their lives in the Caribbean. Vassall and Winslow even had family connections. Winslow's stepson and fellow *Mayflower* passenger Resolved White married Vassall's daughter Judith in 1640.

Despite all they shared, Vassall and Winslow clashed over what sort of liberty the settlers of Plymouth and Massachusetts should have in their churches and civil societies. As far as Vassall was concerned, Winslow and his fellow magistrates imposed a schismatic Congregationalism on people whether they wanted it or not. Vassall pressed New England settlers to embrace a more expansive liberty of conscience. Winslow countered that Vassall's machinations threatened New Englanders' well-worn and well-earned liberty to govern themselves. For Winslow, liberty remained inextricably connected to theological orthodoxy and a godly magistracy.

Winslow called Vassall a "salamander," a creature that thrived in flames, according to many folk traditions. Thomas Walley, later minister at the Cape Cod town of Barnstable, complained about "stirrers up of strife and division . . . salamanders, that love to live in the fire, that are firebrands in church and commonwealth."[2] Vassall was among several New England firebrands who circulated petitions, argued in courtrooms, and formed their own churches. Talk of free grace, religious toleration, and the liberties of freeborn Englishmen thrilled some New Englanders and alarmed others. Most settlers, though, focused on more prosaic tasks. They were not interested in either strengthening or weakening the colony's Congregational churches. In the end, Vassall and other dissenters bent New England's religious and political order but could not break it.

No religious conflict in early New England matched the intensity of what most historians have termed the "antinomian controversy." Kindled in 1636, the theological firestorm engulfed Boston and the Bay Colony for the ensuing two years and reverberated across all of New England for decades to come.[3]

At the heart of the matter was the problem of spiritual anxiety. Along with other Calvinists, puritans insisted that human salvation hinged not on good works or on the ability of humans to respond faithfully to God, but on God's eternal decrees. Ideally, such notions were comforting, especially once individuals reckoned with the true depth of their sinfulness. On the other hand, women and men longed to know that they numbered among God's elect, and puritans insisted that they could not know this with absolute certainty. Nevertheless, most ministers pointed to some benchmark by which believers could gain a reasonable assurance of their salvation. If they truly mourned their sins, if they felt the stirrings of faith within themselves, if they achieved some measure of sanctification, then Christians could trust that God had saved them.

A faction within Boston's church—including its pastor John Cotton, the minister John Wheelwright, new Massachusetts governor Henry Vane, and lay teacher Anne Hutchinson—rejected such notions. For them, reliance on sanctification was a covenant of works, something that smacked of popery and Antichrist. In an echo of Canterbury weaver Gilbert Gore's alleged heresy, Cotton taught that "God may be said to justify me before the habit, or act of faith."[4] Salvation was in God's hands alone. Grace was an entirely free gift. Cotton, Wheelwright, and Hutchinson did believe that women and men could gain the assurance they sought, but for them, such knowledge came through revelation. God's spirit put his seal on his elect. Ravished by his power and grace, they knew they were Christ's.

Cotton's fellow Bay Colony ministers—especially Cambridge's Thomas Shepard—became alarmed at what they heard from Cotton and members of his congregation. If sanctification could not provide assurance, did men and women have any reason to live righteously and to obey those in authority? Moreover, talk of immediate revelation and union with Christ raised the specter of "Familism," a cluster of ideas associated with the German mystic and Anabaptist Hendrick Niclaes and his Family of Love. Niclaes and those he influenced valued individual revelation and union with God over the ordinary means of salvation, such as scripture and the sacraments.

In the spring of 1637, Massachusetts freemen voted Vane out of office. He returned to England. The colony's General Court convicted Wheelwright of sedition and eventually banished him. Hutchinson, whom John Winthrop labeled an "American Jezebel," raised eyebrows because of the number of women and men who visited her home to hear her teachings. Prior to her emigration, Hutchinson had become convinced "that the ministers of England were . . . Antichrists." After she came to Massachusetts Bay, Hutchinson quickly became nearly as concerned about its churches. In November 1637, Massachusetts magistrates accused Hutchinson of slandering other ministers as teachers of a false covenant of works. At the resulting trial, she horrified her accusers with claims of immediate revelation from God. The court banished her, and Boston's church excommunicated her the following March. The magistrates and other ministers reconciled with Cotton, which stabilized the colony.[5]

The ministers, elders, magistrates, and at least some residents of New Plymouth paid close attention to these developments in the Bay Colony. In a display of ecclesiastical cooperation and unity, Plymouth Colony churches sent representatives to a synod at New-towne, Massachusetts, that identified and condemned a long list of alleged theological errors. In February 1638, the Scituate church observed a day of humiliation in which townspeople prayed that God would remove the "spreading opinions" in the Massachusetts Bay churches and prevent them from contaminating those in Plymouth Colony. Even after the controversy began to die down in Massachusetts, Plymouth's magistrates and ministers remained on edge. William Bradford pressed John Winthrop for information about "a monstrous and prodigious birth," a malformed stillborn child of Mary Dyer's that Hutchinson had delivered in her work as a midwife. New England's defenders of theological orthodoxy interpreted the misfortune as God's judgment.[6]

Wheelwright, Hutchinson, and several dozen of their followers took refuge on Rhode Island, to the south of Providence, not far from new English settlements in the western portion of New Plymouth's patent. Because of Plymouth Colony's position between two very different neighboring jurisdictions, moreover, its history increasingly became intertwined with that of Massachusetts Bay and Rhode Island.

Samuel Gorton, an erstwhile London clothier, clashed with the authorities of three New England colonies. A mystic and mischief-maker, Gorton refused to humble himself before any man. He had no respect for university-educated ministers. They quenched the spirit. Nor did Gorton show any deference to magistrates, whom he accused of unjustly punishing those who refused to render obeisance to their unwarranted authority. Whereas puritans preached that the Fifth Commandment required obedience not just to parents but also to magistrates and ministers, Gorton would not submit to anyone.[7]

Gorton, his wife, Mary, and their children came to New England, he said, "only to enjoy the liberty of our consciences." For that pursuit, they picked the wrong place and the wrong time, arriving in

Boston the same month that Bay Colony magistrates found John Wheelwright guilty of sedition. The Gortons prudently relocated to the town of Plymouth.[8]

Ralph Smith, Plymouth's former minister, had known Gorton in England and let a portion of his home to the newcomer and his family. After a year or so, however, Gorton found himself at odds with Smith and with Plymouth's magistrates when he sheltered a woman named Ellen Aldridge. According to Gorton's account, Plymouth's magistrates took umbrage when Aldridge smiled at church. She had arrived in the colony recently, and the magistrates decided to send her back on the ship that had brought her. When the Gortons heard of her plight, they employed her as Mary Gorton's servant and hid her from the colony's constables. Unable to prosecute Aldridge, Plymouth's leaders summoned Gorton. The discussion did not go well. Gorton interrupted one of the magistrates and accused him of hyperbole, whereupon the confused magistrates asked Elder Brewster to define "the meaning of that word." Brewster duly explained that Gorton had called the magistrate a liar. Whatever the particulars of Gorton's behavior, the magistrates fined him and ordered him to appear before the December 1638 General Court.[9]

Meanwhile, Plymouth's leaders concluded that Gorton was making himself an alternative source of religious authority. Ralph Smith's wife, several other members of the Smith family, and a female servant of John Reyner—Smith's successor as Plymouth's pastor—began attending Gorton's "family exercises," times of Bible reading, prayer, and teaching. In 1629 or 1630, Mary Smith had emigrated from Leiden with her first husband, the Sandwich separatist Richard Masterson. According to Gorton, she found "her spirit was refreshed in the ordinances of God as in former days which she said was much decayed and almost worn out of religion since she came to Plymouth." Gorton accused Plymouth's church of having departed from its original purity and spiritual power. They were "an apostatized people fallen from the faith of the gospel," whose leaders now put more stock in the performance of religious obligations than in the freely given grace of Jesus Christ. The critique was similar to what Roger Williams had alleged about the Pilgrim church during his stay in the colony. Not surprisingly, Plymouth's leaders interpreted the meetings as a challenge, to the town's religious order and to that of the Smith household.[10]

Gorton made a memorable appearance before the General Court. According to Winslow, Gorton referred to Governor Bradford as "Satan." Then he addressed the crowd: "Ye see good people how ye are abused! Stand for your liberty; and let them not be parties and judges." It seems that no one stood up in response, but the court fined Gorton for "stirring up the people to mutiny in the face of the court" and gave him two weeks to depart the colony.[11]

In the dead of winter, Gorton joined the recent Bay Colony exiles in the newly established town of Portsmouth on Rhode Island. The Gortons and their servant soon made themselves unwelcome there as well. According to Winslow, Ellen Aldridge beat another woman who strayed onto Gorton's land in pursuit of a cow. Once more haled before a court, Gorton mocked the Rhode Island magistrates as "Just Asses." They did not appreciate his sense of humor. Gorton was banished again, this time after being whipped. He went to Providence, then along with a few followers moved to nearby Shawomet, which they purchased from the Narragansett sachem Miantonomi. Providence settlers opposed to Gorton then traveled to Boston in the company of two other sachems who claimed that Shawomet was their land and had been unlawfully sold. Massachusetts magistrates were eager to assert jurisdiction over Shawomet, which lay outside the Bay Colony's patent. (Plymouth Colony subsequently claimed that its jurisdiction included Shawomet.) When Massachusetts leaders sent messages to Gorton and his followers, they received a flurry of insults in response. The magistrates next sent soldiers to arrest the Gortonists.[12]

The dispute began with property and jurisdiction, but it also involved theology. Gorton emphasized the divinity within all human beings above the earthly incarnation, death, and resurrection of Jesus Christ. In their own version of Christian liberty, the Gortonists had no use for sacraments, for learned ministers, or for magistrates. Narrowly escaping a capital conviction on charges of blasphemy, Gorton was banished from Massachusetts and Shawomet, as were his followers. The now thrice-banished Gorton and two associates sailed for England to seek redress.

While the Gortons were still living in Ralph Smith's house, Plymouth's church invited Charles Chauncy to Plymouth. Church members intended to ordain him as their teacher, a second minister alongside John Reyner. After nearly two decades of absent or largely uninspiring clerical leadership, Chauncy's arrival was a coup for Plymouth. Chauncy had several degrees from Cambridge and had taught Hebrew and Greek at Trinity College. Next came ten tumultuous years of parish ministry, in which Chauncy repeatedly clashed with ecclesiastical officials over everything from the surplice to communion rails. In November 1635, the Court of High Commission suspended him from his ministry and sent him to prison. Two months later, Chauncy got down on bended knee and promised to mend his ways. The next year, however, an official observed that Chauncy "doth mend like sour ale in summer." At this point, Chauncy wisely decided to leave England. Plymouth was a rather precipitous fall for a scholarly and well-connected minister, but Chauncy's abject submission before Laud probably made him less attractive to other New England congregations. For his part, William Bradford was thrilled. Plymouth finally had a preacher whose intellectual chops rivaled those of John Robinson and the ministers of the Bay Colony.[13]

Chauncy may have been learned, but he had not learned to avoid conflict. The prospective pastor had several idiosyncratic ideas about the sacraments, often the seedbed for controversy in seventeenth-century New England. Chauncy taught that Christians should celebrate the Lord's Supper after sundown, in imitation of the last meal shared by Jesus and his disciples. The idea was inconvenient, but not a deal-breaker. If post-sunset communion had been the only sticking point, Plymouth's congregants would have stuck by their prospective teacher. In fact, the newly organized church in the Cape Cod town of Sandwich adopted the practice.[14]

It was Chauncy's ideas about baptism that sank his candidacy. He insisted that "children ought to be dipped and not sprinkled." Even early English opponents of infant baptism, such as John Smyth and Thomas Helwys, had not argued for the necessity of immersion, but there were some recent precedents for Chauncy's stance. In 1633, the English minister Daniel Rogers published a book in which he argued that the Bible commanded baptism by immersion.

Ministers needed to immerse infants in water, hold them in it, and bring them out again in imitation of the life, death, and resurrection of Jesus. Chauncy contended that sprinkling as opposed to dipping was among the "Jesuitical ceremonies" Protestants should reject.[15]

Plymouth's leaders allowed that immersion was permissible according to the Bible, but they did not want infants plunged into frigid New England waters. The congregation tried to find a compromise with Chauncy by proposing that he could baptize those children whose parents opted for immersion, while John Reyner could baptize the rest by sprinkling or pouring. Chauncy, however, could not abide the sprinkling of any Plymouth babies.

The church asked ministers within and beyond the colony to persuade Chauncy to change his mind. There were debates and exchanges of letters, and John Cotton preached on the issue in Boston. "Nakedness of women in the congregation is not civil nor decent," Cotton warned. In the seventeenth century, "naked" generally did not imply a complete absence of clothing. The Boston minister probably meant that dipping would require individuals to remove their outer garments. While most of those baptized would be infants and young children, the idea of Chauncy dipping women into Plymouth's Town Brook was especially disturbing. Cotton, who was probably relieved that someone else's ideas were receiving scrutiny, also asserted that immersion could prove deadly. Chauncy's dipping would endanger the lives of children in winter, and the Bible did not authorize delaying baptisms until summer. Neither Cotton nor anyone else could persuade Chauncy to back down, however.[16]

Churches in New England usually made decisions only after attaining consensus among their members. Bare majorities did not seek to impose their will on minorities, because to do so invited subsequent strife and division. Chauncy thus remained "in suspense" for some time, because significant factions within Plymouth's church both favored and opposed him. He complained that his "long unsettledness hath occasioned great impairing . . . of that little estate I had." Eventually, however, it became clear that he could not become Plymouth's pastor.[17]

The conflict over Chauncy drove a rare wedge between Edward Winslow and William Bradford. Plymouth's governor wanted his colony to find another way to make use of Chauncy's scholarly talents. In 1636, the Bay Colony had established what became Harvard College, but the enterprise had made little headway during its first few years, thus leaving an opening for other initiatives. With John Reyner's support, Bradford proposed that Chauncy start an academy on the Jones River three miles to the north. Winslow foresaw trouble. If situated between Plymouth and Duxbury, Chauncy would "weaken if not destroy both the congregations." Winslow wrote Bay Colony governor John Winthrop and urged him to intervene with Bradford, who shelved the idea.[18]

Chauncy instead became the minister at a divided and diminished congregation in Scituate. The town's first minister was John Lothrop, who prior to his 1634 emigration was the successor to Henry Jacob at the independent congregation in London. After Lothrop came to Scituate, he and a dozen other men and women covenanted with each other to form a church. The congregation grew to sixty members within a few years. In December 1636, the church observed a day of thanksgiving. Congregants and others gathered at their newly built meetinghouse shortly after sunrise. For more than three hours on a frigid morning, they prayed and sang psalms. Lothrop preached. Then they feasted together, "the poorer sort being invited of the richer."[19]

Despite this promising start, both the church and town were soon mired in dissension, some of which stemmed from conflicts over the allocation of land. Lothrop and the majority of Scituate's church members moved to the newly formed Cape Cod town of Barnstable. Out of those who remained, Timothy Hatherly—Scituate's wealthiest man and one of the colony's magistrates—wanted Chauncy. Vassall and several other remaining congregants, however, objected to the candidate's "judgment and practice in the sacraments." Unlike in Plymouth, a small majority imposed its will on a congregation and installed Chauncy as Scituate's pastor.[20]

Chauncy now practiced what he had preached. According to John Winthrop, after Chauncy baptized two of his own children in very cold weather, one died. Another frightened child grabbed hold of Chauncy during a baptism and nearly pulled the minister into the water. At this point, one Scituate woman took matters into her own hands. Anna Stockbridge and her husband, John, had sailed to New England on the same ship as the Vassalls. Anna, but not her husband, joined Scituate's church during Lothrop's pastorate. In July 1642, she demanded that Chauncy provide her with a letter enabling her to take her two-and-a-half-year-old daughter, Elizabeth, elsewhere for baptism. Even in the summer, Stockbridge did not want Elizabeth immersed. Anna Stockbridge must have been a persuasive and forceful woman. In an unusual display of accommodation, Chauncy agreed, and Stockbridge and her husband, John, brought their daughter to Boston. The couple promised to raise Elizabeth "in some church gathered and ordered according to Christ."[21]

Anna Stockbridge died later that summer, but her husband kept their baptismal promise. He joined a church in Scituate, but not Charles Chauncy's. The Stockbridges and the Vassalls were among several Scituate families who in 1643 began holding their own religious meetings. Both their faction and Chauncy's claimed to be Scituate's church. Chauncy insisted that Vassall's followers had unlawfully separated, and he asked churches in Plymouth and Massachusetts Bay to withhold communion from them. According to Chauncy, they no longer belonged to any true church and therefore should not be admitted to the Lord's Supper anywhere.[22]

Vassall was livid. "Is it a small persecution to keep us and ours in the state of heathen [without access to the sacraments]?" he asked. Chauncy and many other puritans had been persecuted in England. Now, Vassall alleged, "the persecuted are become persecutors." Vassall insisted that he should be allowed to worship God according to his conscience without license from anyone else. Accordingly, Vassall and his supporters made plans to ordain their own pastor. They offered the position to William Wetherell, a member of Duxbury's church. After earning two degrees from Cambridge, Wetherell had become a schoolmaster in the Kentish town of Maidstone. After ecclesiastical authorities accused him of using his classroom as a pulpit for nonconformist ideas, Wetherell emigrated to New England. He taught in Charlestown and then Cambridge before moving to Duxbury.[23]

Chauncy was just as outraged. In puritan New England, the liberties of congregations were paramount, not those of individuals. Once individuals swore to a church covenant, they could not join another church without a formal dismissal. Moreover, magistrates and ministers agreed that each town should have—must have—a single, orthodox church. The colony's other churches attempted to apply pressure on Vassall and his followers. Duxbury and its minister Ralph Partridge refused to dismiss Wetherell, and the town of Plymouth's church warned that it would withhold communion from Vassall, Wetherell, and their party should they proceed with their plans. Chauncy threatened to excommunicate Vassall, which would have prevented him from becoming a member or receiving the sacraments at another church. All of these procedures were designed to contain dissent and to encourage disaffected individuals to mend fences with their congregations.

Vassall and Wetherell were undeterred. On September 2, 1645, they and their followers observed a day of fasting, renewed their church covenant (they understood themselves not as a new, separate church, but as the continuation of Scituate's original church), and installed Wetherell as their minister. They held their meetings in the southern portion of Scituate, on the North River. The colony's magistrates and other ministers relented. Chauncy's idiosyncrasies and stubbornness created some sympathy for his Scituate opponents, and at least Vassall and Wetherell had consulted with other churches and had proceeded with some patience.

It was a landmark moment in the early history of New England. One town had two religious options born out of controversy and schism. Wetherell's congregation became known as the "south church," Chauncy's the "north church." Townspeople had the liberty to choose between them.

As Charles Chauncy and William Vassall feuded in Scituate, several chapters of New Plymouth's early history came to an end. Displaying his penchant for going where he was not wanted, Thomas Morton made one final trip to New England. In 1643, he landed in Rhode Island, came to Plymouth, and somehow finagled permission from Governor Bradford to spend the winter. Morton annoyed his old nemesis Myles Standish—"Captain Shrimp"—by going "fowling" on his property in Duxbury. When Morton moved on to Massachusetts Bay the next year, its magistrates were less forgiving of his past transgressions. They jailed him for a winter, decided that he was too "old and crazy [broken down]" to be whipped, fined him one hundred pounds, and released him when he agreed to leave the colony. Morton went to the Maine settlement of Agamenticus (present-day York), whose charter decreed that the non-puritan colony would hold fairs on the feast days of St. James and St. Paul. Perhaps the onetime "host" of Merry Mount found some merriment before his 1647 death.[24]

William Brewster, the Plymouth church's longtime elder, died in April 1644. Brewster had opened his home for separatist meetings in Scrooby, published dissenting literature in Leiden, and, although there is no record of any of their content, had probably preached more sermons than any other man in New England. Brewster was Plymouth's true rock, a pillar of stability who compensated for the early settlement's absence of ministerial leadership. Despite Brewster's death, the Pilgrim core of Plymouth's leadership remained largely intact: *Mayflower* passengers Bradford, Winslow, Standish, and John Alden, along with Thomas Prence, who came on the *Fortune* in 1621 and twice served as governor in the 1630s.

Plymouth's English population expanded rapidly in the early 1640s. In 1643, the colony's towns enumerated around six hundred men of fighting age. In addition to the new towns on the Cape (Sandwich, Barnstable, Yarmouth, and Eastham, the latter incorporated in 1644), settlers established themselves at Cohannet (soon renamed Taunton) and Seekonk (Rehoboth) farther to the west. Prior to the planting of Seekonk and Cohannet, English settlements dotted the coast but had not penetrated the interior. The push into the western lands strained the colony's relationship with Ousamequin and other sachems. While the English brought trading goods, they diminished the region's supply of game and timber, and English horses and livestock trampled Wampanoag crops. The alliance between the Pilgrims and the Wampanoags nevertheless remained firm during these years, in part because English power still helped Ousamequin advance his interests against his Narragansett enemies.[25]

Meanwhile, the peace between Massachusetts Bay and the Narragansetts frayed. The aftermath of the Pequot War badly dispirited the Narragansett sachem Miantonomi, who complained that English settlers "with scythes cut down the grass, and with axes fell the trees; their cows and horses eat the grass, and their hogs spoil our clam banks, and we shall all be starved." Miantonomi proposed that Native peoples from the Hudson to Narragansett Bay join together against the Dutch and the English. "So must we be one as they are," he argued, "otherwise we shall be all gone shortly." The plan foundered in large part because of implacable hostility between the Narragansetts and the Mohegans.[26]

Miantonomi's efforts inadvertently furthered the unity of New England's puritan colonies. In 1643, colonial magistrates formed the United Colonies of New England (or the New England Confederation). Massachusetts Bay, Plymouth, Connecticut, and New Haven agreed to defend each other in the event of war against either Indians or the Dutch. Previously, Massachusetts Bay had refused to assist Plymouth against French raids, and Plymouth had demurred when asked to join the war against the Pequots. Now the colonies had a mutual-defense pact in which each pledged to assist each other with men and money in all instances of "just wars." Partly because they disagreed about whether particular wars were just and looked to their own individual interests, the four colonies struggled to maintain their professed unity in the coming decades. Still, the confederation is a striking example of early cooperation among England's North American colonies.

Miantonomi did not attack the English, but instead was captured while leading his warriors against the Mohegans. In September 1643, the Mohegan sachem Uncas brought his prize captive to the first meeting of the United Colonies, in Hartford. At the session, the delegates agreed that Plymouth should help Ousamequin regain land upon which the Narragansetts allegedly had encroached. As for Miantonomi, the English told Uncas to do as he saw fit. After taking Miantonomi back onto Mohegan lands, Uncas's brother split his head. Fearing Narragansett attacks, Plymouth Colony towns took measures to defend themselves, but Canonicus—who had sent the arrows bundled in snakeskin to Squanto in the winter of 1621–22—and other Narragansett sachems made peace with the English.[27]

During these same years, English society was turned upside down. The late 1630s attempt of Archbishop Laud and King Charles to bring the Church of Scotland into greater conformity with its English counterpart produced a revolt. Now desperate for funds, Charles briefly recalled Parliament in April 1640, then again after the Scots crushed his poorly trained and insufficiently equipped army. The setbacks led to the rapid unraveling of Charles's authority. The

House of Commons impeached Archbishop Laud on charges of treason, accusing him of everything from attempting a reconciliation with Rome to having prodded the king toward war against Scotland. Political conflict between Charles and Parliament intensified. In 1642, Charles fled London, and for several years Royalist and parliamentary armies fought for control of England. Laud was beheaded in January 1645, and the New Model Army—created out of a variety of parliamentary forces—soon closed in on the last Royalist strongholds. By the next year, Charles was Parliament's prisoner.

For New England puritans, Parliament's victory in England's Civil War was the triumph of Christ over Antichrist, a triumph most had expected would not come this side of the millennium. For decades, puritans had watched their version of Reformed Protestantism lose ground both in England and on the continent. Now, with a puritan-dominated Parliament in charge, the hated surplices, prayer books, and even the hierarchy itself were gone. "The tyrannous bishops are ejected," Bradford rejoiced, "their courts dissolved, their canons forceless, their service cashiered, their ceremonies useless and despised; their plots for popery prevented, and all their superstitions discarded, and returned to Rome from whence they came." Plymouth's governor had not expected to live to see what he understood as a harbinger of Christ's millennial reign. "But who hath done it?" Bradford asked, and he used a quote from the Book of Revelation to answer his question. "Who, even he that sitteth on the white horse, who is called faithful, and true, and judgeth, and fighteth righteously." It was Christ's victory, but those who had been willing to suffer for Christ's true church—including the "little handful" at Plymouth—had prepared his way.[28]

Parliament's victory laid bare the fact that puritans did not agree among themselves about how they should reform England's church. Presbyterians and Independents (Congregationalists) jostled for control, and Baptists and a host of radical Protestant sectarians emerged as advocates for a broader religious liberty. This changed situation in England encouraged Scituate's William Vassall to challenge New England's Congregational establishments, which he now regarded as just as tyrannical as the old episcopal hierarchy.[29]

It began in the spring of 1645 with what should have been a

minor dispute in Hingham, the Bay Colony town that bordered Scituate. After reelecting a man who had served for years as their militia captain, Hingham's male residents reversed course and instead chose a new captain. Recriminations and grandstanding ensued. The incumbent militia officer refused to give way, and Hingham's minister threatened to excommunicate him. John Winthrop, then the colony's deputy governor, summoned several Hingham men to explain themselves and jailed two who refused to appear before the magistrates.

In June 1645, eighty-one residents of Hingham sent a petition to the Massachusetts General Court. The petition's single paragraph employed *liberty* or *liberties* eight times. It declared that the magistrates threatened the "liberty and power of the General Court," "the liberty of the churches amongst us," and "the general liberty of the whole country." The petitioners alleged that the magistrates wielded arbitrary power and were tyrannizing the colony's citizens and churches. They asked for the opportunity to plead their case before the bicameral court, hoping that its deputies would reverse the actions of the magistrates.[30]

When the court met, the magistrates agreed to hear the case, and the petitioners named Winthrop himself as the object of their complaints. Winthrop stepped down from his position among the magistrates, sat with his head uncovered, and endured what amounted to an impeachment trial. In the end, the court—magistrates and deputies—acquitted Winthrop and fined the petitioners. Winthrop then asked for the right to deliver a "little speech." In it, Winthrop contrasted two forms of liberty, one "natural" and one "civil or federal." The former was simply the desire of individuals to do whatever they pleased, whether for good or evil. "This liberty," Winthrop warned, "is incompatible and inconsistent with authority." It was a "wild beast which all the ordinances of God are bent against." Civil liberty, by contrast, operated within covenants, both ecclesiastical and civil. It allowed men and women to pursue "that only which is good," and only within the hierarchical relationships that governed human societies. Thus, churches enjoyed liberty under the authority of Christ, citizens enjoyed liberty under the authority of magistrates, and wives found liberty in subjection to their husbands. This same principle of ordered, constrained liberty had guided New

Plymouth's responses to Samuel Gorton and to the schism within Scituate's church.[31]

According to Edward Winslow, it was William Vassall who "blew up this [the Hingham case] to such an height." Apparently, Vassall had lurked in a nearby home, to which the Hingham plaintiffs repeatedly came for advice. Vassall was more open about his activities in Plymouth Colony. At a court of assistants, Bradford introduced what Winslow cryptically referred to as "a matter of great concernment." It was a proposed law to suppress religious dissent, probably aimed at Baptists and anyone whose ideas resembled those of Anne Hutchinson or Samuel Gorton. In October, Plymouth's General Court approved Bradford's measure. One week later, at another court session attended by more magistrates and deputies, Vassall criticized the recently passed statute "as pernicious and destructive to the weal of the government." Vassall and his supporters called for the law to be "defaced and crossed [out]." Bradford, Winslow, and Thomas Prence refused to do so, but they suggested that if the measure proved "prejudicial," it could be repealed in the future.[32]

In the meantime, Vassall circulated his own bill, a law that would "allow and maintain full and free tolerance of religion to all men that would preserve the civil peace, and submit unto government." According to an apoplectic Winslow, Vassall—like Thomas Helwys and Roger Williams before him—made no exceptions for Turks, Jews, Catholics, or Familists. New Plymouth would become a second Rhode Island. Winslow was even more shocked to learn "how sweet this carrion relished to the palates of most of the deputies!" Bradford, Winslow, and Thomas Prence were opposed but feared they would be outvoted. Apparently, three other magistrates—Scituate's Timothy Hatherly, Sandwich's Edmond Freeman, and Taunton's John Browne—backed Vassall. Procedure dictated that the measure receive a vote, but Bradford "would not suffer it to come to vote." Plymouth's governor feared Vassall's bill would "eat out the power of godliness."[33]

Unfortunately, a letter from Winslow to Winthrop provides the only account of the episode, and it raises many questions. If the colony's deputies—and perhaps the townspeople who had elected them—were so enthusiastic about Vassall's proposed toleration, why did the matter drop after Bradford's procedural veto? Perhaps the stature of Plymouth's governor insulated him from any significant protest, but it is also likely that Winslow exaggerated Vassall's support. The next year, the colony's freemen reelected Bradford and all of his assistants, with the exception of Edmond Freeman. The bulk of Plymouth's settlers probably had no interest either in Bradford's measure to strengthen the religious establishment or in Vassall's bill for toleration. The colonists were a mixed multitude. A minority actually belonged to the colony's churches, though more settlers attended them. By this point, only a small number had rejected infant baptism or had embraced the more adventurous ideas of Gorton or the Bay Colony exiles. Many other inhabitants of New Plymouth were not especially attached to the colony's churches, but they were also not opponents of them.

Turning his attention back to the Bay Colony, in the spring of 1646 Vassall supported a group of seven men in another campaign for religious toleration. The principals were Robert Child, who had just returned to Massachusetts with the poorly conceived intention of establishing a vineyard; Samuel Maverick, in the region since the mid-1620s; and John Dand, a London grocer who emigrated in the early 1640s. The seven were not church members. With the exception of Maverick, they were not freemen. As a resident of Plymouth rather than Massachusetts Bay, Vassall could not sign their petition, but Winthrop identified him as the instigator behind the effort.[34]

In their remonstrance, the petitioners asserted that New England's magistrates and ministers had reduced them to "perpetual slavery and bondage." They could not vote, but a government levied taxes and other obligations on them without their consent. In particular, the Massachusetts magistrates' exercise of a veto against the decisions of the deputies amounted to "an over-greedy spirit of arbitrary power" that threatened the liberties they held as "freeborn subjects of the English nation." Likewise, they were forced to attend churches to which they did not belong, and towns forced them to contribute to the support of ministers who would not admit them to the Lord's Supper or baptize their children. The petitioners asked the Massachusetts General Court to compel churches to either admit them as members or grant them the liberty to form their own churches.[35]

John Winthrop understood the conflict similarly but with reversed roles. "They complained of fear of perpetual slavery," the governor countered, "but their intent was, to make us slaves to them." The petitioners wanted to do away with the privileges and power enjoyed by freemen, church members, and magistrates. The court deferred action on the petition until the fall of 1646. The petitioners circulated copies of their remonstrance, but it gained little support among the residents of Massachusetts, who either agreed with their magistrates or realized that to support the petitioners would have exposed themselves to charges of contempt or sedition. The petitioners expected the court to reject their demands. They would then appeal to Parliament.[36]

As the Bay Colony magistrates contemplated how to respond to the petition from Child and Maverick, they were startled by the arrival in Boston of Randall Holden, an associate of Samuel Gorton. After their banishment from Shawomet, Gorton and Holden had gone to England and appealed to the parliamentary Committee for Foreign Plantations, a successor of sorts to the commission over which William Laud had presided. Headed by the Earl of Warwick, the committee's members included Samuel Vassall—William's brother—and former Massachusetts governor Henry Vane. Massachusetts Bay was not prepared to defend itself before the committee, and Gorton benefited from rising English support for religious toleration and the fact that the same committee recently had given Roger Williams a patent for Providence and Rhode Island. In May 1646, the committee sided with the Gortonists and granted them safe passage back to their Shawomet land. Holden's triumphant return to Boston alarmed Bay Colony leaders. If individuals convicted of offenses in New England could appeal to English authorities, the colonies could not properly govern themselves.[37]

Even before the General Court formally rejected their petition, Child and his partners had decided to send Vassall to England. The Massachusetts magistrates countered by sending Edward Winslow on a mission to overturn Gorton's favorable ruling and to defend the Bay Colony against Vassall. Some in the Bay Colony wondered why their government should employ a Plymouth man as their agent, while William Bradford was piqued that Winslow would undertake this errand for Massachusetts. On Winslow's last visit to England, Archbishop Laud had sent him to prison. By the time Winslow set foot on English shores again, Laud was dead and King Charles was Parliament's prisoner. There was no assurance, though, that the committee would favor New England's magistrates over the colonies' religious and political dissenters.

In addition to his appearances before the committee, Winslow engaged in heated printed exchanges with both Gorton and Vassall. While the latter pair aimed most of their criticism at Massachusetts Bay, they informed Parliament that New Plymouth was no better. Gorton alleged that although Plymouth and Bay Colony settlers had once been "pilgrims" who fled persecution, they now had adopted "the selfsame spirit" of their persecutors. Likewise, Vassall asserted that just as Plymouth's leaders imitated the Bay colonists "in their church-ways, so they follow them in their arbitrary government." The complaints of Gorton and Vassall echoed the criticisms the poet John Milton leveled against the puritan Presbyterians who now controlled Parliament. In the early 1640s, Milton had been a fierce critic of Laud and the episcopal hierarchy. Now Milton charged that "new presbyter is but old priest writ large." Likewise, Gorton and Vassall alleged that New England leaders enforced their own version of ecclesiastical and political tyranny.[38]

Winslow scoffed at the notion that New England's settlers were pilgrims turned persecutors. "What greater wrong can be done a poor persecuted people that went into the wilderness to avoid the tyrannical government of the late hierarchy," he asked, "and to enjoy the liberties Christ Jesus hath left unto his churches . . . than to be accounted persecutors of Christ in his saints?" Winslow, like John Winthrop, insisted that true liberty rested on political and ecclesiastical order, and he asserted—with considerable exaggeration—that Presbyterians were welcome anywhere in New England and that New Plymouth left Baptists unmolested. Winslow urged the committee to permit New Englanders to govern themselves. He went so far as to suggest that the colonies were "growing up into a nation," though he stressed—again, with some exaggeration—that they closely adhered to the laws of England.[39]

Winslow's mission was partly successful. He failed to reverse the committee's judgment on Gorton's case, but he prevailed against Vassall. The committee declared that it did not wish to "encourage any appeals" from New England justice. The governments of Massachusetts Bay and New Plymouth governed without interference from England until the restoration of the monarchy under Charles II.[40]

William Vassall probably knew he would be unwelcome back in Scituate or anywhere else in the puritan colonies. Instead, he went to Barbados, where he accumulated land and slaves. He died in late 1655 or 1656.

Winslow remained in London as the Bay Colony's agent, served on several parliamentary committees, defended the commercial interests of New England, and raised money for missionary work among New England's Native peoples. He was also one of many religious dissidents who returned to England after the fall of the church hierarchy made it safe to do so. Winslow's departure was a serious loss for New Plymouth; no one else in the colony matched his transatlantic connections.[41]

When it became clear that he would not come back to New England anytime soon, Winslow's daughter Elizabeth went to England, perhaps to help care for her father, perhaps to find a suitable husband. Winslow's son Josiah, with his wife, Penelope, also journeyed to London. Susanna Winslow never visited her husband. She remained in Marshfield to manage the family's farms and other business in her husband's absence. Edward, Josiah, and Penelope sat for portraits in 1651. The painting of Edward Winslow is the only known contemporary portrait of a *Mayflower* passenger. The three portraits do not depict the austere Pilgrims of the American imagination. The Winslow men sport fancy collars, cuffs, a tassel, and—in Edward Winslow's case—what are probably silver buttons. The Winslow men wear black not to be dour, but because black dye was expensive and signified wealth. Both Josiah and Edward have long hair, of which many puritan moralists disapproved. Penelope Winslow is strikingly fashionable. She holds a velvet or silk wrap around a green dress. A gold-beaded necklace adorns her neck, and a small hood with a row of pearls ornaments her loose, curled hair.[42]

In his portrait, Edward Winslow holds a piece of paper that identifies itself as a "letter from your loving wife Susanna" (see page 175). After he left New England late in 1646, Edward Winslow never saw his Careswell estate or Susanna again. Other settlers felt his absence as well. William Bradford was disappointed when members

Penelope Winslow, 1651. (Pilgrim Hall Museum, Plymouth, Massachusetts.)

of his church moved away to find better land and better prospects. He understood Winslow's decision to stay in England as a betrayal of sacred congregational bonds. Winslow, though, saw no conflict between his religious principles and the pursuit of wealth and parliamentary appointments.

In early 1655, Winslow, now nearly sixty years old, arrived in Barbados as part of Admiral William Penn's campaign against the Spanish West Indies. While there, Winslow crossed paths with William Vassall, his old antagonist.[43] Perhaps he also encountered another man he had once known. If Hope still lived, he probably would have heard that his former master was on the island. After the expedition set sail for Jamaica, Edward Winslow died of a fever and was buried at sea.

In 1646, the commissioners for the United Colonies gathered in New Haven for their annual meeting. Led by the Bay Colony's rep-

Josiah Winslow, 1651. (Pilgrim Hall Museum, Plymouth, Massachusetts.)

resentatives, they discussed proposals to combat the spread of what they understood as heresy. Rhode Island had granted its settlers "a licentious liberty," allowing them to "profess and practice what is good in their own eyes." Now dissenters wanted to bring such chaos to the other colonies. In order to preserve the "liberties of the gospel," the commissioners proposed that the colonies undertake measures to suppress Anabaptism, Familism, antinomianism, and all errors that undermined the Bible and the Sabbath "under a deceitful color of liberty of conscience." Scituate's Timothy Hatherly and Taunton's John Browne represented New Plymouth, and they refused to endorse the motion without advice from their general court. Contrary to the claims of Gorton and Vassall, New Plymouth did not march in lockstep with Massachusetts Bay.

Hatherly and Browne did support a resolution that condemned the oppression of the poor through high prices and low wages, as well as other signs of godlessness, such as drunkenness and showy apparel. The commissioners called on the region's English settlers to live as true Christians. "And though the God of this world (as he is styled) be worshipped . . . in the main and greatest part of America," they concluded, "yet this small part and portion may be vindicated as by the right hand of Jehovah, and justly called Emmanuel's [Christ's] land." All of New Plymouth's leaders shared this vision of a godly New England.[44]

Although events across the Atlantic and the decisions of colonial magistrates influenced the boundaries of religious orthodoxy and toleration, they were also negotiated at a local level. In 1649, Barnstable's church excommunicated Judith Shelley. According to Barnstable minister John Lothrop, "Goody Shelley" became upset when other Barnstable women did not invite her to a "Christian meeting." She allegedly slandered a fellow church member by calling her a proud and dishonest gossip. Shelley also claimed to possess "a spirit of revelation." Because Lothrop at first had acknowledged her gift and then denied it, she asserted that it was her minister who deserved to be cast out of the church. Disparaging ministers and claiming the spirit of revelation had gotten Anne Hutchinson banished from Massachusetts Bay. Judith Shelley's only apparent penalty for her behavior was excommunication. The fact that the women of Barnstable were meeting on their own, moreover, hints at realms of women's religious experience and leadership rarely visible in colonial records.[45]

In 1649, more than a dozen individuals in Rehoboth split from the town's church, denounced its minister, and began holding their own meetings. As William Brewster and John Robinson had done a half century before, the dissenters in Rehoboth separated from a church they regarded as corrupt. The Rehoboth separatists were convinced that the Bible did not authorize infant baptism and that, therefore, their own infant baptisms were invalid. Under the leadership of Obadiah Holmes, they asked a minister from Rhode Island to baptize them. Plymouth's magistrates were not eager to intervene, but after receiving several petitions complaining about the rebaptisms, the General Court threatened individuals who organized unsanctioned religious meetings with disenfranchisement and unspecified further punishments. Holmes and most of his followers soon left for Newport.[46]

While the colony's magistrates and freemen opposed religious toleration, they were far more sluggish in taking action against religious dissidents than their Bay Colony counterparts. When Obadiah Holmes visited the Massachusetts Bay town of Lynn, held meetings, and baptized several persons, he was arrested, taken to Boston, and whipped. The fragile consensus in New Plymouth was that Baptists were to be grudgingly tolerated rather than forcibly corrected. Indeed, in 1655, New Plymouth allowed a prominent Baptist to move to Scituate. The previous fall, Henry Dunster, the first president of Harvard College, had made public his opposition to infant baptism. Forced to resign and leave the colony, he took refuge in Scituate without any apparent controversy. In an ironic development, Harvard recruited as its second president Charles Chauncy, who agreed to keep quiet about his own idiosyncratic baptismal preferences.[47]

Quite literally in between Rhode Island and Massachusetts Bay, New Plymouth came to occupy a middle ground between the former's thoroughgoing toleration and the latter's stricter policing of orthodoxy. Not long after Scituate swapped Chauncy for Dunster, however, a new group of dissidents mounted a much more dramatic challenge to the colony's religious establishment.

CHAPTER THIRTEEN

Friends

THE EVENTS OF EARLY 1649 stunned the English on both sides of the Atlantic. After a parliamentary tribunal convicted King Charles of treason, he was beheaded in public. After the king's execution, the House of Commons abolished the institution of monarchy as "unnecessary, burdensome, and dangerous to the liberty, safety, and public interest of the people." The Commons did away with the House of Lords as well. England was now a commonwealth, a republic.[1]

New Plymouth and the other New England colonies functioned as their own commonwealths, as what historian Michael Winship calls "quasi-republics." William Bradford and Edward Winslow had made clear their sympathy for Parliament during the English Civil War, but the news of regicide led to indecision rather than celebration. In June 1649, Plymouth's General Court canceled the colony's annual elections. Bradford, his assistants, and other officers continued in their positions for the next year. The issue at hand was probably the oath that elected officials swore "to be truly loyal to our sovereign Lord King Charles, his heirs, and successors." There was now no king to whom elected officials could swear their loyalty. In addition to scrapping the election, Plymouth's General Court did not admit any freemen that year.[2]

After the initial shock of the king's decapitation faded, governance in New Plymouth returned to normal. In June 1650, the

General Court reelected all of the existing magistrates and resumed admitting freemen. In the colony's book of laws, Nathaniel Morton crossed out "our sovereign Lord King Charles" and substituted "the state and government of England as it now stands." Colony officials duly added references to "his highness the Lord Protector" once Oliver Cromwell assumed that office in 1653.[3]

Ecclesiastical affairs in England remained chaotic throughout this period. The Presbyterian puritans who controlled Parliament for most of the 1640s eliminated bishops, suppressed the Book of Common Prayer, ejected hundreds of ministers from their positions, and even outlawed Christmas. There was no consensus behind such reforms, however. A large number of English women and men were attached to the Prayer Book, and even more liked Christmas. At the same time, other voices found converts as they took advantage of the freedom to publish their writings and preach in the streets of London and across the countryside. No more than five percent of the populace attended Congregationalist (Independent), Baptist, or other sectarian meetings, but such groups achieved an outsized significance and notoriety.[4]

Presbyterians responded with fierce denunciations of the newfound toleration, and in 1648 Parliament passed a law against blasphemy that required the death penalty for anyone who denied the Trinity. By then, however, the Presbyterians had lost control of English politics to the Independents and radicals that predominated within the New Model Army. Cromwell favored liberty of conscience for at least most Protestants, and while he decried disunity and certain heresies, the net result was an unprecedented religious toleration. In 1650, Parliament eliminated the requirement that individuals attend their parish churches. In the mid-1650s, Cromwell permitted several hundred Jews to settle in England, which had expelled its Jewish population in 1290. In England, a largely puritan revolution had ushered in substantially more religious liberty than was present in most parts of New England.[5]

Back in the mid-1620s, Bradford had reassured the colony's English investors that New Plymouth punished individuals who did not observe the Sabbath and attend worship. However, especially as settlers formed new townships and dispersed into outlying areas, the colony's magistrates did not attempt to enforce religious observance. As long as men and women did not organize their own religious meetings, spout blasphemy, or slander ministers, they could remain quietly indifferent to the colony's churches. Many settlers were indifferent, and some—following the lead of dissenters such as Samuel Gorton and William Vassall—were openly critical of the colony's churches and ministers. In the early 1650s, New Plymouth's leaders attempted to put an end to this relative laxity. In 1650, the General Court mandated a ten-shilling fine for anyone who vilified the colony's churches, ministers, or sacraments. The next year, the court ordered that anyone who skipped church pay a ten-shilling fine or be publicly whipped.[6]

The new laws were out of step with developments in England, and attempts to enforce them sparked discontent and resistance. This was most evident in the Cape Cod town of Sandwich. In October 1651, a grand jury cited Richard Kerby and a dozen other Sandwich residents for not coming to worship. Kerby and Ralph Allen Sr. did more than skip church. They also made "deriding, vild [vile] speeches . . . concerning God's word and ordinances." Presumably they both said a great deal, as the court gave them a few months to pay five pounds or suffer a whipping. Sandwich's minister, William Leverich, complained that many townspeople were "transported with their . . . fancies, to the rejecting of all churches and ordinances." Leverich explained that Satan sought to "undermine all religion, and introduce all atheism and profaneness." Richard Kerby was not an atheist, but he objected to laws that forced him to attend a church he now rejected.[7]

It wasn't just Sandwich. The 1651 grand jury identified transgressions in many towns. Men and women were cited for fraternizing at night and for dancing with each other. The jury cited several individuals for selling strong drink without a license. Much of the misbehavior pertained to religious observance, however. As other residents of the town of Plymouth gathered for worship, Elizabeth Eddy pointedly wrung out and hung out her laundry. Arthur Howland, brother of *Mayflower* passenger John Howland, stopped attending Marshfield's church. In Duxbury, Nathaniel Bassett and Joseph Pryor came to church but disturbed worship. They were given the option of a twenty-shilling fine or being bound to a post with "a paper on their heads on which their capital crime shall be written." The records do not reveal which punishment they chose. The same court that punished Kerby, Allen, Bassett, and Pryor declared a general day of thanksgiving, directing settlers to thank God for Oliver Cromwell's recent victories in Scotland. The religious malcontents of Plymouth Colony surely wondered why they did not enjoy the same liberty of conscience as men and women back in England.[8]

Sandwich remained an epicenter of religious disaffection. In 1655, Ralph Allen, his brother George, and Peter Gaunt—all Sandwich residents previously cited for not attending church—were brought before the General Court for absenting themselves from worship. Asked for an explanation, Gaunt volunteered his opinion that there was "no public visible worship now in the world." In other words, there was no legitimate church or worship for him to attend. Meanwhile, Richard Kerby's eighteen-year-old daughter, Sarah, made dissent a family tradition when she made "suspicious speeches" against a preacher and a magistrate. The court sentenced her to a severe whipping but did not carry it out, hoping that a warning would improve her behavior. The views of the Kerbys and the Allens resembled those of English women and men known as Seekers. These individuals believed that all churches were corrupt; they waited for new revelation or apostles to establish a true church to which they could belong.[9]

The ideal across puritan New England was that each town should have a single, covenanted church with a godly, learned minister. By the mid-1650s, the reality in Plymouth Colony fell far short of this ideal. Several ministers left for opportunities elsewhere, and many communities lacked the money or motivation to build meeting-houses and pay educated clergymen to preach in them. In 1656, the Bay Colony's magistrates complained to the United Colonies commissioners that New Plymouth had failed to secure ministers for its towns. The next year, Plymouth's General Court responded to the chastisement by requiring all townspeople to support orthodox ministers. If a town failed to tax its residents, the magistrates would take it upon themselves to do so. Fourteen residents of Sandwich pledged a paltry fifteen pounds toward the yearly support of a minister, no more than half of what it would take to attract a qualified candidate. The Allens and Kerbys did not give a single shilling. By then, they and others in Sandwich had opened themselves to a new light.[10]

In the spring of 1652, George Fox—the most famous apostle of that light—crossed the River Trent into the town of Gainsborough, where the separatist minister John Smyth had gathered a congregation nearly five decades earlier. One of Fox's followers had already preached in the Gainsborough marketplace. By the time Fox showed up, the town was in an uproar. When Fox took shelter in a sympathetic man's home, people rushed in after him. A man accused Fox of having claimed to be Christ. At that, the people were ready to tear him to pieces. Fox now climbed onto a table and explained himself: "That Christ was in them, except they were reprobates, and it was the eternal power of Christ, and Christ that spoke in me that time to them." The distinction between the historical Jesus, the eternal Christ, and Fox and his followers was not always clear, but his words quieted the mob.[11]

George Fox was the son of a puritan weaver in the English Midlands. He rejected the Presbyterian rigidity of his parish minister, but years of depression and uncertainty followed. Then Fox heard a voice: "There is one, even Christ Jesus, who can speak to your condition." After the Spirit opened him to the "light of Jesus Christ," Fox wandered around the Midlands and the northern counties of England, urging people to experience the same light for themselves. Hundreds of women and men were convinced by his message.[12]

At their meetings, they sometimes sat in silence for hours, but the "power of the Lord" also led to prophesying, exhilaration, and ecstasy. For their trembling and shaking as God's power coursed through their bodies, critics named them Quakers. Fox and his followers referred to themselves as the "Children of Light," the "People of God," and the "Friends of the Truth." By 1655, Friends were holding well-attended meetings in London, Bristol, and other major English cities. Within another five years, there were an estimated forty thousand to sixty thousand Quakers in England. There were more Friends than Baptists.[13]

Much of what the Quakers taught and did had precedents, not only within the religious underground of Familism and antinomianism, but also among separatists, Baptists, and other puritans. As had many sorts of Protestants, so Friends called on individuals "to be delivered from the bondage of corruption into the liberty of the sons of God." The Quakers attracted converts who shared the anti-legalism and anti-ceremonialism that were part of the warp and woof of both separatism and mainstream puritanism, but they articulated a still more radical version of Christian liberty. All of these groups worried that outward forms of religious practice walled off the Spirit and kept individuals from communion with Christ. Rather than wanting to purify the sacraments, though, Friends dispensed with them entirely. In addition to rejecting prayer books and prepared sermons, the Quakers—somewhat like the separatist turned Baptist John Smyth—also did away with psalm singing in favor of "singing with the Spirit." Moreover, what Fox and his missionaries taught undercut key Protestant doctrines about salvation, the Trinity, the Bible, and male religious leadership. Salvation was readily available, the Spirit was more important than the letter of the Bible, the light of Christ within mattered more than the historical person of Jesus, and women could preach and prophesy.[14]

Theology was not the main flash point, however. The Quakers were social revolutionaries who denounced all forms of hierarchy. They believed in the equality of men—and women, to an extent—regardless of class, rank, and title. For instance, etiquette required individuals to use the formal "you" when addressing their superiors. In seventeenth-century English, "thou" was a more familiar form of address. English translations of the Bible used the familiar "thee," "thou," and "thy" when referring to God. The Geneva and the Authorized (King James) translations rendered part of the Lord's Prayer as "hallowed be *thy* name." The Quakers reasoned that if they referred to God as thee and thou, they could hardly address mere mortals as "you." Also offensive to magistrates, judges, and many gentlemen was the refusal of Quakers to remove their hats in the presence of their superiors. Those superiors regarded Quakers as insolent and subversive for this sort of behavior, which resembled that of the Ranters and the Diggers, other radical groups that had appeared in the late 1640s.

The Friends behaved in other ways calculated to provoke maximum hostility. They went into Protestant churches and denounced their worship. They called ministers "hireling priests" and lay Protestants "professors," alleging that they assumed the veneer of Christianity without godliness or spiritual power. They castigated the sinfulness of towns and townspeople in the marketplace. They ignored the Sabbath. They urged people not to pay tithes, often a welcome message among common people who needed every penny they earned. The Friends also refused to swear oaths, a stance inherited from some separatists and Baptists. "Swear not at all," Jesus had commanded, "but let your communication be, Yea, yea; Nay, nay" (Matthew 5:34, 37). The issue of oaths created endless legal problems for the Friends.[15]

Some Quakers made themselves even more conspicuous and offensive. On occasion, the Lord led the Children of Light to perform provocative "signs." In October 1656, as men and women sang hosannas in the midst of a drenching rain, James Nayler—second in influence only to Fox among the early Friends—rode into Bristol mounted on a horse or donkey in an apparent imitation of Jesus's royal entrance into Jerusalem. Other Friends made public displays of penance, wearing white sheets and carrying candles. A few Quakers walked naked through English towns and cities, following what they said was a divine commandment to imitate the prophet Isaiah, who had gone barefoot and without clothes for three whole years.[16]

Outraged ministers, magistrates, and ordinary people accused Quakers of blasphemy, heresy, immorality, witchcraft, and sedition. After one Friend berated a crowd of people about their profaneness, they beat him and his wife and stoned them out of town. Mobs pulled Friends' hair, rubbed excrement on their faces, and ransacked their meetinghouses. Believing that Nayler through his Bristol sign claimed to be Jesus Christ, Parliament convicted him of "horrid blasphemy." Nayler then imitated Christ in his suffering. He was mocked, scourged, branded with a "B" on his forehead, and had his tongue bored through with a red-hot iron. There was more religious toleration during the Interregnum (the years without a king, from 1649 to 1660) than had been the case under the Tudor and Stuart monarchs, but the Quakers transgressed its bounds by a wide margin.

Many Friends welcomed imprisonment and other forms of persecution, as such misfortunes confirmed their union with Christ and participation in his passion. They were soldiers in the "Lamb's War" predicted by the Book of Revelation, willing and sometimes eager to suffer for the savior they loved. They did not fight back, but they would not surrender. If beaten and banished, they would come back for more.[17]

In July 1656, Ann Austin and Mary Fisher came from Barbados to Boston and became New England's first Quaker missionaries and prisoners. Boston's magistrates burned some of their books, imprisoned them, and ordered women to search them for signs of witchcraft. According to a Quaker account, their persecutors "stripped them stark naked, not missing head nor feet, searching betwixt their toes, and amongst their hair, tewing [pulling] and abusing their bodies more than modesty can mention." Although they found no physical clues that Austin and Fisher had made a compact with Satan, the magistrates sent the two missionaries back to Barbados. The magistrates hoped that by promptly banishing Quaker missionaries, they would prevent what they understood as a dangerous contagion from gaining a foothold in their colony. A second, larger group of missionaries arrived two days after Austin and Fisher's departure. The Massachusetts General Court jailed the new arrivals until they could find a way to transport them out of the colony.[18]

New England's magistrates, however, discovered that they could not insulate their colonies from Quaker teachings. Nicholas Upshall, a sixty-year-old Boston innkeeper, had made contact with Austin and Fisher during their brief stay in the city. Like the Kerbys in Sandwich, Upshall was a Seeker who had been disaffected from Boston's church for many years. In 1651, the congregation had excommunicated him after he "denie[d] all the ordinances of Christ in the church." Now Upshall wanted to talk with missionaries who denounced the same ordinances. When he learned of Austin and Fisher's imprisonment, he paid the jailer for their board and presumably found a way to converse with them. When the Massachusetts General Court passed an anti-Quaker act, Upshall spoke out against it. The court banished him too.[19]

Upshall took refuge not in Rhode Island, but in Sandwich. That winter, Henry Fell—a Quaker missionary in Barbados—reported that "in the jurisdiction of Plymouth patent . . . there is a people not so rigid as the other at Boston, and great desires among them after the truth." According to a Quaker publication, the colony's magistrates allowed the refugee innkeeper to stay through the winter over the opposition of Governor Bradford.[20]

Plymouth's leaders soon became less hospitable. They learned that Upshall and others were holding meetings at the home of William Allen, during which those in attendance "inveigh[ed] against ministers and magistrates." Richard Kerby and his family came to the meetings, and Sarah Kerby and her older sister Jane Launder marched into Sandwich's poorly attended church and disturbed the course of Sunday worship. The court heard a complaint that they were "opposing and abusing the speaker," who was probably Richard Bourne, an inhabitant of the town, lay preacher, and missionary to the Wampanoag community at nearby Mashpee. If the sisters proceeded as was customary among the Friends, they endured Bourne's sermon, then stood up and denounced the church, its rituals, and its preacher as worthless and Antichristian. Perhaps they called Bourne a "hireling priest," a "painted beast," or a "deluder of the people." Two years earlier, the court had spared Sarah Kerby a whipping with the hope that she would improve her behavior. This time around, the court let Jane Launder off with a similar warning, but it ordered Sarah Kerby whipped.[21]

Now less inclined toward leniency, New Plymouth's magistrates ordered Upshall to leave the colony. He went to Rhode Island, which Friends termed the "habitation of the hunted-Christ." (Other New Englanders called it the "Island of Errors.") During his brief stay in Sandwich, however, Upshall had convinced others to follow the same principles he had embraced.[22]

One of those convinced—Quakers preferred that term to *converted*—was Edward Perry, who had emigrated from Devon around 1650. Like many other individuals in Sandwich, Perry had already shown signs of disaffection from the colony's political and religious establishment. In 1654, the General Court fined him five pounds because he refused to "have his marriage ratified" before a magistrate. Perry later wrote that despite his faithful attendance at Sandwich's church, he was "not redeemed out of Satan's power, nor come one step nearer unto God." It was not enough for him to know that Christ had died for his sins sixteen centuries ago. He wanted Christ to come to him in the here and now. Searching for salvation, Perry listened to sermons in Plymouth, Scituate, Weymouth, and Boston, but every church left him despondent. He stopped going to worship. When Quaker missionaries arrived in Sandwich, they told him about "Christ Jesus the light within the heart and conscience." Finally, he wrote, God set his soul "at liberty from the power of sin and Satan." He urged his neighbors and others who would listen to cast off their "unprofitable teachers" and search inside themselves for the same light of Christ, which would lead them to the same liberty. Only a small minority of Plymouth's settlers embraced that light, but the Friends gained a foothold in Sandwich and adherents in several other towns.[23]

The convincement of Plymouth's first Friends coincided with a time of political transition in the colony. Myles Standish died in 1656 after what Nathaniel Morton described as "much dolorous pain" caused by kidney or urinary stones.[24] A greater blow came the next year with the May 1657 death of William Bradford, who had served as governor for all but five of the colony's first thirty-six years and had never faced any serious challenges to his leadership.

Bradford's history reveals next to nothing about his family and other private affairs. We do not know anything about his relationships with his wives or his four children. Plymouth's court records document his landholdings, and the inventory of his estate upon his death reveals his accumulation of fine furniture, pewter dishes and silver spoons, well-appointed clothing (a "suit with silver buttons"), and a large library.[25] It is through Bradford's books and writings that we learn about some of the things that animated him. He spent a good portion of his final years studying Hebrew, writing poetry whose banality contrasts with the rich allusiveness of his prose history, and brooding about threats to New England's settlements.

The threats were everywhere. Despite the long peace between Pilgrims and the Wampanoags, Bradford feared that Indians armed with English-made guns would attack colonial settlements, rape English women, and torture other inhabitants before killing them. The greatest danger was within, however. Although graced with a "prudent magistracy" and true churches, New England had become a "mixed multitude," with many settlers motivated by greed rather than by godliness. In verse, Bradford lamented that "whimsy errors have now got such head / And under notion of conscience, do spread." He warned that if New Englanders followed the example of the ancient Israelites and degenerated from their pure foundations, God would sorely chastise them.[26]

Plymouth's governor saw many signs of degeneration. Bradford lamented that Plymouth Colony had developed in ways antithetical to his principles. He cared about the unity of the congregation he had helped transplant from Leiden, and he mourned when its members dispersed to new townships. In the mid-1640s, Plymouth's residents contemplated moving across Cape Cod Bay in order to escape "the straitness and barrenness" of their immediate environment. In the end, the larger portion decided to stay, but several families relocated to what became the town of Eastham. In 1646, the Bay Colony's John Winthrop reported that Plymouth was "now almost deserted." An embittered Bradford compared Plymouth's church to "an ancient mother, grown old, and forsaken of her children . . . like a widow left only to trust in God." In a marginal note in his history, he explained that Satan had "untwiste[d] these sacred bonds and ties" that had bound together the Pilgrims. Bradford added that it was part of his old-age "misery" that he could no longer enjoy "the sweet communion" present in earlier years.[27]

Despite his laments, Bradford's cup did not overflow with bitterness. He sustained his spirit in part by immersing himself in the original languages of the Bible. While Bradford developed some familiarity with Greek, he was more captivated by Hebrew, an interest he shared with other prominent separatists such as John Smyth and Henry Ainsworth. The governor copied Hebrew words, phrases, and biblical verses into the covers and spare pages of his books. "Though I am grown aged," he explained above one such set of exercises, "yet I have had a longing desire, to see with my own eyes, something of that most ancient language, and holy tongue, in which the law and oracles of God were writ." Hebrew brought Plymouth's governor to a more immediate encounter with "the holy text," with its ancient authors, and with God. Bradford persisted with his studies for his "own content[ment]."[28]

Given Plymouth's lack of renowned and well-published ministers, its lack of a college such as Harvard, and its commercial inferi-

Though I am growne aged, yet I haue had a longing desire, to see with my owne eyes, somthing of that most ancient language, and holy tongue, in which the Law and oracles of god were write; and in which god, and angels spake to the holy patriarks of old time; and what names were giuen to things, from the creation. And though I cañot attaine to much herein, yet I am refresh= ed, to haue seen some glimpse hereof; (as moyses saw the land of ca= nan afarr of) my aime and desire is, to see how the words, and phrases lye in the holy texte; and to discerne somewhat of the same, for my owne contente.

William Bradford, "Of plimoth plantation."
(Courtesy of Massachusetts State Library.)

ority to Boston, many historians have described Plymouth Colony as an insignificant backwater. Bradford himself contributed to such views with his description of Plymouth's abandonment and desolation. Once the Pilgrims settled at Patuxet, Bradford never traveled farther from his New England home than Boston and the southeastern shores of Cape Cod. Unlike Edward Winslow, Timothy Hatherly, and Isaac Allerton, he never returned across the Atlantic.

Bradford's outlook, though, was not provincial, either in economic or intellectual terms.[29] Along with Winslow, Hatherly, Thomas Willett, and many others, he participated in transatlantic markets that included New England, New Amsterdam, Europe, and the West Indies. Like many other Plymouth Colony leaders, Bradford maintained a large library, evidence of his ongoing engagement with the larger world of Reformed Protestantism. The hundred or so books inventoried in Bradford's estate include an English translation of Martin Luther's commentary on Galatians, in which the German reformer proclaims Christian liberty from the wrath of God, the power of the devil, and the tyranny of the pope; the works of theologians such as John Calvin and Peter Martyr Vermigli; broadly popular English puritan titles such as John Dod's *Exposition of the Ten Commandments* and the works of William Perkins; several books of his old pastor John Robinson alongside books by the separatists Henry Ainsworth, Henry Barrow, and John Greenwood; and John Cotton's *Bloudy Tenant*, in which Boston's minister maintained that it would be better for magistrates to banish or even execute men and women than to permit "the flock of Christ to be seduced and destroyed by . . . heretical wickedness." Bradford had books in Dutch, and he had English books printed in Amsterdam. William Brewster may have published one or two of the books in Bradford's library. Plymouth Colony's longtime governor understood his plantation's significance within the much broader context of Reformed Protestantism.[30]

When Bradford prepared his will, he asked his friends to pay particular attention to his "little book with a black cover" containing "sundry useful verses," most of which were Bradford's own poems. Nathaniel Morton printed one of Bradford's better efforts in his *New-Englands Memorial*:

> In wilderness he did me guide
> And in strange lands for me provide
> In fears and wants, through weal and woe
> As pilgrim passed I to and fro.

Bradford observed that as "a man of sorrows" (the Book of Isaiah's description of the suffering servant, whom Christians interpreted as Jesus Christ) he had known "wars, wants, peace, plenty." Old age had overtaken him, and he looked forward to the "happy change," the death that would bring him into the presence of Christ.[31]

For New Plymouth, Bradford's death marked the end of an era but was not a rupture with the colony's original principles. Bradford was succeeded as governor by Thomas Prence, the son of a Gloucestershire carriage maker who came to New Plymouth in 1621 aboard the *Fortune*. Prence quickly advanced himself. He married Patience Brewster in 1624, became one of the Undertakers, and served two terms as governor in the 1630s. He moved to Duxbury, then to

Eastham. In the early eighteenth century, Josiah Cotton praised Prence as a "terror to evil doers" (Romans 13:3)—in other words, a biblical magistrate. Prence had supported Bradford's moves against religious dissenters in New Plymouth, and he resolved to take action against the Quakers when they appeared in the colony.[32]

In addition to Prence, *Mayflower* passenger John Alden remained a magistrate, as did Scituate's Timothy Hatherly and James Cudworth. Josiah Winslow and William Bradford Jr. also served among the assistants. So too did Thomas Willett, who belonged to the Leiden congregation in the 1620s and had emigrated on a different *Mayflower* in 1630. Despite the humiliation he endured at the hands of the French at Plymouth's Kennebec trading outpost, Willett succeeded Myles Standish as the colony's military captain in 1648 and gained election as a magistrate beginning in 1651. Like Isaac Allerton, with whom he sometimes did business, Willett spent considerable time in New Amsterdam. He forged close relationships with Willem Kieft and Petrus Stuyvesant and served as a liaison during times of tension between the English and Dutch. Willett grew rich trading in foodstuffs, tobacco, and slaves, and he accumulated land in both New Plymouth and New Amsterdam. Through the 1650s, Willett's views on religious toleration resembled those of Bradford, Prence, and Stuyvesant, all of whom favored firm measures to uphold their established Reformed churches.[33]

For the several years after the arrival of the first Quaker missionaries in 1656, New Plymouth's leaders found themselves consumed by what most of them regarded as a grave crisis. The events in Sandwich prompted Plymouth's General Court to pass a series of anti-Quaker measures. Any person who attended one of the Quakers' "silent meetings" faced a fine of ten shillings and those who hosted such gatherings faced stiffer fines. If inhabitants of the colony became aware of any Quakers in their midst, they had to inform the authorities or else face punishment themselves. When constables apprehended Quaker missionaries, they were to bring them before a magistrate, who would order them imprisoned without access to visitors and with only such food as the court permitted. Jailed Quakers would remain confined until they paid for the costs of their imprisonment and their transportation out of the colony. The General Court made it illegal to be a Quaker, to befriend a Quaker, or even to ignore a Quaker. The missionaries treated the laws like an open invitation.[34]

As Plymouth's court passed its first explicitly anti-Quaker laws, eleven missionaries set sail from England on the *Woodhouse*. In August 1657, the vessel reached New Amsterdam, where its owner, Robert Fowler, refused to remove his hat when summoned to a meeting with Director General Stuyvesant. Meanwhile, two of the missionaries, Mary Wetherhead and Dorothy Waugh, disembarked. According to the account of New Amsterdam's Dutch Reformed clergy, they "began to quake, putting their fury at work, preaching and calling out in the streets that the last day was near." One of the townspeople who came to see the commotion misunderstood the message and cried out, "Fire!" Wetherhead and Waugh continued to preach on their way to jail. Stuyvesant then banished them.[35]

Robert Hodgson, another of the *Woodhouse* missionaries, held meetings in Hempstead (Heemstede) on Long Island. According to his own account, an English magistrate had him arrested and tied to a cart, which hauled him through the woods at night to New Amsterdam. There, the Dutch authorities forcibly removed Hodgson's hat in court. Stuyvesant sentenced him to a fine of six hundred guilders or two years' work "at the wheelbarrow with the Negroes." Hodgson refused to work or pay the fine. Now the violence began. After Hodgson stood for several days chained to a wheelbarrow, Stuyvesant ordered him stripped to the waist with a log tied to his feet. Hodgson related that "the governor then set a strong Negor [Negro] with rods, who laid many stripes upon him both backward and forward, wherewith he cut his flesh very much, and drew much blood upon him; then was he loosed and put into the dungeon, too bad a place for swine, being a stinking hole and full of vermin, not suffering any to come and wash his stripes." The punishment was repeated two days later. Eventually, Hodgson agreed to work. Soon freed by Stuyvesant, he took refuge in Rhode Island.[36]

Plymouth's merchant, magistrate, and militia captain Thomas Willett was in New Amsterdam during Hodgson's imprisonment. In publications designed to sway English opinion against New England's rulers, the Quakers blamed Willett for "incensing the Dutch governor with several false reports of them that are called Quakers."

While Willett probably approved of Stuyvesant's treatment of Hodgson, New Netherland's director general would have acted as he did without the Plymouth magistrate's encouragement. In the fall of 1657, New Netherland's council issued a series of anti-Quaker laws modeled on those enacted by New England's puritan colonies. The Quakers also held Willett responsible for the new measures.[37]

English settlers at Flushing (Vlissingen) sent a remonstrance against the laws to the council. The petitioners maintained that no magistrate was in a position to discern "who is true and who is false." Therefore, all people should enjoy "outward liberty" irrespective of religion. The petitioners noted that the Dutch states granted peace and liberty even to Jews and Muslims. (Stuyvesant had grudgingly obeyed a West India Company directive to allow a group of Jews from Dutch Brazil to take refuge in New Netherland, but he did his best to discourage their continued presence.) Why should New Netherland not welcome Baptists and Quakers? Although the Flushing Remonstrance eventually gained fame as an early American argument for religious liberty, it did not persuade Petrus Stuyvesant. The director general arrested the principle petitioners.[38]

Two other *Woodhouse* missionaries, Christopher Holder and John Copeland, were among those who had been expelled from Boston the previous year. This time, they began their work in Rhode Island, then went to Martha's Vineyard. When they refused to leave the island, its governor arranged for the Wampanoags to transport the pair to Cape Cod by canoe. Holder and Copeland visited Sandwich and then went to Plymouth. Magistrates John Alden and Thomas Southworth ordered them to leave the colony, but the missionaries responded that the Lord had commanded them to return to Sandwich. A constable took them six miles toward Rhode Island, but when he left them, they headed for Sandwich anyway. When they were arrested again, the next escort took them all the way to Rhode Island.

Another *Woodhouse* passenger became New Plymouth's most notorious Quaker missionary. Little is known of Humphrey Norton's life before Quaker records locate him in Durham, Essex, and London in 1655. The next year, Norton penned a letter to the imprisoned George Fox, offering himself to Oliver Cromwell "body for body" if the Protector would grant Fox his freedom. Cromwell reportedly was moved by Norton's spirit of sacrifice but turned down what he considered an unlawful deal. Norton was also bold in ways less helpful to the movement. He accused Quaker organizer Margaret Fell, a close ally of Fox's, of permitting too much speech, prayer, singing, and frivolity at meetings. After a brief mission to Ireland, Norton again stirred dissension within the movement. "Humphrey Norton run out [apostatized]," recorded Fox, "and drew a company after him into his imaginations and self-righteousness and some of them came in again and he came to meetings again." Norton hindered Fox's efforts to impose a measure of order on his fractious movement.[39]

Headstrong spirits were well suited for the mission field, however. When Copeland and Holder came back to Rhode Island with reports of both convincements and persecution, Norton immediately headed east to confront Plymouth's leaders. As did other Friends upon their arrests, Norton complained that the magistrates deprived him of the liberties due any Englishman, such as the right to examine the laws he was charged with violating and the right to due process. "I require of you a public examination," Norton recalled declaring to Thomas Prence, "and if found guilty, [to be] publicly punished, if not, cleared." According to Norton, Prence entirely ignored the legal arguments and banished him. Plymouth's secretary, though, recorded the banishment as the General Court's decision.[40]

Escorted most of the way to Providence, Norton next went to an English settlement on Long Island, where he strolled into a meetinghouse on Sunday and denounced its minister. He was arrested and brought to New Haven, whose magistrates proved much harsher than their Plymouth counterparts. They kept Norton in shackles for three weeks, then charged him with heresy and disturbing the peace. Norton gladly provided evidence against himself by writing papers disparaging ministers, magistrates, and sacraments. The New Haven town records and Norton's own account roughly corroborate each other, though Norton left out the extent to which he made himself obnoxious. Much as separatists and other radical puritans had argued against their opponents in England, Norton alleged that New England's leaders were "all of that cursed stock the Pope, and are guided by the spirit of witchcraft and idolatry." He called the ministers "epicures and belly-gods" and likened the mag-

W. M. Cary, Norton's Punishment, *from William Cullen Bryant and Sydney Howard Gay,* A Popular History of the United States, *vol. 2 (1878).*

istrates to Judas and Cain. They in turn accused him of claiming sinless perfection and promoting anarchy "as if every man should be left to his liberty to do what he would." In court, Norton interrupted anyone speaking against him but refused to say anything when questioned. The next time Norton began his courtroom denunciations, the authorities silenced him by binding "a great iron key" over his mouth. The court then fined Norton ten pounds and ordered him whipped, branded on his writing hand with an "H" for heresy, and banished. After enduring his physical punishments, Norton refused to pay the fine. At that point, a Dutch baker from New Amsterdam intervened. He offered the magistrates two-thirds of what they had assessed Norton, who was then free to return to Rhode Island.[41]

In New Plymouth, the banishment of missionaries and the punishment of settlers who welcomed them failed to put an end to

Quaker meetings. Instead, the anti-Quaker measures revived and deepened divisions among the magistrates themselves. In March 1658, a number of Scituate settlers informed the General Court that magistrate and militia captain James Cudworth had invited the Quakers to hold meetings in his home. Cudworth later explained that he welcomed Quakers because he thought it better to become acquainted with their teachings rather "than with the blind world to censure, condemn, rail, and revile them." The Quakers did not convince Cudworth of their principles, but he was convinced they did not deserve persecution. Cudworth's fellow magistrates stripped him of his captainship, and the colony's freemen did not reelect him as a magistrate in the spring. As usual, the freemen reelected Scituate's Timothy Hatherly as one of the assistants, but he refused to take his customary office in protest against the colony's treatment of the Quakers. The divisions revealed by William Vassall's proposal for religious toleration, apparently dormant for a dozen years, had reemerged.[42]

Despite the opposition from Cudworth and Hatherly, Plymouth Colony further strengthened its anti-Quaker laws. In imitation of English vagrancy laws used to prosecute Quakers, the General Court voted to establish a workhouse for Quaker missionaries, other vagrants, idle persons, and rebellious children and servants, so that imprisoned miscreants would earn their own bread. The court also declared that Quakers could not become freemen, and that freemen who became Quakers would lose that status. Those living in the colony who had not yet taken an oath of fidelity had to do so. If they refused, they could either leave the colony or pay a stiff fine. Furthermore, anyone who had not taken the oath could not participate in local elections or hold any political offices. After passing the new laws, the court summoned Richard Kerby, several members of the Allen family, and other Sandwich men and ordered them to take the oath. The court fined them when they refused to do so.[43]

As Plymouth's political unity frayed, Humphrey Norton returned, this time in the company of fellow missionary John Rous. Norton and Rous came prepared for verbal combat and physical suffering. They got their words in and got what they expected in return.

Norton was the chief combatant. Brought before the General Court on June 1, 1658, he did his utmost to fan the flames of religious and political tension. "Thou liest," he repeatedly told Governor Prence. "Thomas," he added, "thou art a malicious man." Norton had a large stock of such insults, and Prence was one of his favorite targets. In a book published the next year, he characterized Plymouth's governor as "a mad dog, ready to bite at every one that crosseth his way."[44]

The magistrates were unsure how to proceed. They had already banished Norton once, and they could see the H that New Haven's magistrates had burned into his hand. Prence knew that New Plymouth could whip, fine, and banish Norton, and he would keep coming back. If they jailed him, he would refuse to pay the fees that typically accompanied imprisonment. Why should the colony's orthodox settlers pay to feed Norton? If they sentenced him to forced labor, he would refuse to perform it. How could they get rid of him?

Prence contemplated harsher forms of punishment. He obtained a deposition from Christopher Winter, who was not exactly an upstanding member of the community. Scituate's church had once excommunicated Winter for his marriage to a "woman of scandalous carriage," and he later escaped conviction on charges of incest only because his daughter refused to identify him as her infant's father. Nevertheless, Plymouth's leaders asked Winter to converse with Norton and make a record of the imprisoned Quaker's teachings. Winter's deposition began with Norton's assertion that the scriptures "were not for the enlightening of man . . . for he [Norton] said that he had the true light in him and he never had any from the Scriptures." According to Winter, Norton also maintained that "Christ enlightened every man that came into the world and . . . that he that obeyed this light it would save him." In a written response, Norton called Winter a liar but did not back away from his teachings about Christ's light, the Bible, and human salvation.[45]

Plymouth's capital crimes were treason or rebellion, murder, witchcraft or a compact with Satan, the burning of ships or houses, sodomy, rape, and bestiality. In 1642, the colony executed a servant named Thomas Granger, who confessed to sexual intercourse with a variety of animals. Although Plymouth's earliest legal code made adultery punishable by death, a 1658 law decreed instead that adulterers would receive two whippings and wear the letters "AD" sewn on their clothes. Heresy and blasphemy were not capital crimes. In

1655, however, the colony had mandated "corporal punishment" for any who would "deny the Scriptures to be a rule of life," leaving the exact penalty to the magistrate's discretion "so as it shall not extent to life or limb." The court could have used Winter's deposition to convict Norton on this basis, and Prence could have used his discretion to order a more severe whipping or the cropping of Norton's ears. After deputizing men to further investigate Norton's opinions, however, Prence dropped the possibility of a heresy trial.[46]

Brought back into court, Norton resumed his insults. "Thou art like a scolding woman," he chided Prence. Finally, the court demanded that Norton and Rous take an oath of fidelity to the state of England. They refused, saying they would not swear any oath. For that, the court ordered them to be whipped and imprisoned until they paid the marshal's fees. They refused to pay. The magistrates finally gave up and sent them back to Rhode Island.[47]

From there, Norton posted two letters that New Plymouth's secretary termed "railing papers." Norton railed with relish. He arraigned Prence for having "defrauded" the poor by taking their money and goods to satisfy unjust fines. For his sins, the governor would experience "anguish and pain . . . like gnawing worms lodging betwixt [his] heart and liver." Norton also had a special message for John Alden, who apparently had wavered over his colony's treatment of Quakers. He had perceived "a tenderness" in Alden, but the longtime magistrate had now made himself a "packhorse to Thomas Prence" and a "self-conceited fool." Norton encouraged Alden to follow Timothy Hatherly's example, speak for himself, and resign his post, but Alden supported Prence and retained his office.[48]

As they healed from their Plymouth whippings, Norton and Rous concluded that Jesus wanted them in Boston. They reached the town on a lecture day, a weekday worship service attended by ministers from other churches. Norton and Rous waited through the sermon of Boston's John Norton, whom they termed a "painted sepulcher." Then the Quaker Norton stood up and asserted that Boston's church was an "abomination." Norton was arrested on the spot and charged with blasphemy. In court, he claimed the liberty to appeal to England. Governor John Endecott insisted that Norton could not appeal. Boston's magistrates decided that the Quaker prisoners would be whipped twice a week, with the number of stripes increasing by three each time. Rous, Norton, and two other men received one such punishment, thrashed, they reported, "as a cruel man would beat his horse." The magistrates then gave up and released them.[49]

Christopher Holder and John Copeland came to Boston on the heels of Norton and Rous. Unlike the latter pair, Holder and Copeland previously had been banished from the Bay Colony. In September 1657, the Massachusetts General Court had strengthened its anti-Quaker laws by mandating that a banished male Quaker who returned would have one ear "cut off." If he returned again, he would lose another ear. Banished women would be "severely whipped" the first two times they returned. Those who returned a third time, male or female, would "have their tongues bored through with a hot iron." When John Rous heard that Copeland and Holder were in prison, he returned to Boston and was promptly arrested again. The magistrates sentenced the three prisoners to lose their right ears and scoffed at their demand to appeal to Oliver Cromwell. Boston's executioner performed the grisly task.[50]

Fortunately for their welfare, the Lord now directed Rous and Norton to return to England, where they published books with a simple message. England's government should rescue "freeborn English people" from cruel, bloody, and deceitful New England magistrates. Rous and Norton asserted that those leaders denied Friends not only liberty of conscience but also due process and other liberties guaranteed to all Englishmen. In their books, the Quakers included a letter from Scituate's James Cudworth, who had lost his civil offices because he dissented from New Plymouth's anti-Quaker laws and punishments. Cudworth stated that although he "was no Quaker," he would also "be no persecutor." Plymouth had whipped and beggared Quakers, and Massachusetts had done even worse. "We expect that we must do the like," Cudworth predicted, "we must dance after their pipe; now Plymouth-saddle is upon the Bay-horse." Cudworth alluded to the fact that England had scrapped mandatory parish church attendance and had extended liberty of conscience to a wide array of Protestant sects. By contrast, Plymouth had "a state religion . . . a state-minister, and a state-way of maintenance." Plymouth was like England under Charles and Laud, not like England under Cromwell. When the court learned of Cudworth's letter, it imposed a stiff fine and deprived him of his freeman rights.[51]

In September 1658, the United Colonies confederation held its annual meeting, this year in Boston. Noting that all punishments to this point had not deterred the Quakers, the commissioners encouraged general courts to execute banished Quakers who returned and refused to recant. Thomas Prence and Josiah Winslow were New Plymouth's representatives to the United Colonies meeting in 1658; they both signed the document. The Massachusetts General Court passed the proposed law the next month. In 1659, the Bay Colony sentenced three returned Quakers to hang. The condemned included Mary Dyer, whose "monstrous birth" had captivated John Winthrop and William Bradford two decades earlier. After following the Hutchinsons to Rhode Island, the Dyers had eventually returned to England, where Mary Dyer became convinced. In October 1659, Bay Colony authorities executed William Robinson and Marmaduke Stevenson but granted Dyer a reprieve on the scaffold.[52]

Contrary to Cudworth's prediction, New Plymouth did not execute or crop the ears of Quakers. Following her gallows reprieve, Mary Dyer came to Plymouth in the company of Sandwich inhabitant Thomas Greenfield. The court imprisoned the pair and fined Greenfield to pay for Dyer's imprisonment and transportation back to Rhode Island. Choosing martyrdom, Dyer returned to Boston again the following spring and was hanged.[53]

When Mary Dyer passed through Plymouth, two other Quaker missionaries were languishing in its jail. William Leddra and his fellow missionary Peter Peirson had been arrested in June 1659 after visiting meetings in Sandwich. In October, the magistrates asked the pair to pay their fines, leave the colony, and not return. Leddra and Peirson informed their persecutors that they would not submit to unjust laws. Two months later, the magistrates were ready to forget about the fines. They just wanted the missionaries gone. No rush, they assured the pair. They could take a few days, depending on the weather. They simply wanted to know that the missionaries had no intention of returning. Leddra and Peirson refused to make any promises. It was impossible to know how the Lord would direct their movements in the future. They were sent back to prison. The next March, the magistrates tried yet again. "If I were at liberty out of prison," Leddra allowed, "I might depart in the will of God ere long." The hopeful magistrates offered to set them at liberty if they would simply agree to leave and not come back. Peirson again replied that only the will of God dictated their movements. The magistrates told Leddra and Peirson to update them should God intend their departure. In April 1660, they were finally freed and left the colony, though it is unclear whether they, the magistrates, or the Lord backed down. Later that year, Leddra went to Massachusetts, which had already banished him and now sentenced him to hang.[54]

New Plymouth's leaders tried less barbaric ways of extirpating Quakerism. In 1659, the General Court authorized four individuals to attend Quaker meetings in order to "reduce them from the error of their ways." Among those chosen was Isaac Robinson, son of the Leiden separatist minister. Instead of eliminating the alleged errors, the younger Robinson followed Cudworth's example and wrote a letter critical of New Plymouth's magistrates. The court declared Robinson "a manifest opposer of the laws of this government" and sentenced him "to be disfranchised of his freedom." Like Cudworth, Robinson was not convinced by Quaker teachings, only that it was wrong to persecute the Quakers. Robinson moved to Saconeesett (later the Cape Cod town of Falmouth) and Martha's Vineyard, but he remained a member of Barnstable's church.[55]

Sandwich's inhabitants refused to enforce the colony's anti-Quaker laws. The magistrates responded by appointing George Barlow as marshal of Sandwich (and Barnstable and Yarmouth), empowered to act as a constable to make arrests and collect fines. As in the instance of Christopher Winter, Plymouth's godly magistrates had found a very ungodly individual to do their dirty work. Barlow was a cruel and turbulent man who persecuted Quakers in order to enrich himself. (In later years, he was convicted of drunkenness and accused of raping another man's wife.) Humphrey Norton reported that Barlow burst into meetings while the Friends were "sitting still," pulled off their hats, and threatened to put them in the stocks. The Sandwich Quakers began meeting in the woods instead, but Barlow tracked their footprints "as dogs do beasts of prey." Barlow also took property as payment for fines. He deprived Richard Kerby of eight cows, three steers, two calves, and three bushels of corn. The fines were a considerable revenue stream for the colony's government and for Barlow himself. The property seizures impoverished Sandwich Friends but did not end their meetings. In 1660, the General Court ordered the erection of cages in Sandwich (along with Duxbury, Marshfield, and Scituate), and it authorized constables to put those who attended Quaker meetings on public display in the cages.[56]

The magistrates eventually tired of Barlow's zeal, however. In 1661, they fined the marshal for forcing Benjamin Allen to sit in the stocks overnight, and they also ordered Barlow to return a shirt and a few pieces of linen to Ralph Allen. The magistrates did more than upbraid the loathsome Barlow, however. They conceded that their attempt to rid their colony of Quakers had failed.[57]

As New England's Congregational colonies tried in vain to rid themselves of Quakers, the ground of English society shifted dramatically once more. After Oliver Cromwell's 1658 death, his son Richard succeeded him as Lord Protector. The younger Cromwell lacked his father's grip on the army and, needing money, called a Parliament that soon undermined his authority. In May 1660, Parliament declared that Charles II had been England's lawful king since his father's beheading, and the restored monarch returned later that month. In June 1661, two months after his coronation, New Plymouth's General Court recognized Charles II as England's king. Once again, Nathaniel Morton revised the colony's oaths.

Bishops and church courts came back with the Stuart monarchy, but Charles II proclaimed that he would permit "a liberty to tender consciences," promising not to disturb those who held different opinions about religious matters so long as they did not "disturb the peace of the kingdom." In particular, the king was moved by testimonies about the Quaker suffering in Boston, and in 1661 he sent a letter to Massachusetts Bay ordering its government to cease its executions and corporal punishment of the Friends. William Leddra was the last Quaker hanged in the Bay Colony.[58]

Charles II's tenderness proved short lived. In early 1661, former Massachusetts settler Thomas Venner led an uprising against the newly restored monarchy. Venner and like-minded Fifth Monarchists sought to establish a theocracy in which the godly would rule according to biblical law and in which Jesus would be England's only king. Venner paid for his rebellion with his life, but the resulting furor led to the imprisonment of thousands of Quakers as well. According to the 1662 Quaker Act, anyone convicted a third time for refusing to swear a legal oath or for attending a Quaker meeting would be punished by transportation to the colonies. George Fox and Margaret Fell endured long imprisonments in the mid-1660s, hundreds of Friends died in jail, and many more paid fines and suffered other penalties and indignities. Other dissenters, including the Presbyterians who had warmly welcomed the Restoration, also ran afoul of new legislation repressing conventicles. Despite England's own periodic crackdowns against dissent, the crown continued to urge New England magistrates to grant toleration to religious minorities. This was in part because the Congregational magistrates were hostile to Church of England worship, but also because English officials continued to view colonies as ideal destinations for dissenters.[59]

New England had never been an exceptional enclave of persecution within a tolerant transatlantic English world. Certainly, religious dissenters enjoyed more liberty in some parts of England and within some colonies than others, but intolerance and persecution were endemic around the transatlantic English world and in continental Europe as well. New Plymouth was intolerant in comparison with Rhode Island, but what if Laudian or even Restoration England is the benchmark? Religious toleration gained many advocates in the 1640s and 1650s, especially from minorities who feared mistreatment at the hands of those in power. Still, the leaders of England's largest religious groups—the Presbyterians, those who wanted to return to the pre–Civil War episcopal hierarchy, and even many Independents—denounced toleration as a threat to godliness and civil order. The response of Plymouth's leaders to the Friends was not at all unusual within its transatlantic context.

Moreover, New Plymouth had embraced a more moderate approach even before the Restoration and the king's instructions to Massachusetts Bay. In 1659, the colony repealed its compulsory church attendance law. Sabbath laws remained on the books, but in many parts of the colony only flagrant violations produced penalties. After the Restoration, the General Court repealed the measure that permitted constables to place apprehended Quakers in cages, and many other anti-Quaker laws became dead letters. The magistrates tacitly permitted Quakers to hold meetings and no longer fined individuals who refused to swear an oath in court. Partly in response to such developments, the Quakers made themselves easier to tolerate. The monarchy's restoration extinguished some of the movement's apocalyptic fervor, and most Friends now spread their message more quietly. Quaker diatribes in churches and courtrooms became uncommon.[60]

New Plymouth did not promulgate toleration for Quakers, and church taxes in particular became a point of contention for decades to come. Still, communities found ways to limit religious conflict. Many Friends and their sympathizers moved to new settlements away from hostile magistrates and marshals. Richard Kerby bought land in Dartmouth and later on Long Island. His daughter Sarah married Matthew Allen; they also moved to Dartmouth.

Many Quaker missionaries and converts remained in Rhode Island, where they were tolerated if not always welcome. Roger Williams regarded the Friends as rank heretics and was dismayed when they gained control of the colony's government. After Humphrey Norton's restless spirit led him back to Rhode Island, Williams described him as the "Archdeacon," "Archbishop," and "Pope" of the region. Williams observed that as the Fox-led Quakers became more restrained and theologically sophisticated, Norton clung to the older ways and remained an uncompromising nuisance. The year and place of Norton's death are unknown.[61]

In both old England and New England, toleration and persecution depended on local circumstances as much as on royal edicts or the ideas advanced by thinkers such as John Milton, Thomas Hobbes, and John Locke. Outcomes hinged on the behavior and persistence of dissenters, the consensus of magistrates, and the cooperation of constables, marshals, and inhabitants. As much as they disliked the Quakers, New Plymouth's settlers chose to endure the presence of the Friends because attempts to eradicate Quakerism had proven both ineffective and odious.

CHAPTER FOURTEEN

Subjection

IN 1664, KING CHARLES II sent four commissioners to North America on a twofold mission.[1] The first task turned out to be easy. At a time of renewed tension with the Dutch, the king asked Richard Nicolls—one of the commissioners—to conquer New Netherland. Nicolls stopped in Boston, asked its wary magistrates to lend assistance, and then proceeded with three frigates and three hundred soldiers to New Amsterdam. After brief negotiations, Petrus Stuyvesant reluctantly surrendered. Nicolls became the colony's first English governor, and he recruited Plymouth Colony's Thomas Willett as New York City's first mayor. The Dutch-fluent Willett was an ideal choice, as his many commercial visits to the city had earned him the trust and respect of its population.[2]

The second task was much harder. The commissioners were to assess conditions in the various New England colonies and make reports about their loyalty—or lack thereof—to the king. Charles was well aware that the puritan colonies had favored the cause of Parliament during the English Civil War, and the commissioners anticipated that Massachusetts Bay would resist measures designed to promote religious toleration and fidelity to the crown. They were right. The Massachusetts General Court had no intention of complying with requests to alter the colony's laws or to declare annual days of thanksgiving celebrating the king's restoration. The leaders of Connecticut and New Plymouth also feared interference with their established churches and governments. At the same time, they worried about attempts by Massachusetts Bay to encroach on their jurisdictions. Thus, the magistrates of the smaller colonies and the commissioners more readily established good relations and found common ground.

The commissioners chose New Plymouth as the recipient of their first official visit. It was a shrewd choice, as Plymouth Colony's legal standing was more precarious than that of its neighbors. Massachusetts, Connecticut, and Rhode Island all had obtained new charters or royal confirmation of their charters shortly after the Restoration. By contrast, New Plymouth's privileges of self-government and even the settlers' property deeds rested on the flimsy basis of the patent William Bradford had obtained from the long-defunct Council for New England. Unlike their counterparts in other colonies, Plymouth's settlers had not sent an agent to England in the early 1660s.

When commissioners George Cartwright and Robert Carr came to Plymouth in February 1665, the General Court gave them a respectful welcome. Cartwright and Carr delivered a letter from the king, who asked the colony's leaders to require all householders to take the oath of allegiance; to accept men as freemen irrespective of religion; to grant all orthodox men and women free of scandal access to the sacraments, either by admitting them into established churches or by allowing them to form their own congregations; and to repeal any laws derogatory to the king. Plymouth's leaders asked Cartwright to help them obtain a royal charter or at least a confirmation of their patent from the king. In accordance with private instructions from the crown, Cartwright responded that the king would look favorably upon their request if they agreed to permit the crown to appoint the colony's governor. They could even suggest three names from which the king would choose. The commissioners hoped that if New Plymouth agreed to this arrangement, it would pressure the other colonies to accept it as well.[3]

Plymouth's leaders professed their loyalty and politely told the visitors that the General Court would discuss the king's requests. In May 1665, the court approved a cagey response. The magistrates observed that the colony's oath of fidelity already included a profession of loyalty to the king, though that oath bore little resemblance to the much more exhaustive oath of allegiance. On the second point, the General Court promised to welcome as freemen all honest, orthodox men, fully aware that the colony had passed laws excluding Quakers from the franchise. The third point was the trickiest and required the most equivocation. The magistrates suggested that Christians of "different persuasions respecting church government" might establish their own congregations, provided they paid taxes to support the established ministers. It would be better, however, if dissenters went to Rhode Island. The magistrates also promised to repeal any laws repugnant to the king, though they hastened to add that they saw nothing wrong with the United Colonies confederation, which the commissioners understood as an expression of independence from England. With as much politeness as they could muster, New Plymouth's leaders had rejected every single one of the king's demands.[4]

The next month, the General Court discussed the idea of a royally appointed governor and voted that the "particulars be referred to future consideration." It was the most tactful way to reject the king's proposal. New Plymouth's freemen and magistrates emphasized their obedience to the king, but they would not sacrifice the freedom to choose their own governor for a charter that might have further restricted their liberties. Cartwright was piqued, but New Plymouth faced no consequences for its resistance, in part because Massachusetts leaders were far more intransigent. Cartwright reported that the Bay Colonists sheltered regicides, persecuted religious dissenters, and flouted English laws, but he reassured the king of New Plymouth's loyalty.[5]

The commissioners' visit intersected with an important modification to New Plymouth's religious establishment. In 1666, Richard Nicolls wrote Governor Thomas Prence to ask why the General Court had invalidated Rehoboth's election of John Myles as the town's preacher. During the Interregnum, Myles had formed a network of Baptist churches and conventicles centered around the south Wales town of Ilston, near Swansea. "Have we not seen with our eyes in many places of this land," Myles rejoiced, "where Satan's seat hath been for many ages together, that since the enjoyment of our precious liberty . . . many thousands are come to the profession of the Gospel." That liberty came to an end with the Restoration. Myles

had been a staunch supporter of Cromwell and an opponent of epis-
copacy. He was now ejected from his parish and wisely chose to
leave England.[6]

After Myles, his wife and children, and some of his parishioners
came to New England, he received an invitation to become an assistant minister in Rehoboth alongside the Harvard-educated Zecha-
riah Symmes. The town had hired Symmes in 1663, probably on a
probationary basis, as was customary prior to a ministerial call. Either because of ill health or because he did not prove satisfactory,
the town granted Thomas Willett the privilege of finding an assistant for Symmes. Willett selected Myles, who arrived in late 1665 or
early 1666, quickly gained a sizeable following, and stoked a conflict
between supporters and opponents of infant baptism. (Back in 1649,
Obadiah Holmes and a dozen other men and women in Rehoboth
had separated from its Congregational church over the issue of infant baptism.) In the spring or summer of 1666, the colony's magistrates blocked an attempt to replace Symmes with Myles. Willett
asked Richard Nicolls to intervene on his friend's behalf.[7]

Prence informed Nicolls that the vote for Myles had come from
"a promiscuous [male and female] assembly of servants" who had
voted for a stranger and against a man to whom the church and town
had made prior promises. "Such a liberty to call ministers we con-
ceive will hardly be found in old England or new," Prence observed.
Plymouth's governor did not question Myles's theological orthodoxy, but he argued that Myles was unsuitable as a town minister. As
both Prence and Nicolls knew, English ministers and officials often
criticized New England's churches for their stringent membership
standards and for leaving most children unbaptized. How then could
Nicolls sympathize with Myles, who would not baptize any children
at all? Nicolls did not pursue the matter further.[8]

The next year, Plymouth's General Court fined Myles, his Welsh
congregant Nicholas Tanner, and James Browne for organizing their
own religious meetings in Rehoboth. Browne, whose father had supported religious toleration in the 1640s and 1650s, was twice elected
as an assistant to the governor "but not sworn," probably because
of his support for Myles. At this point, however, Plymouth's leaders
proposed a creative solution. With the support of Willett, who con-

trolled large amounts of land in the western portion of the colony, the court invited the Rehoboth Baptists to organize their own town. They accepted the offer, moved south, and established the town and church of Swansea. In 1668, the church proclaimed a day of thanksgiving "to return praise to our god for preserving our liberties." New Plymouth now had a string of town-supported Congregational churches, a single town-supported Baptist church, and several unauthorized Quaker meetings.[9]

Aside from its rejection of infant baptism, Swansea's church closely resembled the colony's Congregational churches. In his understanding of liberty of conscience, John Myles echoed William Bradford and Edward Winslow rather than Thomas Helwys and Roger Williams. The new town's settlers informed Willett that they would bar anyone from their township who denied the Trinity, the divinity of Christ, or the authority of the Bible. Individuals who favored transubstantiation (or consubstantiation) or "any merit of works" were also unwelcome. Some of the above provisions targeted Quakers, but to make themselves abundantly clear, Swansea's settlers added that they didn't want anyone in the new town who would not remove his hat in the presence of a magistrate or who opposed using public money to pay the minister.[10]

By the time that New Plymouth's General Court established Swansea and its Baptist church, Nicolls, Cartwright, and Carr were back in England, and the king's interest in his New England colonies had waned. Plymouth had not tried very hard to obtain a royal charter and still had no legal basis for its government outside of the Bradford patent. At the same time, the colony's magistrates—helped by the surly behavior of Massachusetts officials—had rather deftly convinced the commissioners of their loyalty. They subjected themselves to the king with their words, but not with their actions.

While New Plymouth's magistrates bristled against the prospect of greater royal control, they expected Wampanoag communities within their patent to act like subject peoples. This expectation strained and eventually broke the alliance that the Pilgrims had formed with Ousamequin. While some Wampanoags created new bonds with the English through their acceptance of Christianity, the Pokanokets and other western Wampanoag communities resisted both the English religion and English claims to political supremacy.

The Pokanoket sachems now made Montaup (Mount Hope) their chief place of habitation. A fertile peninsula to the south of Sowams, Mount Hope was relatively sheltered from the problems that accompanied the growth of English settlements across the region, such as the trampling of Native crops by English pigs, cattle, and horses. After Ousamequin's 1660 death, his sons Wamsutta and Metacom reaffirmed their friendship with Plymouth and adopted the English names of Alexander and Philip, respectively.[11]

Wamsutta, however, soon alarmed Plymouth's leaders by selling an enormous tract of land to a Rhode Island settler named Peter Tallman. The deed included all of Sakonnet and a portion of Pocasset, whose sachem, Weetamoo, was Wamsutta's wife. The land in question fell within both Plymouth's patent and Rhode Island's charter. Pocasset and Sakonnet, meanwhile, were home to large Wampanoag communities. While they acknowledged Pokanoket leadership, the Pocasset and Sakonnet sachems did not think that Wamsutta could dispose of their land.[12]

Plymouth's magistrates were not upset that Wamsutta had sold the land, only that he had sold it to Tallman. For decades, Plymouth's leaders had harbored their own designs on Sakonnet. In 1639, the colony's General Court had allowed the "purchasers, or old comers"—William Bradford, Edward Winslow, and John Alden, among others—to choose three large tracts of land. Making their selections, the old comers reserved the area around Sowams and Mount Hope for the Indians as their "chief habitation." For themselves, they selected a sizeable portion of Cape Cod and a large parcel of land that included part of Sakonnet. For two decades, the latter claim was merely aspirational, but in 1661 the General Court stated that servants who had obtained their freedom could acquire land in Sakonnet.[13]

When it learned about Tallman's deed, New Plymouth's General Court instructed Thomas Willett to intervene on Weetamoo's behalf, asking him to confront Wamsutta and Tallman. Willett either could not find Wamsutta or could not get a satisfactory explanation from him. Then in June, Weetamoo and a Sakonnet sachem

named Tatacomuncah traveled to Plymouth to lodge further complaints. The magistrates promised to do their best to void the deed.[14]

Within weeks of Weetamoo and Tatacomuncah's visit, Wamsutta died after his own trip to meet with the colony's leaders. According to two later accounts, the magistrates had deputized Josiah
Winslow to bring Wamsutta before them and to use force if necessary. Massachusetts Bay minister William Hubbard related that Winslow's party surprised Wamsutta and his men after the Pokanokets
had returned from a hunting expedition. After ordering his soldiers
to seize their guns, Winslow informed the sachem "that if he stirred
or refused to go he was a dead man." Increase Mather, another Bay
Colony clergyman, added that after Wamsutta flew into a "raging
passion" at Plymouth's presumptuousness, Winslow pointed his pis-
tol at his breast and demanded a polite and positive answer. For their
part, Plymouth's leaders insisted that Wamsutta's visit had required
no coercion. Regardless of how Winslow fetched him, Wamsutta fell
ill while meeting with the magistrates. The sachem died, either after
he returned home or on the way. Philip (Metacom) later claimed
that his brother "came miserably to die by being forced to court, as
they judge poisoned."[15]

The accounts of Wamsutta's death leave unresolved questions.
Why had Plymouth summoned the sachem? Both Hubbard and
Mather stated that Plymouth's leaders had learned of a conspiracy
between the Pokanokets and the Narragansetts. No contemporary
records support this claim. The issue at hand was Wamsutta's "es-
tranging land, and not selling it to our colony." Plymouth's magistrates regarded the Tallman deed as an economic and political threat.
Did they resort to murder in response? Probably not. In all likelihood, the colony's leaders would have tried other means of making
Wamsutta and Tallman more pliable.[16]

Philip now became sachem and immediately received his own
summons to Plymouth. After denying his complicity in a plot against
the English, he renewed his father's alliance, declared that he would
"forever ever remain subject to the King of England," promised not
to sell or give any of his lands to "strangers" such as Peter Tallman,
and returned home. Several years later, despite a flurry of petitions
from Rhode Islanders, the royal commissioners left Sakonnet, Po-

casset, and Mount Hope within New Plymouth's jurisdiction. The commissioners also met with Philip and resolved a land dispute between the Pokanoket sachem and the Narragansetts in Philip's favor.[17]

Although Philip still perceived benefits from his alliance with the English, the growth of Plymouth's settlements posed a serious threat to his leadership. Ousamequin's treaty with the Pilgrims had ended his subordination to the Narragansetts and strengthened the loose authority he exercised over southeastern New England's Wampanoag communities. Other sachems paid tribute to him, and he in turn sent gifts and promised to protect those communities from attack. Now this political order broke down. More distant Wampanoag communities became detached from the Pokanoket sphere of influence. Ousamequin and his successors stopped sending gifts, and the other sachems stopped sending tribute. The Pokanoket sachems sold distant lands—from Martha's Vineyard to Dedham in Massachusetts Bay—to the English, sometimes without the consent of the Indians who actually lived on the land. By the 1660s, Philip retained influence over Pocasset and Sakonnet, and over Nemasket, whose sachem Tuspaquin (known to the English as the "Black Sachem") had married one of Ousamequin's daughters. The Wampanoag communities on the Cape and the islands, however, declared themselves the subjects of new earthly and heavenly masters.[18]

For the *Mayflower* passengers and other early English settlers in New Plymouth, Indian missions were not a priority. At first, the Pilgrims just tried to survive. At most, they hoped that the Indians would admire English ways and take a corresponding interest in their God.

Such hopes proved groundless. In Massachusetts Bay, the minister John Eliot explained that English settlers could get rid of unwanted Indian visitors by turning the conversation to spiritual matters. "Speak of religion," Eliot explained, "and you were presently rid of them." Christianity so repelled the Indians that they fled from any discussion of God and Jesus, heaven and hell, or sin and salvation. What Eliot observed of other Algonquian peoples was also true of the Wampanoags. They were not enamored of the English or their God. Ousamequin once inquired "what earthly good things" came with Christianity. He could not see any value in "the ways of God." Wampanoags had inherited their cosmology and rituals from their ancestors, and few if any of them contemplated adopting English practices, let alone jettisoning their own.[19]

Despite these substantial barriers to conversion, large numbers of Wampanoags eventually embraced Christianity. This development began not within Plymouth Colony, but on the islands to its south. In 1641, Massachusetts Bay settler Thomas Mayhew purchased a patent to Martha's Vineyard, along with Nantucket and the Elizabeth Islands. Mayhew governed the islands as a proprietary colony, and his namesake son became a missionary to its large Wampanoag communities.

Epidemics followed the arrival of the Mayhews, and about half of the island's Native population perished. During these years of death, a man named Hiacoomes befriended the younger Thomas Mayhew. Hiacoomes taught Mayhew how to speak Wampanoag, and Mayhew taught Hiacoomes how to read English. Hiacoomes soon converted and began preaching Christianity. At first, his evangelistic efforts produced only scorn. "Here comes the Englishman," his neighbors said when Hiacoomes entered their presence. Some did more than mock. After reproaching Hiacoomes for his fellowship with the English, one sachem hit him in the face.[20]

Hiacoomes persisted, and soon his detractors stopped laughing. Nothing the powahs did arrested the epidemics, which happened to spare Hiacoomes. The many deaths called into question the powahs' authority, whereas Hiacoomes rose in status. For the next four decades, Hiacoomes preached on Martha's Vineyard, on neighboring islands, and on the mainland. In 1651, he made a celebrity visit to the Bay Colony and was welcomed into the pews of Boston's First Church. The younger Thomas Mayhew perished at sea in 1657, but the preaching of Hiacoomes and others made steady inroads. Although some sachems on the Vineyard opposed Christianity, by the 1670s the majority of families on the island attended Christian meetings.[21]

Under very different circumstances, large numbers of Massachusett families also aligned themselves with Christianity. John Eliot began preaching to several Native communities and gathered converts into a number of "praying towns." Eliot oversaw the translation of the Christian scriptures into what scholars have called Natick, Massachusett, or—more recently—Wôpanâak. These efforts resulted in the 1663 publication of the first complete Bible printed in the New World. The praying towns and the Bible gained Eliot renown as "the apostle of the American Indians."[22]

More than the Mayhews, Eliot demanded that residents of the towns adopt "civility" alongside Christianity. Eliot's code fined women who did not cover their breasts, men who did not cut their hair, and men or women who killed lice with their teeth. It also required men to work in their fields—instead of leaving agriculture to their wives—and attempted to bring Massachusett sexuality in line with biblical teachings and English law. While few of the families who moved to Eliot's towns desired these elements of English civilization, the Massachusetts had been even more devastated by epidemics and warfare than the Natives on Martha's Vineyard. The relentless expansion of English settlements in the Bay Colony, with the corresponding loss of traditional means of subsistence, left Massachusett communities with few good options and facilitated the development of the praying towns.[23]

As English ministers and Native preachers traveled between Massachusetts Bay and Martha's Vineyard, they evangelized Wampanoags in Plymouth Colony. By 1651, a group of Indians came every week to be taught by William Leverich, then minister at Sandwich. After Leverich left for Long Island, the Sandwich settler Richard Bourne continued the work. Bourne preached at Mashpee (about seven miles south of Sandwich) and traveled to other Wampanoag communities on Cape Cod. He provided support to a network of Wampanoag preachers, who served as evangelists to their own people. One convert, Wuttinnaumatuk, testified that when he had heard John Eliot preach, he "liked not to hear him." When Wuttinnaumatuk "came among the praying Indians," however, he too wanted to pray.[24]

In 1666, Bourne wrote that at Mashpee "and other places near adjoining they are generally praying Indians." Bourne concluded that it was time for the Mashpee Christians to form a church. New Plymouth's magistrates and ministers traveled to Mashpee for the occasion, joined by John Eliot and Thomas Mayhew. The prospective Wampanoag members described how God had wrought a change in their hearts. Paumpmunet explained that he began praying after the deaths of his wife and child. Quoting an array of biblical passages, Paumpmunet affirmed his belief that Christ's death granted life to those who believed in him. "I am become a new creature," he related, "having new understanding, new will, new faith, new hope, new joy, new memory." In his allusion to the fifth chapter of Second Corinthians, Paumpmunet implied that old things had passed away. Pachumu, also known as Hope, recalled the elders of his people warning him as a boy that if he did evil, he "should go to the house of Mattanit." Eliot translated *Mattanit* as "The Devil." As he became older and listened to Christian preaching, Pachumu concluded that he "was under Satan's power and not able to look after God." Reading the Bible and hearing sermons convinced him that Jesus Christ would liberate him from his bondage to sin and grant him eternal life. For unknown reasons, the formation of the Mashpee church did not proceed until 1670, at which time its members ordained Bourne as their minister. By then, large numbers of Cape Cod Wampanoags attended Christian meetings.[25]

Elsewhere in the colony, Christianity gained ground after John Cotton became the town of Plymouth's minister. The namesake son of Boston's renowned minister was a risky choice, as scandal had cost Cotton his first ministerial position. After Cotton graduated from Harvard, the church in Wethersfield, Connecticut, employed him on a probationary basis. Cotton's behavior demonstrated the prudence of this procedure. The young minister allegedly talked his way into one woman's "chamber" by pretending an interest in her furniture. Another woman accused Cotton of "sinful striving." He defended himself by asserting that she had pursued him much as Potiphar's wife had pursued Joseph. In March 1662, a court-appointed committee of two magistrates and two ministers found insufficient evidence that Cotton had committed a "more gross act" but criticized his "sinful, rash, unpeaceable expressions." John Davenport, New Haven's longtime minister and a close friend of John Cotton Sr., wrote the younger Cotton to tell him how poorly he measured up to his father.[26]

Boston's First Church, to which Cotton still belonged, was unambiguous in its judgment. In 1664, the church excommunicated its once-promising member for "lascivious unclean practices with three

women and his horrid lying to hide his sin." Cotton consulted with
Increase Mather, the church's pastor and his brother-in-law. Mather
was "troubled." He wanted to support his relation but did not think
he could in good conscience excuse his "carriage and demeanor."
Mather likely urged Cotton to make a full public confession, which
he did the next day. The social fabric of New England churches and
communities rested not on perfect righteousness, but on the willingness of individuals to confess and repent when they transgressed.
The church promptly restored its prodigal son to full membership.[27]

Attempting to salvage his career, Cotton accepted a post on
Martha's Vineyard. Cotton preached to the island's small number of
English settlers and learned enough Wampanoag to begin preaching to its Native communities. Cotton's wife, Joanna, also received a
stipend from the Society for the Propagation of the Gospel in New
England (or New England Company) for providing medical care to
the Indians. The older, autocratic Thomas Mayhew and the young,
impulsive Cotton were a poor match, however. The commissioners
of the United Colonies soon summoned Cotton to a meeting, where
they lamented that "mutual contentions and invectives one against
another . . . undid what they taught to the Natives." They told Cotton that they did not have enough money to keep paying him. He
should find somewhere else to go. The town of Plymouth, without
a minister since John Reyner's departure in 1654, became Cotton's
next stop. Cotton moved there in 1667, managed to avoid contention for two years, and was installed as the church's minister. In addition to raising a large family, Joanna Cotton worked as a midwife
and healer.[28]

By the time John Cotton arrived in Plymouth, the town's congregation faced a challenge common across New England in the
mid- to late seventeenth century. Only church members could partake of the Lord's Supper and present their children for baptism.
Baptized children did not automatically become full-fledged members of a congregation when they reached a certain age. Instead,
they had to meet the same high requirements for membership as
any other prospective members. In Plymouth, individuals had to
testify to their experience of spiritual regeneration. The church's
practice was for men "orally to make confession of faith and a declaration of their experiences of a work of grace" before the whole

congregation. When women presented themselves as prospective members, they dictated statements then read aloud by the minister or elder. The problem was that many baptized children who came of age did not take this step. Instead, they remained "children of the church," within its covenant and subject to its discipline but excluded from the sacraments. Most glaringly, these men and women could not present their own children for baptism.[29]

In 1662, a synod of Massachusetts Bay ministers had recommended that churches extend baptismal privileges to the grandchildren of members. This solution, called "large Congregationalism" at the time, later became known by the pejorative term "halfway covenant." The proposal sparked a long-lasting debate within New England's Congregational churches, as many laypeople and some ministers maintained that the change imperiled the purity of the churches and was a step back toward the mixed multitude of the Church of England. John Cotton supported the accommodation, but his Plymouth congregation did not. Within the colony, only the church at Yarmouth adopted the practice.[30]

Especially because of his church's stance on baptism, Cotton worked hard to bring adult children to full membership. He and Thomas Cushman, the church's ruling elder, went "through the whole town from family to family to enquire into the state of their souls." In response, twenty-seven men and women were admitted as members during Cotton's first year. Cotton did not want overly strict requirements to discourage individuals from advancing to church membership. In his preaching, he regularly emphasized that God brought women and men to salvation through the ordinances of the church, namely, preaching and the sacraments.[31]

In the fall of 1670, Cotton began preaching to Wampanoags who lived at Manomet, southeast of the town of Plymouth. Within weeks, Cotton recorded the conversions of two men, Occanootus and Wanna. "Occanootus," Cotton wrote in his diary, "did covenant and promise to walk in God's ways and to hate sin and to be a praying man." As had been the case on Martha's Vineyard, Native converts became the most effective apostles to their own people. Cotton noted that Wanna "exhorted the Indians to open their eyes and ears and hearts to hear and receive what was to be taught them." The next year, a self-satisfied Cotton reported that although "there was not one praying Indian when I began with them," there were now thirty. He was also pleased that the New England Company found the money to restore his annual stipend for missionary work.[32]

In Massachusetts, on Martha's Vineyard, and in Plymouth Colony, sachems, families, and individuals aligned themselves with Christianity for a wide variety of reasons. Economic and political motives nudged Natives toward conversion, and the prospect of a salary from benefactors in England no doubt prompted some Indians—and settlers—to undertake missionary work. Furthermore, many praying Indians blended old and new ways, and some moved back and forth between praying towns and prior communities. Still, even though reasons for conversion were complex, contemporary accounts stress religious conviction and spiritual power. Many Native Christians displayed a keen familiarity with the Bible, relished the communal singing of psalms, and asked theologically astute questions of English ministers. While many Wampanoag Christians formed congregations modeled on those of Plymouth Colony, others embraced the ideas of Baptists and Quakers. Regardless of which strain of Protestantism they adopted, Wampanoags made it their own.[33]

Conversions to Christianity reshaped Wampanoag communities. Those who became praying Indians rejected the spiritual authority of powahs and, in some cases, the political and economic authority of sachems. Even if they privately maintained older loyalties, they publicly aligned themselves with the English and their God. Missionaries such as Eliot, Mayhew, and Bourne, meanwhile, promised to help Indians retain at least some of their lands.

While the Cape Cod Wampanoags increasingly accepted Christianity, the western sachems—Philip, Tuspaquin, Weetamoo, and leaders at Sakonnet—were hostile or indifferent to the missionaries and their gospel. John Eliot had tried and failed to convert Ousamequin, and he fantasized for years about converting Philip. In 1664, Eliot asked the United Colonies to provide a stipend for John Sassamon, "who teacheth Phillip and his men to read." Born in eastern Massachusetts, Sassamon was orphaned and indentured to an English settler, fought for the English in the Pequot War, became a schoolmaster in the praying town of Natick, and studied at Harvard College. Sassamon was one of several Native Christians whose skills enabled the publication of Eliot's Bible. Then, in the early

1660s, Sassamon left Eliot's employ and worked for Wamsutta and then Philip. Eliot understood Sassamon as "a means to put life into the work" of converting Philip, and Eliot cheerfully reported that Philip had requested "books to learn to read, in order to [begin] praying unto God." Although the books were sent, Philip did not start praying. The Pokanoket sachem would not submit to the English god.[34]

At the same time, Plymouth's magistrates became more forceful in their insistence that Philip was their subject. In 1667, they summoned Philip to Plymouth to answer charges that he was conspiring with the Dutch or the French in order to recover lands he had sold. Philip rejected the charges, arguing—not unreasonably—that the Narragansett sachem Ninigret had spread the rumors precisely to cause him trouble. He insisted to the colony's magistrates that he remained grateful that Plymouth had preserved his people from the Narragansetts. Plymouth's magistrates concluded that although Philip's "tongue had been running out," there was no evidence of a conspiracy. They fined him forty pounds but offered to remit it if he could prove Ninigret's responsibility for the rumor. Philip resented the presumption of Plymouth's leaders and their pretensions to superiority over him.[35]

In 1671, more rumors of war very nearly led to an actual war. That February, Hugh Cole went from Swansea to a small neck of land along the Taunton River, which flows past Mount Hope and into Narragansett Bay. Plymouth's magistrates had tasked Cole with bringing a group of Wampanoags to answer an allegation—the specifics are unknown—brought by another colonist. The Wampanoags in question refused to go with Cole. Philip then sent a message requesting that Cole pay him a visit. When Cole reached Mount Hope, he saw "many Indians of several places" busy making and repairing weapons. Shortly thereafter, Cole heard reports that Philip had marched toward Swansea with sixty men. Cole delivered his alarming news at New Plymouth's early March General Court.[36]

Plymouth's magistrates imagined the worst. Militia commander Josiah Winslow—Edward Winslow's son—relayed to Governor Prence the highly improbable information that Philip intended to send two hundred men to kidnap them and hold them for ransom.

Another magistrate, Barnstable's Thomas Hinckley, reported rumors that the Narragansetts planned to "kill the men first and then flay the women alive." If outlying English settlers did not flee, the Indians "would slay them as they do cattle." Prence agreed to meet Philip at Taunton, roughly halfway between Plymouth and Mount Hope. Hinckley warned the governor that it was not safe for him to travel across the interior of the colony. Philip worried about his safety as well, but the Pokanoket sachem, Plymouth's governor, and representatives from Massachusetts Bay all came to Taunton on April 12.[37]

At the conference, Philip affixed his mark to a document in which he confessed that he had broken his covenant with the English "by taking up arms with evil intent." The sachem agreed to surrender all of his guns and to assist Massachusetts Bay by turning over several men who were suspects in a murder case within that colony's jurisdiction. The precise language was as important as the terms, however. Philip agreed that the Pokanoket sachems had submitted themselves and their people "unto the king's majesty of England, and to this colony of New Plymouth." At least according to Pilgrim accounts, Ousamequin had declared himself "King James his man," a subject of the distant English monarch. As fellow subjects of English kings, the Pokanoket sachems had seen themselves as equal allies of Plymouth's magistrates. The Pilgrims and their successors, by contrast, saw themselves as the superior party in the alliance and now forced Philip to acknowledge—at least on paper—that he was their subject.[38]

At first it seemed that the Taunton conference had averted war. Some of Philip's men went to Boston and assisted its magistrates with the murder investigation, and the sachem turned over some of his people's guns. Plymouth and Massachusetts declared a day of thanksgiving on May 12, and Prence thanked God and Bay Colony governor Richard Bellingham for their roles in preserving peace. In coming together at Taunton, Prence wrote, they had thwarted "Satan's design . . . to sow discord between brethren." God had not only inclined "the barbarous Indians to peace" but had sweetened the "brotherly love" between the two English colonies.[39]

By the end of the month, Prence was no longer thankful. The governor and his assistants received renewed reports of armed gath-

erings at Mount Hope. It is quite possible that Plymouth's belliger-
ency at the Taunton conference convinced Philip that he had no
choice but to prepare for war. When Plymouth's magistrates heard
that Philip had broken the agreement they had imposed on him, they
reached the same conclusion.

Plymouth's leaders took steps designed to isolate Philip. They
demanded professions of fidelity and submission from Native communities throughout the colony. In June 1671, Wampanoag men
from the Cape put their marks to a document in which they conceded that they had lived "as captives under Satan" and in bondage
to their "sachems." In casting off their old bonds, they accepted new
forms of subjection. They promised to inform the colony's magistrates of any Indian "plot or design contrived against the English."
If war came, they would fight on the side of the English even if it
cost them their lives. After all, according to the Book of Acts, they
and the English were "of one blood."[40]

The next month, other Indians who had aligned themselves
with Christianity declared their fidelity. Among them was Hope
(also known as Pachumu), who had testified publicly about his faith
at Mashpee in 1666. From Manomet came Wanna, whose conversion John Cotton had documented in his journal. Hope, Wanna,
and another six men submitted themselves to New Plymouth's government, explaining that their desire for peace stemmed from their
acceptance of "the gospel of Christ." Like the Cape Cod Wampanoags, they promised to fight any Indians who rose up against New
Plymouth's government. In turn, they asked the settlers to protect
them should "evil persons" persecute them for "seeking after the
knowledge of the true God and his ways."[41]

The western Wampanoag communities, which had not embraced Christianity, refused to submit. Aside from Philip, Plymouth's
leaders worried most about the threat posed by communities at Sakonnet. Sometime shortly before 1671, Awashonks had become what
the English called the "squaw-sachem" of Sakonnet. The English
sometimes called her a "sachem's wife," but she wielded authority in
her own right.[42]

Beginning with the 1671 crisis, Awashonks proved a tenacious
advocate for her people. That tenacity came from watching the
changes in the lands that surrounded Sakonnet. When Awashonks

was younger, the English whom Massasoit had befriended were confined to small coastal communities many miles to the east. They did
not hazard the paths that led to Sakonnet, and they rarely ventured
so far by sea. This was no longer the case. As the English moved
closer to Sakonnet, game became scarce, English cattle trampled
crops, and settlers began traversing paths on horseback. If Awashonks looked from Sakonnet across the water to the west, she could
see the English on Rhode Island. Those settlers eyed Sakonnet, and
they also desired Pocasset and Mount Hope. The Plymouth English
to her east had formed a town they called Dartmouth. Awashonks
knew that the Plymouth settlers and the Rhode Islanders were sometimes rivals, but she also knew that they both envisioned a future in
which they planted crops and raised cattle on her people's land.[43]

In late May, Governor Prence informed Rhode Island officials
that back in March, he had received a letter from Awashonks professing "subjection to the king's majesty and his authority here in
this his colony." However, Prence continued, Plymouth had since
learned that men from Sakonnet continued to plot "mischief" and had
appeared in arms at Taunton. The governor had invited Awashonks
and other Sakonnet sachems to Plymouth to effect peace, but they
had refused to come. Prence concluded that "they give us to understand they are not for peace with us, but war as occasion and opportunity may present."[44]

Plymouth's bellicosity prompted Awashonks to seek new allies.
In April, she sold "a small piece of land" to Peleg Sanford of Rhode
Island. The Sakonnet sachem intended to use the Rhode Island set-
tlers to check what she understood as Plymouth's aggression. Given
Plymouth's vigorous response to Wamsutta's deed back in 1662,
Awashonks's sale probably alarmed the colony's magistrates.[45]

After Awashonks ignored repeated summonses, Plymouth's council of war sent two messengers to Sakonnet in July. They told Awashonks and other Sakonnet leaders that they had four days to surrender their weapons. Furthermore, they were required to come to
Plymouth, acknowledge their offense against the colony, and pledge
their future fidelity. Expecting its demands to be refused, Plymouth
prepared to send Josiah Winslow, one hundred English soldiers, and
forty "of our trustiest Indians" to Sakonnet. The magistrates ap-

pointed August 9 as a day of humiliation. Citizens should gather in their churches, crave God's forgiveness of their sins, and ask the Lord's blessing on the expedition.[46]

Awashonks hesitated. She did not trust the English, but she was not ready to fight them either, especially given Philip's own uncertain intentions. In late July, she came to Plymouth and acceded to the council's demands. The colony's leaders imposed a stiff fine because of her delayed capitulation. She agreed to pay fifty pounds to compensate the colony for its military preparations. Awashonks also "submitted the disposal of her lands to the authority of this government," ostensibly to "regulate such as will not be governed by her." The agreement promised to protect Awashonks should others at Sakonnet attempt to sell land or stir up trouble against the English. At the same time, it gave Plymouth's magistrates power over land they had long coveted. If Awashonks could not pay the fifty pounds, they might sell her land to cover the fine.[47]

Plymouth's magistrates canceled the planned expedition, but they remained wary about Awashonks's compliance. Word soon reached them that Philip had "lately entertained divers of the Sakonnet Indians that were and are our professed enemies, and will accept of no tenders of peace." In response, Plymouth's leaders rescheduled the day of humiliation for August 16 and told Winslow to prepare his troops again. The additional pressure caused another forty individuals from Sakonnet to subscribe their submission. Once again, Plymouth's governor called off the expedition. Later in the fall, Prence pressed Awashonks to secure the submissions of her brother and two sons.[48]

After imposing terms on the Sakonnet communities, Plymouth turned its attention back to Philip. "God calls us by force to endeavor their reducement," Prence wrote his Rhode Island counterpart, informing him that Plymouth intended to send soldiers to Mount Hope. In late August, Plymouth's council of war ordered Philip to appear in Plymouth on September 13 to answer the charges against him. James Browne, who carried the council's letter, found Philip and his "chief men . . . much in drink." Just as Quakers had offended Thomas Prence in the late 1650s, Philip took umbrage because Browne did not remove his hat. The sachem knocked it off Browne's head. The next day, Browne brought Roger Williams as his interlocutor. Philip refused to come to Plymouth. Instead, he planned to go to Boston, where John Eliot had invited him.[49]

Eliot had been intervening on Philip's behalf for some time. Back in June, he had encouraged Prence to return Philip's guns, believing that a gesture of goodwill might induce the Pokanoket sachem to finally embrace the Christian gospel. Then in August, Eliot sent emissaries to both Philip and Prence. The delegation consisted of John Sassamon and two members of the Natick church, William Nahauton and a man named Anthony. Eliot urged Philip to accept peace as mediated by the magistrates of Massachusetts, and he cautioned Prence that Jesus Christ, their "great peacemaker in heaven," would disapprove of Plymouth's preparations for war. Furthermore, he asked Prence "to consider what comfort it will be to kill or be killed when no capital sin hath been committed." In other words, rumors of war were not grounds for war.[50]

Philip had never liked the missionary minister, but the idea that Massachusetts Bay wanted to stop the rush to war made a visit to Boston far more attractive than a summons to Plymouth. Indeed, Bay Colony leaders proved receptive to Philip's stance. "We do not understand how far he hath subjected himself to you," Bay Colony secretary Edward Rawson wrote Prence. Philip's refusal to answer a summons did not justify war, so Massachusetts leaders would not join Plymouth's planned expedition to Mount Hope. "We do not think it is for the common and public interest," Rawson stated, "to put ourselves or be put into blood but upon an unavoidable necessity." He rejected the idea that the Bay Colony's past commitment to the United Colonies bound Massachusetts to support Plymouth in this instance.[51]

The Bay Colony's stance probably had more to do with an ongoing dispute among the puritan colonies than with any matter of principle. The previous year, Massachusetts Bay, Connecticut, and New Plymouth had begun negotiations to revive the United Colonies confederation. Formed in 1643 during a time of tension with the Narragansetts, the confederation had fallen into a state of dormancy. Plymouth had considered it a breach of the confederation's articles when Connecticut had absorbed New Haven in 1664. In September 1670, commissioners from the three colonies had agreed to new articles of confederation, but the respective general courts had not ratified them. The point of contention was the proportional contributions of soldiers and funds that each colony would make in the event of war. Plymouth declared itself "very sensible that we are greatly oppressed by the proportion at first settled" and recommended that each colony bring a count of its adult male population to a planned September meeting. Massachusetts, for its part, was willing to contribute more men but wanted its charges reduced, and its leaders refused to attend a meeting until the issue was resolved. The possibility of war against Philip made the negotiations more tense. Massachusetts governor John Leverett recognized that Plymouth "might be the first that may see or feel the inconvenience" if they failed to reach an agreement. Prence, for his part, suggested that some were "slow to tie the knot again before the storm is blown over." Still, although Leverett urged Prence to avoid war, he reassured Plymouth's governor that "if trouble come the English interest is but one."[52]

Buoyed by his trip to Boston, Philip agreed to a September 24 meeting in Plymouth with representatives of the three colonies. To Philip's surprise and disappointment, Massachusetts Bay now backed Plymouth's demands. Either the confederation's new terms had been ironed out, or Plymouth had convinced Massachusetts leaders of its interpretation of the Taunton agreement. Acting as a tribunal, the English representatives convicted Philip of having broken his past promises. They drew up a new agreement for him to sign. He could take it or leave it. But if he did not make peace now, they warned, "he must expect to smart for it." Philip placed his mark on the document.[53]

It was a humiliation. Philip accepted a fine of a hundred pounds, due within three years. He also had to pay five wolf heads each year, as tribute and as a service to New Plymouth. Philip promised not to make war or sell lands without the colony's permission. Even more explicitly than at Taunton, Philip acknowledged that his people were "subjects to his majesty the king of England, and the government of New Plymouth, and to their laws." The alliance with the Pilgrims had extricated Ousamequin and the Pokanokets from their subordination to the Narragansetts. Now the sons of the Pilgrims reduced Ousamequin's son to subjection.[54]

New Plymouth soon experienced another political transition. Thomas Prence died, and Josiah Winslow succeeded him as the colony's first New England–born and Harvard-educated governor. Like his Pilgrim father, Winslow was a cosmopolitan merchant and politician respected across New England. Connected to Boston's wealthy elite through an uncle and to London merchants through a brother-in-law, Winslow had trade interests that extended across the Atlantic and to the sugar plantations of the West Indies. Along with Thomas Willett, Winslow also bought into the Atherton Company, which purchased vast tracts of New England land and developed them into towns and farms.[55]

Winslow was less interested than his predecessors in the vigorous enforcement of religious orthodoxy, and his election brought about a partial reconciliation with settlers who had lost their civil privileges for sympathizing with the Quakers. Isaac Robinson became a freeman again. Winslow also asked James Cudworth to lead a planned expedition against the Dutch, who recaptured New York in July 1673 (and renamed it New Orange). The now elderly Cudworth, who had lost his militia captaincy because of his opposition to the colony's anti-Quaker policies, declined the offer. He cited poverty and a need to be home to care for his ailing wife, but Cudworth also made it clear that he had not forgiven Winslow and the other magistrates who had "discharged" him of his "military employ" and "of other public concerns." Cudworth could have stayed at home in any event, as the English regained New York through negotiations concluded the next year.[56]

Winslow wanted to mend fences with men such as Robinson and Cudworth, but he did not change his colony's approach to the Wampanoags. The colony's leading men—Winslow, Constant Southworth (William Bradford's stepson), Thomas Cushman, and the younger William Bradford—took every opportunity they could find to purchase lands in Sakonnet and elsewhere. Accordingly, the tensions evident since the early 1660s grew more pronounced.

The terms of the 1671 submissions led to further land sales. Probably because he needed money and English goods in order to maintain his authority, Philip had sold many parcels of land in the 1660s. Although Philip expressed resentment over the loss of land, the one-hundred-pound fine made it necessary for him to continue to sell land. Other sachems faced similar pressures. In March 1672, Josiah Winslow sued Tuspaquin's son William for the nonpayment of a ten-pound debt incurred the previous summer. William could not pay and was forced to sell a parcel of land in order to settle the debt.[57]

At Sakonnet, land sales fueled a leadership contest. There were at least two communities of Indians within what the English considered Sakonnet. Awashonks led a community that lived near the western side of what is now Little Compton, Rhode Island. Another sachem, Mammanuah, led a community farther to the east on the Acoaxet River. In February 1673, several of Mammanuah's brothers affixed their marks to a document recognizing him as the "chief sachem" and "true proprietor" over their lands. Mammanuah aligned himself with the English in ways Awashonks would not. That June, he went to John Cotton's house in Plymouth. According to Cotton, Mammanuah and one of his followers "became praying Indians and desired preaching." His conversion surely made him a more attractive partner for English leaders.[58]

Awashonks tried to outflank her rival. With her son Peter, she signed a deed selling the northern portion of Sakonnet to Southworth and his partners for £75. Not to be outdone, Mammanuah sold overlapping Sakonnet lands to Southworth for £35. At this point, Awashonks and her people confronted Mammanuah directly. They bound and threatened him, trying to force him to relinquish his title to Sakonnet. Instead, Mammanuah sued Awashonks in Plymouth's court for £500. Plymouth's magistrates now referred to Awashonks as the "pretended squaw sachem." After Mammanuah initiated his suit, Southworth obtained Awashonks's agreement to cede all of her lands if she failed to appear in court to defend herself against the suit. When she did not fulfill the condition, Southworth claimed her people's land now belonged to him. For good measure, the court ruled for Mammanuah and awarded him £5 and the cost of the suit. In 1671, Plymouth's magistrates had promised to help Awashonks assert her authority over those who resisted her leadership. Instead, they undermined her and propped up a more compliant sachem. They weaseled, swindled, and browbeat their way into gaining legal title to land they had claimed for several decades.[59]

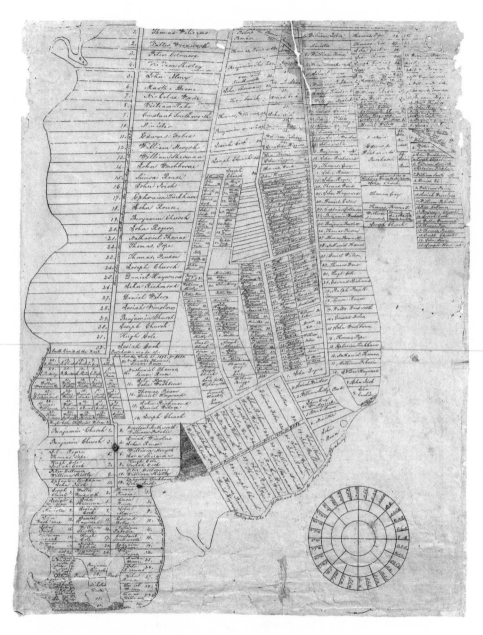

Survey of Little Compton (Sakonnet), nineteenth-century copy of ca. 1681 map.
(Courtesy of John Carter Brown Library.)

Enlarged section of Little Compton survey. Note the names of prominent English proprietors, including Benjamin Church and Governor Josiah Winslow.

Mammanuah kept selling. In April 1675, he sold all of Sakonnet Neck to Southworth, Josiah Winslow, and other purchasers for £80. This included the land on which Awashonks lived. The sale included islands, ponds, coves, rivers, creeks, brooks, mines, and minerals. It included fishing rights in Sakonnet's coastal and inland waters. In other words, Mammanuah deeded everything to the English. The previous month, Plymouth's General Court had granted the purchasers the right to form a township at Sakonnet. They were to oversee an orderly settlement and the eventual establishment of a church.[60]

In fact, a few English were already there. In the summer of 1674, Benjamin Church began developing a Sakonnet farm. Born in Plymouth in 1639, Church had married Alice Southworth, Constant Southworth's daughter. The socially upward marriage made Church a key player in the fulfillment of Plymouth's long-standing territorial ambitions. "I was the first English man that built upon that neck, which was full of Indians," Church later recalled. Church did not move his family to Sakonnet. Instead, like many land proprietors, he hired tenants. Church oversaw the construction of two buildings, and he brought livestock onto his new property.[61]

In May 1675, the Sakonnet proprietors met in Duxbury— probably at Josiah Winslow's Careswell estate—and drew lots, placing names such as Winslow, Church, Southworth, and Almy on eighteen-, thirty-, and fifty-acre portions of Sakonnet. The proprietors reserved a three-quarter-square-mile parcel of land for the use of Awashonks and her people.[62]

"Before these present troubles broke out," Josiah Winslow insisted a few years later, "the English did not possess one foot of land in this colony, but what was fairly obtained by honest purchase of the Indian proprietors." Plymouth's settlers bought land instead of simply taking it, and English purchasers claimed that the low prices paid reflected the unimproved state of the land. More accurately, though, English settlers and magistrates made sure that land they wanted became theirs for next to nothing. If a community rebuffed an offer, the would-be purchasers tried again a few years later. Especially as Rhode Islanders also tried to obtain land in Pocasset and Sakonnet, Plymouth's magistrates became more aggressive. They fined sachems and then took land to settle the debts. If a sachem refused to sell, the magistrates found someone else who was willing to affix a mark to a deed. Those whom "the English had owned for king or queen they would disinherit," Philip explained a few years later, "and make another king that would give or sell them their land." The low prices paid had little to do with the true value of the land but instead reflected the disparities of power between the two peoples. English purchasers paid much more when they bought unimproved "wilderness" from other Englishmen. Certainly some, if not many, purchasers acted with fairness and integrity, and New Plymouth's courts occasionally upheld Wampanoag complaints. At Sakonnet, however, Plymouth's proprietors achieved their objectives through chicanery and ruthless determination and displayed little concern for the communities they disadvantaged and displaced.[63]

Sachems such as Awashonks were hemmed in. English settlers approached and encroached on her lands, and it was increasingly difficult to maintain traditional patterns of authority. Her choices narrowed. She could accede to the dramatic changes reshaping her world and cede her lands and leadership. She could accommodate herself to English ways, embrace Christianity, and hope that English ministers and magistrates would secure a portion of her lands for her people. Or she could fight.

CHAPTER FIFTEEN

War

IN MID-JUNE 1675, BENJAMIN Church received an invitation to a dance. It came from Awashonks, who had called her subjects together so that they could make a momentous decision. Church took an interpreter, went to Awashonks's village, and found "hundreds of Indians gathered together from all parts of her dominion." Awashonks herself was "in a foaming sweat . . . leading the dance." When she saw Church, she stopped moving.[1]

Awashonks told her English guest that Philip had sent representatives to her "to draw her into a confederacy with him in a war with the English." What should she do? Church reassured her that Plymouth's leaders were not preparing for war. She asked for a response from Philip's men, who were still at Sakonnet. They "made a formidable appearance," not least because of their bags full of bullets. Awashonks told Church that Philip had threatened that unless she joined his plot against the English, he would burn English homes near Sakonnet and "provoke the English to fall upon her." Church, a bit uneasily, advised Awashonks to inform Plymouth's governor of her loyalty and to place her people under his protection. Although some of the Sakonnet men made clear their preference for war, the "squaw sachem" asked Church to bear her peaceful tidings to Plymouth.[2]

Historians should use Benjamin Church's self-glorifying memoir with caution, not least because the famed Indian fighter did not write it. Thomas Church wrote up *Entertaining Passages* based on his father's notes shortly before the latter's 1718 death. The elder Church perused the manuscript and had no objections. "And why would he?" asks historian Jill Lepore. The book "paints Church not only as the hero of every battle he fought but as the Puritans' voice of reason and restraint."[3]

Although the Churches blended fact and fancy in their memoir, other sources corroborate the basic contours of the *nickómmo*—an Algonquian dance and feast—that Benjamin Church had witnessed. Roger Williams learned about such occasions from the Narragansetts, but because he feared "partak[ing] of Satan's inventions and worships," he never saw one himself. According to Williams, Algonquian peoples held nickómmos after harvests, successful hunts, and other times of celebration, and also at moments of crisis. As Church observed of Awashonks, Williams wrote that the leader of a nickómmo sweated profusely while making "strange antic [grotesque] gestures, and actions even unto fainting."[4]

A nickómmo served several purposes. The dance and feast confirmed relationships and alliances; sachems such as Awashonks and Philip fed guests and sometimes distributed goods to them. The nickómmo also established a setting in which the community could reach consensus on a decision and access the manitou (spiritual power) needed for its accomplishment. In June 1675, Sakonnet communities faced a grave choice. If Philip and the English went to war, on which side would they fight?

English settlers also held gatherings that month. New Plymouth's magistrates asked John Cotton to draft a proclamation to the colony's churches, asking them to observe a day of humiliation on June 24. Settlers were expected to fast, abstain from work, and beseech God to forgive the sins that had brought about his judgment. In this instance, Cotton declared, it was obvious that "the awful hand of God [was] upon us in permitting the heathen to carry it with great in[solenc]y and rage against us." Cotton's reasoning and language were common among late seventeenth-century New England puritans. If the people repented, God might "be entreated to go forth with our forces" and subdue the rebellious Indians. Otherwise, the wages of their sins might be death.[5]

There was no guarantee that fasting and prayer would produce the desired result, which rested on God's sometimes inscrutable will. Even so, just as William Bradford recounted that badly needed rains followed one drought-inspired day of fasting, many New Englanders linked the communal rituals to the renewal of God's favor. Accordingly, on June 24 in Rehoboth, the minister Noah Newman took Psalm 46:10 as his text. "Be still and know that I am God." Newman reassured his congregants that God would be—as the verse from the Bible promised—"exalted among the heathen."[6]

A puritan day of humiliation was far more reserved and somber than an Algonquian nickómmo. There was fasting instead of feasting, psalm singing instead of dancing. Nevertheless, the two occasions served similar purposes. The nickómmo and the day of humiliation brought communities together in the midst of crisis and steeled them for coming hardships. They were rituals designed to harness supernatural power and curry divine favor. In the months that followed, the prayers of neither people would be answered fully.

The Sakonnet nickómmo came on the heels of a high-stakes murder trial at Plymouth. The dead man was John Sassamon, the scribe and translator who had worked for John Eliot, Wamsutta, and Philip.[7] Several years earlier, Sassamon had moved to Nemasket, roughly halfway between Mount Hope and the town of Plymouth, and preached to groups of praying Indians in the area. In March 1674, the Nemasket sachem Tuspaquin deeded twenty-seven acres of land at Assowamsett Pond to Sassamon. The interpreter's daughter had married a local man, but Tuspaquin probably did not make the "gift" purely as a gesture of goodwill. Rather, a group of New Plymouth land proprietors—including Church, Constant Southworth, and John Thompson—had been pressuring Tuspaquin and others at Nemasket to sell their land, which lay within the newly formed English township of Middleborough. It is possible that Sassamon managed to acquire a prime tract of land for himself before the English proprietors bought it, or he may have tricked Tuspaquin by promising to preserve Nemasket from land-hungry settlers.[8]

In January 1675, Sassamon journeyed to Josiah Winslow's Marshfield home and informed the governor that Philip endeavored "to engage all the sachems round about in a war" against Plymouth. Winslow disregarded Sassamon's intelligence. Surely there was no

Indian conspiracy in the dead of winter, a few months before the Wampanoags would plant their spring crops.[9]

A week or so later, several Native men discovered Sassamon's corpse under the ice of Assowamsett Pond. Given the nature of Sassamon's recent errand, Plymouth's magistrates suspected foul play. Getting wind of the rumors, Philip went to Plymouth of his own accord. According to Winslow and Thomas Hinckley, the magistrates at the time believed Philip was complicit in Sassamon's death but lacked proof. They warned the Pokanoket sachem that if they found incriminating evidence against him, they would "demand his arms to be delivered up," as Plymouth's leaders had required during the 1671 crisis.[10]

Soon there was testimony, not against Philip directly, but against several other men. William Nahauton, one of the Natick evangelists whom Eliot had sent to Philip in 1671, reported that a Christian Indian named Patuckson had witnessed the murder. Patuckson accused three men of having killed Sassamon: Tobias, a trusted counselor of Philip; Wampapaquan, Tobias's son; and Mattashunannamo.

The magistrates sent for the suspects and ordered the exhumation of the corpse. A coroner's inquest affirmed that Sassamon had been murdered. As in the 1655 death of fourteen-year-old John Walker, the magistrates also sought supernatural evidence. When Tobias "came near the dead body," Boston's Increase Mather recounted, "it fell a bleeding on fresh, as if it had been newly slain." The fresh blood was taken as a sign of Tobias's guilt. In an unusual display of leniency toward an accused murderer, the magistrates released Tobias on bond, taking as collateral the Nemasket lands of Tobias and Tuspaquin. Suddenly, land and lives were both at stake. Shortly before the trial, Tuspaquin turned the bond into a deed, making over "all" of his Nemasket land to Constant Southworth and other proprietors. As the historian Lisa Brooks suggests, Tuspaquin probably believed that by selling his lands, he was purchasing Tobias's freedom. If so, he miscalculated.[11]

Plymouth's General Court and magistrates had tried other Native defendants, but mostly for crimes committed against English settlers. On several occasions, the colony's magistrates had supported Wampanoag complaints against settlers. In 1669, for example, they fined Thomas Mathewes for "unreasonably beating of the Indian

Ned." Plymouth had never tried a serious Indian-on-Indian crime, however. Recognizing the unusual and controversial nature of the proceedings, the General Court impaneled six Christian Wampanoag men to confirm the decision of twelve English jurors. Among those chosen were Hope, who had testified to his conversion at Mashpee, and Wanna, whose conversion John Cotton had described in his journal. Both men had sworn their fidelity and obedience to New Plymouth in 1671. Presumably, the jurors heard a report of the coroner's inquest and the testimony of Patuckson. In early June, they convicted the three men, who were sentenced to die by hanging.[12]

In a letter to Connecticut's governor John Winthrop Jr., Roger Williams stated that "many wish that Plymouth had left the Indians alone, at least not to put to death the three Indians upon one Indian's testimony." Plymouth's magistrates, Williams implied, had ignored the Bible's insistence that "at the mouth of one witness [a defendant] shall not die" (Deuteronomy 17:6). When the colony had revised its laws in 1671, it included a set of "General Fundamentals" that defined safeguards and privileges "essential to the just rights, liberties, common good and special end of this colony." The passage from the Book of Deuteronomy was the basis for one of those liberties. In order to convict a defendant of a capital crime, Plymouth required at least two witnesses "or that which is equivalent thereunto." Perhaps the bleeding corpse sufficed as the "equivalent" of a second witness.[13]

Was it an accidental death or murder? If it was murder, did Plymouth have evidence beyond Patuckson's word that the three men were the killers? If they were, had the men acted on orders from Philip?

It is clear that Philip loathed Sassamon. Philip had not changed his mind about Christianity, which he understood as a threat to his authority and the stability of Native communities. There were more particular problems with Sassamon, however. At the height of the 1671 crisis, Philip had complained that his former interpreter had passed intelligence to the English. (Specifically, Sassamon had reported the presence of Narragansett sachems at Mount Hope).[14] Nor did Philip hide his disdain after Sassamon's death. In a mid-June 1675 conversation with Rhode Island's John Easton, Philip alleged that Sassamon had tried to swindle him out of his land while

PHILIP. *KING* of Mount Hope.

Philip (Metacom), engraving by Paul Revere, from Thomas Church,
Entertaining History of King Philip's War *(1772).*
(Courtesy of Yale University Art Gallery.)

working as his scribe. Given such affronts, the Pokanokets told
Easton, Philip would have been within his rights as a sachem to have
ordered Sassamon's death. Philip had means, opportunity, and an
abundance of motives.

While Philip freely confessed his dislike of Sassamon, he insisted
that he and the convicted murderers were innocent. Sassamon had
fallen and drowned. Patuckson owed the defendants money and testified against them to avoid the debt and gain favor with the English.
The Pokanokets insisted that the case was crooked.[15]

On June 8, 1675, Plymouth hanged the three men. Executions
in seventeenth-century New England were public spectacles; one
can presume that a large crowd gathered at the gallows to watch the
three men die. Astonishingly, Wampapaquan's rope broke during
his hanging. He then stated that his co-defendants had murdered

Sassamon but that he had only watched. Of course, the other two men had just died and could not contradict him. Perhaps because the snapped rope suggested divine intervention, Wampapaquan earned a reprieve until the October session of the General Court.[16]

For the time being, Plymouth's magistrates concluded that they lacked sufficient evidence to charge Philip as the mastermind behind Sassamon's death. Roger Williams rejoiced that "the storm" had passed. His relief was premature.[17]

So was Wampapaquan's. His turn of good fortune turned out to be very temporary. Before the end of the month, Plymouth's magistrates no longer felt inclined toward mercy, and they revoked his reprieve. In order to make sure he did not cheat death a second time, they had him shot.

The executions provided the catalyst but were not the cause of the war. The alliance formed between Ousamequin and the Pilgrims had already broken down because of the expansion of English settlements, the pressure of land sales, and the insistence of New Plymouth's magistrates that the Wampanoags were their subjects. Colonial leaders had pushed Philip to the brink of war in 1671 and had then imposed humiliating terms on him. Both sides were now quicker to resort to violence and less open to negotiation and compromise. Across New England, moreover, there were similar strains in the relations between Native peoples and colonial governments.

Whether or not Philip had been plotting against the English in January, he now sought allies for what might occur in the wake of the trial and executions. Just a few days after the hangings, John Browne at Swansea learned that a witness had spotted sixty "double armed men" at Mount Hope. The Pokanokets were on guard because they believed that Governor Winslow "intend[ed] to send for Phillip." As Hugh Cole had reported in 1671, Browne informed Winslow that Indians—including Narragansetts—were streaming to Mount Hope. English settlers heard drums and gunshots. Indians allegedly lay in wait on the paths between Taunton and Swansea. "The truth is they are in a posture of war," Browne concluded.[18]

Plymouth was caught off guard by the news but responded as it had four years earlier. Winslow insisted that other western sachems dissociate themselves from Philip, and the governor gained confirmation from Massachusetts Bay that it would support New Plymouth in the event of war. At the same time, Winslow demanded that Philip surrender his weapons, come to Plymouth, and submit. Philip countered that the allegations against him were false. He asked Winslow to excuse his people from surrendering their guns or paying a fine, and he refused to attend the court. In fact, he expected "great danger" should he venture to Plymouth.[19]

Swansea's English inhabitants were also fearful. They had settled in several clusters, one of which lay on and around the neck of land that leads to Mount Hope. There, on Saturday, June 19, Pokanoket men ransacked the home of Job Winslow, cousin to New Plymouth's governor. The next day, Indians burned two homes. New Plymouth's settlements were vulnerable. According to Josiah Winslow, only a few homes were built with brick or stone. Most houses were "of timber, covered with boards and shingle." They burned readily. Outside of Plymouth itself, most towns had no fortifications, though Swansea had garrisoned a few homes, including the house of the town's Baptist minister, John Myles.[20]

Winslow relayed news of the depredations to Bay Colony governor John Leverett. There were some in Boston who grumbled that Plymouth "had ungroundedly enterprized this war" but, unlike in 1671, Massachusetts quickly sent several units of soldiers. Plymouth's own troops headed west under the command of Captain James Cudworth (soon given the rank of major), who had refused to resume his military responsibilities in 1674 but now volunteered with war possible within the confines of New Plymouth itself. Captain William Bradford—son of the *Mayflower* passenger—was Cudworth's second-in-command. As they reached Swansea, the soldiers joined the settlers huddling in the few safe houses.[21]

Meanwhile, the skirmishes turned deadly. The Natives shot at the garrisoned soldiers, burned more homes, and killed livestock. The first death came on June 23, when an "old man" instructed a young "lad" to shoot at several Indians whom they saw near an English house. A shot mortally wounded one Native man.[22]

The next day, as families across the colony gathered for the court-appointed day of humiliation, Philip's men retaliated. Six or seven Swansea settlers were killed, some while fetching corn from their fields, others while returning from church. Among the casualties were the young man who had fired the previous day's fatal shot and his father. Most of Swansea's inhabitants took refuge in the several garrisons. Even at the safe houses, however, the English were not safe. In a letter to Governor Winslow, Cudworth detailed a night of terror. Gershom Cobb was shot and killed while on sentinel duty, and two other men were gravely wounded. One of the wounded men was Alexander Canady (Kennedy). Cudworth reported that there was "some hope" Canady would recover, and he did. Cudworth said that for the other wounded man, there was "no hope of life." He identified the man only as "Mr. Miles his Negro." Cudworth's letter informs that an enslaved African American man was one of the first to die in what became known as King Philip's War.[23]

The garrison dispatched two men to fetch Matthew Fuller (son of *Mayflower* passenger Edward Fuller; nephew of *Mayflower* passenger, deacon, and physician Samuel Fuller) to treat the wounded. The messengers never reached their destination. As Cudworth reported, "The men were stripped of their upper garments, one having his head cut off and carried a way [and] the other his head flayed, the skin and hair off from his skull and both their right hands cut off and gone." Several representatives from Massachusetts Bay traveling to Mount Hope saw the mutilated corpses, turned around, and headed back to Boston.[24]

On June 26, there was a complete eclipse of the moon. Massachusetts soldiers marching toward Swansea halted as the landscape around them fell dark. It seemed a bad omen. When the moon shone again, some of the men thought they saw an Indian's "scalp" or "bow" in its light. After they resumed their march and reached their destination, Cudworth, Bradford, and their Massachusetts counterparts prepared to attack Mount Hope.[25]

As they passed through the burned-out southernmost settlement of Swansea, the Plymouth and Massachusetts soldiers found pages ripped out of a Bible, scattered on the ground as a symbolic rejection of Christianity. Next, they came to a group of eight poles on which their enemies had mounted five English heads, two scalps, and one set of hands. The shaken and enraged soldiers tossed the remains of their countrymen into the river and then swept across the peninsula. They killed several of Philip's men and ransacked his village, but they failed to capture the Pokanoket sachem. He had crossed to Pocasset.[26]

Throughout the war, English and Natives alike mutilated corpses and hacked off heads and hands. In late June, Roger Williams reported that Philip had sent several English heads as an overture to the Narragansetts. In the town of Plymouth, the authorities executed an Indian spy and took his head to the door of Governor Winslow's Marshfield residence. Severed body parts served diplomatic purposes, functioned as symbols of triumph and warning, and sowed terror.[27]

After failing to catch or kill Philip on Mount Hope, English leaders regrouped and considered how best to pursue their enemies. From Swansea, James Cudworth advised that the English use the Wampanoags' own tactics against them. Small parties of soldiers should "waylay them in the bushes and . . . cut off what we can of them." Cudworth knew that English troops who blundered down paths exposed themselves to ambush and had little chance of locating their intended quarry. Governor Winslow, however, rejected his commander's suggestion, which he considered a "base skulking way" of warfare. Winslow instructed Cudworth to wait for additional troops to relieve Swansea and then make "a more honorable and resolute charge on the enemy's quarters."[28]

In early July, English troops made several irresolute charges into what Captain Bradford described as "great" and "hideous" swamps in search of Philip and the Pocasset sachem Weetamoo. Each time, ambushes forced the inexperienced and confused settlers to retreat. Cudworth soon gave up. "We shall never be able to obtain our end in this way," he stated, "for they fly before us from one swamp to another." English soldiers burned Pocasset homes and found Native encampments, yet both fighting men and noncombatants eluded them. At one point, a frustrated Cudworth went all the way to Plymouth to complain about the need for more supplies. Winslow sent him back west the next day. Cudworth and Bradford decided that their best move was to cordon off Philip and Weetamoo and starve them out. Believing that a smaller number of soldiers could keep Philip and Weetamoo hemmed in, Cudworth and Winslow agreed that most of Plymouth's men should return home. It would soon be harvest time.[29]

While Philip and Weetamoo evaded Cudworth's troops, the Nemasket sachem Tuspaquin looted and burned Middleborough, while another western sachem, Totoson, laid waste to Dartmouth. Totoson's men killed several Dartmouth inhabitants and took captive a woman named Dorothy Hayward. According to Boston minister William Hubbard, her captors soon freed her to repay the kindness she had previously shown in caring for an Indian child. They dressed her wounds and brought her to her town's edge, a rare instance of mercy in a war full of cruelty.[30] Meanwhile, English settlers in other western towns grew desperate. Confined in their garrisons, they watched their homes burn and their crops remain unharvested. Some families in Dartmouth, Middleborough, Swansea, Taunton, and Rehoboth took refuge in Plymouth and other eastern communities.[31]

For several years after the *Mayflower* crossing, the Pilgrims had lived fearfully within their palisaded town. Early settlements dotted the coasts, surrounded by what seemed a vast and almost impenetrably confusing interior. The onset of war partly re-created these circumstances. Many English settlers now lived in hastily fortified towns, not daring to walk along the paths that connected them. They sometimes went long stretches without messengers and mail. "For all travelling was stopped," wrote Benjamin Church, "and no news had passed for a long time." Two Plymouth messengers carrying letters did not reach their destination. "Their horses are found, but no men," informed correspondents in Connecticut. At the same time, Natives hostile to the English seemed to pass through the wilderness undetected.[32]

At the end of July, Philip, Weetamoo, and their people crossed the Taunton River and headed west and then north. Several dozen Mohegan Indians (who had recently come to Boston to confirm their alliance with the English), praying Indians from Natick, and some fresh English recruits tracked the Wampanoags and caught up to them about ten miles north of Providence. Finally getting the open battle they had sought, the English and their allies inflicted casualties. In the end, though, Philip, Weetamoo, and most of their people retreated into yet another swamp and slipped away. Philip headed northwest into Nipmuc country, and Weetamoo turned back toward the Narragansetts.

Despite Benjamin Church's attempt to secure her fidelity to the English, Awashonks also fled. She knew what had occurred in Pocasset, where the English burned homes and executed two "old men." One year later, her son Peter explained that Awashonks's people left because they feared English reprisals. Awashonks first tried to take refuge on Rhode Island. Obstructed by that colony's patrols, they next hid in the swamps while, according to Peter, "the English army came and burnt our houses." With no other favorable alternative, they went to the Narragansetts. As had been the case throughout the early 1670s, the Sakonnets were divided among themselves. Mammanuah fought alongside the English, while others joined Philip and Weetamoo.[33]

With the flight of the western Wampanoag sachems, the fighting moved away from New Plymouth. While colonial leaders discussed how best to pursue Philip, the inhabitants of towns such as Swansea, Dartmouth, and Middleborough returned home, harvested crops, and rebuilt their houses.

For many settlers and many Wampanoags, life did not return to normal. Dartmouth's Dorothy Hayward was only the first of dozens of English to be taken captive during the war. In mid-July, a party of Nipmucs struck the Massachusetts town of Mendon, and English settlements in the Connecticut River Valley came under attack that fall. During the raids, Indians seized captives, mostly women and children. Algonquian peoples had long used captives to replenish populations diminished by war and disease, and they also held prisoners for ransom and as a strategy for negotiation.

The most famous English captive was Mary Rowlandson, a minister's wife taken in February 1676 when Nipmucs and Narragansetts raided Lancaster, Massachusetts. In her enormously popular *The Sovereignty and Goodness of God*, Rowlandson described the horror of the raid in vivid detail. She watched her town's attackers kill a wounded child, and she saw a neighbor "chopped into the head with a hatchet, and stripped naked, and yet was crawling up and down." After choosing captivity over death, she was sold into the household

of Weetamoo and her Narragansett husband Quinnapin. Rowlandson also encountered Philip, who appeared friendly and offered her
tobacco. Her relations with Weetamoo were frosty; her mistress
once snatched a Bible from her hands and threw it outside. Rowlandson described severe hunger, but no torture or abuse. After
three months, she was "redeemed," set free when the English paid a
twenty-pound ransom. "It is good for me that I have been afflicted,"
Rowlandson concluded her narrative by quoting the 119th Psalm.[34]

Some individuals moved from one form of bondage to another.
In June 1676, Narragansett attackers shot to death and then beheaded Hezekiah Willett near his home in Swansea. The Narragansetts took captive Jethro, an African slave attached to the estate
of Thomas Willett, Hezekiah's father. Five days later, Jethro escaped
after spotting English forces nearby. Apparently Jethro had some
facility with the Algonquian language, as he reported that Philip
was "sound and well" and that the Wampanoags and Narragansetts
planned to attack Taunton. With Jethro's information, William Bradford promptly organized an effective defense of the town.[35]

Jethro's service to the colony raised questions about his future
status. Should he be sold? Had he earned his freedom? Would he
now become the property of another descendant of Thomas Willett? Josiah Flynt, minister at Dorcester (in Massachusetts Bay), inquired about Jethro. Flynt was married to Thomas Willett's daughter, Hester. If Jethro was to be sold, Flynt would buy him. If Jethro
was freed, Flynt hoped that Jethro "might be sent to him."[36]

The Boston merchant John Saffin, Thomas Willett's son-in-law
and the administrator of his estate, brokered a deal. Jethro would
"remain a servant unto the successors of the said Captain Willett"
for two years and then be "set at liberty." As was more typical for
indentured servants, the arrangement emphasized the responsibility
of Jethro's master to provide him with meat, drink, and clothing.
In the summer of 1677, Boston's Reverend Increase Mather moved
next door to a house owned by "Jethro the Negro," possibly the
same man.[37]

Although English captives such as Mary Rowlandson gained renown, the English seized a vastly greater number of Native men,
women, and children.[38] Captives were prized booty for soldiers and
their commanders, who received payment for bringing them in. Fol-

lowing precedents established in the wake of the Pequot War, English magistrates and courts consigned many Indian captives to slavery or other forms of servitude. For colonial officials, the opportunity to sell captives yielded funds that helped balance budgets strained by wartime expenditures. Enslavement, and the export of captives in particular, also cleared lands of Native inhabitants and cleared the way for English settlement. These actions resembled those of English officials in other colonies. For instance, in the midst of Bacon's Rebellion, the Virginia legislative assembly in 1676 declared "that all Indians taken in war be held and accounted slaves during life." In other words, captives would be slaves for the rest of their lives, not servants for a fixed term. English settlers in Virginia defended this practice against criticism from royal officials.[39]

Plymouth and Massachusetts forces took captives during their July and August 1675 campaigns at Mount Hope and Pocasset. After the raid on Dartmouth, Wampanoags in the vicinity were fearful of English reprisals, and as many as 160 came to Dartmouth's garrison to surrender. The exact circumstances are unclear. Benjamin Church later claimed that the English had promised favorable terms, but in a contemporary letter, Josiah Winslow stated that the Indians had come "in without any assurance or invitation from us." Regardless, the Wampanoags probably expected to surrender their arms, swear their loyalty, and provide men to serve as scouts and soldiers for the English. Lieutenant John Ellis was unsure how to proceed, so he put the surrenderers on an island and hoped they would stay put until he received orders. Governor Winslow sent Constant Southworth to bring the prisoners to the town of Plymouth. The magistrates were disinclined to show them mercy. "They are known many of them," wrote Winslow, "to be of those that have burned that town, and killed many of the inhabitants." The governor wondered whether it would be possible to "distinguish aright between the innocent and the guilty."[40]

It was easier not to bother with such distinctions. After Southworth brought the captives to Plymouth, the colony's war council decided that they were all guilty. Some had been "actors in the late rising and war." The rest, including the women and children, were "compliers." They had broken their covenants with Plymouth. They had not informed the settlers of Philip's plot. They were rebels and enemies. If the soldiers or magistrates had reason to believe that some of the men had shed English blood or burned houses, they probably executed them. The council decided to sell most of the captives "unto servitude." Similarly, in early September the council condemned to "perpetual servitude" fifty-seven Wampanoags who had "come in a submissive way" to Sandwich. They expected mercy. Instead, New Plymouth's leaders declared that they were now slaves for life.[41]

On September 22, ship captain Thomas Spragg sailed from Boston on the *Sampson* with nearly two hundred Indian slaves, their transport arranged by Massachusetts Bay treasurer John Hull. According to Boston merchant Nathaniel Saltonstall, Spragg's human cargo included eighty Indians from Plymouth Colony captured by the Bay Colony's Samuel Mosely and another forty-five seized by the Mohegans, allies of the English. In all likelihood, some of the Wampanoags who had surrendered at Dartmouth and Sandwich also were aboard the *Sampson*. Spragg was bound for Spain.[42]

A century earlier, Richard Hakluyt—a leading English promoter of colonization—promised that England would help Indians and Africans shake off the shackles of slavery. Hakluyt lamented that the Spanish forced captives "into galleys, where men are tied as slaves, all yell and cry with one voice *Liberta, liberta*, as desirous of liberty and freedom." By contrast, Hakluyt vowed, an English empire would be one of "humanity, courtesy, and freedom." In the 1610s, John Smith objected when Thomas Hunt sold Wampanoags as slaves in Spain. Now, the leaders of New Plymouth and Massachusetts Bay exported captured Indians to the Spanish slave markets.[43]

Spragg unloaded some of the captives in the southwestern Spanish port of Cádiz. The British trader John Mathews acquired the Indians and sold thirty men to Captain Thomas Hamilton, who bought them to pull the oars of his galley. Hamilton, stationed in Tangier, was enthused about his new labor force. Although nine of the Indians had died due to "bad usage on board," he expected the remainder to be "as good if not better than the Moorish slaves." Hamilton hoped that he might purchase a yearly "recruit" of enslaved Natives from across the Atlantic. Given that he pleaded with his superiors to provide the funds he needed for his English crew's provisions and bedding, the conditions for the slaves aboard his gal-

ley must have been wretched. The British Navy decommissioned
the vessel in 1676, and Mathews and Spragg sought to regain possession of the slaves. The whereabouts of the Indians after this time
are unknown.[44]

A few English settlers criticized the enslavement and export of
Indian captives, especially of those who had surrendered to colonial
authorities. In a letter to Bay Colony magistrates, John Eliot warned
that such measures would likely prolong the war—Indians would not
surrender if they feared being sent to Barbados or Cádiz as slaves.
For Eliot, though, it was not just a question of military strategy. "To
sell souls for money seemeth to be a dangerous merchandise," Eliot
upbraided the magistrates and merchants. Eliot observed that the
English had long "condemne[d] the Spaniard for cruelty upon this
point." Bay Colony leaders, he charged, were hypocrites. By export-
ing captives, moreover, colonial leaders removed them from the
blessings of Protestant Christianity.[45]

Barnstable's minister, Thomas Walley, shared Eliot's concerns.
In a letter to Plymouth's John Cotton, Walley lamented "that rash
cruelty of our English toward innocent Indians" and maintained
that "the severity shewed towards the squaws that are sent away"
discouraged those Wampanoags who might have fought as English
allies. Unlike Eliot, though, Walley did not make any formal protest
against the practice. Benjamin Church later claimed that he opposed
the export of Indians, but he played a central role in the subsequent
seizure and enslavement of many Wampanoags and Narragansetts.
Indeed, there was no significant opposition from within New Plymouth to the colony's treatment of captives. In October, the General
Court compensated Josiah Winslow for the "emergent charges" that
had fallen on him over the course of the summer. The governor received "the price of ten Indians, of those savages lately transported
out of the government."[46]

Christian Indians found themselves confronted with other types
of captivity and confinement during the war. This was especially
true in the Bay Colony. Once the Nipmucs began their raids on
Massachusetts towns, English settlers and soldiers regarded all Natives as possible collaborators. At the end of August 1675, the Massachusetts Council declared that Christian Indians had to remain
within a mile of their towns. The magistrates gave permission for

settlers to shoot with impunity any Indians they encountered out-side of those bounds. Beginning in October, Massachusetts removed praying Indians from their communities and interned them on Deer Island in Boston Harbor. Hundreds of men, women, and children suffered a hungry and cold winter. More than half of the island's prisoners perished. Again, John Eliot protested in vain.[47]

At the same time, Nipmucs raided the more western praying towns and offered their inhabitants—many of whom were Nipmucs themselves—a stark choice. They could leave the towns and fight against the English, or they could flee to the English and end up on Deer Island or on Barbados. In response to both English policy and the raids, hundreds of Christian Indians abandoned the praying towns in the fall and winter. Some fled to their kin and former com-munities, and others took their chances with the English. Regard-less of their actions, praying Indians were vulnerable to accusations of disloyalty, caught between two warring peoples who both looked upon them with disdain and suspicion.[48]

New Plymouth also restricted the movement of Indians within its jurisdiction. In December 1675, the colony's war council decreed that the Cape Cod Wampanoags could not come any closer to Plym-outh than the town of Sandwich. Council members worried about the "great damage [that] may accrue to the colony by the southern Indians [in] their frequent resort to Plymouth." What about those Wampanoag communities north of Sandwich? In February, the council commanded the Indians at Nemasket to leave their homes and enter confinement on Clark's Island. It is likely that those in-terned included Christian Wampanoags preached to by John Cot-ton and the late John Sassamon.[49]

Despite the internment and restrictions, on balance Christian Indians in New Plymouth fared better than those in the Bay Colony. Most remained in their communities, and at least in some instances they maintained good relations with the English. For example, even as some Sandwich settlers took refuge in garrisons, the town granted "liberty to the [Mashpee] Indians to set up a house to meet in on the Lord's day."[50] It is difficult to say why Plymouth Colony settlers and officials treated Christian Indians with relatively less suspicion and vindictiveness. The 1671 crisis had already given the colony's Chris-tian Wampanoags an opportunity to demonstrate their fidelity to the English. Also, Richard Bourne had a closer relationship with the Mashpee Wampanoags than any Massachusetts Bay minister had with any single praying town. Bourne was an effective advocate for his congregants, and John Cotton also had a long-established commitment to Indian missions. As was always the case in seventeenth-century New England, local jurisdictions and individual personalities mattered a great deal.

The first several months of the war had brought disaster to numerous English and Wampanoag communities. Both sides endured displacement, the loss of property, captivity, and death. Collectively, however, Wampanoags suffered to a much greater degree. Hundreds had become slaves, and the English had forced many more to abandon their communities. Even so, the fighting was inconclusive. Plymouth and Massachusetts troops had ranged across Mount Hope and Pocasset, but Philip, Weetamoo, and Awashonks had fled. Both they and the war would return.

CHAPTER SIXTEEN

Cannibals

I N November 1675, the United Colonies tapped New Plymouth's governor, Josiah Winslow, to command an English attack against the Narragansetts. Winslow had wanted a resolute charge against hostile Indians, and now he would lead one. The campaign, though, did not target Philip. Instead, the English launched a preemptive strike against a formidable people who had tried hard to stay out of the war.

The Narragansetts were the traditional enemies of the Pokanokets, but mutual grievances against the English and newly formed ties of kinship had sanded away much of that enmity. Still, when the war began, Canonchet (son of Miantonomi, whom the Mohegans had executed in the early 1640s) and other Narragansett sachems wanted to maintain peace with the English. Nevertheless, the English heard multiple reports that armed Narragansett men were gathering with Philip. In the wake of the Swansea raids, for example, Roger Williams denounced Narragansett professions of fidelity as "words of policy [expedience], falsehood, and treachery." When some Narragansett communities sheltered Wampanoags from Pocasset and Sakonnet, English concerns became acute.[1]

The English gave the Narragansett sachems a simple ultimatum. If they did not turn over the Wampanoag refugees, they would make themselves enemies of the English. Under intense pressure, Canonchet and other Narragansett sachems signed an agreement in which they promised to surrender all of the Wampanoags in their midst by October 28. Obligations of kinship and hospitality made it impossible for Canonchet to fulfill the agreement. The Narragansetts knew about the recent English enslavement and export of captive Indians. Narragansett sachems would not betray the Wampanoag refugees to the same fate. After the deadline passed, the commissioners of the United Colonies voted to raise a thousand soldiers and destroy an enemy of their own creation.[2]

Many of the Narragansetts—about a thousand persons in all—were living in a fort they had built in the Great Swamp in present-day South Kingston, Rhode Island. Natives from Pocasset and Sakonnet—including Awashonks—were there as well. During the first months of the war in the summer of 1675, Philip and Weetamoo had eluded the English by retreating into swamps. Canonchet and his people likely felt secure.

Troops from Plymouth and Massachusetts, joined by Pequot and Mohegan allies, converged at Wickford, Rhode Island. While Rhode Island's Quaker-dominated government never allied itself with its puritan neighbors, it gave its blessing to the operation (which would occur within its claimed jurisdiction) and provided logistical support. On Saturday, December 18, the English army marched south and then slept outside during a night of heavy snow. "We lay a thousand in the open field that long night," wrote Massachusetts soldier James Oliver. Well before sunrise the next morning, they resumed their march. A Narragansett captive led them to the fort and showed them the one vulnerable opening in its enormous palisade. After what Oliver described as "sore fighting," English troops pushed their way inside and began setting homes ablaze. Soldiers butchered those who tried to escape. Reports disagree about the number of Narragansett fighters killed in the battle and the blaze, but it is clear that hundreds of noncombatants perished. The English also destroyed "piles of meat and heaps of corn." For the Pequots, the fiery slaughter must have stirred painful memories of how their ancestors had suffered in 1637.[3]

In his memoir, Benjamin Church claimed that he had begged Josiah Winslow to stop the burning of the fort, primarily because it might have sheltered the English soldiers for the night. In the battle's immediate aftermath, the English regretted the loss of shelter and provisions, but they expressed no scruples about the massacre of noncombatants. William Hubbard, minister at Ipswich and an early chronicler of the war, reported that the battle interrupted Narragansett women's preparations for dinner. "They and their mitchin [meat] fried together," he joked. Massachusetts Bay schoolmaster and poet Benjamin Tompson also reveled in the violence. "Here might be heard an hideous Indian cry," Tompson wrote, "Of wounded ones who in the wigwams fry." Tompson added that "had we been cannibals here might we feast." After the many disasters of the war's first six months, English settlers had thirsted for revenge. Now they savored it.[4]

The Great Swamp Fight, however, was not as decisive as the Mystic River massacre had been during the Pequot War. When daylight waned, the English trudged the nearly twenty miles back to Wickford on a "long snowy cold night." About twenty English soldiers died in the battle, and around two hundred were wounded, including Plymouth Colony's William Bradford and Benjamin Church. After reaching Wickford, the English troops buried another forty-two men who died from their wounds. (Bradford and Church recovered.) The soldiers who had survived the Great Swamp—unlike New England's ministers and poets—were in no mood to celebrate. Furthermore, many Narragansetts had escaped. The next month, Narragansett fighters raided Pawtuxet, then fled to central Massachusetts. Winslow at first gave chase but then retreated with his troops to Boston. The army disbanded, having inflicted a heavy blow on the Narragansetts but without having achieved its objective.[5]

Since the Swansea raids, the war had steadily expanded. Half of all English settlements in Plymouth and Massachusetts Bay had been attacked, and in Maine, English settlers precipitated fighting with the Abenaki in much the same way that their southern counterparts had provoked the Narragansetts. Meanwhile, Philip and his warriors had spent the winter in New York, and Canonchet had also given the English the slip. The English suffered further setbacks as the winter came to an end. A large force of Nipmucs burned Sudbury, only twenty miles from Boston.

In the spring of 1676, the war returned to Plymouth Colony. That March, Captain Michael Pierce of Scituate led a small company, including twenty Wampanoags, across the Pawtucket River. In an ambush, possibly organized by Canonchet, "a great multitude of the enemy" slew fifty English soldiers and about half of the Wampanoags. Two days later, the same Narragansetts attacked Rehoboth. Only one man died. The other settlers remained safe in their garrison houses, where they watched thirty-five homes burn. After the destruction, Rehoboth's inhabitants spent three days burying corpses from Pierce's ill-fated offensive. Minister Noah Newman compared the desolation to that which would accompany Christ's Second Coming. He recalled the text he had used for his sermon the first day English blood was shed at Swansea: "Be still and know that I am God." It was harder to retain such faith "in the worst times," but Newman and most other settlers rejected calls to take refuge on the Cape. The minister taught that their suffering would end only when God stopped punishing them for their sins.[6]

The attacks were not limited to the colony's western settlements. Two weeks before the ambush of Pierce's company, the sachem Totoson organized an attack on the house of William Clarke, only two miles south of Plymouth on the Eel River. As with many raids and battles during the war, the strike came on a Sunday. Although Plymouth's government had forbidden Indians to come farther north than Sandwich, one man convicted of the attack said that a Mashpee Wampanoag had visited Clarke to gain knowledge of his home's defenses and stores. While Clarke and most other men attended worship, Natives killed eleven people at the garrison and carried off eight guns along with considerable gunpowder and money. Clarke's wife and all but one of their children died. Boston's Increase Mather explained that Clarke had brought his misery upon himself. The minister related a conversation in which Clarke had wished all of New England's Indians hanged. When Mather objected, Clarke had remained adamant. "Their blood be upon me and my children," he had vowed. Now it was, reasoned Mather. One of Clarke's sons lived despite having been struck on the head by a tomahawk. According to early nineteenth-century historian James Thacher, he "afterwards wore a plate of silver over the wound" and thereby gained the nickname "Silver-Headed Tom." In July, Plymouth convicted and executed several Wampanoags—one by beheading—for the deaths.[7]

In mid-May, Tuspaquin's men raided Scituate, the colony's largest town, killed one man, and burned homes before twenty of the town's inhabitants drove them off.[8] Outside of the Cape, there were no safe havens.

New Plymouth's government struggled to mount a military response. Because men were reluctant to fight, the General Court repeatedly passed laws threatening those who refused impressment with stiff punishments. In the spring, Plymouth's leaders turned down the Bay Colony's request to join an intended offensive to the heart of Nipmuc country. Instead, Plymouth's government begged Massachusetts to send troops to secure Rehoboth and its other western towns. Plymouth also rejected a Massachusetts plan to recruit Indian allies to "range" between Medford and Rehoboth. Colonial secretary Nathaniel Morton feared that Indians sent forth without sufficient English supervision would "be corrupted by the enemy." Furthermore, he added, after Pierce's defeat "we think we must at present do no more but scout about our town with what diligence we can." The people's spirits had begun to "run low," he added. They were "very averse to going forth against the enemy." Plymouth's settlers had no stomach for fresh offensives.[9]

While the English mourned their spring 1676 casualties, the outlook was actually far bleaker for their enemies. The English were more numerous and better armed, and unlike in earlier decades, they controlled the coastal waterways. The Native peoples of southern New England were low on ammunition and provisions. Philip purchased some badly needed supplies from Dutch traders in New York, but the English could obtain food and bullets far more readily. Despite tensions among the colonies, the English were also far more united than their opponents. For the Wampanoags, and for several other peoples, King Philip's War was a civil war. The fact that several Native peoples sided with the English was decisive, moreover. In February, Mohawk forces attacked Philip's men and cost the Pokanoket sachem much of his remaining fighting strength. Two months later, Connecticut soldiers working with Niantic, Pequot, and Mohegan allies captured Canonchet, shot and decapitated him, and sent his head to Hartford.[10]

Even as Natives executed successful raids against the English that spring, many sachems believed that it was time to make peace. Narragansett and Wampanoag peoples began returning to their lands. They needed to plant crops in order to feed themselves. After nearly a year of war, however, colonial leaders wanted nothing less than complete victory and the punishment of those who had shed English blood. In June, Plymouth's settlers finally responded to the depredations of the spring. The General Court voted to raise and send into the field two hundred men, including fifty allied Wampanoags.[11]

Benjamin Church, who had moved his family to Aquidneck Island, now paid another visit to Awashonks. She had returned to Sakonnet. When Church went to an agreed-upon meeting place, her men suddenly rose up out of the grass and surrounded him, brandishing their weapons. Church distributed rum and tobacco and then spoke with Awashonks. After the June 1675 nickómmo, Awashonks had sought to avoid becoming entangled in the war. She had fled to the Narragansetts, may have been present at the Great Swamp Fight, and then went to Wachusett in present-day north-central Massachusetts. In the late winter of 1676, she would have seen Mary Rowlandson and had spent time with Philip and Weetamoo.

After she returned to Sakonnet, Awashonks still did not want her people to take up arms against either Philip or the English. Benjamin Church insisted that she could not escape that choice any longer. He encouraged her to contemplate the example of the Pequots. Church stressed that after the Pequots had subjected themselves to the English, they had received protection against their enemies. They were now allies of the English. Awashonks, of course, knew that during the Pequot War, the English had massacred hundreds of noncombatants and then had enslaved scores of captives. Church urged Awashonks to save her people from the same fate. He promised that if Awashonks and her people submitted to the English, and if Sakonnet men fought against Philip, they "and their wives and children should have their lives spared, and none of them transported out of the country." Church did not offer to help Awashonks retain any land, and he did not even promise that her people would escape enslavement or servitude, just that they would not be executed or exported. What Church pledged was enough. The Sakonnets knew what had become of captives taken by the English the previous summer. They did not trust New Plymouth's officials, but fighting on their side now seemed the only option.[12]

Church sent Awashonks's son Peter to Plymouth to confirm the agreement. Meanwhile, Church marched toward Pocasset with his new allies. On the way, he encountered William Bradford, who greeted Church with marked coolness. The two men did not like each other. Bradford, recently given the rank of major, was a careful and cautious commander. Church was creative and impetuous, and he alleged that Bradford ignored intelligence and squandered opportunities to assault Philip and Weetamoo. In accordance with the colony's law, Bradford ordered Awashonks and her people to turn back and instead walk to Sandwich. He told Church to get Josiah Winslow's approval before taking the Sakonnets into battle.

By that point, Peter and a few companions had reached Plymouth. "We have found you so perfidious," Plymouth's council informed the Sakonnet visitors, "that we must have some good security for your fidelity before we can grant your desires." The Sakonnet men promised that they would fight against Philip, and they offered to turn over Succanowassucke, a Sakonnet man they said had stirred up some of their people to join Philip. The council accepted Peter's offer of renewed and more abject submission, but it kept him as a hostage in order to guarantee Sakonnet compliance. Winslow, meanwhile, confirmed Church's agreement and commissioned him to lead the Sakonnets against Philip and Weetamoo.[13]

Church found Awashonks and her people on the shore of Buzzards Bay feasting on eels, fish, and clams. Another dance followed. The Sakonnets formed rings around a fire. One at a time, leading warriors danced around the fire, named a people at war with the English, and struck their spears and hatchets into the ground. The next day, Church and his Sakonnet recruits returned to Plymouth.[14]

Bradford, Church, and their Native allies spent July pursuing Philip, Weetamoo, Tuspaquin, and the Narragansetts. Although Church later implied that Bradford's caution was either incompetence or cowardice, the major's forces killed dozens and captured scores of Wampanoags and Narragansetts. "I have done my duty and neglected no opportunity to face upon the enemy," he asserted. At the same time, Bradford refused to emulate his more aggressive and vainglorious relation (Church's wife was the granddaughter of

Bradford's stepmother). "I shall not put myself out of breath to get before Ben Church," he vowed.[15]

But if Bradford captured scores, Church seized hundreds and received all of the credit. Church's English and Native troops marched countless prisoners to Plymouth. Some captives then volunteered to switch sides in an attempt to save themselves and their families from foreign slavery. "Those [Indians] that are come in," Barnstable minister Thomas Walley reported, "are conquered and help to conquer others." Walley observed that "throughout the land where Indians are employed there hath been the greatest success if not the only success." It was a "humbling providence of god that we have so much need of them and cannot do our work without them." The English might not have won the war on their own. They certainly would not have won it as quickly.[16]

By the end of July, English troops closed in on their primary human targets. Church's men captured Philip's wife (named Wootonekanuske, according to the nineteenth-century historian Samuel G. Drake) and young son, and Weetamoo perished either during or shortly after a fierce battle near Taunton. Totoson, who had organized the July 1675 raid on Dartmouth and the March 1676 attack on Eel River, also died. Church continued tracking Philip, "putting his Indians in the front." They took more captives, but Philip found refuge in a swamp west of the Titicut River and slipped away. Church returned to Plymouth, then headed west again. He received word that Philip was back near Mount Hope, in a "miry swamp."[17]

This time Philip did not get away. He ran into an ambush, and a Pocasset man named Alderman shot him. During the first weeks of the war, Alderman had fled from Pocasset, taken refuge on Aquidneck Island, and provided intelligence to the English. Now, Alderman's bullet struck Philip's heart. The Pokanoket sachem "fell upon his face in the mud and water with his gun under him."[18]

According to Church, an "Indian executioner" laughed and said that Philip "had been a very great man, and had made many a man afraid of him, but so big as he was he would now chop his ass for him." The scene is probably fanciful, but the morbid humor captures the emotional relief the English experienced at the war's end.[19]

There wasn't anything fanciful about what came next. The executioner beheaded and quartered Philip, meting out the English punishment for treason. Alderman carried Philip's head to Plymouth, and Church sent his "paws"—as Bay Colony secretary Edward Rawson referred to Philip's hands—to Boston. Church's men hung the other pieces of their enemy's corpse on nearby trees.[20]

After Philip's death, Plymouth's forces killed Tuspaquin and several of Philip's other key allies. The western Wampanoag sachems who had outmaneuvered English forces the previous summer succumbed to better-armed, better-fed, and more numerous foes. The English and their Algonquian and Mohawk allies also killed or captured their Nipmuc and Narragansett enemies, but the Bay Colony's struggle against the Abenaki in Maine continued for more than another year. When Massachusetts asked for assistance against the Abenaki, New Plymouth demurred. Although its magistrates affirmed "the common English interest against the barbarous . . . enemy" and wished "to avoid anything that might favor of ingratitude," Plymouth was not certain the lands in question lay within the jurisdiction of Massachusetts Bay. Moreover, Nathaniel Morton explained, Benjamin Church was "the only man with whom our Indians will cheerfully serve," and Church was busy with his family. The United Colonies were never truly united.[21]

The wars of 1675–78 devastated communities across New England. As many as one in every ten adult English men died or suffered captivity, and dozens of English women and children perished. Economic losses were also enormous. In the town of Scituate, for example, twelve homes burned, and Native attackers destroyed crops and livestock. Among those killed at the Great Swamp Fight was Walter Briggs's indentured "Irish man . . . which was his estate." Survivors returned home with maimed bodies and minds haunted by the horrors they had witnessed. Theophilus Witherell, son of the town's longtime minister, was "wholly disabled and so like to be." He lived another quarter-century. Like Witherell, communities bore the scars of war for decades.[22]

Native losses were far more staggering. Many thousands were gone, killed on the battlefield, dead of disease and hunger, living as refugees to the west or north, or transported as slaves out of New England. Whereas the English population rose during the 1670s despite the ravages of war, the Native population of New England fell by half.[23]

In June 1675, the start of fighting in Swansea had coincided with a day of humiliation observed across Plymouth Colony. When New Plymouth's General Court appointed another day of humiliation in June 1676, it also called on church members to "renew a covenant engagement to God for reformation of all provoking evils." By now, the covenant renewal was a familiar ritual in New England. Church members confessed their apostasy from their founding ideals, asked God to forgive their sins, and renewed the covenant that bound them to each other and to God. The hope was that the occasion would remove a crisis and mark a new beginning for the community.[24]

In the town of Plymouth, the congregation observed a day of prayer, then called a meeting a week later at which members listened to the covenant they had entered into when they had joined the church. Minister John Cotton and Elder Thomas Cushman arraigned the people for having broken the covenant. The evidence was obvious. God had afflicted them with a year of war. God had used the Indians to slay settlers and destroy their livelihoods. In fact, they deserved more severe punishment, but God in his mercy now gave them an opportunity to repent and to stay his wrath. Congregants affirmed that they had violated the covenant, and they agreed to renew their bonds with God and with each other.

The church set aside an entire day in mid-July for the renewal. On that morning, Cotton preached on a text from Psalm 56: "Thy vows are upon me, O God." Then in the afternoon, Cushman read an extensive confession on behalf of full church members, who acknowledged their manifold sins. They had engaged in frivolous conversation, quarreled with each other, neglected family prayers, kept away from the Lord's Supper, and broken the Sabbath. Cushman urged them to reform and live as God required. In response, church members stood up, signifying their consent.

Cotton then read a second document on behalf of the church's "[adult] children," individuals who had come of age but had not owned its covenant for themselves. Some men and women were not sure that they had experienced spiritual regeneration. Others trembled at the thought of partaking of the Lord's Supper unworthily because to do so might lead to their damnation. In the first few years after John Cotton's installation, the church had admitted dozens of new members, but that momentum had dissipated. Many young men had died "by the rage of the enemy," Cotton observed, but halfway members were really fighting against God. Cotton used words from the Book of Jeremiah to liken them to "a degenerate plant" descended from "a noble vine." Now, they should promise "to walk steadfastly in that good old way." If they could qualify themselves for full membership and the sacraments, they should not hold back. As the members had done, these women and men all stood up to signify their consent. Eight became full church members over the next two years.

Cotton insisted that the covenant renewals worked wonders. "God turned his hand against our heathen enemies and subdued them wonderfully," he wrote. Within a month, Philip was dead. The magistrates decreed a day of thanksgiving.[25]

Plymouth's residents assembled to pray, sing psalms, and listen to John Cotton's sermon. Then Alderman and some of Church's soldiers arrived with Philip's head. Puritans described their days of thanksgiving as "solemn" gatherings. One suspects this day was unusually joyous.

According to Benjamin Church, Plymouth's government paid Alderman the standard and "scanty" rate of thirty shillings for Philip's head. English settlers knew what to do with the bloody prize. Just as the Pilgrims had done with Wituwamat's head, Plymouth's soldiers placed the heads of Philip and other enemy sachems on the town's fort. Visitors saw Philip's desiccated head for decades. Cotton Mather, who had an advanced sense of self-entitlement, "took off the jaw from the exposed skull" on one of his visits to see his Plymouth relations.[26]

"Our eyes saw the salvation of God," John Cotton commented on the head's timely arrival. It was a sign that God had finally answered their prayers. "Thus did God break the head of that leviathan," Boston's Increase Mather wrote, "and gave it to be meat to the people inhabiting the wilderness." Twenty-five years later, Cotton Mather put it more bluntly: "God sent 'em in the head of a leviathan for a thanksgiving feast." God had succored the Pilgrims with a harvest in 1621. Now he nourished his people with Philip's head.[27]

CHAPTER SEVENTEEN

Children of Life and Death

NEW ENGLAND'S SEVENTEENTH-CENTURY settlers lived longer and healthier lives than their counterparts in Europe. The historian John Demos found that Plymouth Colony men and women who reached maturity lived to an average of sixty-nine and sixty-two years of age, respectively. Infant mortality rates, however, were only slightly better in New England than in many parts of England. The mortality rates for young children also remained stubbornly high. While available records permit only rough approximations, around a tenth of New England infants died before their first birthday, and a quarter did not reach the age of ten.[1] Young children were "like as a bubble, or the brittle glass," wrote the Massachusetts Bay poet Anne Bradstreet after the death of her three-year-old granddaughter.[2]

The emotions of bereaved parents were similarly brittle. Mothers and fathers were not desensitized to grief because they lost so many children. Instead, each successive death was a heavier blow, and some New England couples buried child after child. Half of Boston merchant Samuel Sewall's fourteen children died before the age of three. At one point, he dreamed that they were all dead. John Saffin, raised in the Plymouth Colony town of Scituate, outlived every single one of his eight children.[3]

Plymouth's John and Joanna Cotton endured several painful losses. Over the first twenty-two years of their marriage, Joanna brought eleven children into the world, the expansion of the family uninterrupted by her husband's sexual indiscretions and career transitions. The first death came in 1669. The couple left their four-year-old daughter, Sarah, with Joanna's parents in Guilford, Connecticut. Several months after John's installation as Plymouth's pastor, Sarah perished in the midst of an epidemic that also claimed Joanna's mother and one of her sisters. "Our graves are multiplied and fresh earth heaps increased," lamented Joanna's father, Bryan Rosseter. "Coffins again and again have been carried out of my doors." Weeks later, Joanna learned that she was pregnant again. When she gave birth to a daughter the next spring, they named her Sarah after her deceased sister.[4]

Five years later, Joanna delivered a son who died one day after his birth. This time, because she was not nursing, she quickly became pregnant again. In August 1675, the Cottons moved to Boston for the remainder of her pregnancy. In all likelihood, they did so because they feared for her health and safety after the war's outbreak. While away from his own congregation, John Cotton preached regularly at his brother-in-law Increase Mather's North Church and filled other pulpit invitations. He probably aspired to a more prestigious and better-compensated position in the Bay Colony. Also, his eldest and namesake son had begun his studies at Harvard. In September, Joanna gave birth to another son, whom the couple named Josiah.[5]

By December, the Cottons and their infant son had returned to Plymouth. They all survived a wave of sickness that swept through the colony that winter, but a "malignant fever" the next year did not spare one-year-old Josiah. During his illness, the Cottons would have maintained a long vigil at Josiah's bedside. John would have read from the Bible and prayed. Others from the community would have come to pray over Josiah as well, with the belief that if God did not heal him, their prayers would lift his soul into God's presence. After a death, a midwife customarily washed the corpse and wrapped it in linen. Perhaps Joanna did the work herself in this case. John Cotton probably fasted from Josiah's death until his son's burial.[6]

Some Reformed Protestants rejected graveside services, eulogies, and rituals of mourning as unbiblical, and puritans were especially zealous against anything that smacked of Catholicism. In old

England and New England, puritans buried their dead in a timely and simple manner. Things were changing by the time of Josiah Cotton's death, however. Especially when wealthy individuals died, families staged elaborate processions and then held lavish feasts. The bereaved sometimes sent gloves as invitations to a funeral—or at least provided them for pallbearers and other dignitaries—and gave engraved rings, scarves, and other tokens of grief to those who attended. Ministers prayed before a procession or at the grave, and they delivered eulogies, either during a Sunday service or on the day of the funeral itself. It is unlikely, however, that tiny Josiah Cotton's burial involved much pageantry.[7]

After the boy's death, his father's ministerial colleagues wrote to express their condolences and offer advice. Barnstable's Thomas Walley reminded the Cottons that "the affliction you have at present is no new or strange affliction but that which is common to the children of God." Joanna, however, remained inconsolable ten days after young Josiah's death. John confided to his brother-in-law Increase Mather that his wife was "most desolate and pensive." The previous night, she had "fall[en] afresh to mourning, as if she had nothing else to do."[8]

John Cotton worried because he knew that Christians were not supposed to mourn, at least not for too long or to excess. New England Congregationalists understood hardships as expressions of God's sovereign will. Just as God had afflicted the colonies with the scourge of war, God had willed Josiah's death. God's will was inscrutable, but puritans reminded themselves that God was merciful. Even the deaths of children were part of that mercy, a painful way that God reminded men and women of their sinfulness and mortality. Josiah was God's, and God had taken him. Excessive grief betrayed an idolatrous attachment to the things of this world.

John Cotton's nephew Cotton Mather later warned against this sin in one of colonial New England's most poignant sermons. His first child, a daughter named Abigail, died on the morning of December 25, 1687. For New England Congregationalists, who did not celebrate Christmas, it was a regular Sabbath day. Mather preached that afternoon. "A dead child," he stated, "is a sight no more surprising than a broken pitcher, or a blasted flower." Even so, he conceded that Abigail's death was almost unbearable. His heart was "tempestuous [and] rebellious," but he reminded himself and his congregants that God was the only proper object of their devotion. "It is a blasted banned soul," warned Mather, "that sets up a creature in the room, [on] the throne of the great God, that gives unto a creature those loves and those cares which are due unto the great God alone." Furthermore, Christians should remember that it was their idolatrous love for their children that prompted God's punishment. Mourners should repent. "'Twas that sin that killed thy child," Mather taught. When he published his sermon, he dedicated it to his friend Samuel Sewall, who was well acquainted with the same grief.[9]

John and Joanna Cotton received similar counsel after Josiah's death. "A great part of our obedience," Thomas Walley wrote, "lies in our submission to the will of God and being graciously quiet under his hand." When Cotton informed Increase Mather of his wife's desolation, his brother-in-law instructed Joanna that she needed "patience and moderation in respect of grief . . . otherwise you will despond . . . and wrong yourself, your family, your body, your soul, and it may be provoke the Lord." If Joanna did not quiet her rebellious heart, Mather warned, God might further punish her family. The lives of her other children were at stake. Furthermore, Mather and Walley both suggested that the Cottons should thank God that Josiah did not die at the hands of cruel Indians.[10]

Puritans are known more for their doctrinal rigidity than for their tenderness. Though they argued among themselves about the finer points of predestination, they agreed that prior to the world's creation, God had elected some individuals to salvation and others to damnation. In his wildly popular *The Day of Doom*, Massachusetts minister and poet Michael Wigglesworth summarized the doctrine:

> He that may choose, or else refuse,
> all men to save or spill,
> May this man choose, and that refuse,
> redeeming whom he will.

For seventeenth-century Congregationalists, moreover, hell was much more crowded than heaven. God chose to damn most human beings.[11]

Reformed theologians presumed that infants shared in the human predicament of original sin and thus were among the objects of God's wrath. John Calvin was adamant on the point. "Even though the fruits of their iniquity have not yet come forth," he maintained, "they have the seed enclosed within them. Indeed, their whole nature is a seed of sin . . . hateful and abhorrent to God." As sinful humans, infants also shared in God's decrees of salvation and reprobation. This was not cruelty on God's part, but equity. God treated perishing infants just as he treated all other human beings. In fact, infant deaths proved that God elected individuals irrespective of their merits. He did not save some infants for the good works they would have done had they lived to maturity. God simply picked and chose according to his will and for his own purposes. It was a stark theology, capable of providing hope to sinners already convinced they could not earn their salvation, but also capable of plunging individuals into despair.[12]

At least some of the time, though, Congregational ministers soothed souls made anxious by these doctrines. Ministers preached that those men and women who faithfully attended God's ordinances and lived righteously should not despair. Especially because individuals had to testify to an experience of regeneration in order to join churches, church membership conveyed a probability of salvation. "Church membership was not a guarantee that one was elect," explains the historian Baird Tipson, "but anyone seeking assurance was far better in than out." Much better. Congregationalists never fully resolved the paradoxes in their theology, but ministers such as John Cotton (of Plymouth) preached comforting messages to church members. "Though you are not so rich in faith as Abraham was," Cotton encouraged those he termed "weak Christians," "though you don't make so much haste as other Christians do, yet if you seriously follow after Christ you shall be crowned. Every true Christian shall get safe to heaven." Those who had owned the church covenant had testified to God's work of grace in their hearts. They should trust God.[13]

In particular, the deaths of children bent Calvinist theology toward mercy. Samuel Stone, Cotton's theological mentor in Connecticut, affirmed that "election hath no dependence upon prevision, of any gracious qualifications, good works, and grace, faith, or any good in the creatures." Yet Stone suggested that "God doth

constantly convert children . . . there are more souls of infants in
heaven, than of any other age." Similarly, Michael Wigglesworth
referenced

> an infant throng
> of babes, for whom Christ died
> whom for his own, by ways unknown
> to men, he sanctified.

Heaven might not be as crowded as hell, but it was full of children.
Therefore, ministers reassured grieving church members that their
infants and very young children enjoyed God's salvation.[14]

"A child is gone," Thomas Walley wrote to John and Joanna
Cotton, "but God is not gone, grace is not gone, nor yet the child
lost." Bridgewater's James Keith was similarly definite in his encouragement. "Our Lord Jesus Christ," Keith reassured the Cottons,
"hath said suffer little children to come to me, he is the great and
good shepherd, who hath a favor for poor children and doth gather
the lambs unto his bosom." In addition to telling Joanna Cotton to
restrain her grief, Increase Mather also offered her comfort. "God
had made you an instrument," Mather wrote, "to replenish heaven,
and bring forth an heir for the kingdom of God." Josiah Cotton
was not lost. He had preceded John and Joanna into the presence
of God.[15]

A few months after Josiah's death, Joanna Cotton became pregnant again. She conceived after returning from a trip to visit her
relatives in Connecticut, a trip she could not have made during the
war. The next winter, she gave birth to a son the couple named
Samuel, who died shortly before his sixth birthday. By the time of
Samuel's death, Joanna had delivered two more sons, one of whom
she named Josiah after his deceased brother.

It was relatively easy for church members to leave the salvation
of infants and very young children in God's hands. As sons and
daughters matured, though, parents worried about their spiritual
development. On both sides of the Atlantic, books about pious children were popular and served as both an inspiration and a warning
to parents. Scituate's John Clap, who died at the age of thirteen,

served as an exemplar in one such manual. Although free from any obvious transgressions, Clap mourned his sinfulness, and he longed to be with Christ. When he worked in the fields with his father, he asked questions to deepen his knowledge of God. When he came to church, he stood for the entire two or three hours in order to better concentrate on the sermon and prayers. Clap then patiently bore a long illness, showing no distress even when he could no longer open his mouth. Just before he breathed his last, "his teeth were opened," giving him a final chance to rejoice in Christ's blood and commend his own spirit to his Lord. Clap then "quietly breathed his soul into the arms of his blessed savior." Urian Oakes, minister at Cambridge and president of Harvard College, praised the strange lad as a "young old man, full of grace, though not full of days."[16]

Few children died like John Clap, and fewer lived like him. Many parents had a keen sense of how far their own children fell short of such ideals. The Cottons, for instance, repeatedly heard troubling news about their eldest son, John. In July 1675, Increase Mather recorded in his journal that his son Cotton was "being abused by John Cotton and some other scholars at the college." Apparently, upperclassmen expected freshmen—such as Cotton Mather—to run errands for them and beat or otherwise abused them if they refused. Increase Mather, a nonteaching fellow at Harvard and intimately involved in the college's administration, summoned the younger John Cotton and told him to stop the practice.[17]

Mather kept his Plymouth relations informed about their son, and late in 1676, John and Joanna received word of something that brought "much grief and bitterness." It is not clear what their son had done, but the couple regarded it as a serious transgression. Joanna worried about her son's soul, though she found some comfort in the New Testament's promise that "Christ Jesus came into the world to save sinners." Her anxious husband asked Mather to invite his son for a weekly chat. Even better, perhaps young John could live with the Mathers that winter or spring. That way, he would be under Mather's "roof and eye." John Cotton sent a barrel of beef to his brother-in-law and promised to pay any expenses that his son would incur. "Who knows," he wrote, "but God may make you his father?" Ministers often placed their sons with their colleagues, who became surrogate fathers and mentors to the next generation of clergy. The Cottons went to great length to promote their children's spiritual well-being.[18]

While John and Joanna Cotton mourned Josiah's death in January 1677, they had two Native boys with them as temporary members of the household. Increase Mather had asked John Cotton to obtain a captive Indian boy and groom him as a servant. As it turned out, Cotton acquired two boys: a "little one" from Benjamin Church and a six-year-old named Jether from New Plymouth's treasurer, Constant Southworth. Cotton informed Mather that Jether was "a pretty little boy," but that it would be "some time before he do you service." In the meantime, Cotton was instructing him in the basics of Christianity. "I hope he will be soon capable of good instruction," Cotton wrote. "He can truly answer that question: who made him?" Cotton's facility with the Wampanoag language made him ideal for this role.[19]

Two months later, Cotton reported to Mather that he had returned the other boy to Church but that Jether was "now fit to cut your wood, and go to mill." Cotton was uncertain whether he should send him to Boston or await word from Mather, and he apologized that in his wife's absence, he could not properly clothe the boy. Joanna was with her relatives in Connecticut. "I received him meanly clad," Cotton explained, "and cannot put on him more than these black rags for want of my wife." It is a strange comment. Plymouth's minister could surely have arranged clothing for Jether had he cared to do so.[20]

In July, Increase Mather asked for the "Indian lad" to be sent to him on the "next vessel." Mather had arranged for Jether to serve a family in Dorchester for a few months and then enter service in his household. "By that time," Mather wrote, "I hope he will be able to speak English."[21]

Jether left the Cotton household. Did he indeed go to Dorchester and then Boston? Did he survive an epidemic of smallpox that caused John Cotton to bring his namesake son home the next winter? Did he run away from service? In his short life, Jether had known little but disruption and tumult. What macabre sights had he witnessed during the previous two years? Were his parents slaves in the

Caribbean or the Mediterranean? Was he an orphan? Did he have siblings? Known documents offer no insight into his experiences or background, a sharp contrast with the abundance of materials that chronicle the lives of the Cottons and the Mathers.

Jether was among the many hundreds of Native men, women, and children who had surrendered or been captured during the closing months of the war. English jurisdictions across the region distributed and sold captives. In Providence, for instance, Roger Williams presided over a court that condemned one man to immediate execution, sold others, and then sent the remaining prisoners to Newport for sale. Existing records do not reveal any slave auctions within Plymouth Colony. Field commanders such as Benjamin Church distributed or sold prisoners on their own. The colony's magistrates also sent large numbers to Boston. There, captives were held in some sort of slave pen and auctioned off.[22]

Bay Colony treasurer John Hull presided over several sales of captives. On August 24, 1676, Hull sold approximately one hundred captives for just over £160. Healthy adults, boys, and girls fetched about £2 each, while one group of thirteen "squaws and papooses wounded, one sick" sold for £20. The Boston merchant and mariner Thomas Smith was the biggest buyer. He purchased three men, one girl, two "lads," eleven "squaws," eight "papooses," and four "little children," twenty-nine slaves in all. One month later, Hull recorded another sale, this time of around one hundred captives. Thomas Smith bought forty-one of them for £82.[23]

African slaves sold in Boston or Newport fetched much higher prices. "Our Negroes, men and boys," Governor Josiah Winslow informed English officials in 1680, "are valued at twenty, twenty-five, [or] thirty pounds per head as they seem to be better or worse." Why were Indian captives sold for a fraction of that cost? New Englanders understood that for Africans, slavery was a permanent and inheritable condition. There was consensus across New England that Indian captives should be reduced to servitude, but—especially in the case of children—perhaps only for a fixed number of years or until they reached a certain age. The flood of captives seized in the closing months of the war also lowered their value.[24]

Further depressing prices was the fact that some Caribbean colonies closed themselves to Native slaves. In mid-June 1676, Barbados not only outlawed the further import of New England Indians, but also required masters to send away within six months any they had previously purchased. Barbados's assembly declared that Indians from New England were "of a subtle and dangerous nature and able more cunningly to contrive and carry on those dangerous designs which our Negroes of their own nature are prone unto." The previous year, white Barbadian planters had learned of a planned African slave revolt and had executed several dozen alleged conspirators. They feared that New England Indians would make their slave population even more rebellious.[25]

Despite the news from Barbados, Thomas Smith crammed nearly 200 enslaved Indians into the hold of his ship, the *Seaflower*. Of these, 110 came from New Plymouth; the others were Bay Colony captives. In order to protect Smith and prospective buyers from charges of man-stealing, governors Josiah Winslow and John Leverett provided certificates that explained that Philip and other sachems had rebelled against the authority of the king and had broken their covenants with his colonies. They had committed "murders, villainies, and outrages" and had intended to utterly destroy or expel all English settlers. Therefore, the governors concluded, "by due and legal procedure the said heathen malefactors, men, women, and children, have been sentenced and condemned to perpetual servitude and slavery." The governors authorized Smith to sell them in any English colony or in "the dominions of any other Christian prince." Smith apparently tried to sell his human cargo in the Caribbean, then sailed to Tangier.[26]

The fate of one captive prompted an unusual debate. Shortly before Benjamin Church's forces tracked and ambushed Philip, they had seized Philip's wife and son. Church stated that Philip's son was nine years of age; his name is unknown. In other instances, magistrates sold the children of enemy sachems and shipped them out of New England. Philip, though, represented all of New England's enemies and all of its people's afflictions, making his son a special case. Plymouth's leaders asked the colony's ministers if he was a "child of death." In other words, should they kill him?[27]

John Cotton and Marshfield's Samuel Arnold voted for execution. True, the Bible instructed that children should not be "put to death for the fathers" but rather that "every man shall be put to death for his own sin" (Deuteronomy 24:16). Cotton and Arnold did not think that magistrates should execute the children of ordinary capital criminals. Philip, however, was no ordinary criminal. Instead, he had been among the "principal leaders and actors in such horrid villainies . . . against a whole country, yea the whole interest of God." Philip had been God's enemy, and the "sword of justice" might slay his son. The ministers pointed to several instances in the Bible in which the Israelites killed the children of their enemies, sometimes on God's command.[28]

Increase Mather, John Cotton's brother-in-law, urged that "some effectual course be taken" with Philip's son. He pointed to the biblical example of Hadad, "who was a little child when his father, chief sachem of the Edomites, was killed by Joab." During the reign of King David, the Israelites under the command of Joab had spent six months killing all of the men in Edom. Hadad escaped to Egypt with some of his father's officials and later became an adversary of David's son Solomon. Had he been in a position to do so, surely David would have acted with prudence and killed Hadad in order to forestall future trouble. Likewise, Philip's son might seek vengeance if Plymouth's magistrates spared his life.[29]

James Keith at Bridgewater dissented from the position of his fellow ministers. He acknowledged that Psalm 137 posed some difficulty ("Blessed shall he be that taketh and dasheth thy children against the stones"). Nevertheless, Keith suggested that Plymouth should follow the example of King Amaziah, who out of obedience to the Mosaic Law did not slay his enemies' children.[30]

Plymouth's magistrates could not decide what to do, so Philip's son languished in jail over the course of the winter. Finally, in March 1677 they settled on what they probably regarded as an act of mercy. They enslaved the boy instead of killing him. "Philip's boy goes now to be sold," John Cotton informed Increase Mather. In all likelihood, Plymouth's authorities arranged for their enemy's son to be exported far from New England.[31]

In the first months of the war, Plymouth's magistrates did not distinguish between captured noncombatants and those Wampanoags who had voluntarily surrendered themselves. Likewise, even as the war came to an end, colonial leaders enslaved and exported noncombatant children alongside their parents. It was simpler—and more profitable—to enslave and export as many Indians as possible. As the immediate English thirst for vengeance and profits waned, however, distinctions emerged among different categories of captives.

In July 1676, New Plymouth's war council resolved to enslave and remove from the colony all men above the age of fourteen who had been captured in battle or who had returned home "in a clandestine way." Women and children taken in like circumstances were considered slaves for life but were not necessarily banished from the colony. Plymouth's leaders now extended some mercy to surrenderers. In the summer of 1676, the war council voted to confine the latter group on what amounted to a reservation on land to the east of Dartmouth.[32]

Children were a more complex case. The war council decreed that the children of surrenderers would be placed with English households as servants until the age of twenty-five, "especially their parents consenting thereunto." The language suggested that such consent was not strictly necessary. In March 1677, New Plymouth's General Court required English masters who had received Indian children to sign indentures. The documents would make clear that the children's servitude would end when they reached twenty-five. The next year, the court forbade settlers from buying and selling "our captive savages." The ban did not mean that their labor was never transferable. As was the case with English indentured servants, masters might send them to other households or bequeath their remaining years of labor to their heirs. The court's intention was that the children not become chattel akin to African slaves.[33]

The statutes left considerable ambiguity, however. What about those Indians condemned to be slaves in perpetuity? Were they like African slaves? Could they be bought and sold? Would Native children inherit their mothers' condition of slavery? The result of this ambiguity was that many Wampanoags toiled for English households in a murky and ill-defined capacity. Whether their masters called them "servants" or "slaves," they were in bondage, and they were vulnerable to the machinations of settlers who might circumvent the law in order to retain their labor.

Nearly all of these servants and slaves remain anonymous, but a few diaries and legal records hint at their experiences. In October

1679, the young minister Peter Thacher moved his family from Boston to Barnstable on a probationary basis. Thacher was the son of Thomas Thacher, the pastor of Boston's Third Church. After the elder Thacher's 1678 death, the inheritance of his estate stoked tension between his children and his widow. Margaret Thacher's marriage to Thomas Thacher was her second, and she brought considerable assets to the match, including at least two slaves of African descent. In September 1679, she took legal measures to recover what she felt was hers. "This day mother Thacher arrested me for two Negroes," Peter Thacher wrote in his diary. Within a few years, the younger Thacher had either recovered the slaves from his stepmother or had acquired replacements.[34]

Peter Thacher's household also included his wife, Theodora, an infant daughter (also Theodora), an English servant named Lydia Chapin, and an Indian servant or slave, Margaret. In his diary, Peter Thacher expressed a deep concern for Lydia's health and spiritual condition. In the spring of 1679, Lydia collapsed and appeared to be dead, then suffered from violent fits all night long. The next winter, Lydia "was ready to draw up deadly conclusions against herself." Thacher called her into his study and counseled her to resist Satan's temptation to suicide. A few weeks later, Lydia was so morose or incapacitated that she let young Theodora cry. The Thachers took the baby to bed with them, and Lydia sat up that night in anguish. Shortly thereafter, a relative came to bring Lydia back to Boston. Her family had placed her with the Thachers, but she was not psychologically fit for service.[35]

Peter Thacher purchased Margaret from Lydia Checkley—the wife of merchant Anthony Checkley of Boston—for ten pounds. She came to the household in June 1679, shortly before the Thachers moved to Barnstable. Margaret helped care for the baby, knitted and sewed, and performed other household tasks. "The Lord make her a blessing to the family," Thacher wrote, "and her coming under my roof a blessing to her soul that she may learn to know and fear the Lord her master and [her] God." She at least learned to fear her earthly master. "I came home," wrote Thacher two months later, "and found that my Indian girl had like to have knocked my Theodora in [the] head by letting her fall." Thacher punished Margaret by beating her with "a good walnut stick."[36]

It is quite possible that Thacher would have beaten any servant who dropped Theodora, but the Thachers did not punish Lydia when she neglected the baby. Indeed, Peter Thacher's diary documents a stark divide between the experiences of the two servants. Lydia may or may not have wanted to become a servant to the Thachers, but her family retrieved her as her mental health faltered. (Lydia subsequently returned to the family's service.) By contrast, Peter Thacher bought Margaret. Regardless of how she fared, she would serve the minister and his family at least into her adulthood or until the Thachers sold her. Peter Thacher displayed an unusual solicitude for Lydia's spiritual well-being, but despite his initial hopes for Margaret's soul, he made no attempt to instruct Margaret in Christianity. (Massachusetts Bay, but not Plymouth, had a law that required masters to instruct Indian servant children in the "Christian religion.") In fact, outside of the accident with Theodora, he seems to have paid very little attention to Margaret at all. She was not worth mentioning unless she caused a problem.[37]

A few documents trace the movements of enslaved Wampanoags within New Plymouth. In March 1677, Duxbury's Adam Right acquired a woman named Hannah from Benjamin Church. "Taken and captivated" toward the end of the war, she had been condemned to "perpetual servitude and slavery." The next winter, Right sold Hannah for four pounds and ten shillings to William Woddell, a Portsmouth (Rhode Island) official who trafficked in Indian servants and slaves. Hannah came with a bill of sale that clarified her status as a slave. She was chattel, property that English settlers could buy and sell.[38]

Woddell also acquired a Pocasset woman named Meequapew and her two children. Most likely, Meequapew had taken refuge with the Narragansetts during the war. After English troops rounded up many Narragansetts in the closing months of the war, Rhode Island's government bound her and her children to Woddell. In this instance, he received her labor for three years, that of her fourteen-year-old son, Peter, for ten years, and that of her six-year-old daughter, Hannah, for fifteen years. In contrast to indentures for English servants, Woddell had no obligation to provide his Indian servants with clothing or any other benefits upon their freedom.[39]

Like the Thachers, members of the Almy family owned both

Indian and African slaves. After several decades in the Plymouth Colony town of Sandwich, William Almy, his wife, Audrey, and their children moved to Portsmouth and also acquired land in Pocasset and Sakonnet. When William Almy died in 1677, his estate included an Indian couple and their child. Seven years later, Almy's son Job bequeathed a number of "servants" to his heirs. One inventory of his estate identified two "Negro servants" valued at £42 and an unspecified number of "Indian servants" worth £35. A second inventory the next year itemized "one negro woman" at £15 and "Indian servants" at £25. Nowhere did the inventories state the number of years the individuals had left to serve. Presumably they were slaves for life. Unless they succeeded in running away, the adults involved would never become free.[40]

The first person of African descent to appear in New Plymouth's records is an unnamed "blackamore" included on a 1643 list of men able to bear arms in the town of Plymouth.[41] It is unclear whether the man was a slave, a servant, or a free man. Ten years later, a "negro maidservant of John Barnes" accused a man of stealing from her master. She too could have been a servant or slave. As African slavery became more prevalent in southern New England, some of the Plymouth Colony's wealthiest men acquired slaves. At the time of his 1674 death, for instance, Thomas Willett owned eight slaves, including Jethro. John Myles, whose unnamed "Negro" was one of the first casualties of King Philip's War, possessed five slaves at the time of his death. Listed on the inventory of his estate right after his pigs, horses, and cattle, they were his most valuable possessions, collectively worth £72. "Our blacks . . . are very few," Governor Winslow reported in 1680, "and of them fewer breeders." That was true in New Plymouth's eastern towns, but when Rhode Island settlers moved to Mount Hope, Pocasset, and Sakonnet after the war, the number of slaves of African descent within the colony increased.[42]

Plymouth Colony's settlers typically acquired African slaves from Newport, New Amsterdam, or Boston. In one instance, however, the Boston merchant John Saffin directed a cargo of slaves to the out-of-the-way town of Swansea. Saffin's life straddled the colonies of Plymouth and Massachusetts Bay and intersected with slavery at several points. It was Saffin who had negotiated Jethro's status at the end of King Philip's War, and one of his own slaves successfully sued him for freedom at the turn of the eighteenth century. In 1681, he and several of his fellow merchants tried to circumvent the Royal African Company's crown-granted monopoly on the slave trade. Saffin and his partners sent a vessel—the *Elizabeth*—to Guinea and directed its master to head for Swansea on his return to New England. Getting wind that Rhode Island officials planned to interdict the *Elizabeth*, Saffin gave instructions to divert the vessel to Nantasket. He urged the ship's master to anchor offshore and "take in such Negroes" under the cover of darkness. The fate of the *Elizabeth* and the slaves it carried remains unknown.[43]

Other than the laws limiting the terms of service for captive children, New Plymouth did not codify either African or Native slavery. One significant difference between the two types of bondage emerged over time, though. English settlers understood that the children of enslaved African mothers would be slaves, but in the case of Indian slaves and servants, there was no presumption of heritability. Masters sometimes claimed the progeny of their female Native slaves, but some of those children successfully contested such claims in court.

Nevertheless, for the remainder of the seventeenth century there were far more Indians than Africans in various forms of bondage to New Plymouth families. Especially as fewer English servants came to New England, enslaved and indentured Wampanoags provided an inexpensive source of labor for Plymouth Colony households. The 1694 estate of Scituate's John Williams included three Indian "servants" collectively valued at £60. Even as English settlers sold many Indians out of the colony, they imported others from Maine, from Carolina, from Florida, and from more distant places. For instance, when Scituate's Anthony Collamore died in January 1694, his estate included a "Spanish Indian servant" worth £20. Native slaves and servants were a ubiquitous presence in English households.[44]

In June 1677, Governor Josiah Winslow wrote King Charles to assure the crown that New Plymouth's settlers had not provoked the "rebellion" of Philip and other Native peoples. He promised that his colony had done its utmost to defend the king's interest in the recent war. As a token of his fidelity to the king, Winslow sent what he termed the "best of the ornaments and treasure of sachem Philip, the grand rebel." The "spoils" consisted of what Winslow described as Philip's "crown, his gorge [staff], and two [wampum] belts of their own making, of their gold and silver." Winslow sent his letter and gifts by way of Waldegrave Pelham, his brother-in-law. They never reached the king. Pelham may have kept them for himself. Alternatively, he or another courier lost them.[45]

For New Englanders, captives and land were the chief spoils of war, and because of its good harbor and fertile land, Mount Hope was the jewel among those prizes. After King Charles confirmed New Plymouth's jurisdiction over the peninsula in 1679, Plymouth's magistrates sold it to a group of wealthy proprietors from Boston. There was a Pokanoket remnant on Mount Hope, but settlers from Rhode Island, Massachusetts Bay, and Plymouth purchased lots, planted crops, and brought Indian and African slaves and servants onto their properties. In 1681, Mount Hope became the township of Bristol.

The situation in Sakonnet was different. Its Native men had fought on both sides of King Philip's War. While Plymouth's magistrates permitted both Mammanuah and Awashonks to return to their land, they did not treat the two rival sachems and their respective communities equally. Mammanuah, who had embraced Christianity prior to the war and adhered to the English for its duration, still controlled substantial land at Acoaxet and continued to sell portions of it into the mid-1690s. In keeping with the agreement between Benjamin Church and Awashonks, Plymouth's magistrates and the Sakonnet proprietors allowed the sachem and her people to remain, but only at their discretion. Unlike Mammanuah, Awashonks soon owned no land at all. Whether they obtained it through purchase or through confiscation, the Sakonnet proprietors divvied up the parcel of land they previously had reserved for Awashonks. In 1682, Plymouth's General Court declared that Sakonnet would become the township of Little Compton.

Many of the Native men and women who remained at Sakonnet and Acoaxet now aligned themselves with Christianity. According to Cotton Mather, Native missionaries from Martha's Vineyard traveled to Sakonnet and made many converts. John Cotton also went to Sakonnet. In 1678, he preached twice to a crowd of some 150 individuals. Cotton made a list of more than eighty men and women at Sakonnet who had become praying Indians. In 1680, the English appointed a man named Isaac as "Indian magistrate at Sakonnet," noting that he gave "good grounds of hope that he is religiously affected." Even though Isaac had fought against the English during the war, he gained permission from the General Court to carry a gun.[46]

Awashonks lived at Sakonnet for at least a dozen years after the end of the war. In 1683, colonial authorities brought Awashonks, her daughter Betty, and her son Peter to Plymouth and imprisoned them. They were accused of infanticide, of having murdered Betty's "young child." Both Awashonks and Betty insisted that the child had been stillborn. Lacking witnesses or other evidence, the magistrates felt obliged to dismiss the charge of murder.

The acquittal did not end the matter, however. Betty was not married, and Awashonks and Betty had punished another woman— the wife of a man named Sam—who had commented on her pregnancy. At Awashonks's behest, Sam's wife had been whipped. For that, the magistrates fined the sachem, her son, and her daughter. They also ordered the "Indians at Sakonnet" to whip Betty for her fornication. Plymouth's leaders still suspected that Awashonks and Betty might be guilty of the capital crime of murder. They resolved to seek further evidence but apparently never found it. Awashonks was still alive as of 1688, when she made a request through her son Peter for her community's sixty-seven families to be given land on which to plant crops. The request illustrates the extent of the dispossession experienced by Awashonks and her people. It is unclear whether English officials granted the requested land.[47]

Words etched into a boulder in Little Compton's Wilbour Woods commemorate Awashonks as "queen of Sogkonate [Sakonnet] and friend of the white man." Compared to the statues of men such as Myles Standish and Ousamequin, it is an obscure and crude tribute to one of the most significant figures in the Wampanoag-English conflicts of the 1670s. The etching was made in the late nineteenth century; the words are now barely legible. They are also inaccurate. Awashonks was not a queen but one of several individuals who claimed leadership of Sakonnet communities during these years. Nor was she a friend of the English, who despite her resistance claimed all of her people's land.

Awashonks rock, Wilbour Woods, Little Compton, Rhode Island.
(Courtesy of the Rhode Island Historical Society [RHi X17 473].)

Without land ownership, Awashonks's people faced a difficult future. By the mid-1690s, Peter, Awashonks's son, was indentured—or
possibly enslaved—to Edward Richmond, who had moved from
Rhode Island to Sakonnet after the war. Peter and two other Indians
were valued at three pounds each. Awashonks had not been able to
save her land, and she could not save her son from servitude.[48]

While Plymouth's settlers regarded the western Wampanoags as
conquered peoples after the war, most Wampanoag communities
had not been conquered. Native men from Cape Cod had fought
for rather than against the English, and Wampanoags on the islands
to the south had cooperated with English authorities but had otherwise kept out of the fighting.

Christian Wampanoag communities in New Plymouth continued to fare better than their counterparts in Massachusetts Bay.
Whereas several of John Eliot's praying towns disappeared and

Natick's population contracted, the community at Mashpee grew over the last quarter of the seventeenth century. In the mid-1680s, Plymouth's government promised that the land would belong to the Mashpee Wampanoags and their children forever. As the historian David Silverman has argued, without its people's embrace of Christianity, Mashpee probably would not have remained Wampanoag land. Rowland Cotton, a son of John Cotton who became minister at Sandwich, counted around two hundred adult members of Mashpee's church in 1693.[49]

Although some English ministers and other settlers continued to preach to Wampanoag communities, Native evangelists—as at Sakonnet—usually took the lead. Following Richard Bourne's death in 1685, Simon Popmonit became Mashpee's minister for the next thirty-five years. Son of a sachem, Popmonit was respected among his own people and by English magistrates. As sachemships collapsed, churches provided alternative opportunities for Wampanoags to exercise leadership and forge connections with English ministers and settlers. As Wampanoags had once traveled great distances to gather for nickómmos like the one Benjamin Church had witnessed, they now gathered for ordinations or celebrations of the Lord's Supper.

Wampanoags who embraced Christianity made it their own and kept it that way, a fact remarked on by English settlers and visitors. In 1708, when his ship ran into danger in the shallow waters to the south of Cape Cod, Lord John Lovelace—on his way to New Jersey as its next governor—was forced to put in near Dartmouth. Lovelace met a Christian Wampanoag and asked for the name of the man's English minister. The man replied that Dartmouth's minister was "a worthy and hopeful young gentleman" but that he himself had "been under none . . . but Indian instruction." His faith came from his own people, not from the English. After Simon Popmonit died in 1720, the New England Company sent Joseph Bourne (Richard Bourne's great-grandson) to Mashpee as its minister. Because few Mashpee Wampanoags spoke English, they refused to come to church unless Bourne learned their language. The young English minister complied.[50]

While it provided space for Native leadership and community, Christianity was not a panacea for the challenges Wampanoags faced after the war. As the English population continued to increase, new

Whaling ship's figurehead, ca. 1830.
(Courtesy of the New Bedford Whaling Museum.)

townships formed on the Cape and elsewhere, and settlers moved onto Wampanoag lands. Many Native enclaves disappeared; their inhabitants moved to larger communities such as Mashpee, which remained vigilant against English encroachment. In 1710, Simon Popmonit petitioned the Massachusetts government (in 1692, Plymouth Colony was absorbed into a larger Province of Massachusetts Bay). He complained that residents of Barnstable had "appropriated to themselves a considerable part" of his people's land and had begun building houses on it. It is unclear whether the Mashpee Wampanoags succeeded in getting redress, but Popmonit could at least command attention from colonial officials.[51]

Land was only one challenge. As traditional means of subsistence disappeared, Indians faced limited prospects. Many parents indentured their children to English families, and many men found themselves reduced to servitude when they borrowed money and could not repay it. Others worked as day laborers and lived on the outskirts of English towns. On the Cape, Wampanoag men became workers on whaling ships, and debt forced them to remain in such positions indefinitely.[52]

Some Wampanoag parents wanted to place their children with English families. They understood both the immediate benefits—one less mouth to feed—and the usefulness of language skills and cultural fluency. Devout, or perhaps savvy, Christian Wampanoags were especially keen to send their children to the homes of English ministers. In other instances, Indian servitude was debt peonage orchestrated by settlers eager to obtain cheap labor. Simon Popmonit lamented in a petition that "ourselves and our poor children are frequently made servants for an unreasonable time." He maintained that Indians sometimes contracted debts out of ignorance or foolishness, and he asked that such indentures be permitted only with the consent of two English justices of the peace. In this case, the Massachusetts government passed the requested law, but two generations later, an English minister reported that most Mashpee boys were indentured to English masters.[53]

Through their embrace of Christianity and their willingness to fight alongside English soldiers, Wampanoags at Mashpee and elsewhere on the Cape retained their leaders, their language, and at least some of their land. These communities remained vital at the end of the seventeenth century. They were unconquered, and they maintained a substantial degree of autonomy. Over time, though, many Wampanoag men, women, and children found themselves in bondage to English families and whalers. The English did not call them slaves, but they were not free.

CHAPTER EIGHTEEN

Bitter Cups

T HE NUMBER OF QUAKERS and Baptists in New Plymouth grew significantly in the years after King Philip's War,
especially in the western portion of the colony. As was the
case in England and in many other colonies, religious dissenters in Plymouth Colony were second-class citizens, grudgingly
tolerated but subject to significant civil disadvantages. In the years
after 1660, New Plymouth's settlers were free to attend or ignore
the established churches as they saw fit, and Quakers and Baptists
usually could meet openly for their own religious services. In this
respect, dissenters and the religiously indifferent enjoyed liberty of
conscience.

As historian Alexandra Walsham explains, however, this degree
of toleration "emphatically did not mean religious freedom" as that
term would be understood in later centuries. The colony's Congregational ministers and magistrates did not abandon the goal of religious uniformity or their antipathy toward alleged heresy. They
understood the established churches as a public good, providing sacred functions for entire communities. The General Court required
towns to levy taxes toward ministerial salaries and the construction
and upkeep of meetinghouses. Dissenters received no exemptions
from church taxes and suffered fines and imprisonment if they refused to pay. They also could not become freemen or, at least in
many parts of the colony, participate in town affairs.[1]

In Scituate, there had been two churches ever since the early 1640s split over Charles Chauncy's baptismal practices. Once Chauncy left for Harvard in 1654, nothing separated the two congregations except geography and lingering resentments. Especially after Nicholas Baker became minister of the north church in 1660, the town's ecclesiastical relations gradually improved. With a heavy dose of condescension, Cotton Mather praised Baker's "good natural parts," which compensated for his merely "private education." Baker had been a farmer and probably a lay preacher before his ordination. In Massachusetts Bay, councils of clergy assessed the learning and orthodoxy of ministerial candidates before ordaining them. Baker would not have become a minister in the Bay Colony. In New Plymouth, by contrast, laypeople ordained their ministers, and they sometimes elected men who lacked a university education. Baker and William Wetherell, still pastor of the south church, effected a reconciliation that was completed in April 1675. "We desire," Baker declared that month, "God to forgive you and us whatsoever may have been displeasing to him." The congregations did not reunite, but Scituate's church members could now take the Lord's Supper at either meetinghouse.[2]

In towns such as Scituate, Quakers faced less hostility for a stretch of years between 1660 and the start of the war. The most prominent Friend in Scituate was Edward Wanton. According to early nineteenth-century chronicler Caleb Hopkins Snow, Wanton had been one of the "officers under the gallows" at the time of Mary Dyer's execution and "was so affected by the sight, that he became a convert." Wanton prudently relocated to Scituate. He worked as a carpenter and shipbuilder and accumulated substantial property, including at least one African slave. Over Wanton's forty-five years in Scituate, he hosted countless religious meetings at his home.[3]

When the Quaker missionary John Burnyeat toured New England in 1672, he spoke to a large crowd in Scituate that gathered in an orchard to hear him. According to Burnyeat, "some of the elders of their church" interrupted the meeting to dispute with him. Burnyeat maintained that New Plymouth's 1657 banishment of Nicholas Upshall in the dead of winter had been cruel and "inconsistent with the gospel dispensation." Ousamequin had acted more like a Christian than had William Bradford, Burnyeat charged. For their part,

Scituate's church leaders accused Burnyeat of heresy. Animosity remained, but New Plymouth leaders had abandoned severe forms of anti-Quaker persecution, and the Friends in turn backed away from their most aggressive forms of public witness. Quaker missionaries did not visit churches to rail against the colony's ministers, and constables did not interfere with Quaker meetings.[4]

In Scituate and elsewhere, King Philip's War stoked renewed tension between the Friends and other settlers. Congregational ministers preached that God was punishing New England because of its toleration of heresy and wickedness. The Quakers agreed that God was punishing New England, but they identified different sins as the cause. Magistrates and ministers had offended God by persecuting his Friends, and now God was taking vengeance. In March 1676, Edward Perry of Sandwich reported hearing a divine voice: "Blood for blood, and cruelty for cruelty." Echoing the sentiments of other Friends, Perry lamented that a people who had gone "over the great ocean into this land . . . that they might have the liberty of their consciences to worship" now prevented others from exercising that same liberty. Perry maintained that New England's afflictions would not end until the persecutors repented, but he promised that God would protect and deliver his faithful remnant—the Friends—from the carnage that surrounded them.[5]

Many Plymouth Colony Friends refused military service during the war. From the start of the movement, some Quakers had insisted that the Children of Light could not bear arms or in any way contribute to violence and warfare. After the restoration of the monarchy, pacifism increasingly became a movement-wide principle. In order to discourage persecution, Quakers leaders wanted to reassure King Charles II that they were not revolutionaries and posed no threat to his government. George Fox and other leading Friends declared in January 1661 that "all bloody principles, we . . . do utterly deny, with all outward wars and strife and fightings with outward weapons, for any end or under any pretense." Jesus had commanded Peter to sheathe his sword, and Friends should follow the spirit of Christ. Prior to King Philip's War, a few Quakers in Plymouth Colony were fined for their refusal to participate in militia training, but for the most part towns found ways to limit conflict over the issue.[6]

When the colony drafted men after the March 1676 raid on

Rehoboth, the war council noted that "many of the soldiers that were pressed came not to go forth, especially Scituate and Sandwich proved very deficient." Not all of these men were Quakers. Many men were loath to leave their families and farms; others simply wanted to avoid the horrors of war and possible death. Quakers in Sandwich, however, insisted that unlike others who only looked to their "own bodily interest," their refusal was in obedience to "the command of Christ Jesus and a tender conscience towards God." They were not at liberty to fight.[7]

Especially after the costly Native raid on Scituate in May 1676, townspeople resented the tender consciences in their midst. After the war, therefore, town leaders were less inclined to ignore Quaker violations of laws and communal expectations. In 1665, a town meeting had appointed men to rate—assess—each household to determine its portion of Scituate's ministerial salaries. (Nicholas Baker and William Wetherell received £60 and £45 each year, respectively.) Constables then visited households to collect the tax. Quakers invariably refused to pay taxes to support churches and ministers they rejected as false. As in the case of militia service, prior to 1675 communities had avoided prolonged conflict over church taxes. Now the church rate provided an easy way to punish Quakers. In December 1676, for example, constables seized five pewter platters from Edward Wanton to satisfy his share of the rate. The next year, a constable took five yards of broadcloth.[8]

Another Scituate Friend, John Rance, refused both taxes and military service. Rance's background is obscure. Sometime during the Massachusetts Bay governorship of Richard Bellingham (1665–72), Rance came to that colony from England as a Quaker missionary. He was imprisoned, and he moved to Scituate after his release. During King Philip's War, Rance was among the town's "delinquent soldiers." In March 1676, the council fined him eight pounds. Later that year, constables seized some of Rance's corn and sheep to satisfy his church taxes.[9]

In the summer of 1677, the constables returned. They demanded two shillings toward Nicholas Baker's salary. Rance would not pay what he termed "the priest's rate," so the constables took a kettle from him. The outraged Rance followed them to the minister's home and watched them give the kettle to Baker. The next Sunday, Rance marched into the north church meetinghouse. Alluding to the books of Jeremiah and Ezekiel, he denounced Baker as "no true minister but one of that sort of false prophets which the Lord sent his servants to cry woe against." Rance cried woe, warning that God would punish false teachers who enriched themselves at the expense of God's Friends. Baker was a wolf and a thief, Rance alleged.[10]

Magistrate James Cudworth called for the constable. Rance now had a second object for his scorn. "The Lord will meet with all hypocrites," Rance told Cudworth. In the late 1650s, Cudworth had opposed the whipping and imprisonment of Quakers, and he had even hosted meetings of the Friends in his home. Cudworth wanted concord, not conflict, however. He had no patience with Rance, whom he ordered removed from the church. The next day, Rance was placed in the stocks. Cudworth then ordered Scituate's constable to bring him to Plymouth, where Governor Josiah Winslow ordered his hat removed.[11]

In the meantime, Nicholas Baker sent a letter to the colony's leaders. While Baker insisted that he was "far from a harsh rigid persecuting spirit," he maintained that Quakers like Rance went too far. Rance and other Quakers openly spouted "damnable and blasphemous doc[trines]," peddled heretical books, and invited Scituate's young people to their "diabolical worship." Even worse, the Quakers had the temerity to meet near Baker's church between its two services. As "nursing fathers to the churches of Christ," the magistrates should not overlook the offenses committed against their children. They should punish John Rance, and two or three hours in the stocks would not suffice. The General Court agreed. New Plymouth's magistrates and deputies convicted Rance of slandering Baker and Cudworth and of enticing young persons to hear "false teachers." The penalty was twenty lashes. According to Rance, Governor Winslow commuted the sentence after ten blows.[12]

As Plymouth's General Court punished John Rance, its leading citizens were contemplating new legislation designed to shore up the established churches. The previous month, the court had asked the colony's ministers to help them define "those due bounds and limits which ought to be set to a toleration in matters of religion."

John Cotton canvassed his colleagues and drew up a list of essential doctrines. They proposed that "none be tolerated to set up any public worship" who did not accept the Bible as God's word, the Trinity as defined in the ancient ecumenical confessions, and the justification of sinners as an act of grace irrespective of human merit. Moreover, the ministers rejected toleration for dissenters who accepted excommunicated persons into their communion, who disturbed approved worship services, or who denounced the established churches as "sinful and Antichristian." (The latter point was ironic considering that the Pilgrim separatists, at least while in England and Leiden, had rejected the Church of England as Antichristian.) The statement was pointedly silent on the issue of baptism and thus did not target John Myles's church in Swansea. Without mentioning them by name, the ministers made it clear that the Friends remained far outside the acceptable limits of toleration.[13]

A few days after John Rance's whipping, the General Court passed additional legislation requiring towns to build meetinghouses and employ ministers. In particular, the court ordered that towns collect a single rate that would include the minister's salary with the community's other expenses. The court also threatened to take charge of local taxation should towns fail to meet these obligations. Some ministers were upset that the court did not adopt harsher measures. Why had the General Court asked about the proper limits of toleration if it intended to tolerate heresy anyway? "It makes my loins at a stand," fumed Taunton's George Shove. "I never was more disappointed." The new laws did not interfere with Quaker meetings or proselytizing.[14]

Shove was disappointed, but so were the Friends. In communities such as Scituate, constables seized cows, sheep, cloth, corn, barley, sugar, kettles, cups, platters, and porringers. In June 1678, Edward Wanton and several other Quakers petitioned the General Court. "Christ Jesus invites people freely," they maintained. "His ministers ought not to make people pay." Ministerial rates smacked of Jewish tithes and Catholic tyranny. Wanton and his fellow petitioners minced no words in their rejection of New Plymouth's churches. "We do really believe your preachers are none of the true ministers of Christ," they informed the magistrates. They also reminded their persecutors that they enjoyed their own "liberty but

upon sufferance" of a king who found New England's Congregational churches "repugnant."[15]

The court ignored the petition, but it made its displeasure known
by fining Wanton ten pounds for a "disorderly" marriage. Plymouth
law required the public announcement of betrothals and permitted
only magistrates or persons authorized by them to join couples in
marriage. (Plymouth Colony ministers did not perform marriages.)
Quakers contravened the law when they married privately in their
own ceremonies. Wanton would not pay the fine, so a constable
seized two oxen and a cow from him to satisfy it. When Wanton
refused to contribute his assigned portion to Scituate's meetinghouses, town leaders jailed him for six weeks.[16]

Arthur Howland Jr.—nephew of *Mayflower* passenger John
Howland—also ran afoul of the more stringent enforcement of
church taxes. The family had a long tradition of civil disobedience
and resistance to authority. Howland's father had broken with Marshfield's church in the 1650s, hosted Quaker meetings, become convinced, and allegedly threatened to kill the town constable who tried
to arrest him. In March 1667, the General Court fined the younger
Arthur Howland five pounds "for inveigling of Mistress Elizabeth
Prence and making motion of marriage to her, and prosecuting the
same contrary to her parents' liking." Elizabeth Prence was the
daughter of then governor Thomas Prence, who probably opposed
the match because of the Howland family's involvement with the
Friends. Howland trudged back to Plymouth a few months later
and promised the court to "wholly desist" from his efforts to marry
Elizabeth. He promptly broke his promise; the couple married that
December. Prence apparently forgave his daughter for her disobedience. When Prence died, Elizabeth Howland inherited a share of
his considerable estate equal to that of her six sisters. The governor
also left her a silver saltcellar and a black cow.[17]

Arthur Howland Jr. was not a Friend at the time of his marriage,
but a decade later he became convinced. Samuel Arnold, Marshfield's minister, ordered Howland to come before the church to answer congregational charges against him. Howland agreed to appear
if he could have "liberty to read" a statement he had written explaining his new principles. Arnold would not grant that liberty, so Howland refused to come, stating that Arnold would require him "to put

off my hat and stand before the church." The Marshfield church then excommunicated Howland in absentia. Arnold warned the congregants that "they should not eat or drink with" Howland, and church leaders even cautioned Elizabeth Howland against eating with her excommunicated husband.[18]

While they continued sharing meals, the Howlands soon had less to eat. Excommunication did not absolve Arthur Howland of his civic responsibility toward Marshfield's church. In the summer of 1682, the town tasked Richard French with collecting the town-mandated rate for Arnold's salary. Arnold received fifty pounds a year, half paid in either corn or cattle, and the other half paid in wheat, barley, pork, butter, or silver money. The arrangement was typical. Inhabitants of Plymouth Colony had little hard money, so governments permitted payments in kind. Given his wife's inheritance, Arthur Howland could have afforded to pay the fifteen shillings that Marshfield expected him to contribute. Howland, however, was not about to pay a penny. French responded by seizing property. According to Howland, French "took away our butter scarce leaving us a convenient dish or basin to eat our vittles in."[19]

Two years later, French was back. This time, he took Howland himself and brought him to Plymouth. According to Howland, he was jailed without a hearing before a court or magistrate. He was "not allowed neither bread nor water, nor anything to lie on but the floor, nor anything to cover me with, nor liberty to go . . . to get anything for my money." If his case resembled that of other Friends, Howland probably languished in jail for about a month.[20]

Some non-Quakers also opposed the General Court's heavy-handed oversight of the colony's churches. In Scituate, it was burdensome and complicated to maintain two buildings and two ministers. By the late 1670s, Nicholas Baker had died, William Wetherell was infirm, and the south church's meetinghouse had fallen into disrepair. Now that the two churches were no longer at odds, townspeople discussed the possibility of reuniting the two congregations. The south church sought advice from neighboring ministers, who recommended that the town maintain both churches and that the south church raise a new building and obtain an assistant for Wetherell. The town ignored the expensive advice and voted to "reduce the

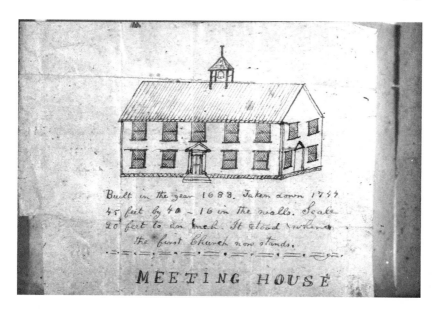

Built in the year 1683. Taken down 1744
45 feet by 40 – 16 in the walls. Scale
20 feet to an inch. It stood where
the first Church now stands.

MEETING HOUSE

Sketch of Plymouth's 1683 meetinghouse.
(Pilgrim Hall Museum, Plymouth, Massachusetts.)

whole inhabitants into one congregation." Why should Scituate's taxpayers support two churches no longer separated by the old dispute over baptism?[21]

The General Court then invalidated the town vote and appointed a committee of three ministers and three magistrates to oversee the construction of a new meetinghouse for the south church. In a June 1680 petition, twenty Scituate men argued that the General Court's action was "contrary to the due liberties of our town." Why should the colony's magistrates tell them what to do about their meetinghouses? If townspeople wanted a single church, surely that was their prerogative. Although they did not belong to either church, the petitioners professed themselves willing to contribute "in a regular way for the maintaining the worship of God without any such forcible means." Recently, however, the General Court had assumed control of the collection of Scituate's church taxes. The twenty men asked why the court treated them "as children under age." In other words, they were taxed without their consent or representation. Despite the objections, Scituate's south church built its new meetinghouse in 1681.[22]

The situation in Sandwich was very different from that in Marshfield or Scituate. Following the departure of William Leverich in the mid-1650s, Sandwich lacked a regular minister for nearly two decades. The town also ignored the law that long-standing male inhabitants take the oath of fidelity, and more than a dozen Friends voted in town affairs and retained their right to future divisions of town land. The Quaker Edward Perry held a number of offices in the 1660s and 1670s; he was one of several men who set the tax rates for Sandwich's contribution to the colony's wartime expenditures.[23]

In 1678, Sandwich church members asked the General Court to put an end to this permissiveness. The petitioners alleged that their Quaker neighbors impoverished newly recruited minister John Smith and neglected the glaring need for a new meetinghouse. Apparently, the building was so dilapidated and cramped that some individuals had to stand or lie down outside during services. (Given the long-standing apathy in Sandwich toward the established church, it is hard to imagine that the meetinghouse could not contain the town's worshippers.) Church members in Sandwich could not redress the situation because the Friends and those sympathetic to them "over voted" them at town meetings. "That such persons should have liberty by voting" offended God, the petitioners warned. They begged the General Court to take action. The colony's freemen complied with the request and ordered the town to administer the oath, which Quakers refused to swear. Many of the Friends then lost the right to vote and to participate in future divisions of town property.[24]

Sandwich Friends repeatedly petitioned the General Court to restore their civic privileges. In 1681, four Quakers—William Newland, William and Ralph Allen, and Edward Perry—complained that they remained in "many ways deprived of that just and free liberty which by the law of our native land we are born heirs unto." The Sandwich petitioners denied any interest in "licentious practices" or "pretended liberty." They only wanted "the liberty that is pure and peaceable," a spiritual liberty that purified individuals from sin and a political liberty that allowed them to enjoy their "natural privileges." They noted that other New England jurisdictions—Rhode Island—permitted Friends to "engage" their loyalty to the king, absolving them of the need to swear an oath. Sandwich's Friends asked for a similar accommodation and an end to the measures that made them a political underclass.

A threat followed. If Plymouth's magistrates and freemen rebuffed their request, they would appeal to the king. As Edward Wanton and his fellow petitioners had done in 1678, the Sandwich Friends reminded Plymouth's leaders that their own freedoms were fragile. "The liberty you enjoy," they wrote, "is but by license and leave" from the English king. The magistrates would be more likely to keep their liberty if they extended it to others.[25]

The threat was not idle. The colony's authority to govern itself hung in the balance for fifteen years following the end of King Philip's War. Prior to this time, English officials and monarchs had paid only occasional attention to their North American colonies. In the mid-1630s, Charles I had consented to New England's reorganization under a single governor-general, but the plan lost traction with Thomas Gorges's failure and the onset of the Civil War. During the Interregnum, Parliament passed the first of a series of Navigation Acts that regulated colonial shipping and trade, and the crown seized New Netherland soon after the Restoration. Only in the mid-1670s, however, did royal officials develop a more sustained interest in their North American colonies, an interest that came about in part because of England's transatlantic rivalry with France and in part because of the wars and rebellions that wracked New England and Virginia. Charles II and his officials concluded that if they wanted to keep their empire, they would have to govern and defend it.[26]

As a sign of England's newfound imperial consciousness, the Privy Council's Committee on Trade and Foreign Plantations (known as the Lords of Trade) dispatched Edward Randolph to Massachusetts Bay in 1676. Approximately forty-five years of age, the Canterbury-born Randolph had held several minor positions, first with the Cinque Ports and then with the navy. Randolph's financial compensation did not match his aspirations, and he was now looking across the Atlantic to find more lucrative opportunities. For the next fifteen years, Randolph played a significant role in mediating royal policy toward the New England colonies.

Randolph's immediate task was to deliver a letter about his cousin by marriage Robert Mason's proprietary claims to New Hampshire, but he also prepared detailed reports on the colonies he visited. Randolph informed English officials that the Bay Colony was a den of antimonarchical and duplicitous politicians, seditious ministers, and brazen smugglers. He blamed Massachusetts settlers and politicians for the wars against Natives across New England, accurately charged that colonists sheltered some of the regicides responsible for King Charles I's execution, and alleged—also accurately—that Boston merchants ignored the duties and requirements of the Navigation Acts. Over the next decade, Randolph repeatedly urged English officials to consolidate New England into a smaller number of colonies with royally appointed governors. While some Massachusetts settlers favored warmer relations with the crown and welcomed royal assistance against the Indians and the French, most of the Bay Colony's ministers and elected leaders regarded the combative Randolph and his proposals with intense suspicion and disdain.[27]

Given the enmity he faced in Massachusetts and his allegations against Bay Colony leaders, Randolph sought allies elsewhere. In July, he went to Plymouth at Governor Josiah Winslow's invitation. Randolph did not stay long enough to gain a deep understanding of the colony. For instance, he observed inaccurately that in New Plymouth there were "no slaves, only hired servants." Randolph praised New Plymouth's governor as a "stout commander" who was "eminently popular and beloved in all the colonies." Winslow was a loyal royal subject, a counterweight to the seditious Bostonians. According to Randolph, Winslow chafed against the Bay Colony's "encroaching upon the rights, trades, and possessions of the neighboring colonies" and believed "that New England could never be secure, flourish, nor be serviceable" until "reduced" to royal government. Randolph sailed for England in the fall of 1676 convinced of the Bay Colony's disloyalty and of Winslow's goodwill. It is unlikely that Winslow felt any genuine desire for royal government. His obsequiousness stemmed from a recognition of New Plymouth's weakness, and he was willing to advance his own colony's interests at the expense of Massachusetts.[28]

Winslow's approach paid dividends. Even though New Plymouth did not send an agent of its own to England, and despite the fact that its gifts and letters sometimes failed to reach their intended recipients, Charles confirmed New Plymouth's jurisdiction over Mount Hope, Sakonnet, and Pocasset, and the king suggested that he soon would give the colony its charter. Randolph's advocacy is the most reasonable explanation for this success.

New Plymouth's prospects had never been so bright. In a 1680 report to the Privy Council, Winslow estimated that the colony's settlers included twelve hundred men between the ages of sixteen and sixty, and he counted eight hundred births in the past seven years. Settlers, from other colonies and from Plymouth's own towns, were moving onto the newly conquered lands. Massachusetts Bay buffered New Plymouth from the threat of Abenaki raids or French incursions. Although many inhabitants still eked out a living on land of dubious fertility, the colony was stable and secure and enjoying the favor of English officials.[29]

Randolph returned to Boston in 1679 as the royal customs agent for New England. The new position made him even less popular in Massachusetts Bay. Two months later, Randolph confided to Winslow that if the crown consolidated the New England colonies, he hoped it would attach the southern portion of Massachusetts Bay to New Plymouth and appoint Winslow as governor. Winslow would obtain a significant salary increase with the preferment. Perhaps it was a stretch to think that the king would grant such an honor to the son of a man—Edward Winslow—who had accepted appointments from Oliver Cromwell. Nevertheless, Randolph asked Winslow to travel to England in his company and present the case to the Lords of Trade. For his part, Winslow praised Randolph in letters to English officials as "faithful and careful in what he is betrusted" and lamented that he endures "many unkindnesses and disappointments in our neighbor colony." In July 1680, Plymouth's General Court honored Randolph by making him a freeman of the colony.[30]

Winslow, though, declined the trip to England, citing ill health and a fear of Turkish pirates. By the fall, the colony's leaders had decided not to send anyone at all and instead to rely on the services of William Blathwayt, an ambitious young Privy Council clerk and secretary to the Lords of Trade. Winslow understood that obtaining a charter would require what amounted to bribes, so he made arrangements to pay Blathwayt for his services. Had Blathwayt wished to advance New Plymouth's interests, he probably could have done so. Over the next decade, Blathwayt acquired a rich wife, numerous offices (including secretary at war), and the confidence of three very different kings. While he was happy to take some of Plymouth's money, Blathwayt concentrated on advancing himself rather than a tiny, remote Congregational colony.[31]

Winslow further disrupted Randolph's plans by dying in December 1680 at the age of fifty-two. His end was painful. He suffered from "gout and griping [bowel spasms]," Boston's Samuel Sewall reported, and the "flesh was opened to the bone on his legs before he died." Like his Pilgrim father, Josiah Winslow was savvy, energetic, and widely traveled. His parentage, wealth, and bearing had commanded respect from his fellow New England magistrates and made a positive impression on Edward Randolph. For New Plymouth, Winslow's death was a heavy blow. Deputy Governor Thomas Hinckley praised him as a "noble, gallant, and accomplished gentleman." The General Court allocated forty pounds toward Winslow's funeral expenses.[32]

Longtime colony secretary Nathaniel Morton wrote letters to Penelope Winslow to express his condolences and provide her with some theological comfort. Morton closed one of his letters with a quotation from John Robinson's popular *Observations Divine and Moral*. "We are not to mourn for the death of our Christian friends," Robinson taught, "as they which are without hope." There was no reason to mourn on behalf of the deceased, as God would raise them to a more glorious life. Nor should bereaved Christians feel abandoned by God. "But we should take occasion by their deaths," instructed the Pilgrim pastor, "to love this world the less, out of which they are taken, and heaven the more, whither they are gone before us, and where we shall ever enjoy them."[33]

The next June, Plymouth's freemen chose Hinckley as Winslow's successor. Born around 1620 in a Kentish village, Hinckley moved with his parents and siblings to Scituate and then to Barnstable. The family had been members of John Lothrop's church in London, and Thomas Hinckley remained—according to Edward Randolph—a "rigid Independent [Congregationalist]." Edward Cranfield, the crown-appointed governor of New Hampshire, informed the Lords of Trade that Hinckley and his assistant Barnabas Lothrop were "weak men and very unfit to be concerned in government." Cranfield was a vigorous defender of royal prerogative in New England, and he loathed nearly all of the region's magistrates and ministers. At least some of those ministers, however, agreed with Cranfield's assessment of Hinckley. Cotton Mather jabbed that in New Plymouth, a "*nullus*"—a nobody—had succeeded Winslow's lion. Hinckley proved entirely incapable of shepherding his colony through the political tumults of the next decade. Whereas Winslow could build ties with men such as Randolph, Hinckley antagonized English officials and eventually alienated many of his own colony's settlers as well.[34]

New Plymouth had not had an effective and loyal agent working on its behalf in England since Edward Winslow had represented the colony. Finally, in the summer of 1681, Hinckley asked James Cudworth—recently elected as deputy governor—to sail to England. More than any other magistrate, Cudworth might have alleviated royal concerns about the colony's religious establishment and its treatment of Quakers. Cudworth, however, was nearly seventy years of age, and he died of smallpox soon after he reached London. His modest estate included "one Indian boy," worth—along with a "case" and some "bottles"—six pounds. In 1683, the magistrates asked Ichabod Wiswall, Duxbury's minister, to replace Cudworth. Led by octogenarian John Alden, the former *Mayflower* cooper, Duxbury's householders—church members and others—voted against releasing Wiswall for the assignment. Plymouth thus left its interests in the hands of William Blathwayt, to whom Hinckley sent fifty guineas in March 1683.[35]

While Blathwayt promised New Plymouth "a pre-eminence before others, whose behavior has been less dutiful," both he and Randolph soon became less encouraging. One issue was the colony's ongoing persecution of Quakers. Winslow explained in a 1680 report to the Privy Council that New Plymouth gave "equal respect and encouragement" to all Protestants "except the Quakers, and them we disturb not if they do not disturb our peace." Winslow and Hinckley did not feel any need to hide their distaste for Quakers, probably because their colony's treatment of the Friends was not harsh by English standards. While some English communities no longer persecuted Quakers, officials elsewhere seized their property, and some Friends fell victim to mobs as well. During episodic crackdowns on religious dissenters, English authorities imprisoned hundreds of Quakers. Scores died in prison. The king, however, expected Quakers in his colonies to have more liberty than those in England. Hinckley reassured Blathwayt in 1683 that "since we had any hints of his majesty's indulgence to them," New Plymouth had treated the Friends with more forbearance. The governor noted that the colony fined Quakers for disorderly marriages, but he offered to tolerate such marriages if the king so desired.[36]

Randolph also criticized Hinckley for countenancing "the late arbitrary, and till now unheard-of, proceedings" against the merchant John Saffin, who had purchased land on Mount Hope (Bristol) but continued to live in Boston. In 1682, Bristol's constable, Increase Robinson, sought to collect Saffin's portion of the town rate, which included money toward a house for the town's first minister. Saffin refused to pay and refused to let Robinson take any of his property. Hinckley ordered Saffin kept in Plymouth's jail until he paid the rate and fees related to his arrest and confinement.[37]

Randolph and Blathwayt decided that their earlier assessments were wrong. Plymouth Colony's government and church establishment resembled those of Massachusetts Bay. And unlike the Bay Colony, Plymouth Colony did not have a charter. "All you can pretend to by your grant from the Earl of Warwick [the 1630 patent] is only the soil in your colony," Randolph leveled with Hinckley, "and no color for government." Blathwayt informed Plymouth that its charter would have to wait until the crown resolved what to do about the Bay Colony. "From hence it will be that your patent will receive its model," he told Hinckley.[38]

The king and his officials decided to bring Massachusetts Bay to heel. The Lords of Trade obtained a quo warranto, which ordered the Bay Colony to defend its actions—and, by extension, its charter—in court. At the same time, Charles promised the recalcitrant Bostonians that if they resigned their charter, he would make minimal changes to it and their form of government. If they refused to cooperate, they would lose their charter anyway, and more sweeping changes would be made. Massachusetts leaders preferred to be bent

rather than to bend. In November 1684, the Court of Chancery invalidated the Massachusetts Bay charter. Plymouth's northern neighbors now had no legal basis for their government. That same month,
the Lords of Trade recommended that New Plymouth be joined to
Massachusetts. The Pilgrim colony's loss of self-government seemed
assured.[39]

By this point, Plymouth's governor understood the possible results of royal control. In New Hampshire, crown-appointed governor Edward Cranfield jailed minister Joshua Moodey when the latter refused to celebrate the Lord's Supper according to the Book of
Common Prayer. "The good Lord prepare poor New England for
the bitter cup," Moodey wrote Hinckley.[40]

CHAPTER NINETEEN

Taxation and Representation

As New England settlers waited to learn how the crown would reshape their governments and possibly their churches, Plymouth's leaders blithely decided to revise the colony's laws. In June 1685, the General Court approved the new edition.

In a preface, the laws referenced the compact that the *Mayflower* passengers had entered into some sixty-five years earlier. Next came a list of "general fundamentals," a bill of rights. It began with the declaration the freemen had made in 1636, that "no act, imposition, law or ordinance be made or imposed upon us . . . but such as shall be enacted by consent of the body of freemen or associates, or their representatives legally assembled, which is according to the free liberties of the freeborn people of England." In keeping with developments in English rhetoric and political thought, New Plymouth's freemen now referred to themselves not as "freeborn subjects" but as "freeborn people." Other fundamentals followed, including rights to annual elections, the impartial administration of justice, and jury trials.

The last substantive fundamental pertained to the colony's Congregational churches. Because the "first comers" had braved the wilderness that they "might with the liberty of a good conscience enjoy the pure scriptural worship of God, without the mixture of humane inventions and impositions," the laws called on the colony's govern-

Drawing of the Plymouth Colony seal, from The Book of the General
Laws of the Inhabitants of the Jurisdiction of New-Plimouth *(1685).*
(Courtesy of Library of Congress.)

ment to protect and encourage the established churches. Correspond-
ingly, if there was a "defect of church order" in a town, the General
Court should compel it to employ an able, orthodox minister.

On some matters of liberty, there was considerable consensus
among New Plymouth's freeborn people. The colony had conducted annual elections for more than six decades. The right to a
trial by jury had been codified in 1636. Furthermore, most of New
Plymouth's inhabitants cherished some form of Christian liberty.
They desired freedom from ecclesiastical hierarchy and any nonbiblical elements of worship, though Congregationalists, Baptists, and
Quakers disagreed about what constituted pure worship. Plymouth's
settlers also disagreed about the meaning and extent of liberty of
conscience. Congregationalists and John Myles's Baptists wanted
town governments to protect their own consciences but did not believe that liberty of conscience required exempting dissenters from
church taxes or the toleration of heresy. Both the Friends and a growing number of Baptists in the western portion of the colony favored

a broader liberty that would end church taxes and allow a wider variety of religious groups to meet for worship.

In a departure from prior practice, the 1685 laws divided the colony into three counties, named for county seats Plymouth, Bristol, and Barnstable. The magistrates who lived in each county would comprise its court, though others could attend if needed. The county courts were given the authority to try most civil and criminal cases (excluding divorce and crimes for which execution or banishment could result). The new laws also empowered county courts to record deeds, settle estates, and raise taxes for bridges, roads, and prisons. Furthermore, if communities did not tax their residents according to the colony's laws, the courts would appoint men to complete the task.

Scituate's householders complained that the new courts deprived both freemen and towns of their "ancient liberties." The crux of the objection was that inhabitants would be taxed without their consent, an example of arbitrary government that New Englanders had long feared. As far as Scituate's townspeople were concerned, the establishment of county courts with the power to tax violated the first of the general fundamentals enshrined in the colony's laws.[1]

By the time New Plymouth's General Court arranged for the publication and distribution of the revised laws, it was clear that they would not remain in effect for very long. A new form of arbitrary government was coming to New England.

In May 1686, Edward Randolph arrived in Boston with the news that the Bay Colony's government had been replaced by a provisional council headed by Joseph Dudley, a Massachusetts politician who favored accommodation with the crown. The provisional council had no authority over New Plymouth, but Dudley and Randolph informed Governor Thomas Hinckley that his colony would be attached to Massachusetts as soon as a crown-appointed governor reached Boston.

Randolph, now secretary to Dudley's council, brought with him a Church of England minister named Robert Ratcliffe and asked that one of the city's three meetinghouses be set aside for worship according to the Book of Common Prayer. He might as well have asked Boston's ministers to dance around a maypole. He also asked the council to fund Ratcliffe's salary. Its members told him that in Boston, church members made voluntary contributions. Those who supported Ratcliffe could pay his salary. (Boston was an exception to the general Massachusetts Bay and Plymouth Colony rule of church taxes.) Relegated to a small room in the Town House, Ratcliffe, Randolph, and a few others met for worship. The piqued secretary informed the archbishop of Canterbury that the city's ministers denounced their liturgy as "leeks, garlic, and trash."[2]

In Plymouth Colony, towns continued to rate their inhabitants to support the Congregational churches and their ministers. Edward Wanton once again refused to pay his portion of Scituate's rate and received his customary constabulary visit. Randolph heard of Wanton's treatment and upbraided Hinckley for violating the "liberty of conscience" that the crown promised New Englanders. "Let us bring the matter to the square," Randolph explained to Hinckley. Would Plymouth's Congregationalists "be rated to pay our minister of the Church of England who now preaches in Boston?" If not, they should not tax Quakers who had no desire to hear Scituate's ministers. The governor ignored Randolph's warning.[3]

Soon Hinckley and New Plymouth's other magistrates received more than counsel. On December 19, 1686, the tenth anniversary of the Great Swamp battle and massacre, Boston's inhabitants heard a "great gun or two." They could see the frigate carrying New England's newly appointed governor to their shores. The next day, clad in a "scarlet coat laced," the aristocratic and authoritarian Sir Edmund Andros landed at Boston. According to Peter Thacher, minister in the town of Milton, the "rabble" greeted the governor with "three shouts," but the city's ministers and former magistrates looked on with stony disapproval. Andros then marched through Boston, entered the Town House, kept his hat on, and began imposing his will on colonies whose religion and independent spirit he had long disdained.[4]

Andros had begun his adult life as a soldier. He cut his teeth in battle by fighting in the employ of the Dutch, then commanded an English regiment on Barbados. Through the patronage of James, Duke of York, Andros became governor of New York and obtained a knighthood. The formation of the Covenant Chain alliance with the Iroquois kept New York's settlers safe during King Philip's War, and Andros gained a reputation as an efficient administrator loyal to the crown.[5]

In 1686, his old patron, now King James II, commissioned him as captain general, vice admiral, and governor in chief of a "Dominion of New England" that at first encompassed Massachusetts Bay, New Plymouth, New Hampshire, Maine, and Rhode Island. Over the next two years the crown added Connecticut, New York, and the two Jerseys to the Dominion. Andros's chief task was to defend New England against the French and hostile Indians. The king and the Lords of Trade also instructed him to enforce the Navigation Acts, to ensure liberty of conscience, and to encourage those individuals who wished to conform to the Church of England. The king's commission empowered Andros to make laws and levy taxes with his appointed council's "advice and consent." The council, however, was unelected, and Andros could dismiss its members for any cause. Thus, Andros governed without any checks on his power beyond those that might come from England.[6]

The Plymouth men on the council included Hinckley and magistrates Barnabas Lothrop, William Bradford, John Walley, and Daniel Smith, as well as Nathaniel Clarke, the colony's former secretary. The appointees did not include the venerable John Alden, who was too frail to attend meetings in Boston. The last of the Pilgrim leaders, Alden finally died in September 1687, nearly ninety years of age. At an unknown date, Priscilla Alden had predeceased her husband. In an elegy, John Cotton praised Alden and subtly criticized the new order:

> whilst to choose they had their liberty
> Within the limits of this colony
> their civil leaders, him they ever chose.

For more than half a century, New Plymouth's freemen had elected the *Mayflower* cooper as one of their magistrates. Cotton used the occasion of his death to remind New Plymouth's settlers that they no longer possessed that liberty.[7]

One day after Andros's dramatic entrance in Boston, he sent letters to Rhode Island and New Plymouth, ordering their appointees to appear on December 30. Hinckley and his fellow councilors complied, came to Boston, took the oath of allegiance to the king, and also swore an oath to uphold their new offices. The colony founded by the Pilgrims no longer existed.[8]

In some ways, the transition to the new regime was smooth. Andros left county courts and militia officers in place, and he had instructions to accept the validity of marriages contracted by magistrates.

The new governor represented a king who favored a broad religious toleration. Around the year 1670, the future James II had been received into the Catholic Church. Shortly after his conversion became public knowledge, English Protestants grew alarmed about a "Popish Plot" to assassinate Charles II and place his Catholic son on the throne. A parliamentary faction made an unsuccessful bid to exclude James from the succession. Once he became king, however, James needed allies, and he hoped that Protestant dissenters (those who refused to conform to the Church of England) would support toleration for Catholics if they received it themselves. In March 1686, James pardoned dissenters in prison, and his April 1687 Declaration of Indulgence suspended the ecclesiastical penal laws and opened public offices to Catholics and all Protestants. While Catholics and some dissenters celebrated James's religious policies, the crown's imposition of religious toleration horrified many other Protestants.[9]

In keeping with his instructions, Governor Andros insisted that New England towns stop taxing their inhabitants to pay ministers. He also forced the issue of space for Church of England worship in Boston. In March 1687, Andros sent the widely reviled Randolph to ask for the keys to the city's Third Church. At first, the church's officers refused, but the sexton finally gave way on Good Friday. Thereafter, the church provided space for both Congregational and Church of England services on Sundays, with congregants sometimes waiting outside for the previous minister to conclude a long sermon. The scene was not repeated in towns such as Plymouth or Scituate, which lacked both a Church of England minister and prospective parishioners.[10]

There were other important changes. Partly on the basis of existing Massachusetts laws, Andros raised revenue through a penny-a-pound tax on property, plus twenty pennies for each free man aged sixteen or older. The council also imposed duties on wine, rum, and other liquor. The Lords of Trade also encouraged Andros to introduce a system of quitrents, nominal payments made by landowners to their lords or governors. Going forward, inhabitants could obtain land only from Andros and only if they agreed to pay a bit more than two shillings per one hundred acres each year. What about lands already granted? At issue here was the fact that many inhabitants of Plymouth Colony—and other parts of the Dominion—had never obtained title to their land from the crown or a corporation specifically empowered by the crown to make lawful grants of land. According to Andros, grants from town governments were invalid, as were land purchases from Indians. Implying that there had been no legal basis for most prior grants, Andros suggested that settlers should petition him to confirm their grants and agree to the same quitrents.[11]

Many New England settlers and their former magistrates objected to Andros's policies. In February 1687, Thomas Hinckley petitioned Andros that the settlers of New Plymouth be allowed to retain "their ancient rights." In particular, he asked that all of the inhabitants of each town support "godly, able, orthodox ministers or preachers of the gospel." Andros rejected the request. The next month, Hinckley tried again. He read a statement in favor of ministerial rates at a council meeting. Rhode Island's former governor, Walter Clarke, countered that persons "who had not actually obliged themselves . . . to maintain the minister should be left at their liberty and not be pressed to pay against their wills." Andros confiscated Hinckley's paper. Plymouth's former governor next sent a petition to William Blathwayt, asking that laws mandating church taxes remain in effect. Otherwise, Hinckley warned, Andros would "starve out the ministry, and the people thereby exposed to turn heathen or atheists." Blathwayt, now secretary to the Lords of Trade, was not at all concerned about the potential starvation of New England ministers. He ignored Hinckley's petition.[12]

Several towns—including Scituate, Duxbury, and Eastham—contravened Andros's orders and continued to rate their inhabitants to support their churches. As usual, Scituate's Edward Wanton would not pay the church tax, and as usual a constable came and seized

some of his "goods and chattels." Andros and his council declared
that Scituate's rate was "without any legal proceedings or authority
. . . and contrary to his Majesty's gracious indulgence [of April 1687]
to all his loving subjects." They ordered the confiscated goods returned to Wanton. Scituate then found a more creative way to punish recalcitrant Friends. Scituate appointed Wanton and his fellow
Quaker Joseph Coleman as town constables, knowing that they would
refuse the office. Coleman explained that his conscience would not
permit him to fine men who did not participate in militia training.
The town fined the Friends when they rejected their appointments.
A county sheriff seized thirty sheep and lambs from Coleman, and
he took nearly 150 pounds of wool from Wanton.[13]

In the town of Plymouth, John Cotton's salary became a point of
contention. Cotton's £90 annual salary was a princely sum by Plymouth Colony standards. By comparison, Duxbury's Ichabod Wiswall
and Marshfield's Samuel Arnold each received £50. At an August
1687 meeting, Plymouth's householders discussed whether they
should collect Cotton's usual amount. Only a few men voted to do so.
"The negative vote being called for," recorded town clerk Thomas
Faunce, "many more hands were held up." Town leaders declared
that their promises to Cotton would instead be met "by the free sub-
scription of everyone," and they appointed men to learn how much
individuals would pledge.[14]

Cotton, who expected to receive about half of his customary
amount, was beside himself. He fingered Isaac Cushman—son of
Plymouth's longtime elder Thomas Cushman and *Mayflower* passenger Mary (Allerton) Cushman—as the "ring leader" of those who
"voted down a rate." Throughout the 1680s, Plymouth's church was
roiled by strife and factionalism. In his letters and church records,
Cotton made only cryptic references to the troubles, which stemmed
from conflict between the minister and Elder Cushman. By January
1684, things were bad enough that Cotton raised the idea that the
congregation might dismiss him as its minister. Church members
had a contentious meeting in his absence, but they neither granted a
dismissal nor restored peace. Finally, two months later, neighboring
churches effected a tenuous reconciliation, but Cotton continued to
feud with the Cushmans and with Ephraim Morton Sr., the brother
of colonial secretary Nathaniel Morton. Thus, when Andros made

church contributions voluntary, Cotton's opponents—along with many other townspeople—were happy to keep their money.[15]

Cotton informed his son Rowland that he now would "be poorly able to maintain [him] at [Harvard] College." Perhaps it was time for Rowland to find a pulpit. The next year, Plymouth's townspeople promised John Cotton even less money. "People being left to their liberty," the minister warned, "maintenance of the ministry is likely to be brought to nothing very speedily." For John Cotton and Thomas Hinckley, liberty properly understood was inextricably connected to social order and religious orthodoxy. Liberty meant the cultivation and preservation of churches where Christians worshipped according to the Bible as Plymouth's Congregationalists understood it. What Randolph and Andros had ushered in, as far as Cotton and Hinckley were concerned, was license for religious indifference and chaos.[16]

Given the reduction of his salary, Cotton sought supplements to his income. The Society for the Propagation of the Gospel in New England (often called the New England Company) still paid Cotton an annual stipend for his work with the Wampanoags. Cotton now asked for a raise. In a letter to Increase Mather, then in England, Cotton noted that John Eliot drew fifty pounds a year from the society. The aged Eliot, Cotton reported, was "hastening to his journey's end." Perhaps Mather could help Plymouth's minister assume Eliot's higher stipend after the latter's death. Cotton was nothing if not presumptuous. Longtime New Plymouth magistrate John Freeman (of Eastham) once lamented to Thomas Hinckley that "English ministers go away with too great an allowance for the little service they do for" the Indians. Wampanoag ministers who were "constant teacher[s]" received only three or four pounds a year. The New England Company, however, continued to reward English ministers more handsomely than their Native counterparts. After Eliot died in 1690, John Cotton obtained his requested increase.[17]

While Cotton worried about his salary, many of Plymouth's inhabitants objected to the poll tax and property taxes. Hinckley complained to Blathwayt that "it seemed neither just or legal to impose that law, made by another colony, on us in our colony, who never had any hand in the making of it." Taxing freemen without their consent was arbitrary government. Moreover, the former governor insisted that Plymouth's settlers could not afford to pay the new taxes. "Poverty is like to come upon us like an armed man," he warned, alluding to the Book of Proverbs (6:11 and 24:34). Rather brazenly, given the demise of New Plymouth's government and in light of his own place on Andros's council, Hinckley also sent a petition to James II in which he repeated his objections to the taxes. Hinckley begged the king to reverse course and grant New Plymouth's settlers a charter that would prevent "burdensome taxes or other uneasy things [being] imposed on them without their consent." It was another futile protest. Nothing in Andros's commission required him to obtain the consent of New England settlers for the taxes he decided they should pay.[18]

Some New England communities refused to collect Andros's taxes, among them the Massachusetts town of Ipswich. Andros ordered the arrest of thirty individuals there, including the minister John Wise. At the resulting trial, presided over by Joseph Dudley, Wise asserted that the taxes and arrests violated the rights of Englishmen enshrined in Magna Carta. According to Wise, Dudley countered that England's laws did not follow men to the ends of the earth. "You have no more privileges left you," he threatened Wise, "than not to be sold for slaves." The respective positions of Wise and Dudley represented two sides in an ongoing debate about whether the laws and liberty of England extended to its colonies. The judges handed down large fines and compelled Wise to apologize to Andros.[19]

In New Plymouth, Shadrach Wilbore—Taunton's town clerk—became a symbol of resistance. On behalf of the town's inhabitants, Wilbore drafted a petition that questioned the legality of the new taxes and sent it to New England treasurer John Usher. According to Boston's Edward Rawson and Samuel Sewall, it was a "modest paper signifying their not being free to raise money on the inhabitants without their own consent by an assembly." Andros, who did not suffer challenges to his authority, considered Taunton's paper decidedly immodest, a "scandalous, factious, and seditious writing." The governor issued a warrant for Wilbore's arrest and ordered him to stand trial in Bristol. Andros also took action against several other officeholders in Taunton who had supported the protest. After the county court dutifully sent Wilbore to prison, Taunton ceased its resistance and collected the tax. By mid-November, after five weeks in jail, Wilbore's courage was thoroughly daunted. He wrote Andros and begged for a pardon, noting that it was "very cold" and he had "a great family of children." He promised to be more circumspect with his writing in the future. Andros let him go.[20]

It was Andros's land policies that created the most stubborn opposition. Some New Plymouth landowners petitioned Andros to confirm their grants, but most settlers hesitated to do so, partly because of the expense and partly because taking that action would have conceded the governor's view of existing deeds. Andros, meanwhile, made grants of land that towns had reserved as commons or had in some cases granted to others. For instance, the governor granted Clark's Island to Nathaniel Clarke. The town of Plymouth claimed title to the uninhabited island, named for John Clarke, who had guided the Pilgrim shallop to shelter during the December 1620 exploration of Plymouth Bay. It is possible, but not certain, that Nathaniel Clarke was the grandson of the *Mayflower* pilot.[21]

Clarke had once been a respected member of Plymouth's town and church. In 1685, New Plymouth's freemen elected him as the colony's secretary, replacing the recently deceased Nathaniel Morton. Then, the next spring, Clarke's life unraveled. His wife, Dorothy, moved out of their home, taking with her considerable "money, rings, and treasure," assets from her first marriage. She also petitioned the General Court for a divorce, accusing her husband of impotency by reason of deformity. Puritans expected married couples to maintain conjugal relations, for pleasure as well as procreation. Unlike their civil and ecclesiastical counterparts in England, magistrates and ministers in New England accepted sexual impotence, insufficiency, or refusal as grounds for divorce or annulment. New Plymouth never passed a statute governing divorce, but its General Court granted divorces in cases of desertion, bigamy (one man had other wives in Boston, Barbados, and England), and adultery. In at least one other instance, an accusation of impotency led to a couple's separation, though apparently not a formal divorce. The magistrates accordingly took Dorothy Clarke's allegations seriously. They also decided that Nathaniel Clarke should not continue as the colony's secretary. He lost the position and the fifteen-pound salary that accompanied it. Thomas Hinckley ordered Clarke to surrender the colony's records.[22]

The court appointed three physicians to examine Nathaniel Clarke's genitals (at his expense), which they judged to be without defect. As a result, the magistrates would not grant a divorce, but they feared that the Clarkes would "ruin each other in their estates." The colony's leaders therefore brokered an agreement. Each spouse would live in one half of their newly built house. Dorothy Clarke would keep her estate, except for one hogshead of rum to pay for the finishing of the new house, and three barrels of cider for Nathaniel Clarke to drink.[23]

Once the civil proceedings ended, congregational discipline began. Dorothy Clarke was a full member of Plymouth's church, whereas Nathaniel Clarke had been born within its covenant but had not advanced to full membership. Church leaders called the couple to appear before the congregation. Cotton and Elder Thomas Cushman spoke to Dorothy about "some breach of rule in the management" of her differences with Nathaniel. She confessed her transgressions, and the church declared itself satisfied. Cushman then spoke "a few serious words" to Nathaniel Clarke, who flew into a "wicked passion," upset that "the church would clear the guilty and condemn the innocent." He declared that he would no longer have anything to do with the congregation. Nathaniel Clarke blamed his wife for both their marital strife and the divorce suit. Perhaps because they agreed with him, church members let the matter drop. Remarkably, the Clarkes seem to have lived together more amicably after the unusual court settlement. Nathaniel, however, resented the town and church leaders who had contributed to his private examination and public humiliation.[24]

Thoroughly alienated from Plymouth's other leaders, Clarke curried favor with Andros. In late 1687, he petitioned the governor for the island. Andros sent notice to the town of Plymouth informing its settlers of Clarke's request and asking whether any individuals claimed title to the island. In response, the town appointed a seven-man committee to defend its claim and agreed to raise ten pounds to defray the committee's expenses. Plymouth's objections did not sway Andros's decision. By the spring of 1688, Nathaniel Clarke owned the island.[25]

In response to resistance from towns such as Ipswich, Taunton, and Plymouth, Andros's council in March 1688 made it unlawful "for

the inhabitants of any town . . . to meet or convene themselves together at a town meeting, upon any pretense or color whatsoever."
The only exception was an appointed day each May for the election
of town officers. In the summer of 1688, Andros signed warrants for
the arrest of the Clark's Island committee members, along with Plymouth town clerk and deacon Thomas Faunce. They were accused of
holding illegal meetings and of raising unauthorized taxes. Andros
also charged Duxbury's minister, Ichabod Wiswall, because he had
authored the town's defense of its claim. A court in Boston meted
out stiff fines to the defendants and ordered them to appear again
that fall. Plymouth's John Cotton reported in September that "hard
measure is expected." Cotton worried that "our people are so impoverished by the management of this unhappy island" that they
had promised him an even more meager salary. Plymouth's church
set aside October 30 as a fast day and instructed townspeople to pray
for their "brethren and neighbors" appearing before the court.[26]

By the late summer of 1688, New Englanders had more pressing
concerns than Clark's Island or John Cotton's salary. Fighting had
resumed between English settlers and Abenakis in Maine, and Indians razed the Massachusetts towns of Deerfield and Springfield.
James II had consolidated the colonies and appointed Andros in
large part to secure the New England frontier. The governor responded to the raids by impressing hundreds of Massachusetts men
and sending them to Maine. At the same time, Andros tried but
failed to mend relations with the Abenaki.

While Plymouth's settlers lived far from the fighting, they shared
in the region's fear of a conspiracy that involved not only the French
and their Indian allies, but allegedly extended to Andros himself.
The town of Rochester's Samuel Eldred Jr. heard a rumor of sixteen
hundred armed Wampanoags on Martha's Vineyard and the other
islands to the south of Cape Cod. A Native man named Joseph told
Eldred that the "governor did not dare to disarm them for the governor had more love for them, the said Indians, than for his Majesty's
subjects the English." The rumor was sheer fancy, but many New
Englanders suspected that a governor appointed by a Catholic king
worked for rather than against their enemies.[27]

Fears of Catholic conspiracies were even more advanced on the

other side of the Atlantic. In June 1688, James II's wife, Mary of
Modena, gave birth to a son. The birth meant that a Catholic prince
rather than the Protestant daughter of the late Charles II was now
next in the line of succession. Attempting to discredit the newborn
heir, some Protestants outlandishly claimed that it was a sham birth,
that the queen had never been pregnant, and that palace courtiers had
smuggled an imposter infant into the royal birth chamber. Church
of England leaders, meanwhile, took the birth as a signal to stiffen
their resistance to toleration. Later that same month, a jury acquitted seven bishops—including the archbishop of Canterbury—who
had refused to read the king's Declaration of Indulgence. By the fall,
both James and his opponents anticipated that William of Orange
would invade England. William was married to King Charles II's
daughter Mary, and he now sought his uncle's throne. James prepared to fight, then fled to France when his allies deserted him soon
after William's landing, amid massive displays of popular support
for the usurper.[28]

In February 1689, Parliament declared the throne vacant and
offered it to William and Mary as joint monarchs. A Bill of Rights
placed limits on royal prerogative, upheld the liberties of Parliament, and barred Catholics from attaining the throne. The goal was
the creation of a constitutional, staunchly Protestant monarchy.
Those who celebrated the accession of William and Mary called it
a "Glorious Revolution."

In the winter of 1688–89, rumors of revolution crossed the Atlantic, but confirmation of James's flight did not reach New England
for quite some time. John Winslow, whose grandmother Mary Chilton and great-uncle Edward Winslow had been *Mayflower* passengers, arrived in Boston from Nevis on April 4 with news of "happy
proceedings in England." Andros jailed young Winslow. Soon, however, town militia companies and mutinous soldiers from the Maine
campaign were marching toward Boston. Sensing opportunity and
wishing to avoid bloodshed, Boston town leaders arrested Andros,
Randolph, and other members of the Dominion government. They
forced Randolph to arrange the surrender of the Redcoats, both
those at the town's fort and those on Castle Island. From Boston,
William Bradford informed Thomas Hinckley that Andros was now
"in irons."[29]

It was by no means clear that any of the Dominion colonies could simply revive their prior governments without the sanction of the crown. The accession of William and Mary did not invalidate the decisions their predecessors had made about New England. Nevertheless, New Plymouth's freemen met in early June, voted to resume their "former way of government" that had been interrupted "by the illegal arbitrary power" of Andros, and reelected all of their former magistrates (with the exception of the late John Alden). The colony held a day of thanksgiving later in the month. For his resistance to Andros, the town of Taunton thanked Shadrach Wilbore, compensating him for his imprisonment with a grant of one hundred acres of land. Similarly, Plymouth sold land to reimburse the men who had suffered fines and incurred other expenses defending the town's ownership of Clark's Island.[30]

Not everyone was thankful. Nathaniel Clarke had been in Boston at the time of the uprising. He made plans to flee New England but was arrested and brought to Plymouth. After the colony's June 1689 election, the first act of the reestablished General Court was to declare Clarke a "public enemy." The court required that he post a bond of two hundred pounds, promise to appear before the magistrates in October, and behave well until then.[31]

Plymouth's church leaders also examined the Clarke family's recent behavior. They accused Dorothy Clarke of "encouraging her husband to get Clark's Island from the town" and of abusing John and Joanna Cotton's nine-year-old son, Josiah. The boy had climbed into a tree on the Clarke property, and Dorothy Clarke allegedly had pulled him out of the tree and thrown him over her fence. In her defense, she claimed that she had gently removed Josiah from the tree and that Joanna Cotton had caused her son's bleeding by "putting a key into Josiah's mouth." The church ordered Dorothy Clarke to repent and ordered Nathaniel Clarke to appear before the congregation. He twice refused, cleverly stating that "he could not speak, because he was under [court] bonds" for good behavior. The church voted to disown Nathaniel Clarke as a child of the church, declaring that he, like Esau, had "despised his birthright." The next spring, Dorothy Clarke confessed her sin and was forgiven. Her husband eventually made his peace with the town's church, which he joined nine months before his January 1718 death.[32]

Punishing Nathaniel and Dorothy Clarke was easy. Resuming effective self-government proved difficult, and the colony's decision to support Massachusetts and New York in wars against the French and Indians made it almost impossible. The revolution against Andros had left frontier communities in Maine undefended, and raids in the summer of 1689 alarmed settlers across northern New England. The Bay Colony quickly requested the services of Little Compton's Benjamin Church, the Plymouth Colony hero of King Philip's War. With a mixture of English and Wampanoag recruits, Church headed north to Casco Bay. Church and his men successfully defended the town of Falmouth against an Abenaki attack. Eleven of Church's men died in the expedition, including one Wampanoag and one "negro" from Plymouth Colony. In 1690 and 1692, Church returned to Maine to lead English raids against the Abenaki.[33]

What became known as King William's War—the North American counterpart to a war in Europe between France and an alliance of England, the Dutch Republic, and the Hapsburgs—soon widened. French and Indian raids against Schenectady in New York and Salmon Falls in New Hampshire prompted the Bay Colony to send an expedition commanded by Sir William Phips against Port Royal on French Acadia. The Maine-born Phips had made his mark in 1687 by discovering a sunken Spanish galleon, which netted him some £11,000 and a knighthood. His good fortune continued against the French, who quickly surrendered. Breaking the terms of the surrender, Phips allowed his troops to plunder the settlement.

Buoyed by his conquest of Port Royal, Phips next led a campaign against Quebec, where his luck came to an inglorious end. Two hundred Plymouth Colony men, including fifty Wampanoags, sailed north as part of a twenty-three-hundred-man force. Lieutenant General John Walley, son of Barnstable's late minister Thomas Walley, played a pivotal and controversial role in the operation. Walley had been a militia captain in Bristol and a member of Andros's council during the Dominion. Phips gave him the critical task of leading the land assault on Quebec. After Walley's troops went ashore, they repulsed the French, but Walley did not press his advantage and move toward the city. John Wise, the former Ipswich tax resister and a chaplain on the expedition, confronted Walley about his failure to advance. "I cannot rule them," Walley said of his troops. Nor did he wish to rule them. After several days of indecision, Walley pushed for a retreat and became one of the first into the boats. "What is an army of lions," wrote another member of the expedition, "when they must not go on except a frighted hart [deer] shall lead them?" Walley's soldiers were not lions. They were hungry and weak. Many died of smallpox on their homebound ships, which encountered a storm that wrecked one and blew others clear to the Caribbean.[34]

Wise put the blame for the defeat, deaths, and the abandonment of considerable artillery squarely on John Walley. The loss of pay or having to wear the "wooden sword" as a badge of cowardice would be insufficient punishments, Wise asserted. "There is no less than death deserved," the minister concluded. Walley countered that the fleet should not have spent three weeks within three days' sail of Quebec, giving the enemy ample notice of the planned assault. "Our consciences do not accuse us," Walley wrote. In abandoning an attack against a well-fortified city whose defenders outnumbered the New Englanders, Walley probably saved his troops from an even greater disaster.[35]

Around two dozen Plymouth Colony settlers died in the 1689–90 campaigns, along with an unknown number of Wampanoag volunteers. In addition to these human losses, King William's War was a financial and political debacle for the colony. Unlike his predecessor Josiah Winslow, Thomas Hinckley had not hesitated when Bay Colony governor Simon Bradstreet requested his help. With Hinckley's support, the General Court repeatedly voted to raise troops and money for the war. The tax burden proved crushing, with communities in 1690 being asked to raise five to ten times the amounts they had paid in 1685. The war threatened to bankrupt the Bay Colony as well, but New Plymouth's government was especially fragile.

The result was a tax revolt that spread across the colony, from Bristol to the Cape Cod town of Eastham.[36] By the summer of 1690, six communities—out of the colony's twenty towns and villages—"neglected" to choose officials to rate inhabitants. There were multiple reasons for the recalcitrance. Some inhabitants questioned the government's legitimacy, and there were rumors that the crown would soon attach New Plymouth to either New York or Massachusetts Bay. Why pay taxes to a government that might cease to exist? Moreover, the sheer size of the rates collided with the colony's limited resources. Even with representation, settlers could endure only so much taxation.

The General Court threatened fines against delinquent individuals and reluctant communities, and it considered taking tax collection into its own hands. In the end, though, the tax revolt succeeded. Hinckley reported in the fall of 1691 that inhabitants were "riotously assembling in considerable numbers at Dartmouth to resist" constables. He feared similar displays of unrest and revolt in other communities, including Little Compton. "It's thought there would be bloodshed," he informed Duxbury's Ichabod Wiswall, "if means should be used to reduce them to order and their duty." Hinckley and his fellow magistrates felt powerless to collect the taxes needed to meet the colony's obligations.[37]

The political disarray contributed to the colony's final dissolution. After the collapse of the Dominion, Plymouth's leaders petitioned the new king—whom they flattered as a second Joshua, Constantine, Theodosius, and Augustus, all in one obsequious letter—for the resumption of their "former enjoyed liberties and privileges, both sacred and civil." It quickly became clear, however, that William agreed with his predecessors about the need for greater royal control over England's colonies. Massachusetts Bay, for example, did not get its old charter back.[38]

What would happen to New Plymouth, the only New England colony whose government had never rested upon a charter? The most likely outcome was that the 1684 decision to attach New Plymouth to Massachusetts Bay would stand. In the meantime, the colony's leaders made yet another half-hearted attempt to secure their own charter. The General Court sent no agent to England, instead relying on Boston's Increase Mather and Sir Henry Ashurst, a baronet and member of Parliament. Mather had encouraged Hinckley to sever his attachment to William Blathwayt; he chided Hinckley for wasting fifty guineas on someone who would "make you purchase your own slavery with your own money." He recommended that New Plymouth instead distribute money to Ashurst. Hinckley took the advice about Blathwayt to heart. The colony's leaders sent their future petitions to Ashurst.[39]

In February 1690, Duxbury's Ichabod Wiswall sailed to England (on the same boat as Edmund Andros and Edward Randolph). Despite his lack of influence and access, Wiswall was the closest thing to an advocate and agent for New Plymouth in England. He agreed with Mather that funds were essential, reminding Hinckley of Ecclesiastes 10:19 ("Money answereth all things" in the King James version). New Plymouth needed to secure access to the king and his council by paying bribes to men with influence.

Wiswall grew frustrated when New Plymouth failed to provide the bribes. The General Court voted to collect a modest sum through voluntary contributions, but the freemen would "raise but little to send upon an uncertainty." Wiswall could not believe his colony's apparent indifference, terming it a "great riddle." "If you desire to return to the late experience of the miseries of an arbitrary government," he told Hinckley, "a little longer neglect of your opportunity may hasten it." He wondered how it was that Plymouth's current leaders ventured so little for "their civil and religious privileges" when the Pilgrims had risked everything. Wiswall was not alone in his exasperation. John Cotton also urged the governor to provide more leadership for the charter effort. "Stand forth, and play the man," he wrote him in February 1691, "for our God and for the cities of our God." Despite the prodding of Wiswall and Cotton, the neglect continued. Hinckley conceded that his government had no ability to procure the needed money.[40]

Other colonies were less neglectful of their interests. Henry Sloughter, soon to become governor of New York, made a bid to have New Plymouth attached to his colony. Despite their geographic separation, the idea was not farfetched. Some settlers in the western towns of New Plymouth favored the plan, and Martha's Vineyard was already under New York's jurisdiction. Mather parried the scheme and instead asked officials to include Plymouth within a new Massachusetts Bay charter. Wiswall alleged that "the rashness and imprudence of one, at least, who went from New England in disguise by night, hath not a little contributed to our general disappointment." The cryptic reference was to Mather, who had slipped away from Boston at night to avoid Andros's warrant for his arrest.

What Wiswall understood as betrayal may have been unavoidable. Mather's son Cotton informed Hinckley that Plymouth had no chance of obtaining its own charter. It was only a matter of whether Massachusetts or New York would absorb the small colony. In the fall of 1691, the crown attached Plymouth and the islands to its south to an expanded Province of Massachusetts Bay.[41]

Even before English officials settled its fate, the Pilgrim colony had ceased to govern itself. Some communities did not send deputies or freemen to the June 1691 election, causing the magistrates to reschedule it for later in the summer. The last action of New Plymouth's General Court came in July 1691, when it appointed a day of fasting and prayer. During the final months of the colony's existence, there were no general courts or courts of assistants.

Increase Mather received the honor of recommending the new province's first governor and the members of his council. As governor, he proposed William Phips, who had returned to England to answer critics of the failed campaign against Quebec. As members of Phips's council, Mather recommended Hinckley, Walley, Barnabas Lothrop, and William Bradford, men who had held office under Andros and during the colony's final years of self-government. Shortly after Governor Phips reached Boston in May 1692, he appointed a special court to prosecute cases of alleged witchcraft at Salem, then focused his own attentions on the ongoing war against the French-backed Abenaki.

While representatives from Plymouth, Barnstable, and Bristol Counties had little clout in the expanded Massachusetts, its charter guaranteed that colonists could elect a House of Representatives each year, that the members of that House could elect the governor's council (subject to the governor's veto), and that the king would appoint someone from Massachusetts rather than a stranger as governor. The new Massachusetts Assembly (House, council, and governor) declared that it alone could levy taxes, direct expenditures, and oversee the colony's courts, but the new charter allowed the Privy Council to veto any colonial laws within three years of their passage.

Both in Massachusetts Bay and New Plymouth, there was far more quiescence than had been the case during the Dominion. In his diary, John Paine of Eastham lauded King William as "a bulwark

to their castle's walls," a monarch appointed by God to protect Protestants from "the heathen and Antichristians [Catholics]." Rather
than fearing bishops and royal governors as agents of Antichrist,
settlers increasingly saw themselves as members of a Protestant empire with a shared interest in advancing the cause of Christ against
France and Spain.[42]

The Massachusetts Assembly required communities to support an
"able, learned and orthodox minister." In other words, the church
taxes that Edmund Andros had scuttled were back. By adding Plymouth Colony to its territory, though, Massachusetts Bay had absorbed hundreds of religious dissenters into its jurisdiction. The historian William McLoughlin estimates that approximately one-third
of Bristol County's population consisted of Baptists and Quakers.
As had been the case during the 1670s and 1680s, men who refused
to pay ministerial rates had their property seized by constables, and
some ended up in prison. For decades, Baptists, Quakers, and Angli-
cans fought for exemptions from laws that required them to support
ministers and churches they rejected.[43]

   The new charter was good news for John Cotton, as Plymouth
resumed its collection of his salary. Cotton's ministry came to an
ignominious end a few years later, however. In addition to the conflicts with members of the Cushman and Morton families, there had
been other signs of trouble. In 1691, John Gray accosted Cotton in
the street. "Thou, a minister of the gospel," Gray railed. "Thou art
a dirty fellow." Then in June 1697, Plymouth's church members assembled to consider "some miscarriages in the pastor towards Re-
bekah Morton." He confessed to one of her charges and denied everything else. The church voted to continue him in office, but when
rumors of Cotton's indiscretions spread across New England, other
ministers intervened. According to Boston's Samuel Sewall, a council of neighboring churches found him guilty of "notorious breaches
of the Seventh Commandment [against adultery], and undue carriage in choosing elders." The more salacious accusations extended
beyond Rebecca Morton to include other women. Cotton's friends
and ministerial colleagues advised him to make a full confession and
ask for a dismissal. Cotton partly capitulated. He agreed that his

ministry in Plymouth was over, but he now refused to admit any wrongdoing.[44]

Joanna Cotton had borne her husband's scandalous behavior in Connecticut. She had moved with him to Martha's Vineyard, then to Plymouth. For decades, she had raised and mourned children, all the while continuing her work as a midwife and healer. She visited the sick, made remedies, and sent recipes and advice in letters. In the 1690s, she coexisted uneasily with a French Catholic physician—Francis LeBaron—who had moved to Plymouth. Joanna sometimes recommended bloodletting, but customarily only after "physick"—medicine—had been tried. John once informed one of his sons that LeBaron was "very sullen and surly" toward Joanna. Most towns-people probably preferred her ministrations.[45]

As John stewed over his most recent humiliation, Joanna's work was unremitting. In February 1698, Robert Bartlett asked her to come to his family. Joanna spent the night. Sarah Bartlett had just given birth to a "lovely boy . . . both its feet bending inwards, likely to be a cripple." She spent the night with the Bartletts and returned home early the next morning. (The Bartlett baby died several days later.) There was no time to rest, however. Joseph Churchill needed her help with his twenty-year-old son. At the same time, two men wanted her to visit their pregnant wives. William Ring fetched her on horseback to tend to his sick daughter. Finally, she visited Mercy Wood and treated an infection that eventually proved fatal. "She was never more willing to do and run as now," John Cotton observed, even though Joanna was "tired with serving."[46]

Joanna was also tired of her husband's inability to own up to his transgressions. Shortly after Joanna's spate of work in late February and early March, Boston's Samuel Sewall visited Plymouth. He dined with the town's new minister, but he also called on John and Joanna. "A free confession was the best way," Sewall urged John Cotton repeatedly, bringing up the example of David's adultery, suffering, repentance, and redemption. The deposed minister would not budge. "Some of my last words to him was," Sewall wrote, "kiss the Son [Christ], lest he be angry."[47]

In an attempt to salvage his reputation, especially with Joanna, John Cotton blamed his dismissal on the circumstances surrounding

*Gravestone of Joanna Cotton (1642–1702), Sandwich, Massachusetts.
The epitaph reads: "The memory of the just is blessed." The winged skull
represents the flight of the soul to heaven. (Photograph by author.)*

New Plymouth's failure to obtain its own charter. He explained that when his brother-in-law Increase Mather had returned from England with the new Massachusetts Bay charter, "our people were all in a rage at him [Mather]." They accused Mather of having pretended friendship to New Plymouth and then of having "take[n] them in to be slaves." Cotton fingered Ichabod Wiswall as the source of the contention. "When another man [Wiswall] came home from old England," Cotton continued, "he made it his work . . . to traduce Brother Mather." What did any of this have to do with John Cotton? Plymouth's now former minister had defended Mather against his critics. Five years later, Cotton suggested, those grudge-bearing critics sought revenge with their trumped-up charges. It seems highly unlikely that the machinations surrounding the charter had much if anything to do with Cotton's travails. Most damning is the fact that the Mathers themselves accepted his guilt. Increase Mather thought the council of ministers had been too lenient on Cotton.[48]

Plymouth Colony had dissolved, and so did John and Joanna Cotton's marriage. Joanna could have sued John for divorce on the grounds of adultery, but she did not want to expose herself and her family to further humiliation. Instead, she separated from John by moving to her son Rowland's home in Sandwich. Joanna's withdrawal stung John. Churches and communities expected couples to cohabit. Wives were bound to their husbands, bound to obey and follow them. By the summer of 1698, John complained to Joanna about "aspersions, grounded upon your living so long at Sandwich." She was unmoved.[49]

In the wake of John Cotton's dismissal, no other congregation in New England would employ him. Then a call came from Charlestown (later Charleston), South Carolina, founded some two decades earlier. Congregationalists there were forming a church and needed a pastor. When John Cotton left for South Carolina in 1698, Joanna remained in Massachusetts. "Mother seems not to know what to do about coming to you," Rowland Cotton wrote to his father. It seems, however, that she knew exactly what she wanted to do. By staying in Sandwich, Joanna Cotton exercised a measure of liberty.[50]

Conclusion

C APTAIN WILLIAM COIT IS a Revolutionary War foot-
note. He was from New London, Connecticut, fought at
Bunker Hill, drifted in and out of the army for a few
years, and was captured by the British in 1781. An aide to
George Washington once dismissed him as "a mere blubber."

Coit had one success to his credit, though. In the fall of 1775, he
took command of a privateer and sailed out to look for British ships
bringing provisions to the encircled Redcoats at Boston. Coit's vessel was barely seaworthy. The mainmast had rotted off. The deck,
he joked, was new "when it was first made" and now "ashamed of
being old." His cannons were artifacts from the early days of English Connecticut. He warned that firing them might split his ship
in two. He reassured his commanding officers, however, that as long
as he encountered only "unarmed vessels," he would keep his ship
afloat. It worked out. As Washington reported, Coit "blundered upon
two vessels from Nova Scotia." He took the ships, their crews, and
his modest plunder—hay, livestock, and chickens—to the nearest
port, which was Plymouth.

Once there, he had some fun at his prisoners' expense. He made
them "land upon the same rock our ancestors first trod when they
landed in America." From upon the rock, either Coit's men or his
prisoners—the account is unclear—"gave three cheers, and wished
success to American arms." Coit and his crew soon abandoned their
ship, which was put out of service the next year.[1]

362

During the Revolutionary era, New Englanders revived their interest in the Pilgrims, and many of them took the "Forefathers" far more seriously than did William Coit. In Massachusetts, Patriots yoked the Forefathers to the cause of American independence, and by the early nineteenth century, the Pilgrims had become symbols of republicanism, democracy, and religious toleration. "We have come to this Rock," Daniel Webster proclaimed at the bicentennial of the Pilgrim landing, "to record here our homage for our Pilgrim Fathers; our sympathy in their sufferings; our gratitude for their labors; our admiration of their virtues; our veneration for their piety; and our attachment to those principles of civil and religious liberty." Americans did not always agree on what exact forms of liberty the Pilgrims had established. Webster, for instance, called on Americans to pledge themselves "upon the Rock of Plymouth, to extirpate and destroy" the slave trade. Unitarian ministers stressed Pilgrim tolerance, whereas more conservative Congregationalists praised the Pilgrims' adherence to Calvinist verities. Depending on the time, place, and political party, the Pilgrims stood for social order, democratic equality, or even secession (because of their separatism). Regardless of how they refashioned them, however, nearly all white Americans lauded the Forefathers as the forerunners of ideals they themselves cherished.[2]

By the time Webster delivered his bicentennial oration, Plymouth Rock was no longer the massive granite boulder the Pilgrims would have seen in 1620. In or around 1775, independence-minded townspeople led by Colonel Theophilus Cotton—a grandson of John and Joanna Cotton—decided "to consecrate the rock on which [the Pilgrims] landed to the shrine of liberty." Cotton's act of consecration was to move the rock to the "liberty pole square" in front of Plymouth's meetinghouse. Plymouth's townspeople were not as adept with giant screws as their Forefathers had been. In their attempt to raise the boulder, they split it in two. The upper portion went to the liberty pole; the larger base remained at the wharf.[3]

As new generations of politicians and ministers heaped praised on the Pilgrims, the rock itself became smaller and more fragile. People sat on the rock, wrote on it, chipped off bits of it as souvenirs, and moved the two remaining halves around. On July 4, 1834, townspeople transported the rock's upper portion from the town square to the front of Pilgrim Hall. Meanwhile, the rock's base remained exposed at the wharf and was subject to many indignities. When the base was moved under a canopy completed in 1867, a considerable portion was removed to make it fit. One large hunk of the rock ended up as a doorstep at the Harlow House in Plymouth. In 1880, the Pilgrim Society reunited the two halves of the rock. Finally, on the occasion of the Pilgrim tercentennial in 1920, the town built the stately portico that has housed Plymouth Rock for the last hundred years. Many of the million or so tourists who come to Plymouth each year peer at the rock and wonder why it isn't bigger. It is remarkable that there is anything left at all. The boulder has had a rough last few centuries.[4]

Just as some Americans chipped away at Plymouth Rock, so others have chiseled away at the mythology surrounding the Pilgrims. The Mayflower Compact? The terse document had no influence on the political theory of the American founding. The landing on the rock? There are no references to the rock as the Pilgrim landing spot until 150 years after the *Mayflower*. The First Thanksgiving? Not a proper thanksgiving, and even if it had been, not the first. What about religious toleration and friendship with the Indians? In the years that followed the compact, the landing, and the 1621 harvest, Plymouth Colony leaders beheaded Indians and took their land, fined Baptists, and whipped Quakers.

Some Americans never bought into the myths fashioned by men like Daniel Webster. "The pilgrims landed at Plymouth," stated William Apess, an early nineteenth-century Methodist minister of mixed Pequot ancestry, "and without asking liberty from anyone, they possessed themselves of a portion of the country, and built themselves houses, and then made a treaty, and commanded them [the Wampanoags] to accede to it."[5] Apess pointed out that if the New Englanders of his day faced such an invasion, they would rush to defend their country. Yet with no awareness of their hypocrisy, Apess's white neighbors celebrated the Pilgrim invaders. Apess's argument now gains a broader hearing. Each year, the United American Indians of New England holds a National Day of Mourning above Plymouth Rock on Cole's Hill. Speakers talk about "Thankstaking" instead of "Thanksgiving" and link New England's seventeenth-century history to ongoing Native American struggles for justice. The National Day of Mourning gathering now draws larger crowds than the Pilgrim Progress procession held the same day.

Perhaps the Pilgrims and the colony they founded are like Plymouth Rock, diminished and disappointing. Yet when Pilgrim mythology is stripped away, the more expansive and colorful history of Plymouth Colony remains, like the base of the rock buried underneath the sand. The Mayflower Compact and the 1621 harvest are still significant, if not in the same ways that nineteenth-century politicians and painters imagined them. Moreover, these well-known founding moments have obscured the colony's subsequent history, including the decades-long Quaker struggle against persecution and the resilience of the Sakonnet community amid war and dispossession.

What about the contribution of the Pilgrims to American "principles of civil and religious liberty?" The Pilgrims and their successors cared a great deal about liberty, but they understood it in particular, seventeenth-century ways. Over the colony's seven-decade history, there were ongoing contests over the meanings of Christian liberty, liberty of conscience, and the political liberties of "freeborn English people." At the same time, settlers left no record of any debate about African slavery, and there are only a few hints of controversy among English settlers about their reduction of Wampanoags and other Native peoples to servitude, slavery, and subjection. Plymouth Colony leaders took it for granted that some groups of people were entitled to more liberties than others, while English dissenters and Natives pushed back against these assumptions. Rather than bequeathing to later generations of Americans a simple story of democracy and freedom, the Pilgrims and the other inhabitants of Plymouth Colony left behind both a complicated legacy of human bondage and unresolved debates about liberty.

Abbreviations

ANB	*American National Biography Online.*
Bangs, *Indian Deeds*	Jeremy Dupertuis Bangs, *Indian Deeds: Land Transactions in Plymouth Colony, 1620–1691* (Boston, Mass.: New England Historical Genealogical Society, 2002).
Bangs, *PCPL*	Jeremy Dupertuis Bangs, *Plymouth Colony Private Libraries: As Recorded in Wills and Inventories, 1633–1692*, rev. ed. (Leiden: Leiden American Pilgrim Museum, 2018).
Bangs, *S&P*	Jeremy Dupertuis Bangs, *Strangers and Pilgrims, Travelers and Sojourners: Leiden and the Foundations of Plymouth Plantation* (Plymouth, Mass.: General Society of Mayflower Descendants, 2009).
Bangs, *Sandwich*	Jeremy Dupertuis Bangs, *The Town Records of Sandwich during the Time of Plymouth Colony, 1620–1692* (Leiden: Leiden American Pilgrim Museum, 2014).
Bangs, *Scituate*	Jeremy Dupertuis Bangs, *The Seventeenth-Century Town Records of Scituate, Massachusetts*, 3 vols. (Boston: New England Historical Genealogical Society, 1997–2001).
Bangs, *Winslow*	Jeremy Dupertuis Bangs, *Pilgrim Edward Winslow, New England's First International*

	Diplomat (Boston: New England Historical Genealogical Society, 2004).
BL	British Library, London.
BLB	*Governor William Bradford's Letter Book* (Boston: Massachusetts Society of Mayflower Descendants, 1906).
Bunker	Nick Bunker, *Making Haste from Babylon: The* Mayflower *Pilgrims and Their World* (New York: Knopf, 2010).
CCA	Canterbury Cathedral Archives, Canterbury, U.K.
Church, *EP*	T[homas] C[hurch], *Entertaining Passages Relating to Philip's War* ... (Boston: B. Green, 1716).
CJCJ	Sheila McIntyre and Len Travers, eds., *The Correspondence of John Cotton Jr.* (Boston: Colonial Society of Massachusetts, 2009).
CMHS	*Collections of the Massachusetts Historical Society.*
CPC	Williston Walker, *The Creeds and Platforms of Congregationalism* (New York: Charles Scribner's Sons, 1893).
CRW	Glenn W. LaFantasie, ed., *The Correspondence of Roger Williams*, 2 vols. (Providence, R.I.: Brown University and the Rhode Island Historical Society, 1988).
CSP	*Colonial State Papers* database.
Deane, *Scituate*	Samuel Deane, *History of Scituate, Massachusetts* ... (Boston: James Loring, 1831).
DNB	*Oxford Dictionary of National Biography Online.*
EED	Champlin Burrage, *The Early English Dissenters in the Light of Recent Research (1550–1641)*, 2 vols. (Cambridge: Cambridge University Press, 1912).
ER	Robert N. Toppan and Alfred T. S. Goodrick, eds., *Edward Randolph: Including His Letters and Official Papers* ... , 7 vols. (Boston: Prince Society, 1898–1909).

FPCN	Parish Records, book 1, First Parish Church of Norwell, James Library, Norwell, Mass.
GMB	Robert Charles Anderson, ed., *The Great Migration Begins: Immigrants to New England, 1620–1633,* 3 vols. (Boston: New England Historic Genealogical Society, 1995).
GN	Kelly Wisecup, ed., *"Good News from New England" by Edward Winslow* (Amherst: University of Massachusetts Press, 2014).
HP	"The Hinckley Papers," in *CMHS,* 4th ser., 5 (1861): 1–308.
JJW	Richard S. Dunn, James Savage, and Laetitia Yeandle, eds., *The Journal of John Winthrop, 1630–1649* (Cambridge, Mass.: Harvard University Press, 1996).
Langdon	George D. Langdon Jr., *Pilgrim Colony: A History of New Plymouth, 1620–1691* (New Haven: Yale University Press, 1966).
Magnalia	Cotton Mather, *Magnalia Christi Americana: or, the Ecclesiastical History of New-England* (London: Thomas Parkhurst, 1702).
MD	*Mayflower Descendant.*
MHS	Massachusetts Historical Society.
MR	[George Morton et al.], *A Relation or Journall of the beginning and proceedings of the English Plantation setled at Plimoth in New England* ... (London: John Bellamie, 1622), commonly known as *Mourt's Relation.*
MSAC	Massachusetts State Archives Collection, Massachusetts State Archives, Boston, accessed via familysearch.org.
NAK	National Archives, Kew, U.K.
NEC	Thomas Morton, *New English Canaan* ... (London: Charles Greene, n.d.).
NEHGR	*New England Historical and Genealogical Register.*
NEM	Nathaniel Morton, *New-Englands Memoriall* ... (Cambridge, Mass.: S.G. and M.J., 1669).

NEQ	*New England Quarterly.*
NEYM	New England Yearly Meeting Records, Special Collections and University Archives, University of Massachusetts, Amherst.
OPP	Worthington Chauncey Ford, ed., *History of Plymouth Plantation by William Bradford*, 2 vols. (Boston: Massachusetts Historical Society, 1912).
PAAS	*Proceedings of the American Antiquarian Society.*
PChR	Arthur Lord, ed., *Plymouth Church Records, Part I* (Boston: Colonial Society of Massachusetts, 1920).
PCR	Nathaniel B. Shurtleff, *Records of the Colony of New Plymouth . . .*, 12 vols. (Boston: W. White, 1855–61).
PMHS	*Proceedings of the Massachusetts Historical Society.*
PTR	William T. Davis, ed., *Records of the Town of Plymouth* (Plymouth: Avery & Doten, 1889), vol. 1.
RAN	Records of the Archdeaconry of Nottingham, University of Nottingham Special Collections, Nottingham, U.K.
RGCMB	Nathaniel B. Shurtleff, ed., *Records of the Governor and Company of the Massachusetts Bay . . .*, 5 vols. (Boston: W. White, 1853–54).
SBCR	Scituate and Barnstable Church Records, transcription by Ezra Stiles, MS Vault Stiles, Beinecke Rare Book and Manuscript Library, Yale University, New Haven, Conn.
Simmons	C. H. Simmons, ed., *Plymouth Colony Records*, vol. 1, *Wills and Inventories, 1633–1699* (Camden, Maine: Picton, 1996).
SPO	*State Papers Online* database.
Stratton	Eugene Aubrey Stratton, *Plymouth Colony:*

	Its History & People, 1620–1691 (Salt Lake City: Ancestry, 1986).
WJS	Philip L. Barbour, ed., *The Complete Works of Captain John Smith (1580–1631)*, 3 vols. (Chapel Hill: University of North Carolina Press, 1986).
WMQ	*William and Mary Quarterly.*
WP	*Winthrop Papers, 1498–1654*, 6 vols. (Boston: Massachusetts Historical Society, 1929–68).

Notes

Introduction

1. There has been no end to the writing of books about the Pilgrims and the early years of Plymouth Colony. Several of the most significant recent entries include Nick Bunker, *Making Haste from Babylon: The Mayflower Pilgrims and Their World* (New York: Knopf, 2010); Jeremy Dupertuis Bangs, *Strangers and Pilgrims, Travellers and Sojourners: Leiden and the Foundations of Plymouth Plantation* (Plymouth, Mass.: General Society of Mayflower Descendants, 2009); Nathaniel Philbrick, *Mayflower: A Story of Courage, Community, and War* (New York: Penguin, 2006). The two most recent accounts of the colony's history as a whole are George D. Langdon Jr., *Pilgrim Colony: A History of New Plymouth, 1620–1691* (New Haven: Yale University Press, 1966); Eugene Aubrey Stratton, *Plymouth Colony: Its History and People, 1620–1691* (Salt Lake City: Ancestry, 1986). Other valuable studies include John Demos, *A Little Commonwealth: Family Life in Plymouth Colony* (New York: Oxford University Press, 1970); Darren B. Rutman, *Husbandmen of Plymouth: Farms and Villages in the Old Colony, 1620–1692* (Boston: Beacon, 1967).
2. OPP, 1:xvii.
3. Miller, *The New England Mind: The Seventeenth Century* (New York: Macmillan, 1939); Miller, *Orthodoxy in Massachusetts, 1630–1650* (Cambridge, Mass.: Harvard University Press, 1933); Bozeman, *To Live Ancient Lives: The Primitivist Dimension in Puritanism* (Chapel Hill: University of North Carolina Press, 1988), 115; Morison, *By Land and by Sea: Essays and Addresses by Samuel Eliot Morison* (New York: Knopf, 1953), 234. This scholarly neglect is not universal. In recent years, several historians have integrated Plymouth Colony into larger narratives of the early English settlement of New England. See, for example, Andrew Lipman, *The Saltwater Frontier: Indians and the Contest for the American Coast* (New Haven: Yale University Press, 2015); Michael P. Winship, *Godly Republicanism:*

Puritans, Pilgrims, and a City on a Hill (Cambridge, Mass.: Harvard University Press, 2012); David D. Hall, *A Reforming People: Puritanism and the Transformation of Public Life in New England* (New York: Knopf, 2011).

4. See Charles E. Hambrick-Stowe, *The Practice of Piety: Puritan Devotional Disciplines in Seventeenth-Century New England* (Chapel Hill: University of North Carolina Press, 1982), esp. chapter 3.

5. Walsham, *Charitable Hatred: Tolerance and Intolerance in England, 1500–1700* (Manchester: Manchester University Press, 2006), 3.

6. Hall, *A Reforming People;* Winship, *Godly Republicanism.*

Chapter One. The Lord's Free People

1. Elizabeth French, "Genealogical Research in England," *NEHGR* 68 (Apr. 1914): 182. Cushman was baptized on 9 Feb. 1577/78. On Cushman's Canterbury years, I have relied on Robert C. Cushman and Michael R. Paulick, "Robert Cushman, Mayflower Pilgrim in Canterbury, 1596–1607," *Mayflower Quarterly* 79 (Sept. 2013): 226–35; Paulick, "Pilgrim Robert Cushman's Book, *The Cry of a Stone*," *MD* 60 (Spring 2011): 31–35.

2. R[obert] Campbell, *The London Tradesman* ... (London: T. Gardner, 1747), 271. On the grocer trade in early modern England, see Jon Stobart, *Sugar and Spice: Grocers and Groceries in Provincial England, 1650–1830* (Oxford: Oxford University Press, 2013), chapter 1; J. Aubrey Rees, *The Grocery Trade: Its History and Romance*, vol. 1 (London: Duckworth, 1910), esp. chapters 10–17. On the 1603 plague in Canterbury, see Charles Creighton, *A History of Epidemics in Britain* (Cambridge: Cambridge University Press, 1891), 498.

3. [Wiburn], *A Checke or reproofe of M. Howlets untimely shreeching* (London: Thomas Dawson, 1581), 15v. On the term *puritan*, see Patrick Collinson, "A Comment: Concerning the Name Puritan," *Journal of Ecclesiastical History* 31 (Oct. 1980): 483–88.

4. John Bruce, ed., *The Diary of John Manningham* ... *1602–1603* (Westminster, U.K.: J. B. Nichols and Sons, 1868), 156. See Peter Lake with Michael Questier, *The Antichrist's Lewd Hat: Protestants, Papists and Players in Post-Reformation England* (New Haven: Yale University Press, 2002), chapters 13 and 14.

5. Luther, *The Freedom of a Christian*, in Harold J. Grimm, ed., *Career of the Reformer: I*, vol. 31 of *Luther's Works*, ed. Jaroslav Pelikan and Helmut T. Lehman (Philadelphia: Fortress, 1957), 344, 356. Calvin, *Institutes of the Christian Religion*, trans. Ford Lewis Battles, ed. John T. McNeill (Philadelphia: Westminster, 1960), book 3, 19, 1, 1:833.

6. Luther, *Freedom of a Christian*, 344; Ozment, "Martin Luther on Religious Liberty," in Noel B. Reynolds and W. Cole Durham Jr., eds., *Religious Liberty in Western Thought* (Grand Rapids, Mich.: Eerdmans, 1996), 77.

See the discussion in Benjamin J. Kaplan, *Divided by Faith: Religious Conflict and the Practice of Toleration in Early Modern Europe* (Cambridge, Mass.: Harvard University Press, 2007), 22–24.

7. The most helpful introductions to late sixteenth-century English separatism remain Stephen Brachlow, *The Communion of Saints: Radical Puritan and Separatist Ecclesiology* (London: Oxford University Press, 1988); B. R. White, *The English Separatist Tradition: From the Marian Martyrs to the Pilgrim Fathers* (London: Oxford University Press, 1971).

8. Browne, *Reformation without Tarrying for Anie* [1582], in Albert Peel and Leland H. Carlson, eds., *The Writings of Robert Harrison and Robert Browne* (London: George Allen and Unwin, 1953), 164. On the "Bury Stirs," see John Craig, *Reformation, Politics and Polemics: The Growth of Protestantism in East Anglian Market Towns, 1500–1610* (Aldershot: Ashgate, 2001), chapter 4.

9. [Barrow and Greenwood], *A True Description* [1589], in *CPC*, 33–40. See Brachlow, *Communion of Saints*, esp. chapters 1 and 3.

10. Barrow, *A Brief Discoverie of the False Church* [1590], in Leland H. Carlson, ed., *The Writings of Henry Barrow, 1587–1590* (London: George Allen and Unwin, 1962), 347 ("neglected"), 511 ("full power"). See Francis Bremer, *Lay Empowerment and the Development of Puritanism* (New York: Palgrave Macmillan, 2015), 51–52; Michael P. Winship, *Godly Republicanism: Puritans, Pilgrims, and a City on a Hill* (Cambridge, Mass.: Harvard University Press, 2012), 51–60.

11. T. E. Hartley, ed., *Proceedings in the Parliaments of Elizabeth I* (London: Leicester University Press, 1995), 3:162–68.

12. William Barlow, *The Summe and Substance of the Conference . . .* (London: V.S. for Mathew Law, 1605), 36 ("no bishop"), 83 ("harry"); James to Lord Henry Howard, undated letter, ca. 17 Jan. 1604/05, in G.P.V. Akrigg, ed., *Letters of King James VI & I* (Berkeley: University of California Press, 1984), 221. See Alan Cromartie, "King James and the Hampton Court Conference," in Ralph Houlbrooke, ed., *James VI and I: Ideas, Authority, and Government* (Aldershot: Ashgate, 2006), 61–80.

13. "Apology and Satisfaction," in J. P. Kenyon, ed., *The Stuart Constitution, 1603–1688: Documents and Commentary* (Cambridge: Cambridge University Press, 1986), 32. See Patrick Collinson, *Richard Bancroft and Elizabethan Anti-Puritanism* (Cambridge: Cambridge University Press, 2013), chapter 11; Stuart Barton Babbage, *Puritanism and Richard Bancroft* (London: SPCK, 1962), esp. chapters 3–7.

14. Letter from Richard Bancroft et al., 18 Nov. 1603, in minutes of the Canterbury diocesan Court of High Commission, DCb/PRC/44/3, p. 7, CCA. Since I examined them, some of the materials cited in this chapter have moved from the Canterbury Cathedral Archives to the Kent History and Library Centre in Maidstone.

15. Minutes of the Canterbury diocesan Court of High Commission, Nov.–

Dec. 1603, pp. 125–33, CCA, published in Michael R. Paulick and Simon Neal, "Canterbury Cathedral Archives: Robert Cushman's Libels of 1603," *MD* 60 (Spring 2011): 36–49.

16. Archdeacon's Court Comperta et Detecta, 1603–1607, cases of Thomas Hunt and Robert Cushman, DCb-J/X/.4.4b, ff. 30–31, CCA. See French, "Genealogical Research in England," 183.

17. Precedent Book, DCb-J/Z/3.26, ff. 37v–38v, CCA. I am grateful to Michael R. Paulick for sharing a transcript of these pages.

18. Thirty-Nine Articles (1671), in G. R. Evans and J. Robert Wright, eds., *The Anglican Tradition: A Handbook of Sources* (London: SPCK, 1991), 160.

19. David R. Como, *Blown by the Spirit: Puritanism and the Emergence of an Antinomian Underground in Pre-Civil-War England* (Stanford: Stanford University Press, 2004), chapter 6, esp. 200–211. Gore is an early example of those whom Como categorizes as "imputative" antinomians.

20. Deposition Registers, 1606–1609, DCb-PRC/39/30, ff. 166r–173v, CCA. I am grateful to Michael R. Paulick for sharing a transcript of these pages.

21. "in the most contemptuous manner" in Precedent Book, DCb-J/Z/3.26, f. 38r.

22. Robert Coachman [Cushman], *The Cry of a Stone* . . . (London: R. Oulton and G. Dexter, 1642), 36; Wilson, *A Dialogue About Justification by Faith* . . . (London: William Hall, 1610), preface ("wantonnesse") and 99–100.

23. Cushman, *The Cry of a Stone*, 17.

24. Michael R. Paulick, "The 1609–1610 Excommunications of *Mayflower* Pilgrims Mrs. Chilton and Moses Fletcher," *NEHGR* 153 (Oct. 1999): 407–12.

25. Henry Barrow, *A Brief Discoverie of the False Church* [1590], in Leland H. Carlson, ed., *The Writings of Henry Barrow, 1587–1590* (London: George Allen and Unwin, 1962), 458–60. See David Cressy, *Birth, Marriage, and Death: Ritual, Religion, and the Life-Cycle in Tudor and Stuart England* (Oxford: Oxford University Press, 1997) 403–9.

26. Paulick, "The 1609–1610 Excommunications."

27. On the Helwys family, see Bunker, chapter 8; Walter H. Burgess, *John Smith the Se-Baptist, Thomas Helwys, and the First Baptist Church in England* (London: James Clarke, 1911), chapter 7.

28. Complaint of Robert Beresford, 20 Nov. 1593, C3/232/3, NAK; complaint of Robert Beresford, C2/Eliz/B16/48, NAK. I am grateful to Sue Allan for providing me with a transcription of these documents.

29. Anne Greene, libel against Thomas Elwayes [Helwys], undated, ca. 1591–99, LB 245/2/23, RAN. I am grateful to Sue Allan for providing me with a transcription of this document. On the will, see Walter H. Burgess, "The Helwys Family, with Pedigree," *Transactions of the Baptist Historical Society* 3 (1912–13): 18–30.

30. Presentment, 8 May 1596, PB 292/5/53, RAN.

31. W. P. W. Phillimore and George Fellows, eds., *Nottinghamshire Parish Registers* (London: Phillimore, 1904), 6:94; Cressy, *Birth, Marriage, and Death*, 298–305. The poem was inscribed in the parish register of Everton, forty miles to the north of Bilborough.

32. Presentment, 20 Apr. 1598, PB 292/6/12, RAN; presentment, 9 Feb. 1613, PB 295/3/69, RAN.

33. On Brewster's family and childhood, see Sue Allan, *William Brewster: The Making of a Pilgrim* (Burgess Hill, U.K.: Domtom, 2016).

34. Simon Adams, "William Davison," *DNB*.

35. Presentment, 27 Apr. 1598, PB 292/7/46, RAN. See discussion in Ronald A. Marchant, *The Puritans and the Church Courts in the Diocese of York, 1560–1642* (London: Longmans, 1960), 141–42.

36. See Jason K. Lee, *The Theology of John Smyth: Puritan, Separatist, Baptist, Mennonite* (Macon, Ga.: Mercer University Press, 2003), chapter 2; Stephen Wright, "John Smyth," *DNB*; Burgess, *John Smith the Se-Baptist*, chapters 2 and 3.

37. Presentment, 26 July 1603, PB 294/1/119, RAN; Smith [Smyth], "To the Christian Reader," in *A Paterne of True Prayer* ... (London: Felix Kyngston, 1605). See White, *English Separatist Tradition*, 119–20.

38. On Robinson, see Timothy George, *John Robinson and the English Separatist Tradition* (Macon, Ga.: Mercer University Press, 1982); Walter H. Burgess, *The Pastor of the Pilgrims: A Biography of John Robinson* (New York: Harcourt, Brace and Howe, 1920). As demonstrated by Matthew Reynolds, many historians have misidentified Robinson as the "Dr. Robinson" of Cambridge's Emmanuel College who in 1603 preached a fiery sermon at St. Andrew's Church in Norwich. The John Robinson of Sturton, Scrooby, and Leiden was of Corpus Christi College and was not "Dr." See Reynolds, *Godly Reformers and Their Opponents in Early Modern England: Religion in Norwich, c. 1560–1643* (Woodbridge: Boydell, 2005), 97–99.

39. Marchant, *Puritans and the Church Courts*, 152.

40. Marchant, *Puritans and the Church Courts*, 299, 296. On Bernard, see Amy Gant Tan, "Richard Bernard and His Publics: A Puritan Minister as Author" (Ph.D. diss., Vanderbilt University, 2015), esp. chapters 1 and 2.

41. On Robinson's possible participation, see George, *John Robinson*, 82–83.

42. Robinson, *A Justification of Separation from the Church of England* ... ([Amsterdam: G. Thorp], 1610), 94. Robinson's tract was a sharp critique of Bernard.

43. "nine months" in Smyth, *Paralleles, Censures, Observations* ... ([Middelburg: R. Schilders], 1609), 128–29; illness in Bernard, *Christian Advertisements and Counsels of Peace* ... (London: Felix Kyngston, 1608), 37; with Helwys in Smyth, *Propositions and Conclusions* (n.p., ca. 1613), C2r.

44. OPP, 1:20–22.

45. Smyth, *Paralleles*, 5.

46. Diary of Tobie Matthew, 10 Sept. 1607, transcript by Thomas Wilson, York Minster Library, accessed on microfilm; OPP, 1:25.

47. Bradford's two accounts of this episode are in OPP, 1:30–31 ("courteously") and 2:347; presentment for an illicit conventicle, undated, Spalding Sewers/460/1/15, Lincolnshire Archives, Lincoln, U.K. I am grateful to Sue Allan for providing a transcript of this document. See Bunker, 187.

48. OPP, 1:24–25. See Marchant, *Puritans and the Church Courts*, chapter 8.

49. Barrow, *Brief Discoverie*, 668. See Roland G. Usher, *The Rise and Fall of the High Commission* (Oxford: Oxford University Press, 1913); Winship, *Godly Republicanism*, 31.

50. High Commission Act Book, quoted in Henry Martyn Dexter and Morton Dexter, *The England and Holland of the Pilgrims* (Boston: Houghton, Mifflin, 1905), 392–93.

51. Marchant, *Puritans and the Church Courts*, 162–63; presentment of 11 Apr. 1608, PB 294/2/100, RAN.

52. OPP, 1:24.

53. Robinson, *Of Religious Communion Private, & Publique* ([Amsterdam], ca. 1614), 41. The most detailed account of the separatists' flight is in Bunker, chapter 9. The most extensive source is OPP, 1:31–34.

54. Testimonies of Edward Armfield (Helwys's servant), Henry Spencer (the ship's captain), and Robert Barnby (a crewmember) are in SP 14/32/46 and 47, 13 May 1608, accessed via *SPO*; "sacremente" is in OPP, 1:33.

55. See the analysis in Douglas Anderson, *William Bradford's Books: Of Plimmoth Plantation and the Printed Word* (Baltimore: Johns Hopkins University Press, 2003), 26–28.

56. Abstract of the Registers of the Privy Council, 1550–1610, Add. Ms. 11402, f. 147r, BL. See Bunker, 197. I am grateful to Sue Allan for sharing a transcription of this document.

Chapter Two. Leiden

1. See Jonathan Israel, *The Dutch Republic: Its Rise, Greatness, and Fall, 1477–1806* (Oxford: Clarendon, 1995), chapters 7–17.

2. Christine Kooi, *Liberty and Religion: Church and State in Leiden's Reformation, 1572–1620* (Leiden: Brill, 2000), 6–9.

3. Benjamin J. Kaplan, *Calvinists and Libertines: Confession and Community in Utrecht, 1578–1620* (Oxford: Clarendon, 1995), esp. chapter 2; Kooi, *Liberty and Religion*, 10–12.

4. See Jeremy Dupertuis Bangs, "Dutch Contributions to Religious Toleration," *Church History* 79 (Sept. 2010): 585–613; Evan Haefeli, *New Netherland and the Dutch Origins of American Religious Liberty* (Philadelphia: University of Pennsylvania Press, 2012), esp. chapters 1–3; Benjamin J. Kaplan, *Divided by Faith: Religious Conflict and the Practice of Toleration in*

Early Modern Europe (Cambridge, Mass.: Harvard University Press, 2007), 172–83.

5. Howell, *Epistolae Ho-Elianae: Familiar Letters Domestic and Forren* . . . (London: Humphrey Moseley, 1645), 14 (C2v). In the 1640s, Howell edited or simply invented these letters for publication, but his descriptions reflect his travels to Amsterdam and Leiden in the late 1610s.

6. Smyth, *The Differences of the Churches of the separation* . . . (n.p., 1608), 3 ("at liberty"), 6 ("merely" and "shut"). See also Helwys letter of 26 Sept. 1608, *EED*, 2:167–68. On relations among Smyth, Helwys, Robinson, and the Ancient Church, see Stephen Wright, *The Early English Baptists, 1603–1649* (Woodbridge: Boydell, 2006), 22–32.

7. *PChR*, 136. See Christopher Marsh, *Music and Society in Early Modern England* (Cambridge: Cambridge University Press, 2010), chapter 8.

8. Ainsworth, *Counterpoyson* . . . (n.p., 1608), 177; Smyth, *Paralleles, Censures, Observations* . . . ([Middelburg: R. Schilders], 1609), 54–55.

9. See Keith L. Sprunger, *Dutch Puritanism: A History of English and Scottish Churches of the Netherlands in the Sixteenth and Seventeenth Centuries* (Leiden: Brill, 1982), 76–90; Wright, *Early English Baptists*, 33–44.

10. Helwys, *A Short Declaration of the mistery of iniquity* (n.p., 1612), 57 ("consciences"), 69 ("betwixt"); *The Kinges Maiesties Speach To the Lords and Commons* . . . (London: Robert Barker, [c. 1610]), A4v. The copy of Helwys's *Declaration* with his inscription is at the Bodleian Library.

11. Christopher Lawne et al., *The Prophane Schism of the Brownists* . . . (n.p., 1612), 15–16. See Scott Culpepper, *Francis Johnson and the English Separatist Influence: The Bishop of Brownism's Life, Writings, and Controversies* (Macon, Ga.: Mercer University Press, 2011), chapters 3 and 4.

12. D. Plooij and J. Rendel Harris, eds. and trans., *Leyden Documents Relating to the Pilgrim Fathers* (Leiden: Brill, 1920), I–II; OPP, 1:39.

13. See Bangs, *S&P*, chapter 3; population statistics from Kooi, *Liberty and Religion*, 22.

14. Bangs, *S&P*, chapter 11.

15. Plooij and Harris, *Leyden Documents*, LXX. See *Magnalia*, book 2, 4.

16. Bangs, *S&P*, 318–22; Plooij and Harris, *Leyden Documents*, XXX.

17. Bangs, *S&P*, 261–71.

18. Robinson, *The Peoples Plea for the Exercise of Prophesie* (n.p., 1618), A3r. See Francis J. Bremer, *Lay Empowerment and the Development of Puritanism* (New York: Palgrave Macmillan, 2015), 59–62; Timothy George, *John Robinson and the English Separatist Tradition* (Macon, Ga.: Mercer University Press, 1982), 148–50.

19. Ames-Robinson correspondence in Lawne, *Prophane Schisme*, 47–54.

20. Cushman letter, undated, ca. 1620, in OPP, 1:114.

21. Robinson, *A Just and Necessarie Apologie* . . . (n.p., 1625), 62 ("will he, nill he"), 16 ("common In"), 39 ("debarred"), 38 ("after a sort"). Robinson originally published this book in Latin in 1619.

22. Robinson, *A Justification of Separation from the Church of England* (n.p., 1610), 212 ("heavenly") and 122 ("heaven"); Winslow, *Hypocrisie Unmasked* . . . (London: Richard Cotes, 1646), 88.

23. OPP, 1:53.

24. Winslow, *Hypocrisie*, 89. See Bangs, *S&P*, 572.

25. Cushman letter of 8 May 1619, in OPP, 1:87.

26. On the religious and political developments within the Dutch Republic between 1609 and 1619, I am relying on Israel, *The Dutch Republic*, 393–94 and chapters 18–20; Maarten Prak, *The Dutch Republic in the Seventeenth Century: The Golden Age*, trans. Diane Webb (Cambridge: Cambridge University Press, 2005), chapter 1; Bangs, *S&P*, chapters 12–13.

27. The fullest study of Arminius's life and thought remains Carl Bangs, *Arminius: A Study in the Dutch Reformation* (Nashville: Abingdon, 1971). On the theological debate over predestination in the Dutch Republic, see also Jan Rohls, "Calvinism, Arminianism and Socinianism in the Netherlands until the Synod of Dort," in Martin Mulsow and Rohls, eds., *Socinianism and Arminianism: Antitrinitarians, Calvinists and Cultural Exchange in Seventeenth Century Europe* (Leiden: Brill, 2005), chapter 1.

28. Eric Platt, *Britain and the Bestandstwisten: The Causes, Course and Consequences of British Involvement in the Dutch Religious and Political Disputes of the Early Seventeenth Century* (Göttingen: Vandenhoeck and Ruprecht, 2015).

29. OPP, 1:49–50; Bangs, *S&P*, 501–4. See Rendel Harris and Stephen K. Jones, *The Pilgrim Press: A Bibliographical and Historical Memorial of the Books Printed at Leyden by the Pilgrim Fathers*, ed. Ronald Breugelmans (Nieuwkoop: De Graaf, 1987), 74–75.

30. Kooi, *Liberty and Religion*, chapter 5.

31. On the attack against Chilton, see *S&P*, 278–79, 552. I am grateful to Michael R. Paulick for sharing a translation of James Chilton's deposition.

32. OPP, 1:60.

33. Theodore Rabb, *Jacobean Gentleman: Sir Edwin Sandys, 1561–1629* (Princeton: Princeton University Press, 1998), 16, chapters 12–13.

34. George Bancroft, ed., "Articles from the Church of Leyden," *Collections of the New-York Historical Society*, 2nd ser., 3 (1857): 301–2.

35. OPP, 1:78–83. See Michael P. Winship, *Godly Republicanism: Puritans, Pilgrims, and a City on a Hill* (Cambridge, Mass.: Harvard University Press, 2012), 113–15.

36. Winslow, *Hypocrisie*, 90; "not molest" in OPP, 1:68.

37. Paget, *An Arrow against the Separation of the Brownists* . . . (Amsterdam: George Veseler, 1618, 7; Foxe, *The First Volume of the Ecclesiasticall history contayning the Actes and Monumentes* . . . (London: John Daye, 1570), 837. On what Edward Arber christened the "Pilgrim Press," I am relying on Bangs, *S&P*, 542–45, 555–68; Keith L. Sprunger, *Trumpets from the Tower: English Puritan Printing in the Netherlands, 1600–1640* (Leiden: Brill, 1994),

133–44; Harris and Jones, *The Pilgrim Press.* See also Douglas Anderson, *William Bradford's Books:* Of Plimmoth Plantation *and the Printed Word* (Baltimore: Johns Hopkins University Press, 2003), 5.

38. Carleton to Naunton, 18 Sept. 1619, in *Letters from and to Sir Dudley Carleton, Knt. during His Embassy in Holland* (London: n.p., 1757), 390.

39. E. B. O'Callaghan, ed., *Documents Relative to the Colonial History of the State of New-York* (Albany: Weed, Parsons, 1856), 1:22–24.

40. Bunker, 249–59.

41. OPP, 1:121; Winslow, *Hypocrisie*, 91.

42. Winslow, *Hypocrisie*, 97–98. See George, *John Robinson*, 150.

43. OPP, 1:124.

Chapter Three. *Mayflower*

1. "fitter" in Cushman letter of ca. mid-June 1620, OPP, 1:111–14; Robinson to Carver, 14 June 1620 (possibly misdated), OPP, 1:106–9.

2. "unfit" in Robinson to Carver, 14 June 1620; Fuller et al. to Carver and Cushman, 10 June 1620, OPP, 1:109–11.

3. Cushman letter of ca. mid-June 1620. Presumably the letter came into Bradford's possession after Carver's death.

4. Cushman to Carver, 10 June 1620, OPP, 1:118–19.

5. OPP, 1:127.

6. Cushman to Edward Southworth, 17 Aug. 1620, OPP, 1:141–46.

7. See Nathaniel Philbrick, Mayflower: *A Story of Courage, Community, and War* (New York: Penguin, 2006), 28.

8. OPP, 1:139–40.

9. OPP, 2:351.

10. See George Willison, *Saints and Strangers* (New York: Reynal and Hitchcock, 1945), 130–33.

11. Robinson to Bradford, 19 Dec. 1623, OPP, 1:368; Simmons, 313; Bangs, *PCPL*, 214. See Bangs, *S&P,* chapter 6, esp. 177–88.

12. Strachey's report is in Samuel Purchas, *Purchas His Pilgrimes* (London: William Stansby, 1625), 4:1735 ("hell of darkness") and 4:1744 ("moan"). See Hobson Woodward, *A Brave Vessel: The True Tale of the Castaways Who Rescued Jamestown and Inspired Shakespeare's* The Tempest (New York: Viking, 2009), esp. chapters 3–9.

13. On Hopkins, see Caleb H. Johnson, *Here Shall I Die Ashore, Stephen Hopkins: Bermuda Castaway, Jamestown Survivor, and* Mayflower *Pilgrim* (Xlibris, 2007).

14. Stratton, 179.

15. David Lindsay, Mayflower *Bastard: A Stranger among the Pilgrims* (New York: Thomas Dunne, 2002), chapters 1–2 ("brood" on 15); Caleb H. Johnson, *The* Mayflower *and Her Passengers* (Xlibris, 2006), 191 ("blots and blemishes").

16. James Boswell, *Life of Samuel Johnson* (London: Henry Baldwin, 1791), 1:189.
17. Donald R. Dickson, *John Donne's Poetry* (New York: Norton, 2007), 50.
18. OPP, 1:150. Contrary to the speculation of some historians, the "great screw" was not part of a printing press. See Bangs, *S&P,* 607–9.
19. OPP, 1:149.
20. OPP, 1:151.
21. See Alexandra Walsham, *Providence in Early Modern England* (Oxford: Oxford University Press, 1999), esp. chapters 1 and 2.
22. OPP, 1:155–58. See the analysis in Ursula Brumm, "Did the Pilgrims Fall upon Their Knees When They Arrived in the New World?" *Early American Literature* 12 (Spring 1977): 25–35.
23. "some of the strangers" and "liberty" in OPP, 1:189; "faction" in *MR,* 2.
24. "association" and "agreement" in *MR,* 3; "combination" in OPP, 1:189. An early reference to a "compact" appears in Alden Bradford, "A Topographical Description of Duxborough in the County of Plymouth," *CMHS,* 1st ser., 2 (1793): 6.
25. The earliest text of the compact is in *MR,* 3. The earliest list of the men who signed the compact is in *NEM,* 15–16.
26. See Bangs, *S&P,* 620.
27. The Bermuda articles are in Purchas, *Purchas His Pilgrimes,* 4:1795–96.
28. Susan Myra Kingsbury, ed., *The Records of the Virginia Company of London* (Washington, D.C.: Government Printing Office, 1906), 303. See Bangs, *S&P,* 623–25.
29. Mark L. Sargent, "The Conservative Covenant: The Rise of the Mayflower Compact in American Myth," *New England Quarterly* 61 (June 1988): 233–51.
30. Willison, *Saints and Strangers,* 144.
31. Philbrick, Mayflower, 40. See the discussion in Steven K. Green, *Inventing a Christian America: The Myth of the Religious Founding* (New York: Oxford University Press, 2015), 74–77.
32. Bradford and Isaac Allerton to James Sherley, 8 Sept. 1623, in R. G. Marsden, ed., "A Letter of William Bradford and Isaac Allerton, 1623," *American Historical Review* 8 (Jan. 1903): 299.
33. *MR,* 3.
34. Smith, *De Republica Anglorum* ... (London: Henry Midleton, 1583), 10–12. See John Donoghue, *Fire under the Ashes: An Atlantic History of the English Revolution* (Chicago: University of Chicago Press, 2013), chapter 1.
35. OPP, 1:192.

Chapter Four. Thanksgiving

1. On the peoples and cultures of southern New England, see Andrew Lipman, *The Saltwater Frontier: Indians and the Contest for the American Coast*

(New Haven: Yale University Press, 2015); Kathleen J. Bragdon, *Native People of Southern New England, 1500–1650* (Norman: University of Oklahoma Press, 1996).

2. On developments in North American agriculture during the Medieval Warm Period, see Daniel K. Richter, *Before the Revolution: America's Ancient Pasts* (Cambridge, Mass.: Harvard University Press, 2011), chapter 1.

3. Account by Gabriel Archer in David B. Quinn and Alison M. Quinn, eds., *The English New England Voyages, 1602–1608* (London: Hakluyt Society, 1983), 118.

4. James Rosier, *A True Relation* [1605], in Quinn and Quinn, *The English New England Voyages*, 283–84. See Alden T. Vaughan, *Transatlantic Encounters: American Indians in Britain, 1500–1776* (Cambridge: Cambridge University Press, 2006), chapter 4.

5. Gorges, *A Briefe Narration* [1658], in James Phinney Baxter, *Sir Ferdinando Gorges and His Province of Maine . . .* (Boston: Prince Society, 1890), 2:8. On Gorges, see Richard Arthur Preston, *Gorges of Plymouth Fort: A Life of Sir Ferdinando Gorges, Captain of Plymouth Fort, Governor of New England, and Lord of the Province of Maine* (Toronto: University of Toronto Press, 1953); Charles E. Clark, "Sir Ferdinando Gorges," *DNB*.

6. Gorges, *Briefe Narration*, 2:20–21. On Epenow, see Vaughan, *Transatlantic Encounters*, 65–67; David J. Silverman, *Faith and Boundaries: Colonists, Christianity, and Community among the Wampanoag Indians of Martha's Vineyard, 1600–1871* (Cambridge: Cambridge University Press, 2005), 1–5. The reliability of Gorges's *Briefe Narration* may be questioned by the fact that Gorges or his grandson confused the circumstances of Epenow's abduction with the 1614 actions of Thomas Hunt. Ferdinando Gorges wrote a much sparser account of Epenow in a 1622 report. Nevertheless, Indian captives were frequently exhibited in London, so there is no reason to doubt this aspect of Epenow's experience.

7. Gorges, *Briefe Narration*, 2:24–25.

8. Smith, *A Description of New England* [1616], in *WJS*, 1:330, 329.

9. Gorges, *A Briefe Relation of the Discovery and Plantation of New England* [1622], in Baxter, *Sir Ferdinando Gorges*, 1:210. On Squanto, see Neal Salisbury, "Squanto: Last of the Patuxets," in David G. Sweet and Gary B. Nash, eds., *Struggle and Survival in Colonial America* (Berkeley: University of California Press, 1981), 228–46.

10. Smith, *Description of New England*, 1:352–53; Gorges, *Briefe Relation*, 1:209–10.

11. Dermer to Samuel Purchas, 27 Dec. 1619, in Purchas, *Purchas His Pilgrimes* (London: William Stansby, 1625), 4:1778–79. On leptospirosis, see John S. Marr and John T. Cathey, "New Hypothesis for Cause of Epidemic among Native Americans, New England, 1616–1619," *Emerging Infectious Diseases* 16 (Feb. 2010): 281–86. On the connection between epidemics and declines in indigenous population, see Alfred W. Crosby,

"Virgin Soil Epidemics as a Factor in the Aboriginal Depopulation in America," *WMQ* 33 (Apr. 1976): 289–99.

12. Gorges, *Briefe Narration*, 2:29; Dermer letter of 30 June 1620, in OPP, 1:206–10. Neal Salisbury asserts that the Pokanokets took Squanto prisoner after Epenow's assault on Dermer's party. See Salisbury, "Squanto," 237. Other than an uncertain reference in Thomas Morton's *New English Canaan*, however, there is a lack of evidence on this point. See *NEC*, 103–5. Because Bradford included Dermer's last letter in his history, Salisbury claims that the Pilgrims took a copy of it with them on the *Mayflower* and used it to select "the depopulated site of Squanto's Patuxet." Salisbury, *Manitou and Providence: Indians, Europeans, and the Making of New England, 1500–1643* (New York: Oxford University Press, 1982), 109. However, the Pilgrims' several descriptions of their initial explorations betray no knowledge of Dermer's experiences. Bradford probably obtained a copy of the letter after the Pilgrims' first year in New England.

13. The quotations in this and the following paragraphs are from an account published in 1622. Although the work is called *Mourt's Relation* for a foreword penned by a "G. Mourt" (believed to be George Morton), most historians suggest that William Bradford and Edward Winslow wrote the bulk of its contents. See *MR*, C2r–21.

14. See Christopher Heaney, "A Peru of Their Own: English Grave-Opening and Indian Sovereignty in Early America," *WMQ* 73 (Oct. 2016): 609–46; Erik R. Seeman, *Death in the New World: Cross-Cultural Encounters, 1492–1800* (Philadelphia: University of Pennsylvania Press, 2010), 86–87, 145–48.

15. See Charles C. Mann, *1491: New Revelations of the Americas Before Columbus* (New York: Random House, 2005), 40–41.

16. *NEM*, 21.

17. 21 Dec. according to the New Style.

18. Date of death in Thomas Prince, "New England Chronology," in *A Chronological History of New-England In the Form of Annals . . .* (Boston: Kneeland & Green, 1736), 76; OPP, 2:404; *Magnalia*, book 2, 4; Jane G. Austin, "William Bradford's Love Life," *Harper's New Monthly*, June 1869, 135–40. For instance, Samuel Eliot Morison speculated that Dorothy Bradford "took her own life," having "grown faint and sick when [she] first beheld that wild-looking northern land, so different from the green and cultivated England they had left." Nathaniel Philbrick similarly argues that "just because Austin misrepresented the facts does not eliminate the possibility that Dorothy Bradford killed herself." It is a possibility entirely undocumented in the historical record, however, and the idea that a woman would lose courage when faced with either a forbidding wilderness or persistent heartache fits rather well with nineteenth- and

twentieth-century American notions about female emotional instability. Morison, ed., *Of Plymouth Plantation* (New York: Knopf, 1952), xxiv; Philbrick, Mayflower: *A Story of Courage, Community, and War* (New York: Penguin, 2006), 76–77, 379–80. See the discussion in Stratton, 324–26; George Bowman, "Governor William Bradford's First Wife Dorothy (May) Bradford Did Not Commit Suicide," *MD* 29 (July 1931): 97–102. I am grateful to Donna Curtin for her suggestions on this subject.

19. Deaths and births in Prince, "New England Chronology," 76.

20. OPP, 1:193–94. See Sam White, *A Cold Welcome: The Little Ice Age and Europe's Encounter with North America* (Cambridge, Mass.: Harvard University Press, 2017), 193.

21. OPP, 1:196, 194.

22. OPP, 1:197–98; M. Pierce Rucker, "Giles Heale, the *Mayflower* Surgeon," *Bulletin of the History of Medicine* 20 (July 1946): 216–31.

23. Prince, "New England Chronology," 96–103; Bradford to Thomas Weston, Nov. 1621, in OPP, 1:238. Prince's source for this information is what he identifies as William Bradford's "Register," which is not extant.

24. See Kathleen Donegan, *Seasons of Misery: Catastrophe and Colonial Settlement in Early America* (Philadelphia: University of Pennsylvania Press, 2014), esp. chapters 2 and 3.

25. OPP, 2:352.

26. Mark Nicholls, ed., "George Percy's 'Trewe Relacyon': A Primary Source for the Jamestown Settlement," *Virginia Magazine of History and Biography* 113 (2005): 249–51.

27. Pratt, "Declaration of the Affairs of the English People that first inhabited New England," *CMHS*, 4th ser., 4 (1858): 478. See the reflections in John McWilliams, *New England's Crises and Cultural Memory: Literature, Politics, History, Religion, 1620–1860* (Cambridge: Cambridge University Press, 2004), chapter 1.

28. *MR*, 32.

29. *MR*, 33.

30. *MR*, 37; Emmanuel Altham to Edward Altham, Sept. 1623, in Sydney V. James Jr., ed., *Three Visitors to Early Plymouth* . . . (Plymouth, Mass.: Plimoth Plantation, 1963), 30. When the English used the term "naked" or even "stark naked," they meant very little clothing, in the latter case perhaps only a fringe about the waist. See Karen Ordahl Kupperman, *Indians and English: Facing off in Early America* (Ithaca, N.Y.: Cornell University Press, 2000), chapter 2.

31. *MR*, 37; OPP, 1:201–2. In his history, composed about a quarter-century later, Bradford recorded that the Indians promised "that when their men came to them, they should leave their bows and arrows behind them." Unlike the account in *Mourt's Relation*, Bradford omitted the Pilgrims' corresponding obligation to do the same. See the analysis in Jenny Hale

Pulsipher, *Subjects unto the Same King: Indians, English, and the Contest for Authority in Colonial New England* (Philadelphia: University of Pennsylvania Press, 2005), 18–19; Salisbury, *Manitou and Providence*, 114–16.

32. Simon Neal and Caleb H. Johnson, "The Brewster Book: A Pilgrim Letter Written in December 1621," *MD* 60 (Autumn 2011): 117–21. Johnson suggests Edward Winslow as the letter's author.

33. OPP, 1:220 ("skulls and bones"); *MR*, 46.

34. *MR*, 40, 45. See the analysis in Pulsipher, *Subjects unto the Same King*, 19–20.

35. *MR*, 49–52.

36. *MR*, 61; OPP, 1:230.

37. See Charles E. Hambrick-Stowe, *The Practice of Piety: Puritan Devotional Disciplines in Seventeenth-Century New England* (Chapel Hill: University of North Carolina Press, 1982), 100–103.

38. "goodness" in *MR*, 61; "diplomatic event" in Lipman, *Saltwater Frontier*, 101. The adjective "secular" appears in both Philbrick, *Mayflower*, 117; and James Deetz and Patricia Scott Deetz, *The Times of Their Lives: Life, Love, and Death in Plymouth Colony* (New York: Anchor, 2001), 9.

39. James W. Baker, *Thanksgiving: The Biography of an American Holiday* (Durham: University of New Hampshire Press, 2009); Anne Blue Wills, "Pilgrims and Progress: How Magazines Made Thanksgiving," *Church History* 72 (Mar. 2003): 138–58.

40. *MR*, 61.

Chapter Five. Good News

1. OPP, 1:231–32.

2. Weston to John Carver, 6 July 1621, OPP, 1:233–35; estimate of a thousand skins a year from Caleb H. Johnson et al., "The Brewster Book Returns," *MD* 60 (Spring 2011): 24.

3. Weston to John Carver, 6 July 1621.

4. OPP, 1:238 ("recompense"), 236 ("speedy").

5. "tied boughs" in *MR*, 59; "there seated" in OPP, 1:229; "jump" in *GN*, 114.

6. Rathband, *A Briefe Narration of Some Church Courses Held in Opinion and Practise in the Churches lately erected in New England* (London: G.M. for Edward Brewster, 1644), 46.

7. Cushman, *A Sermon Preached at Plimmoth in New-England . . .* (London: J.D. for John Bellamie, 1622). See David A. Lupher, *Greeks, Romans, and Pilgrims: Classical Receptions in Early New England* (Leiden: Brill, 2017), 294; David S. Lovejoy, "Plain Englishmen at Plymouth," *NEQ* 63 (June 1990): 232–48.

8. Michael McGiffert, "Religion and Profit Do Jump Together: The First American Pilgrim," *Reflections* 87 (Summer–Fall 1992): 17; "lights, livers"

in "The complainte of certaine Adventurers and Inhabitants of the Plantation in Newe England," CO 1/5, n. 112, f. 249, NAK.

9. See the discussion in Bangs, *S&P*, 300–301, 647.

10. OPP, 1:244–46.

11. The episode is discussed in *GN*, 59–60 ("no small terror"); OPP, 1:240–41. See Jeffrey Glover, *Paper Sovereigns: Anglo-Native Treaties and the Law of Nations, 1604–1664* (Philadelphia: University of Pennsylvania Press, 2014), chapter 3. See also Kelly Wisecup's analysis in *GN*, 39, n. 114.

12. *MR*, L2v.

13. The following paragraphs rely on the accounts by Bradford, OPP, 1:252–84; and Winslow, *GN*, 61–66. Quotations are from these sources unless otherwise indicated.

14. Phinehas Pratt, "A Declaration of the Affairs of the English People that First Inhabited New England" [1662], *CMHS*, 4th ser., 4 (1858): 482. Both Bradford and Winslow assert that Wessagusset leaders executed one thief. OPP, 1:291; *GN*, 91. Thomas Morton alleges that they planned to sacrifice an "old and impotent" but innocent man in place of the thief, who was young and vigorous. After becoming worried that the stratagem would enrage the Indians, they hanged the thief. *NEC*, 110.

15. Winslow narrates the visits to Massasoit and Corbitant in *GN*, 79–87, the source of the below quotations unless otherwise noted.

16. *GN*, 105. On powahs, see Kathleen J. Bragdon, *Native People of Southern New England, 1500–1650* (Norman: University of Oklahoma Press, 1996), 200–208; Jenny Hale Pulsipher, *Swindler Sachem: The American Indian Who Sold His Birthright, Dropped out of Harvard, and Conned the King of England* (New Haven: Yale University Press, 2018), 21–22.

17. See Martha L. Finch, *Dissenting Bodies: Corporealities in Early New England* (New York: Columbia University Press, 2010), 38–46.

18. Winslow's discussion of these beliefs and practices is in *GN*, 102–6. See the analysis in Neal Salisbury, *Manitou and Providence: Indians, Europeans, and the Making of New England, 1500–1643* (New York: Oxford University Press, 1982), 135–38.

19. *GN*, 90.

20. *GN*, 77.

21. "turned savage" in *GN*, 91; "kill all" in Pratt, "Declaration," 483.

22. *GN*, 93.

23. In Pratt's narrative, it is Pecksuot who makes very similar remarks. It is possible Winslow's *Good News* influenced Pratt's later reconstruction of events. See Pratt, "Declaration," 481.

24. *GN*, 94; Hubbard, *A General History of New England* [ca. 1682] (Boston: Charles C. Little and James Brown, 1848), 111.

25. *GN*, 95–96.

26. Bradford and Isaac Allerton to James Sherley, 8 Sept. 1623, in R. G. Marsden, ed., "A Letter of William Bradford and Isaac Allerton, 1623," *Amer-*

ican Historical Review 8 (Jan. 1903): 299. See Erik R. Seeman, *Death in the New World: Cross-Cultural Encounters, 1492–1800* (Philadelphia: University of Pennsylvania Press, 2010), 75–77; Andrew Lipman, *The Saltwater Frontier: Indians and the Contest for the American Coast* (New Haven: Yale University Press, 2015), 137–38.

27. *GN*, 116.

28. *GN*, 72.

29. Robinson to Bradford, 19 Dec. 1623, OPP, 1:367–69.

30. *NEC*, 111–12; "stink" in *GN*, 57. See Karen Ordahl Kupperman, "Thomas Morton, Historian," *NEQ* 50 (Dec. 1977): 660–64. On the grave-desecration allegation, see *NEC*, 106; Seeman, *Death in the New World*, 151–53.

31. Francis Jennings, *The Invasion of America: Indians, Colonialism, and the Cant of Conquest* (New York: Norton, 1976), 187. George Willison's 1945 critique of the Wessagusset operation set the tone for subsequent criticism. See Willison, *Saints and Strangers, Being the Lives of the Pilgrim Fathers and Their Families . . .* (New York: Reynal and Hitchcock, 1945), chapter 15. See also Salisbury, *Manitou and Providence*, 125–40.

32. *GN*, 102.

33. OPP, 1:301–2.

34. Cushman, *A Sermon*, 17 (emphasis in original); OPP, 1:303. See the analysis in Lupher, *Greeks, Romans, and Pilgrims*, 284–316; Bangs, *S&P*, 653–55.

35. OPP, 1:325; *GN*, 101.

36. Emmanuel Altham to Edward Altham, Sept. 1623, in Sydney V. James Jr., ed., *Three Visitors to Early Plymouth* (Plymouth, Mass.: Plimoth Plantation, 1963), 24.

37. OPP, 1:325–26.

Chapter Six. Sacraments

1. Robinson, *A Justification of Separation from the Church of England* (Amsterdam: n.p., 1610), 344–45.

2. Hilton letter, ca. Dec. 1621, in *WJS*, 1:430–31. On Hilton, see *GMB*, 2:951–57.

3. Bunker, 292–93, 317.

4. This and the next several paragraphs rely on Richard Arthur Preston, *Gorges of Plymouth Fort: A Life of Sir Ferdinando Gorges, Captain of Plymouth Fort, Governor of New England, and Lord of the Province of Maine* (Toronto: University of Toronto Press, 1953), chapters 10 and 11; Charles M. Andrews, *The Colonial Period of American History* (New Haven: Yale University Press, 1934), vol. 1, chapter 16; Charles Francis Adams, *Three Episodes of Massachusetts History* (Boston: Houghton, Mifflin, 1896), vol. 1, chapters 8 and 9.

5. Charles Deane, ed., "Records of the Council for New England," *Proceedings of the American Antiquarian Society* (1867): 964.

6. OPP, 1:338.

7. OPP, 1:362–67.

8. Robinson, *Of Religious Communion Private and Publique* (Amsterdam, 1614), 60 (emphasis in original).

9. Barrow, *A Brief Discoverie of the False Church* [1590], in Leland H. Carlson, ed., *The Writings of Henry Barrow, 1587–1590* (London: George Allen and Unwin, 1962), 451.

10. Robinson, *A Justification*, 92. See E. Brooks Holifield, *The Covenant Sealed: The Development of Puritan Sacramental Theology in Old and New England, 1570–1720* (New Haven: Yale University Press, 1974), 61–73.

11. Robinson to Brewster, 20 Dec. 1623, OPP, 1:369–72.

12. OPP, 1:357–58. In my discussion of the conflict between the Pilgrims and John Lyford, I am relying on the analysis in Michael P. Winship, *Godly Republicanism: Puritans, Pilgrims, and a City on a Hill* (Cambridge, Mass.: Harvard University Press, 2012), 122–31. Winship and Nick Bunker correctly revise earlier portraits of John Lyford as an "Anglican" or conformist.

13. Bunker, 343–49.

14. Quotations in this and the following paragraphs are from OPP, 1:380–414; *NEC*, 118–19.

15. On Peirce, see David A. Lupher, *Greeks, Romans, and Pilgrims: Classical Receptions in Early New England* (Leiden: Brill, 2017), 187–94.

16. "Episcopal calling" in OPP, 1:395. See William Hubbard, *A General History of New England* [ca. 1682] (Boston: Charles C. Little and James Brown, 1848), 93–94.

17. OPP, 1:384–85; *NEC*, 119.

18. See Charles Edward Banks, "Bradford's Portrayal of a Religious Rival," *PMHS* 62 (Oct. 1928–June 1929): 51–52.

19. OPP, 1:415–17.

20. *NEC*, 119. Morton's allusion is to Exodus 12:5.

21. Hubbard, *A General History of New England*, 93–94.

22. OPP, 1:418.

23. Sherley et al. to Bradford et al., 18 Dec. 1624, in *BLB*, 4.

24. OPP, 1:436.

25. Town of Plymouth "Black Book," 1/46, Plymouth and West Devon Record Office, Plymouth, U.K.; OPP, 1:443. Leiden statistics from Jonathan Israel, *The Dutch Republic: Its Rise, Greatness, and Fall, 1477–1806* (Oxford: Clarendon, 1995), 625.

26. Sherley to Bradford, 18 Dec. 1624.

Chapter Seven. The Lord of Misrule

1. Hawthorne, *Twice-Told Tales* (Boston: American Stationers, 1837), 77–94; Williams, *In the American Grain* (New York: Albert and Charles Boni,

1925), 75. On the many ways Americans have remembered Thomas Morton, see John McWilliams, *New England's Crises and Cultural Memory: Literature, Politics, History, Religion, 1620–1860* (Cambridge: Cambridge University Press, 2004), chapter 2.

2. *NEC*, 142. The most comprehensive examinations of Thomas Morton and *New English Canaan* are Jack Dempsey, *New English Canaan . . .* (Stoneham, Mass.: Jack Dempsey, 1999); Donald F. Connors, *Thomas Morton* (New York: Twayne, 1969); Minor Wallace Major, "Thomas Morton and His New English Canaan" (Ph.D. diss., University of Colorado, 1957). For a shorter biography and interpretation, see Charlotte Carrington, "Thomas Morton," in Jeffrey A. Fortin and Mark Meuwese, eds., *Atlantic Biographies: Individuals and Peoples in the Atlantic World* (Leiden: Brill, 2014), 32–68.

3. Jonson's quote is from a dedication to *Every Man Out of His Humour.* Clifford's Inn was an Inn of Chancery, located near the Inner Temple and the Inns of Court. See Wilfrid R. Prest, *The Rise of the Barristers: A Social History of the English Bar, 1590–1640* (Oxford: Clarendon, 1986), 107–15.

4. Philip J. Finkelpearl, *John Marston of the Middle Temple: An Elizabethan Dramatist in His Social Setting* (Cambridge, Mass.: Harvard University Press, 1969), chapters 1–6, quote on 80.

5. The court records have been transcribed and published in Charles Edward Banks, "Thomas Morton of Merry Mount," *PMHS*, 3rd ser., 58 (Oct. 1924—June 1925): 147–93.

6. Russell M. Lawson, *The Sea Mark: Captain John Smith's Voyage to New England* (Hanover, N.H.: University Press of New England), 152–54.

7. H. Hobart Holly, "Wollaston of Mount Wollaston," *American Neptune* 37 (Jan. 1977): 5–25.

8. OPP, 2:47–48.

9. On the name Ma-re Mount, see David A. Lupher, *Greeks, Romans, and Pilgrims: Classical Receptions in Early New England* (Leiden: Brill, 2017), 104–5; John P. McWilliams Jr., "Fictions of Merry Mount," *American Quarterly* 29 (Spring 1977): 6–7; Adams Jr., ed., *The New English Canaan of Thomas Morton* (Boston: Prince Society, 1883), 14–15, n. 4.

10. Donne, "A Sermon Preached to the Honorable Company of the Virginian Plantation," in Logan Pearsall Smith, ed., *Donne's Sermons* (Oxford: Clarendon, 1919), 52. See John Donoghue, *Fire under the Ashes: An Atlantic History of the English Revolution* (Chicago: University of Chicago Press, 2013), 21–24.

11. "scum" in OPP, 2:54; "inveigled" in *BLB*, 41.

12. Bunker, 363.

13. Value based on seven hundred pounds of fur at eight shillings a pound. On the development of the beaver trade in the early seventeenth century, see Eric Jay Dolin, *Fur, Fortune, and Empire: The Epic History of the Fur Trade in America* (New York: Norton, 2010), chapters 1–4.

14. See Caleb H. Johnson, *The* Mayflower *and Her Passengers* (Xlibris, 2006), 59–70.

15. Ruth A. McIntyre, *Debts Hopeful and Desperate: Financing the Plymouth Colony* (Plymouth, Mass.: Plimoth Plantation, 1963), 32, 47–48; Langdon, chapter 3.

16. *NEC*, 41. See Kathleen J. Bragdon, *Native People of Southern New England, 1500–1650* (Norman: University of Oklahoma Press, 1996), 97–98; Bragdon, *Native People of Southern New England, 1650–1775* (Norman: University of Oklahoma Press, 2009), 104–5; Andrew Lipman, *The Saltwater Frontier: Indians and the Contest for the American Coast* (New Haven: Yale University Press, 2015), 105–12.

17. De Rasière to the Amsterdam Chamber of the West India Company, 23 Sept. 1626, in A.J.F. van Laer, trans. and ed., *Documents Relating to New Netherland, 1624–1626* (San Marino, Calif.: Henry E. Huntington Library, 1924), 224.

18. De Rasière to Samuel Blommaert, ca. 1628, in Sydney V. James Jr., ed., *Three Visitors to Early Plymouth* (Plymouth, Mass.: Plimoth Plantation, 1963), 76–77; H. R. McIlwaine, *Journals of the House of Burgesses of Virginia, 1619–1658/59* (Richmond, Va.: n.p., 1915), 14.

19. OPP, 2:44; board members of the West Indian Company to the States-General, 16 Nov. 1627, in E. B. O'Callaghan, ed., *Documents Relative to the Colonial History of the State of New-York . . .* (Albany: Weed, Parsons, 1856), 1:38.

20. *NEC*, 60.

21. *NEC*, 60 ("masterpiece" and "rich"), 10 ("virgin" and "industry").

22. *NEC*, 15 ("sweep away"); 24 (more fit), 57 ("more happy"), 17 ("two sorts").

23. *NEC*, 132–35.

24. *NEC*, 133.

25. *NEC*, 136–37; Edith Murphy, "'A Rich Widow, Now to Be Tane Up or Laid Downe': Solving the Riddle of Thomas Morton's 'Rise Oedipeus,'" *WMQ* 53 (Oct. 1996): 755–68.

26. *NEC*, 134; OPP, 2:48; *Magnalia*, book 3, 75.

27. Phinehas Pratt, "Declaration of the Affairs of the English People that First Inhabited New England" [1662], *CMHS*, 4th ser., 4 (1858): 478.

28. *BLB*, 15 June 1627 and 9 June 1628, 35–36, 41–44. See Daniel Walden, "'The Very Hydra of the Time': Morton's *New English Canaan* and Atlantic Trade," *Early American Literature* 48 (2013): 315–36.

29. *NEC*, 138. See David J. Silverman, *Thundersticks: Firearms and the Violent Transformation of Native America* (Cambridge, Mass.: Harvard University Press, 2016), chapter 1 and 92–101.

30. *NEC*, 137 ("prosperity" and "good way"), 149 ("gleaned").

31. OPP, 2:56–57.

32. *NEC*, 138–45.

33. OPP, 2:50.

34. The text of the Bradford patent is in Ebenezer Hazard, *Historical Collections; Consisting of State Papers* . . . (Philadelphia: T. Dobson, 1792), 1:298–304.

35. OPP, 2:58–60.

36. OPP, 2:74; *NEC*, 162.

37. John Noble, ed., *Records of the Court of Assistants of the Colony of the Massachusetts Bay, 1630–1692* (Boston: County of Suffolk, 1904): 2:4; Morton, 21 June 1636 petition to Court of Requests, published in *PMHS*, 3rd ser., 59 (Oct. 1925—June 1926): 95.

38. Aug. 1630, *WP*, 2:267; 21 Nov. 1627 notebook entry, *WP*, 2:44; OPP, 2:76. See also Thomas Wiggin to John Coke, 19 Nov. 1632, *CMHS*, 3rd ser., 8 (1843): 323.

39. Maverick to the Earl of Clarendon, undated, ca. 1662, in Clarendon MS 74, f. 248, Bodleian Library, Oxford. The letter is published in *Collections of the New-York Historical Society for the Year 1869* (New York: Printed for the Society, 1870), 40. Maverick was an opponent of Massachusetts's puritan magistrates and encouraged the Restoration government to take steps to check the colony's alleged cruelty and disloyalty.

40. Zuckerman, "Pilgrims in the Wilderness: Community, Modernity, and the Maypole at Merry Mount," *NEQ* 50 (June 1977): 255–77 (quote on 275).

Chapter Eight. Out of Small Beginnings

1. David Cressy, *Charles I and the People of England* (Oxford: Oxford University Press, 2015); chapter 3.

2. Hooker, *The Danger of Desertion: or a Far[e]well Sermon of Mr. Thomas Hooker* (London: G.M., 1641), 15.

3. Cotton to Thomas Hooker, 3 Dec. 1634, in Thomas Hutchinson, ed., *A Collection of Original Papers Relative to the History of the Colony of Massachusets-Bay* (Boston: Thomas and John Fleet, 1769), 57.

4. See Francis J. Bremer, *First Founders: American Puritans and Puritanism in an Atlantic World* (Durham, N.H.: University of New Hampshire Press, 2012), chapter 2.

5. OPP, 2:89. See Caleb H. Johnson, *The* Mayflower *and Her Passengers* (Xlibris, 2006), 146–51.

6. Bangs, *PCPL* 25; *NEC*, 153 ("quacksalver"), 161 ("Doctor Noddy"), 152 ("called a wife"). On Fuller's practice of medicine, see Norman Gevitz, "Samuel Fuller of Plymouth Plantation: A 'Skillful Physician' or 'Quacksalver'?" *Journal of the History of Medicine and Allied Sciences* 47 (Jan. 1992): 29–48.

7. Bangs, *PCPL*, 24–30. See the discussion in Michael P. Winship, *Godly*

Republicanism: Puritans, Pilgrims, and a City on a Hill (Cambridge, Mass.: Harvard University Press, 2012), 141–42.

8. Endecott to Bradford, 11 May 1629, OPP, 2:90–92.
9. *CPC*, 116.
10. Letter of Charles Gott to Bradford, 30 July 1629, in *BLB*, 47–48; "right hand" in *NEM*, 75; Fuller to Bradford, 28 June 1630, in *BLB*, 57.
11. *NEM*, 76–77.
12. *NEM*, 77; *Archaeologia Americana: Transactions and Collections of the American Antiquarian Society* 3 (1857): 52–54 ("rash innovations" on 54), 76.
13. Cotton to Skelton, 2 Oct. 1630, in David D. Hall, "John Cotton's Letter to Samuel Skelton," *WMQ* 22 (July 1965): 478–85. See the analysis in Slayden Yarbrough, "The Influence of Plymouth Colony Separatism on Salem: An Interpretation of John Cotton's Letter of 1630 to Samuel Skelton," *Church History* 51 (Sept. 1982): 290–303.
14. Cotton to Skelton, 2 Oct. 1630, 481. On Jacob, see Stephen Wright, "Henry Jacob," *DNB*; Scott Culpepper, *Francis Johnson and the English Separatist Influence* (Macon, Ga.: Mercer University Press, 2011), 153–68.
15. See the analysis in Winship, *Godly Republicanism*, 153–54.
16. Miller, *Orthodoxy in Massachusetts, 1630–1650* (Cambridge, Mass.: Harvard University Press, 1933), xiii. For a more recent version of Miller's argument, see Stephen Foster, *The Long Argument: English Puritanism and the Shaping of New England Culture, 1570–1700* (Chapel Hill: University of North Carolina Press, 1991), 153–54.
17. The argument here relies on Winship, *Godly Republicanism*, chapter 6; Yarbrough, "The Influence of Plymouth Colony on Salem."
18. *PChR*, 116.
19. OPP, 2:117.

Chapter Nine. Soul Liberty

1. *PChR*, 64.
2. OPP, 2:58.
3. New England Company to Endecott, 17 Apr. 1629, in *RGCMB*, 1:390.
4. Biographies of Roger Williams include Edwin S. Gaustad, *Liberty of Conscience: Roger Williams in America* (Grand Rapids, Mich.: Eerdmans, 1991); John M. Barry, *Roger Williams and the Creation of the American Soul: Church, State, and the Birth of Liberty* (New York: Viking, 2012); and the editorial notes in Glenn W. LaFantasie's edition of Williams's correspondence (*CRW*).
5. Williams, *The Bloody Tenent Yet More Bloody . . .* (London: Giles Calvert, 1652), 12.
6. "still my soul" in Williams to Barrington, ca. Apr. 1629, *CRW*, 1:2; "in the heavens" in Williams to Barrington, 2 May 1629, *CRW*, 1:4.

7.	*Magnalia*, book 7, 7.

8.	Williams to Cotton Jr., 25 Mar. 1671, *CRW*, 2:630; *JJW*, 12 Apr. 1631, 50.

9.	Williams to Cotton Jr., 25 Mar. 1671, 2:630; OPP, 2:161–62.

10.	*JJW*, Oct. 1632, 82.

11.	*Magnalia*, book 2, 13–14.

12.	"further" in Williams to Winthrop, undated [ca. late 1632], *CRW*, 1:9; "yet communicating" in Williams to John Cotton Jr., 25 Mar. 1671.

13.	Cotton, *A Reply to Mr. Williams*, in *The Bloudy Tenent . . .* (London: Matthew Symmons, 1647), 4; *NEM*, 78.

14.	OPP, 2:162; Winthrop to John Endecott, 3 Jan. 1633/34, *WP*, 3:146–49.

15.	Winthrop to Endecott, 3 Jan. 1633/34.

16.	Winthrop to Endecott, 3 Jan. 1633/34.

17.	*JJW* 30 Apr. 1635, 144.

18.	*JJW*, Aug. 1635 and 1 Nov. 1635, 153, 158 ("pollution").

19.	*JJW*, Jan. 1635/36, 163–64. For Winthrop as Williams's benefactor, see Williams to John Mason and Thomas Prence, 22 June 1670, *CRW*, 2:610.

20.	"loth to displease" and "gold" in Williams to Mason and Prence, 22 June 1670, 2:610–11.

21.	Barry, *Roger Williams*, 224–26. See also Timothy L. Hall, *Separating Church and State: Roger Williams and Religious Liberty* (Urbana: University of Illinois Press, 1998), chapter 3.

22.	Williams, *The Bloudy Tenent of Persecution . . .* (London: n.p., 1644), 195 ("soul liberty"), 232 ("owne soules"), 94 ("rape").

23.	Williams to Mason and Prence, 22 June 1670, 2:617.

24.	*JJW*, Dec. 1638, 276.

Chapter Ten. Hope

1.	Population figure in Stratton, 50. The most complete discussion of New Plymouth's expansion beyond its initial settlement is found in Bangs, *Indian Deeds*, 1–225.

2.	PCR, 28 Oct. 1633, 1:17; "good farms" in OPP, 2:152–53.

3.	OPP, 2:106.

4.	OPP, 2:132, 130. See Ruth A. McIntyre, *Debts Hopeful and Desperate: Financing the Plymouth Colony* (Plymouth, Mass.: Plimoth Plantation, 1963), part 2.

5.	OPP, 2:126, 134; Winslow to Winthrop, 1 July 1637, *WP*, 3:437.

6.	Bradford misplaces this episode in his narrative as occurring in 1631. See OPP, 2:134–35. Winthrop's journal dates it to June 1632. See *JJW*, 14 June 1632, 70.

7.	*JJW*, 12 July 1633, 92. See OPP, 2:166–67.

8.	See the account in Alfred A. Cave, *The Pequot War* (Amherst: University of Massachusetts Press, 1996), 77–87.

9. *JJW*, Oct. 1633, 99; OPP, 2:172–73.

10. OPP, 2:194.

11. OPP, 2:171. On the difficulties Plymouth faced in defending its Kennebec trade, see Roger Bradley, "Empty Promises: Plymouth Colony's Kennebec Fur Monopoly," *Mayflower Journal* 1 (Spring 2016): 51–72.

12. OPP, 2:176; deposition, 1634, in Simmons, PCR, 1:25–26. Although the latter document does not identify the deponent, it was most likely Howland.

13. Winthrop to Nathaniel Rich, 22 May 1634, *WP*, 3:166–68. See also OPP, 2:176–83; *RGCMB*, 14 May 1634, 1:119.

14. *JJW*, 15 May 1634, 115; Winthrop to Rich, 22 May 1634.

15. *JJW*, 9 July 1634, 122.

16. Winthrop to Rich, 22 May 1634; *JJW*, Aug. 1634, 125.

17. "Act for the Resignation of the Great Charter of New England," 25 Apr. 1635, in *PAAS* (1867): 124–25. The discussion here and in the following paragraphs relies on Charles M. Andrews, *The Colonial Period of American History* (New Haven: Yale University Press, 1934), 1:400–423; Richard Arthur Preston, *Gorges of Plymouth Fort: A Life of Sir Ferdinando Gorges, Captain of Plymouth Fort, Governor of New England, and Lord of the Province of Maine* (Toronto: University of Toronto Press, 1953), chapters 13 and 14.

18. "comely young woman" and "note book" in OPP, 2:136–40. See also Thomas Dudley to Countess of Lincoln, 12–28 Mar. 1630/31, in *Collections of the New-Hampshire Historical Society* 4 (1834): 244–46; *RGCMB*, 1 Mar. 1630/1631, 1:83; *JJW*, 25 June 1631, 53. On Gardiner, see Charles Francis Adams, *Three Episodes of Massachusetts History* (Boston: Houghton, Mifflin, 1892), 1:251–63; Philip Ranlet, "Sir Christopher Gardiner," *ANB*.

19. OPP, 2:183–86.

20. OPP, 2:198.

21. Gorges, "Considerations necessarie to be resolved uppon in settling the Governor for New England," 3 Nov. 1634, CO 1/8, n. 34, ff. 95–96, NAK, transcript in Bangs, *Winslow*, 147–48.

22. Winslow, undated petition, CO 1/6, n. 69, f. 185, NAK, transcript in Bangs, *Winslow*, 149–52.

23. OPP, 2:209.

24. *JJW*, Sept. 1633, 97.

25. OPP, 2: 217 ("daily"), 221 ("Lord's waste"), 233 ("controversy"), 167 ("thrust out").

26. On the developments that led to the Pequot War, see Cave, *Pequot War*, chapter 3; Katherine A. Grandjean, "New World Tempests: Environment, Scarcity, and the Coming of the Pequot War," *WMQ* 68 (Jan. 2011): 75–100.

27. OPP, 1:413.

28. OPP, 2:244–46. See Cave, *Pequot War*, 137–38.

29. Mason, *A Brief History of the Pequot War* [ca. 1670], in Charles Orr, ed.,

History of the Pequot War: The Contemporary Accounts of Mason, Underhill, Vincent and Gardener (Cleveland: Helman-Taylor, 1897), 28, 30; *Magnalia*, book 7, chapter 6, 43.

30. OPP, 2:250–51. See Susan Juster, *Sacred Violence in Early America* (Philadelphia: University of Pennsylvania Press, 2016), chapter 1.

31. PCR, 7 June 1637, 1:60; OPP, 2:247–48.

32. On the enslavement and export of Pequots, see Michael L. Fickes, "'They Could Not Endure That Yoke': The Captivity of Pequot Women and Children After the War of 1637," *NEQ* 73 (Mar. 2000): 58–81; Margaret Ellen Newell, *Brethren by Nature: New England Indians, Colonists, and the Origins of American Slavery* (Ithaca, N.Y.: Cornell University Press, 2015), chapters 1–3.

33. Stoughton to Winthrop, ca. 28 June 1637, *WP*, 3:435–36; branded in *JJW*, 6 July 1637, 225; Karen Ordahl Kupperman, *Providence Island, 1630–1641: The Other Puritan Colony* (Cambridge: Cambridge University Press, 1993), 178.

34. Michael Guasco, *Slaves and Englishmen: Human Bondage in the Early Modern Atlantic World* (Philadelphia: University of Pennsylvania Press, 2014), chapters 1 and 2 ("too pure," 45).

35. See Guasco, *Slaves and Englishmen*, 180–87, 284–85, n. 101; Rebecca Anne Goetz, *The Baptism of Early Virginia: How Christianity Created Race* (Baltimore: Johns Hopkins University Press, 2012), 57–59.

36. *The Book of the General Lawwes and Libertyes concerning the Inhabitants of the Massachusetts* (Cambridge: s.n., 1648), 4. See Newell, *Brethren by Nature*, 53.

37. Williams to Winthrop, 21 June 1637, *CRW*, 1:86–87 ("be not enslaved"); Williams to Winthrop, 31 July 1637, *CRW*, 1:109 ("perpetual").

38. Williams to Winthrop, 30 June 1637, *CRW*, 1:88; Williams to Winthrop, ca. 1 Aug. 1638, *CRW*, 1:173.

39. Williams to Winthrop, 10 Nov. 1637, *CRW*, 1:132. See Newell, *Brethren by Nature*, 82.

40. PCR, 1 Dec. 1640, 2:4. See Newell, *Brethren by Nature*, 83.

41. "Bill of Sale," 12 Jan. 1647/48, *WP*, 5:196–97. On the trade of goods and slaves between New England and the Caribbean, see Newell, *Brethren by Nature*, chapter 2.

Chapter Eleven. Freemen and Freedom

1. Joseph Meadows Cowper, ed., *The Roll of the Freemen of the City of Canterbury . . .* (Canterbury: Cross and Jackman, 1903), viii–ix. See Michael Guasco, *Slaves and Englishmen: Human Bondage in the Early Modern Atlantic World* (Philadelphia: University of Pennsylvania Press, 2014), chapter 1.

2. See Rachel Foxley, *The Levellers: Radical Political Thought in the English Revolution* (Manchester: Manchester University Press, 2013).

3. David D. Hall, *A Reforming People: Puritanism and the Transformation of Public Life in New England* (New York: Knopf, 2011), chapter 1.

4. PCR, 15 Nov. 1636, 11:6.

5. Winthrop, "General Observations for the Plantation of New England [1629], *WP,* 2:114; Winthrop's defense of the negative vote [1643], *WP,* 4:382. See the discussion in Hall, *A Reforming People*, chapter 1.

6. PCR, 15 Nov. 1636 and 5 Mar. 1638/39, 11:7 ("double voice") and 35 ("residue"). See Hall, *Reforming People*, 43.

7. PCR, 15 Nov. 1636, 11:11. See the discussions in Stratton, 143–49; Langdon, chapter 7; Langdon, "The Franchise and Political Democracy in Plymouth Colony," *WMQ* 20 (Oct. 1963): 513–26.

8. PTR, 18 Feb. 1649/50, 29–30. See Hall, *Reforming People*, chapter 2 (esp. 56, 95).

9. On servants in Plymouth Colony, see John Demos, *A Little Commonwealth: Family Life in Plymouth Colony* (New York: Oxford University Press, 1970), chapter 7.

10. Thomas Prince, "New England Chronology," in *A Chronological History of New-England In the Form of Annals* (Boston: Kneeland & Green, 1736), 105. On Doty, see Caleb H. Johnson, *The* Mayflower *and Her Passengers* (Xlibris, 2006), 132–37; *GMB*, 1:573–77.

11. PCR, 1 Feb. 1642, 2:33 (cattle); 24 Mar. 1633/34, 1:26 (blood); 2 Jan. 1637/38, 7:6 (assault on Clarke).

12. PCR, 2 Jan. 1633/34, 1:23.

13. PCR, 5 June 1678, 5:262. The case of John Sassamon is the most famous instance, but see also *Magnalia*, book 6, 34. On the practice, see David D. Hall, *Worlds of Wonder, Days of Judgment: Popular Religious Belief in Early New England* (Cambridge, Mass.: Harvard University Press, 1989), 176.

14. PCR, 6 Feb. and 6 Mar. 1654/55, 3:71–73. See James Deetz and Patricia Scott Deetz, *The Times of Their Lives: Life, Love, and Death in Plymouth Colony* (New York: Anchor, 2000), 119–21.

15. PCR, 8:178. On benefit of clergy in colonial America, see Edgar J. McManus, *Law and Liberty in Early New England: Criminal Justice and Due Process, 1620–1692* (Amherst: University of Massachusetts Press, 1993), 112–14; Jeffrey K. Sawyer, "'Benefit of Clergy' in Maryland and Virginia," *American Journal of Legal History* 34 (Jan. 1990): 49–68.

16. PCR, 4 Dec. 1638, 11:29.

17. I have relied on the careful reconstructions of this case in Glenn W. LaFantasie, "Murder of an Indian, 1638," *Rhode Island History* 38 (Aug. 1979): 67–77; Katherine Grandjean, *American Passage: The Communications Frontier in Early New England* (Cambridge, Mass.: Harvard University Press, 2015), 1–14.

18. Wood, *New England's Prospect* [1634], ed. Alden T. Vaughan (Amherst: University of Massachusetts Press, 1977), 90.

19. OPP, 2:264.

20. See Williams to Winthrop, ca. 1 Aug. 1638, *CRW*, 1:171–73.

21. *JJW*, Aug. 1638, 260; OPP, 2:267–68.

22. PCR, 5 June 1638, 1:87; PCR, 7 Oct. 1639, 1:135. See Mark Valeri, *Heavenly Merchandize: How Religion Shaped Commerce in Puritan America* (Princeton: Princeton University Press, 2010), chapters 1 and 2. On Hopkins during these years, see Caleb H. Johnson, *Here Shall I Die Ashore: Stephen Hopkins; Bermuda Castaway, Jamestown Survivor, and* Mayflower *Pilgrim* (Xlibris, 2007), chapter 18.

23. PCR, Feb. 1638/39, 1:111–13.

24. PCR, 4 June 1639, 1:127.

25. For a brief sketch, see *GMB*, 1:12–14. He sometimes appears as Addy Webb in colonial records.

26. PCR, 25 Mar. 1633, 1:11; PCR, 7 Nov. 1636, 1:46.

27. PCR, 2 Oct. 1637, 1:68; PCR, 5 June 1638, 1:86–87.

28. PCR, 6 Aug. 1637, 1:64. See Robert F. Oaks, "'Things Fearful to Name': Sodomy and Buggery in Seventeenth-Century New England," *Journal of Social History* 12 (Winter 1978): 272; Deetz and Deetz, *The Times of Their Lives*, 139–40.

29. Bradford et al. to John Winthrop and council, 6 Feb. 1631/32, *WP*, 3:64–65; PCR, 1 Jan. 1633/34, 1:21.

30. On the significance of an ordered and godly body in Plymouth, see Martha L. Finch, *Dissenting Bodies: Corporealities in Early New England* (New York: Columbia University Press, 2010), esp. 77–80. On witchcraft in Plymouth Colony, see Deetz and Deetz, *The Times of Their Lives*, 92–97.

31. PCR, 2 July 1638, 1:91; PCR, 29 Aug. 1638, 12:35.

32. PCR, 24 Sept. 1645, 12:113–14; Adey [Audey] will of 4 Mar. 1651/52, in Simmons, 215–16.

Chapter Twelve. Salamanders

1. On Vassall, see John C. Appleby, "John Vassall" and "Samuel Vassall," *DNB*; *GMB*, 3:1871–1875.

2. Walley, *Balm in Gilead to Heal Sions Wounds* . . . (Cambridge, Mass.: S.G. and M.J., 1669), 14.

3. In the next several paragraphs, I rely most heavily on Michael P. Winship, *Making Heretics: Militant Protestantism and Free Grace in Massachusetts, 1636–1641* (Princeton: Princeton University Press, 2002).

4. Cotton, *The Way of Congregational Churches Cleared* [1648], in David D. Hall, *The Antinomian Controversy, 1636–1638: A Documentary History* (Middletown, Conn.: Wesleyan University Press, 1968), 411.

5. Winthrop, *A Short Story of the Rise, reign, and ruine of the Antinomians, Familists & Libertines* [1644], in Hall, *The Antinomian Controversy*, 310 ("Jezebel"), 272 ("Antichrists").

6. Plymouth representatives at synod in Charles Chauncy (1705–87), *Sea-*

sonable Thoughts on the State of Religion in New-England (Boston: Rogers and Fowle, 1743), vii; SBCR, 24; Bradford to Winthrop, 11 Apr. 1638, *WP*, 4:23–24. In 1769, Stiles transcribed the Scituate and Barnstable records from a manuscript in the handwriting of John Lothrop. See a transcription in *NEHGR* 9 (1855): 279–87; *NEHGR* 10 (1856): 37–43, 345–51.

7. On Gorton, see Philip F. Gura, *A Glimpse of Sion's Glory: Puritan Radicalism in New England, 1620–1660* (Middletown, Conn.: Wesleyan University Press, 1984), chapter 10; John Donoghue, *Fire under the Ashes: An Atlantic History of the English Revolution* (Chicago: University of Chicago Press, 2013), chapter 12; Michelle Burnham, "Samuel Gorton's Leveller Aesthetics and the Economics of Colonial Dissent," *WMQ* 67 (July 2010): 433–58.

8. Gorton, *Simplicities Defence against Seven-Headed Policy* . . . (London: John Macock, 1646), 2. John Cotton alleged that Gorton left Boston to avoid paying a debt to a minister back in England who had advanced him £100. See Cotton, *A Reply to Mr. Williams*, in *The Bloudy Tenent* . . . (London: Matthew Symmons, 1647), 5.

9. Winslow, *Hypocrisie Unmasked* . . . (London: Richard Cotes, 1646), 67; Gorton to Nathaniel Morton, 30 June 1669, in Peter Force, ed., *Tracts and Other Papers, Relating Principally to the Origin, Settlement, and Progress of the Colonies in North America* . . . (Washington, D.C.: Wm. Q. Force, 1846), vol. 4., tract 7, p. 6; PCR, 5 Nov. 1638, 1:100.

10. Gorton to Morton, 30 June 1669, 7 ("refreshed"), 12 ("apostatized").

11. Winslow, *Hypocrisie*, 67–68; PCR, 4 Dec. 1638, 1:105.

12. Winslow, *Hypocrisie*, 52–55.

13. Letter of Samuel Clerke, 12 June 1637, SP 16/361/67 (accessed via *SPO*).

14. *JJW*, Mar. 1640, 322.

15. "dipped" in *JJW*, Mar. 1640, 322; Rogers, *A Treatise of the Two Sacraments of the Gospell* . . . (London: Thomas Cotes, 1633), B3v, 77–78; Chauncy to John Davenport, 1640, month obscured, Thomas Prince manuscripts, MS Am. 1506, pt. 2, no. 20, Boston Public Library.

16. Robert Keayne, notebook of sermons preached by John Cotton, 21 June 1640, MS N-1517, MHS. I am grateful to Merja Kytö for providing me with a copy of her transcript of these notes.

17. Chauncy to John Davenport, 1640. On the Congregational practice of consensus, see James F. Cooper Jr., *Tenacious of Their Liberties: The Congregationalists in Colonial Massachusetts* (New York: Oxford University Press, 1999), esp. 42–43.

18. Winslow to Winthrop, 10 Oct. 1640, *WP*, 4:292.

19. SBCR, 31.

20. Vassall [to John Wilson], June 1643, FPCN, transcription in Bangs, *Scituate*, 3:354.

21. *JJW*, 7 July 1642, 398–99; Richard D. Pierce, ed., *Records of the First Church*

in Boston, 1630–1868 (Boston: Colonial Society of Massachusetts, 1961), 1:289–90. See Alison Games, *Migration and the Origins of the English Atlantic World* (Cambridge, Mass.: Harvard University Press, 1999), 150–51; Joseph B. Felt, *The Ecclesiastical History of New England . . .* (Boston: Congregational Library Association, 1855), 1:497.

22. Chauncy letter of 22 Feb. 1642/43, FPCN, in Bangs, *Scituate*, 3:357.

23. Vassall [to Ralph Partridge], n.d. [in response to a letter of 9 Apr. 1645], FPCN, in Bangs, *Scituate*, 3:374–75. See Peter Clark, *English Provincial Society from the Reformation to the Revolution: Religion, Politics and Society in Kent, 1500–1640* (Rutherford, N.J.: Fairleigh Dickinson University Press, 1977), 199, 372; Samuel G. Drake, *Result of Some Researches among the British Archives for Information Relative to the Founders of New England . . .* (Boston: New England Historical and Genealogical Register, 1860), 83.

24. Winslow to Winthrop, 7 Jan. 1643/44, *WP*, 4:428; *JJW*, Sept. 1644, 535–39. See Charlotte Carrington, "Thomas Morton," in Jeffrey A. Fortin and Mark Meuwese, eds., *Atlantic Biographies: Individuals and Peoples in the Atlantic World* (Leiden: Brill, 2014), 64–66.

25. See William Cronon, *Changes in the Land: Indians, Colonists, and the Ecology of New England* (New York: Hill and Wang, 1983), esp. chapter 7.

26. Miantonomi as reported by Lion Gardener, *CMHS*, 3rd ser., 3 (1833): 154. See the discussion in Andrew Lipman, *The Saltwater Frontier: Indians and the Contest for the American Coast* (New Haven: Yale University Press, 2015), 153–56.

27. See Michael Leroy Oberg, *Uncas: First of the Mohegans* (Ithaca, N.Y.: Cornell University Press, 2003), chapter 4.

28. OPP, 1:14–16.

29. The next several paragraphs rely on Francis J. Bremer, *John Winthrop: America's Forgotten Founding Father* (New York: Oxford University Press, 2003), 360–65; Robert Emmet Wall Jr., *Massachusetts Bay: The Crucial Decade, 1640–1650* (New Haven: Yale University Press, 1972), chapter 3.

30. Petition in John Child [William Vassall], *New-Englands Jonas Cast up at London . . .* (London: T.R. and E.M., 1647), 3–4. Although published under John Child's name, most historians attribute this tract to Vassall.

31. *JJW*, June 1645, 579–91.

32. Winslow, *New-Englands Salamander, Discovered . . .* (London: Richard Cotes, 1647), 4–6; Winslow to Winthrop, 24 Nov. 1645, *WP*, 5:55–56.

33. Winslow to Winthrop, 24 Nov. 1645.

34. For this and subsequent discussion of the remonstrance, see the discussion in Wall, *Massachusetts Bay*, chapter 5.

35. Child, *New-Englands Jonas*, 8–13.

36. *JJW*, Nov. 1646, 656.

37. See Wall, *Massachusetts Bay*, chapter 4.

38. Gorton, *Simplicities Defence*, 2; Child, *New-Englands Jonas*, 13.

39. Winslow, *Hypocrisie*, A2v.

40. Winslow, *New-Englands Salamander*, 22; *JJW*, July 1647, 703.

41. See Bangs, *Winslow*, chapters 8–11; Rebecca Fraser, *The* Mayflower: *The Families, the Voyage, and the Founding of America* (New York: St. Martin's, 2017), chapters 14–15. On the reverse migration of New England puritans to England in the 1640s, see Susan Hardman Moore, *Pilgrims: New World Settlers & the Call of Home* (New Haven: Yale University Press, 2007), chapters 4 and 5.

42. See the interpretation of the paintings in Martha L. Finch, *Dissenting Bodies: Corporealities in Early New England* (New York: Columbia University Press, 2010), 107–16.

43. Bangs, *Winslow*, 393–94.

44. PCR, 18 Sept. 1646, 9:81–82.

45. SBCR, 37–38.

46. *RGCMB*, 18 Oct. 1649, 3:173–74; PCR, 10 June 1650, 11:57. See William G. McLoughlin, *New England Dissent, 1630–1833: The Baptists and the Separation of Church and State* (Cambridge, Mass.: Harvard University Press, 1971), 1:19–21, 128–29, n. 2.

47. See Jonathan den Hartog, "'National and Provinciall Churches Are Nullityes': Henry Dunster's Puritan Argument against the Puritan Established Church," *Journal of Church and State* 56 (Autumn 2014): 691–710.

Chapter Thirteen. Friends

1. 7 Feb. 1648/49, *Journal of the House of Commons*, vol. 6, *1648–1651* (London: H.M. Stationery Office, 1803), 133. The Commons passed the act the next month.

2. Winship, *Hot Protestants: A History of Puritanism in England and America* (New Haven: Yale University Press, 2018), 1; PCR, 6 June 1649, 2:139; oath in PCR, 11:8. I see no evidence to support Carla Gardina Pestana's claim for "the closet monarchical tendencies of the separatist Plymouth Plantation." See Pestana, *The English Atlantic in an Age of Revolution, 1640–1661* (Cambridge, Mass.: Harvard University Press, 2004), 84.

3. PCR, 11:8.

4. John Morrill, "The Church in England, 1642–9," in Morrill, ed., *Reactions to the English Civil War, 1642–1649* (New York: St. Martin's, 1983), 90.

5. On Cromwell, liberty of conscience, and toleration, see Blair Worden, "Toleration and the Cromwellian Protectorate," in W. J. Sheils, ed., *Persecution and Toleration* . . . (Oxford: Ecclesiastical Historical Society, 1984), 199–233; cf. J. C. Davis, "Cromwell's Religion," in John Morrill, ed., *Oliver Cromwell and the English Revolution* (London: Longman, 1990), chapter 7.

6. PCR, 10 June 1650 and 6 June 1651, 11:57–58.

7. PCR, 7 Oct. 1651, 2:172–73; PCR, 2 Mar. 1651/52, 3:4; Leverich to John Wilson, 22 Sept. 1651, in *Strength out of Weakness. Or a Glorious Manifes-*

tation Of the further Progresse of the Gospel amongst the Indians in New-England . . . (London: M. Simmons, 1652), 21.

8. PCR, 7 Oct. 1651, 2:172–74; 2 Mar. 1651/52, 3:4–5. A decade later, the court cited Elizabeth Eddy (then spelled Eedey) for traveling from Plymouth to Boston on Sunday. She explained that Martha Saffin had asked her to visit her in her illness. PCR, 1 May 1660, 3:186.

9. PCR, 6 Mar. 1654/55, 3:74; PCR, 5 Mar. 1655/56, 3:96. On Seekers, see Christopher Hill, *The World Turned Upside Down: Radical Ideas during the English Revolution* (London: Temple Smith, 1972), chapter 9.

10. PCR, Sept. 1656, 10:156; PCR, 3 June 1657, 11:67; Bangs, *Sandwich*, 17 July 1657, 279–80.

11. Norman Penney, ed., *The Journal of George Fox* (Cambridge: Cambridge University Press, 1911), 1:33–34.

12. On Fox, see H. Larry Ingle, *First among Friends: George Fox and the Creation of Quakerism* (New York: Oxford University Press, 1994), quote on 49.

13. On early Quaker spirituality and worship practices, see Rosemary Moore, *The Light in Their Consciences: The Early Quakers in Britain, 1646–1666* (University Park: Pennsylvania State University Press, 2000), chapters 6 and 9–11. On the growth of the movement, see Barry Reay, *The Quakers and the English Revolution* (New York: St. Martin's, 1985), 8–11.

14. Moore, *The Light in Their Consciences*, 90, 152–53.

15. See John Miller, "'A Suffering People': English Quakers and Their Neighbours, c. 1650–c. 1700," *Past & Present* 188 (Aug. 2005): 71–103.

16. Leo Damrosch, *The Sorrows of the Quaker Jesus: James Nayler and the Puritan Crackdown on the Free Spirit* (Cambridge, Mass.: Harvard University Press, 1996).

17. On the significance of suffering for Quakers, see Adrian Chastain Weimer, *Martyrs' Mirror: Persecution and Holiness in Early New England* (New York: Oxford University Press, 2011), chapter 5.

18. [Humphrey Norton and John Rous], *New-England's Ensigne* . . . (London: T.L., 1659), 6–7. See Arthur J. Worrall, *Quakers in the Colonial Northeast* (Hanover, N.H.: University Press of New England, 1980); Carla Gardina Pestana, *Quakers and Baptists in Colonial Massachusetts* (Cambridge: Cambridge University Press, 1991); Jonathan M. Chu, *Neighbors, Friends, or Madmen: The Puritan Adjustment to Quakerism in Seventeenth-Century Massachusetts Bay* (Westport, Conn.: Greenwood, 1985). The classic account by Rufus M. Jones also remains valuable. See Jones, *The Quakers in the American Colonies* (London: Macmillan, 1911), chapters 3–6.

19. Richard D. Pierce, ed., *The Records of the First Church in Boston, 1630–1868* (Boston: Colonial Society, 1961), 54.

20. Henry Fell to Margaret Fell, 19 Feb. 1656/57, Swarthmore Manuscripts, vol. 1, 68, Friends House Library, London; [George Fox and John Rous], *The Secret Workes of a Cruel People Made manifest* . . . (London: 1659), 2.

21. PCR, 3 Feb. and 5 Mar. 1656/57, 3:111–12.

22. PCR, 5 Mar. 1656/57, 3:113; Norton and Rous, *Ensigne*, 14; "Errors" in Henry Fell to Margaret Fell, 19 Feb. 1656/57.

23. PCR, 6 June 1654, 3:52. *Account of the Christian Experiences and Living Testimonies of that faithful Servant of Christ Edward Perry* (n.p., 1726), 4 ("not redeemed"), 7 ("Christ Jesus the Light"), 11 ("set my Soul"), 25 ("unprofitable").

24. *NEM*, 144.

25. Inventory of Bradford estate, 22 May 1657, in Simmons, 332–37.

26. Bradford, "A Descriptive and Historical Account of New England in verse, ca. 1650," MHS; cf. Michael G. Runyan, ed., *William Bradford: The Collected Verse* (St. Paul, Minn.: John Colet, 1974), 218, 224. See the discussion in David D. Hall, *Ways of Writing: The Practice and Politics of Text-Making in Seventeenth-Century New England* (Philadelphia: University of Pennsylvania Press, 2008), 74.

27. *JJW*, May 1646, 626; OPP, 2:367–69, 1:76.

28. Bradford, Manuscript 198 (including "Of plimoth plantation"), State Library of Massachusetts, Boston, viewed as .pdf. See the commentary in David A. Lupher, *Greeks, Romans, and Pilgrims: Classical Receptions in Early New England* (Leiden: Brill, 2017), 317–59.

29. See Jeremy Dupertuis Bangs, "Re-bunking the Pilgrims," *Historically Speaking* 6 (Sept./Oct. 2004): 2–5.

30. Cotton, *The Bloudy Tenent, Washed, And made white in the bloud of the Lambe* . . . (London: Matthew Symmons, 1647), 10. The inventory lists around forty volumes, which Jeremy Bangs has painstakingly identified. It also references "three and fifty small books" and "divers other Dutch books." See Bangs, *PCPL*, 216–31.

31. Bradford will of 9 May 1657, Simmons, 331; *NEM*, 144–45.

32. "Terror" in Morton, *New-England's Memorial* . . ., rev. ed. (Boston: Nicholas Boone, 1721), 244. On Prence, see *GMB*, 3:1518–24.

33. Elizur Yale Smith, "Captain Thomas Willett: First Mayor of New York," *New York History* 21 (Oct. 1940): 404–17.

34. PCR, 1657, 11:100–101. See also PCR, 3 June 1657, 11:68.

35. Johannes Megapolensis and Samuel Drisius to the classis of Amsterdam, 14 Aug. 1657, in Jaap Jacobs, *New Netherland: A Dutch Colony in Seventeenth-Century America* (Leiden: Brill, 2005), 306.

36. Norton and Rous, *Ensigne*, 16–18. See Evan Haefeli, *New Netherland and the Dutch Origins of American Religious Liberty* (Philadelphia: University of Pennsylvania Press, 2012), 161–67. A year's salary for a skilled worker in New Amsterdam was around two hundred guilders. See Jacobs, *New Netherland*, 328–47.

37. Fox and Rous, *Secret Workes*, 11–12.

38. Remonstrance of 27 Dec. 1657, in Charles T. Gehring and Janny Venema, *Council Minutes, 1656–1658* (Syracuse, N.Y.: Syracuse University Press, 2018), 330–33. See the analysis in Haefeli, *New Netherland*, 167–85;

Jeremy Dupertuis Bangs, "Dutch Contributions to Religious Toleration," 79 (Sept. 2010): 585–613.

39. Norton to Fox, 4 Apr. 1656, in *Journal of George Fox*, 1:245–46; "run out" in *Journal of George Fox*, 2:314. See also Fell to Norton, ca. Apr. 1656, Spence MS, vol. 3, n. 41, Friends House, London, printed in Elsa F. Glines, ed., *Undaunted Zeal: The Letters of Margaret Fell* (Richmond, Ind.: Friends United Press), 186–88. On Norton, see Steven C. Harper and I. Gadd, "Humphrey Norton," *DNB*.

40. Norton and Rous, *Ensigne*, 25; PCR, 6 Oct. 1657, 3:123. On Friends' use of these legal arguments against their New England persecutors, see Nan Goodman, *Banished: Common Law and the Rhetoric of Social Exclusion in Early New England* (Philadelphia: University of Pennsylvania Press, 2012), chapter 3.

41. Norton and Rous, *Ensigne*, 50–51, 105; Franklin Bowditch Dexter, ed., *New Haven Town Records, 1649–1662* (New Haven: New Haven Colony Historical Society, 1917), 339–43.

42. PCR, 2 Mar. 1657/58, 3:130 (Cudworth); Rous et al. *New-England, A Degenerate Plant* (London: n.p., 1659), 14; PCR, 1 June 1658, 3:134 (Hatherly). See Robert Charles Anderson, *Puritan Pedigrees: The Deep Roots of the Great Migration of New England* (Boston: New England Historic Genealogical Society, 2018), chapter 8.

43. PCR, 1658, 11:120 (workhouse), 101 (Quakers and freeman status); PCR, 1 June 1658, 3:138 (Richard Kerby, oath of fidelity).

44. PCR, 1 June 1658, 3:139; Norton and Rous, *Ensigne*, 25.

45. SBCR, 34; PCR, 2 Mar. 1668/69, 5:13–14; Winter deposition and Norton response in Simmons, 548–50. On the case of alleged incest, see James Deetz and Patricia Scott Deetz, *The Times of Their Lives: Life, Love, and Death in Plymouth Colony* (New York: Anchor, 2000), 146–47.

46. PCR, 1658, 11:95 (adultery); PCR, 1 June 1655, 11:64 ("rule of life"). On capital crimes in the New England colonies, see Edgar J. McManus, *Law and Liberty in Early New England: Criminal Justice and Due Process, 1620–1692* (Amherst: University of Massachusetts Press, 1993), chapter 2.

47. PCR, 1 June 1658, 3:140.

48. Simmons, 545–47.

49. Norton and Rous, *Ensigne*, 79–81.

50. *RGCMB*, 14 Oct. 1657, 4:308–9; Norton and Rous, *Ensigne*, 82–93.

51. Norton and Rous, *Ensigne*, 4; Rous, *Degenerate Plant*, 14–20.

52. PCR, Sept. 1658, 10:212.

53. PCR, 6 Dec. 1659, 3:178.

54. PCR, 6 Oct. and 6 Dec. 1659, 7 Mar. 1659/60, 3:176, 178, 184.

55. PCR, 11:124; PCR, 6 June 1660, 3:189; undated entry, Barnstable, Mass. West Parish Church records, 1639–1853, RG5285, p. 20, Congregational Library & Archives, Boston, Mass. (accessed via http://congregational library.org/nehh/main).

56. "sitting still" in Norton and Rous, *Ensigne*, 47; "dogs" in George Bishop, *New England Judged . . .* (London: Robert Wilson, 1661), 143; PCR, 10 June 1660, 11:125–26. On Barlow, see Ellen F. O'Flaherty, "George Barlow, the Marshal of Sandwich, Massachusetts, and His Descendants for Three Generations," *NEHGR* 171 (Fall 2017), 307–14.

57. PCR, 5 Mar. 1661, 3:206.

58. See Adrian Chastain Weimer, "Elizabeth Hooton and the Lived Politics of Toleration in Massachusetts Bay," *WMQ* 74 (Jan. 2017): 43–76. On toleration and persecution during the Restoration, see John Coffey, *Persecution and Toleration in Protestant England, 1558–1689* (Harlow, U.K.: Longman, 2000), chapter 7.

59. Miller, "'A Suffering People,'" 78.

60. See Carla Gardina Pestana, "The Quaker Executions as Myth and History," *Journal of American History* 80 (Sept. 1993): 441–69.

61. Williams, *George Fox Digg'd Out of his Burrowes* (Boston: John Foster, 1676), 86, 250.

Chapter Fourteen. Subjection

1. On the visit of the royal commissioners, see Jenny Hale Pulsipher, *Subjects unto the Same King: Indians, English, and the Contest for Authority in Colonial New England* (Philadelphia: University of Pennsylvania Press, 2005), chapter 2.

2. See Robert C. Ritchie, *The Duke's Province: A Study of New York Politics and Society, 1664–1691* (Chapel Hill: University of North Carolina Press, 1977), chapters 1–3.

3. See Henry Bennett to Nicolls, 23 Apr. 1664, in John R. Brodhead, ed., *Documents Relative to the Colonial History of New-York* (Albany: Weed, Parsons, 1853), 3:58.

4. "The propositions made by his Ma[jes]ties Commissioners" and "The Courts Answer," 4 May 1665, Winslow Papers, MHS. They are printed in PCR, 4:85–87. I am grateful to Adrian Weimer for alerting me to the distinction between the oath of allegiance and Plymouth's own oath of fidelity.

5. PCR, 7 June 1655, 4:92; Cartwright to Prence, 8 July 1665, Winslow Papers, MHS.

6. [Myles], *An Antidote Against The Infection of the Times* (London: T. Brewster, 1656), 16. On Myles, see Philip Jenkins, "Infidels, Demons, Witches, and Quakers: The Affair of Colonel Bowen," *Fides et Historia* 49 (Summer/Fall 2017): 1–15; Glanmôr Williams, "John Miles, Ilston, and the Baptist Denomination in Wales," *Minerva* 7 (1999): 11–18; William G. McLoughlin, *New England Dissent, 1630–1833: The Baptists and the Separation of Church and State* (Cambridge, Mass.: Harvard University Press, 1971), 1:128–35.

7. Richard LeBaron Bowen, *Early Rehoboth: Documented Historical Studies of Families and Events in This Plymouth Colony Township* (Rehoboth, Mass.: n.p., 1945), 1:32–33.

8. Prence to Nicolls, 4 July 1666, CO 1/20, n. 110, NAK, accessed via *CSP.* There is a transcript of this letter in the Frederick Lewis Gay transcripts, Plymouth Papers, vol. 1, ff. 24–27, Ms. N-2012, MHS.

9. "not sworn" in PCR, 7 June 1665, 4:90; PCR, 2 July 1667, 4:162; Swansea church meeting of 9 Mar. 1667/68, in Robert Charles Anderson, "Swansea, Massachusetts, Baptist Church Records," *NEHGR* 139 (Jan. 1985): 29.

10. Anderson, "Swansea, Massachusetts, Baptist Church Records," 27–29.

11. Massasoit Ousamequin's death is documented in PCR, 13 June 1660, 3:192.

12. Original deed of 20 Jan. 1661/62, Boston Athanaeum; copy (with some alterations) and attestation of Richard Bulgar and Thomas Durfee, 10 Aug. 1679, MSAC, 30:102 and 102a. See the discussion in Lisa Brooks, *Our Beloved Kin: A New History of King Philip's War* (New Haven: Yale University Press, 2018), 45–50.

13. PCR, 1 Dec. 1640, 2:4–5; PCR, 4 June 1661, 3:216.

14. PCR, 4 Mar. 1661/62 and 3 June 1662, 4:8, 16–18.

15. Hubbard, *A Narrative of the Troubles with the Indians* ... (Boston: John Foster, 1677), 9–10; Mather, *A Relation of the Troubles which have hapned in New-England* ... (Boston: John Foster, 1677), 71; John Cotton Jr. to Increase Mather, 19 and 20 Mar. 1676/77, in *CJCJ*, 187–89; "poisoned" in John Easton, "A Relacion of the Indyan Warre" [1675], in Charles H. Lincoln, ed., *Narratives of the Indian Wars, 1675–1699* (New York: Scribner, 1913), 10–11.

16. PCR, 4 Mar. 1661/62, 4:8. See the analysis in Brooks, *Our Beloved Kin,* 50–53.

17. PCR, 6 Aug. 1662, 4:25–26; Roger Williams to a Special Court of Commissioners, 18 Aug. [Oct.] 1677, *CRW*, 2:741. See Pulsipher, *Subjects*, 57.

18. See David J. Silverman, *Faith and Boundaries: Colonists, Christianity, and Community among the Wampanoag Indians of Martha's Vineyard, 1600–1871* (Cambridge: Cambridge University Press, 2005), 38–48.

19. Eliot to Richard Baxter, 7 Oct. 1657, in F. J. Powicke, "Some Unpublished Correspondence of the Rev. Richard Baxter and the Rev. John Eliot, 'The Apostle to the American Indians,' 1656–1682," *Bulletin of the John Rylands Library* 15 (Jan. 1931): 158; Massasoit in Henry Whitfield, *The Light appearing more and more towards the perfect Day* ... (London: T.R. and E.M., 1651), 12.

20. "English man" in Mayhew Jr. letter of 7 Sept. 1650, in Whitfield, *Light appearing*, 4.

21. 1651 visit to Massachusetts in letter of John Wilson, 27 Oct. 1651, in Society for the Propagation of the Gospel in New England, *Strength out*

of Weaknesse ... (London: M. Simmons, 1652), 16. On Hiacoomes and the establishment of Wampanoag Christianity on Martha's Vineyard, see Silverman, *Faith and Boundaries,* chapter 1; Edward E. Andrews, *Native Apostles: Black and Indian Missionaries in the British Atlantic World* (Cambridge, Mass.: Harvard University Press, 2013), 29–34, 43–44. On the growth of Wampanoag Christianity on Martha's Vineyard by the 1670s, see Silverman, "The Church in New England Indian Community Life: A View from the Islands and Cape Cod," in Colin G. Calloway and Neal Salisbury, ed., *Reinterpreting New England Indians and the Colonial Experience* (Boston: Colonial Society of Massachusetts, 2003), 267.

22. [Increase Mather], *A Brief Relation of the State of New England* ... (London: Richard Baldwine, 1689), 16. On the "Indian Bible," see Kristina Bross, *Dry Bones and Indian Sermons: Praying Indians in Colonial America* (Ithaca, N.Y.: Cornell University Press, 2004), chapter 3.

23. See Richard W. Cogley, *John Eliot's Mission to the Indians Before King Philip's War* (Cambridge, Mass.: Harvard University Press, 1999), chapter 3; Jean M. O'Brien, *Dispossession by Degrees: Indian Land and Identity in Natick, Massachusetts, 1650–1790* (Cambridge: Cambridge University Press, 1997), esp. 42–51.

24. On the growth of Wampanoag Christianity at Mashpee, see J. Patrick Cesarini, "John Eliot's 'A Brief History of the Mashepog Indians,' 1666," *WMQ* 65 (Jan. 2008): 101–34 (Wuttinnaumatuk quoted on 128); Silverman, "The Church in New England Indian Community Life."

25. Richard Bourne to the Commissioners of the New England Company, 6 Sept. 1666, Records of the New England Company, no. 7957, p. 1, Guildhall Library, London (consulted on microfilm copy); Cesarini, "'Brief History,'" 126–34; Eliot, *The Indian Grammar Begun* ... (Cambridge, Mass.: Marmaduke Johnson, 1666), 9. See Silverman, "The Church in New England Indian Community Life," 267.

26. Samuel Willis et al., report of 20 Mar. 1661/62, in Andrews-Eliot Correspondence, Ms. N-1774, box 1, MHS, printed in *CJCJ,* 44–45; John Davenport to John Cotton, 23 Mar. 1662/63, in *CJCJ,* 47. On Cotton, see the introduction to *CJCJ.*

27. Richard D. Pierce, ed., *The Records of the First Church in Boston, 1630–1686,* Publications of the Colonial Society of Massachusetts (Boston: Colonial Society of Massachusetts, 1961), 60–61; Mather Diary, 11 June 1664, typescript by Michael G. Hall in Mather Papers, American Antiquarian Society, Worcester, Mass.

28. PCR, Sept. 1667, 10:329.

29. *PChR,* 145.

30. For Cotton's support of the practice, see Cotton to Increase Mather, 26 Aug. 1678, *CJCJ,* 239. See Michael P. Winship, *Hot Protestants: A History of Puritanism in England and America* (New Haven: Yale University Press, 2018), 236–40. On developments within Plymouth Colony, see J. M.

Bumsted, "A Well-Bounded Toleration: Church and State in the Plymouth Colony," *Journal of Church and State* 10 (Spring 1968): 267.

31. *PChR*, 144–45.

32. John Cotton Jr., Journal, 15 Nov. 1670 and 29 Mar. 1671, in Len Travers, ed., "The Missionary Journal of John Cotton, Jr., 1666–1678," *PMHS*, 3rd ser., 109 (1997): 89–90; Cotton to Commissioners of the United Colonies, 7 Sept. 1671, *CJCJ*, 85.

33. On the creation of distinctively Wampanoag forms of Christianity, see David J. Silverman, "Indians, Missionaries, and Religious Translation: Creating Wampanoag Christianity in Seventeenth-Century Martha's Vineyard," *WMQ* 62 (Apr. 2005): 141–74.

34. Eliot to the commissioners of the United Colonies, 25 Aug. 1664, in PCR, 10:383–86. On Sassamon, see Jill Lepore, *The Name of War: King Philip's War and the Origins of American Identity* (New York: Knopf, 1998), chapter 1.

35. PCR, 2 July 1667, 4:164–66. See Julie A. Fisher and David J. Silverman, *Ninigret, Sachem of the Niantics and Narragansetts: Diplomacy, War, and the Balance of Power in Seventeenth-Century New England and Indian Country* (Ithaca, N.Y.: Cornell University Press, 2014), 100–103; James D. Drake, *King Philip's War: Civil War in New England, 1675–1676* (Amherst: University of Massachusetts Press, 1999), 65.

36. Cole deposition of 8 Mar. 1670/71, *CMHS*, 1st ser., 6 (1800): 211.

37. Winslow to Prence, included in Richard Bellingham to Prence, 24 Mar. 1670/71, Winslow Papers, MHS; Hinckley and Nathaniel Bacon to Prence, 6 Apr. 1671, Winslow Papers, MHS.

38. Record of 10 Apr. 1671 with Philip's mark, in Increase Mather, *A Brief History of the Warr with the Indians in New-England* (Boston: John Foster, 1676), postscript, 7. See Pulsipher, *Subjects*, chapter 3.

39. Prence to Bellingham, 5 May 1671, Miscellaneous Bound, MHS.

40. PCR, 7 June 1671, 5:66–67.

41. PCR, 5–7 July 1671, 5:70–72.

42. See Samuel G. Drake, *The Book of the Indians of North America* (Boston: Antiquarian Bookstore, 1833), 62–64. The fullest treatment of Awashonks (or Awashunkes) is Ann Marie Plane, "Putting a Face on Colonization: Factionalism and Gender Politics in the Life History of Awashunkes, the 'Squaw Sachem' of Saconet," in Robert S. Grumet, ed., *Northeastern Indian Lives, 1632–1816* (Amherst: University of Massachusetts Press, 1996), 140–65.

43. On the rise of horseback travel, mail, and commerce, see Katherine Grandjean, *American Passage: The Communications Frontier in Early New England* (Cambridge, Mass.: Harvard University Press, 2015), 123–37.

44. Prence to Rhode Island, 28 May 1671, Winslow Papers, MHS. In his letter, Prence refers to "a letter from seoconet sachim." Because Plymouth officials regarded Awashonks as the most influential sachem at Sa-

konnet in 1671, the reference is most likely to her. It is possible, however, that Prence referred to another Sakonnet sachem.

45. John Cranston et al. to Thomas Prence, 26 Oct. 1671, Winslow Papers, MHS.

46. PCR, 8 July 1671, 5:73–75.

47. PCR, 24 July 1671, 5:75. On the practice in New Plymouth of attaching mortgages to debts in the 1660s and 1670s, see Bangs, *Indian Deeds*, 140–54, 188–90, 223–24.

48. "enemies" in Thomas Prence to Rhode Island, 23 Aug. 1671, Winslow Papers, MHS. See also Nathaniel Morton to John Cotton and Thomas Cushman, ca. Aug. 1671, *CJCJ* 81–82; Prence to Awashonks, 20 Oct. 1671, in *CMHS*, 1st ser., 5 (1799): 197.

49. Prence to Rhode Island, 23 Aug. 1671; James Walker to Prence, 1 Sept. 1671, in *CMHS*, 1st ser., 6 (1800): 197–98. See the analysis in Pulsipher, *Subjects*, 95–96.

50. Eliot to Prence, 16 June 1671, John Davis Papers, MHS; "Instructions," 1 Aug. 1671, in *CMHS*, 1st ser., 6 (1800): 201–3.

51. Rawson to Prence, 8 and 9 Sept. 1671, Winslow Papers, MHS.

52. "sensible" and "blown over" in Prence to John Winthrop Jr. and Samuel Willis, 7 Sept. 1671, Winslow Papers, MHS; "the inconvenience" and "but one" in Leverett to Prence, 6 Sept. 1671, Winslow Papers, MHS. See also Edward Rawson to John Winthrop Jr., 6 June 1671, Colonial Boundaries, n. 2, Connecticut State Archives, Hartford. On the United Colonies, see Harry M. Ward, *The United Colonies of New England: 1643–90* (New York: Vantage, 1961), chapter 12.

53. PCR, 24 Sept. 1671, 5:78–79.

54. PCR, 29 Sept. 1671, 5:79. See the analysis in Pulsipher, *Subjects*, 99–100.

55. Rebecca Fraser, *The Mayflower: The Families, the Voyage, and the Founding of America* (New York: St. Martin's, 2017), chapter 15; John Frederick Martin, *Profits in the Wilderness: Entrepreneurship and the Founding of New England Towns in the Seventeenth Century* (Chapel Hill: University of North Carolina Press, 1991), 62–78.

56. Cudworth to Josiah Winslow, 16 Jan. 1673/74, Winslow Papers, MHS.

57. PCR, 5 Mar. 1671/72, 5:89.

58. Record of 11 Feb. 1672/73, in Bangs, *Indian Deeds*, 452; Cotton Journal of 5 June 1673, in Travers, "The Missionary Journal," 94.

59. Deed of 31 July 1673, in Philip B. Simonds, ed., *Purchase of the Lands in Little Compton 1672/1673 from the Saconet Indians* (Providence: for the Winter Court, 1977); deed of 1 Nov. 1673, in Bangs, *Indian Deeds*, 465–67; deed of 29 May 1674, in Benjamin Franklin Wilbour, *Notes on Little Compton* (Little Compton: Little Compton Historical Society, 1970), 7; PCR, 7 July 1674, 7:191. See Brooks, *Our Beloved Kin*, 119–20. See also the discussion by Brooks at https://ourbelovedkin.com/awikhigan/awash onks (accessed 27 Aug. 2018).

60. Deed of 9 Apr. 1675, in Bangs, *Indian Deeds*, 477–79; PCR, Mar. 1674/75, 5:162.
61. Church, *EP*, A2.
62. Nineteenth-century copy of ca. 1681 map of Sakonnet, John Carter Brown Library, Providence, Rhode Island; Meeting of 21 May 1675, Proprietors' Records, vol. 1, p. 5, Town Offices, Little Compton, Rhode Island. I am grateful to Marjory O'Toole for helping me make sense of the Sakonnet deeds.
63. Josiah Winslow to Increase Mather, 1 May 1676, in Mather, *A Brief History of the Warr*, postscript, 2–3; Easton, "Relacion," 11. See Jenny Hale Pulsipher, "Defending and Defrauding the Indians: John Wompas, Legal Hybridity, and the Sale of Indian Land," in Brian P. Owensby and Richard J. Ross, eds., *Justice in a New World: Negotiating Legal Intelligibility in British, Iberian, and Indigenous America* (New York: New York University Press, 2018), chapter 3.

Chapter Fifteen. War

1. This chapter and the next rely on Douglas Leach's chronology and narrative history of King Philip's War. See Leach, *Flintlock and Tomahawk: New England in King Philip's War* (New York: Macmillan, 1958). Although I place less weight on "cultural anxieties" and more on the encroachment of English settlements, my thinking about the war has also been shaped by Jill Lepore, *The Name of War: King Philip's War and the Origins of American Identity* (New York: Knopf, 1998). Lisa Brooks's reconstruction of the experiences of individuals such as Weetamoo and James Printer provides an invaluable perspective on how different peoples made choices and interpreted the events around them during the war. See Brooks, *Our Beloved Kin: A New History of King Philip's War* (New Haven: Yale University Press, 2018).
2. Church, *EP*, 2–3.
3. Lepore, "Plymouth Rocked," *New Yorker*, 24 Apr. 2006, 164–70.
4. Williams, *Key into the Language of America* . . . (London: Gregory Dexter, 1643), 119. See Heather Miyano Kopelson, *Faithful Bodies: Performing Religion and Race in the Puritan Atlantic* (New York: New York University Press, 2014), 51–63; Kathleen J. Bragdon, *Native People of Southern New England, 1500–1650* (Norman: University of Oklahoma Press, 1996), 226–28.
5. Proclamation of 22 June 1675, *CJCJ*, 108.
6. Newman to John Cotton, 19 Apr. 1676, *CJCJ*, 150.
7. On Sassamon's death and the resulting trial and executions, see Yasuhide Kawashima, *Igniting King Philip's War: The John Sassamon Murder Trial* (Lawrence: University of Kansas Press, 2001); Jill Lepore, "Dead Men

Tell No Tales: John Sassamon and the Fatal Consequences of Literacy," *American Quarterly* 46 (Dec. 1994): 479–512; James P. Ronda and Jeanne Ronda, "The Death of John Sassamon: An Exploration in Writing New England Indian History," *American Indian Quarterly* 1 (Summer 1974): 91–102.

8. Tuspaquin deed of ca. Mar. 1673/74, in Bangs, *Indian Deeds*, 469–70; Len Travers, ed., "The Missionary Journal of John Cotton, Jr., 1666–1678," *PMHS*, 3rd ser., 109 (1997): 94. See the analysis in Brooks, *Our Beloved Kin*, 121–24.

9. Josiah Winslow and Thomas Hinckley, "A Breiff Narrative of the beginning and progresse of the present trouble between us and the Indians," ca. fall 1675, in PCR, 10:362–64.

10. Winslow and Hinckley, "A Breiff Narrative."

11. Mather, *A Relation of the Troubles which have hapned in New-England . . .* (Boston: John Foster, 1677), 75; PCR, 1 Mar. 1674/75, 5:159; deed of 14 May 1675, in Bangs, *Indian Deeds*, 482–84. See Brooks, *Our Beloved Kin*, 123–24.

12. PCR, 1 Mar. 1669, 5:31; PCR, 1 June 1675, 5:167–68.

13. Williams to John Winthrop Jr., 27 June 1675, in *CRW*, 2:698–701; *The Generall Laws and Liberties of New-Plimouth Colony* (n.p., 1672), 1–3.

14. James Walker to Thomas Prence, 1 Sept. 1671, *CMHS*, 1st ser., 6 (1799): 198.

15. Easton, "A Relacion of the Indyan Warre" [1675], in Charles H. Lincoln, ed., *Narratives of the Indian Wars, 1675–1699* (New York: Scribner, 1913), 7–8.

16. PCR, 1 June 1675, 5:167; Roger Williams to John Winthrop Jr., 25 June 1675, *CRW*, 2:693–97; Increase Mather, *A Brief History of the Warr With the Indians in New-England . . .* (Boston: John Foster, 1676), 2. On the ritual of executions, see David D. Hall, *Worlds of Wonder, Days of Judgment: Popular Religious Belief in Early New England* (Cambridge, Mass.: Harvard University Press, 1989), 168, 179–84.

17. Williams to Winthrop Jr., 13 June 1675, *CRW*, 2:690–93.

18. John Brown to Josiah Winslow, 11 June 1675, Winslow Papers, MHS.

19. Samuel Gorton Jr. to Winslow, undated [June 1675], Miscellaneous Bound Manuscripts, MHS.

20. Winslow to Lord Henry Coventry, 1 May 1680, CO 1/44, n. 55, f. 395r, NAK, accessed via *CSP*.

21. Winslow to Leverett, 6 July 1675, Davis Papers, MHS.

22. Easton, "Relacion," 12.

23. Death of father and son in Easton, "Relacion," 12; Cudworth to Winslow, 27 June 1675, Boston Athanaeum. I am grateful to Thomas Kidd and Jenny Pulsipher for their help in the transcription of Cudworth's letter. On the death of Myles's slave, see also William Hubbard, *A Narrative of*

the Troubles with the Indians in New-England ... (Boston: John Foster, 1677), first page of "The Table."

24. Cudworth to Winslow, 27 June 1675.

25. Hubbard, *Narrative*, 17–18.

26. Bible in Hubbard, *Narrative*, 19; poles and body parts in Massachusetts Council to John Pynchon, 10 July 1675, box 20, Winthrop Papers, MHS.

27. Heads to Narragansetts in Williams to Winthrop Jr., 27 June 1675; spy in Benjamin Batten to Thomas Allin, ca. July 1675, in Douglas E. Leach, "Benjamin Batten and the *London Gazette* Report on King Philip's War," *NEQ* 36 (Dec. 1963): 512. On the similar functions of mutilation and body parts during an earlier war, see Andrew Lipman, "'A meanes to knitt them togeather': The Exchange of Body Parts in the Pequot War," *WMQ* 65 (Jan. 2008): 3–28.

28. Cudworth to Winslow, 27 June 1675; Winslow to Leverett, 28 June 1675, Davis Papers, MHS.

29. Bradford to John Cotton, 21 July 1675, *CJCJ*, 109; Cudworth to Winslow, 20 July 1675, Winslow Papers, MHS.

30. Deposition of Dorothy Hayard [Hayward], 25 June 1677, Davis Papers, MHS; Hubbard, *Narrative*, first page of "The Table."

31. See the letters of John Freeman to Winslow, 3 and 18 July 1675, Winslow Papers, MHS.

32. Church, *EP*, 20; Thomas Stanton and Thomas Minor to John Winthrop Jr. and Council of Connecticut, 30 June 1675, box 20, Winthrop Papers, MHS. See Katherine Grandjean, *American Passage: The Communications Frontier in Early New England* (Cambridge, Mass.: Harvard University Press, 2015), 160.

33. Bradford to Cotton, 21 July 1675; PCR, 28 June 1676, 5:201–3.

34. Rowlandson, *The Soveraignty and Goodness of God* . . ., 2nd ed. (Cambridge: Samuel Green, 1682), 5 ("chopped"), 73 ("good for me"). The latter phrase is from Psalm 119:71.

35. "sound and well" in M. Halsey Thomas, ed., *The Diary of Samuel Sewall, 1674–1729* (New York: Farrar, Straus and Giroux, 1973), 1:18.

36. Newman to John Cotton, 3 Aug. 1676, *CJCJ*, 166.

37. "remain" and "set at liberty" in PCR, 1 Nov. 1676, 5:216; house in Boston in Michael G. Hall, *The Last American Puritan: The Life of Increase Mather, 1639–1723* (Middletown, Conn.: Wesleyan University Press, 1988), 129. See also William Bradford to John Cotton, 18 July 1676, *CJCJ*, 159. On Saffin, see Albert J. Von Frank, "John Saffin: Slavery and Racism in Colonial Massachusetts," *Early American Literature* 29 (Jan. 1994): 254–72.

38. On the enslavement and export of Natives during and after King Philip's War, see Lepore, *The Name of War*, chapter 6; Margaret Ellen Newell, *Brethren by Nature: New England Indians, Colonists, and the Origins of*

American Slavery (Ithaca, N.Y.: Cornell University Press, 2015), chapters 6 and 7.

39. Statute of 5 June 1676, in William Waller Hening, ed., *The Statutes at Large; Being a Collection of all the Laws of Virginia* (Richmond: Samuel Pleasants Jr., 1810), 2:346. See Michael Guasco, *Slaves and Englishmen: Human Bondage in the Early Modern Atlantic World* (Philadelphia: University of Pennsylvania Press, 2014), chapter 3.

40. Winslow to John Leverett, 28 July 1675, MSAC, 67:229. The figure of 160 comes from Church, *EP*, 13. See the analysis in Linford D. Fisher, "'Why shall wee have peace to bee made slaves': Indian Surrenderers during and after King Philip's War," *Ethnohistory* 64 (Jan. 2017): 91–114.

41. PCR, 4 Aug. and 2 Sept. 1675, 5:173–74.

42. [Saltonstall], *The Present State of New-England with Respect to the Indian War* (London: Dorman Newman, 1676), 6, 9.

43. Hakluyt [1584] in Charles Deane, ed., *Discourse Concerning Western Planting* (Cambridge, Mass.: John Wilson, 1877), 159. See Guasco, *Slaves and Englishmen*, 12–14.

44. Thomas Hamilton to "the Right and Principall Officers and Commissioners of His Majesty's Navy," 15 Dec. 1675, ADM 106/311, National Archives, Kew; memo of 29 Apr. 1676 at http://images.library.yale.edu:8080/neips/data/html/1676.04.29.00/1676.04.29.00.html (accessed 11 Sept. 2018). See the discussion in Newell, *Brethren by Nature*, 174–79.

45. Eliot to Massachusetts Bay governor and council, 13 Aug. 1675, PCR 10:451–53.

46. Walley to John Cotton, 18 Nov. 1675 and 17 Apr. 1676, *CJCJ*, 119 ("rash"), 144 ("squaws"); Church, *EP*, 13; PCR, 1 Oct. 1675, 5:175.

47. On the exile to Deer Island, see Christine M. DeLucia's *Memory Lands: King Philip's War and the Place of Violence in the Northeast* (New Haven: Yale University Press, 2018), chapter 1; Lepore, *The Name of War*, 136–41.

48. See Jenny Hale Pulsipher, "Massacre at Hurtleberry Hill: Christian Indians and English Authority in Metacom's War," *WMQ* 53 (July 1996): 461–62.

49. PCR, 6 Dec. 1675 and 29 Feb. 1675/76, 5:183, 187.

50. Record of 22 Feb. 1675/76 town meeting, in Bangs, *Sandwich*, 24, 278.

Chapter Sixteen. Cannibals

1. Williams to John Winthrop Jr., 27 June 1675, *CRW*, 2:698.

2. PCR, 18 Oct. and 2 Nov. 1675, 10:360–61, 357. See Jenny Hale Pulsipher, *Subjects unto the Same King: Indians, English, and the Contest for Authority in Colonial New England* (Philadelphia: University of Pennsylvania Press, 2005), chapter 5.

3. Oliver to John Cotton, transcription by John Cotton, 14 Jan. 1675/76,

CJCJ, 132; "piles of meat" in Joseph Dudley, letter of 21 Dec. 1675, in George M. Bodge, "Soldiers in King Philip's War," *NEHGR* 40 (Jan. 1886): 89–90.

4. Church, *EP*, 16–17; Hubbard, *A Narrative of the Troubles with the Indians in New-England* . . . (Boston: John Foster, 1677), 53; Tompson, *New Englands Crisis* . . . (Boston: John Foster, 1676), 19. In his "nomenclature," William Wood translated *mitchin* as "meat." Wood, *New Englands Prospect* . . . (London: Thomas Cotes, 1634), aftertext, p. 2. See Jill Lepore, *The Name of War: King Philip's War and the Origins of American Identity* (New York: Knopf, 1998), chapter 3; Susan Juster, *Sacred Violence in Early America* (Philadelphia: University of Pennsylvania Press, 2016), 62–66.

5. Oliver to Cotton, 14 Jan. 1675/76. On the battle and its aftermath, see Douglas Leach, *Flintlock and Tomahawk: New England in King Philip's War* (New York: Macmillan, 1958), chapter 7.

6. Newman to Cotton, 27 Mar. and 19 Apr. 1676, *CJCJ*, 141, 150.

7. PCR, 7 and 21 July 1676, 5:204–6; Mather Diary, 12 Mar. 1675/76, in Samuel A. Green, ed., *Diary by Increase Mather* . . . (Cambridge, Mass.: John Wilson and Son, 1900), 45; James Thacher, *History of the Town of Plymouth* . . ., 2nd ed. (Boston: Marsh, Capen & Lyon, 1835), 387. See also Nathaniel Saltonstall, *A New and Further Narrative of the State of New-England* . . . (London: F.B., 1676), 5.

8. Nathaniel Morton to Massachusetts Bay council, 21 Apr. 1676, MSAC, 68:234. See also Scituate petition of 16 Feb. 1676/77, Davis Papers, MHS.

9. Plymouth's refusal in Thomas Savage to John Leverett and council, 16 Mar. 1675/76, MSAC, 241:279; request for assistance in Hinckley to John Leverett, ca. 1 Apr. 1676, Davis Papers, MHS; Morton to Massachusetts council, 26 Apr. 1676. I am grateful to Jeremy Bangs for his help in transcribing the last letter. See Leach, *Flintlock*, 161–62.

10. James D. Drake, *King Philip's War: Civil War in New England, 1675–1676* (Amherst: University of Massachusetts Press, 1999).

11. PCR, 7 June 1676, 5:197. See discussion of the peace initiatives in Lisa Brooks, *Our Beloved Kin: A New History of King Philip's War* (New Haven: Yale University Press, 2018), chapter 8.

12. Church, *EP*, 21–27.

13. PCR, 28 June 1676, 5:201–3.

14. Church, *EP*, 28–30.

15. Bradford to Cotton, 24 July 1676, *CJCJ*, 164.

16. Walley to Cotton, 18 July 1676, *CJCJ*, 158.

17. Church, *EP*, 34. On Weetamoo's death, see Brooks, *Our Beloved Kin*, 323–26. Wootonekanuske identified in Samuel G. Drake, *The Book of the Indians of North America* . . . (Boston: Josiah Drake, 1833), book 3, 13.

18. On Alderman and Philip's death, see Church, *EP*, 11, 44; Increase Ma-

ther, *A Brief History of the Warr With the Indians in New-England . . .* (Boston: John Foster, 1676), 46–47.

19. Church, *EP*, 45.

20. Rawson to Josiah Winslow, 20 Aug. 1676, Winslow Papers, MHS.

21. Morton to John Leverett, 8 June 1677, Davis Papers, MHS.

22. Scituate petition of 26 Jan. 1676/77.

23. See Drake, *King Philip's War*, 168–69.

24. *PChR*, 148. See Stephen Foster, *The Long Argument: English Puritanism and the Shaping of New England Culture, 1570–1700* (Chapel Hill: University of North Carolina Press, 1991), 223–27.

25. *PChR*, 148–52.

26. Church, *EP*, 45; *Magnalia*, book 3, 199.

27. *PChR*, 153; Mather, *A Brief History*, 47; *Magnalia*, book 7, 54. See John McWilliams, *New England's Crises and Cultural Memory: Literature, Politics, History* (Cambridge: Cambridge University Press, 2004), 120.

Chapter Seventeen. Children of Life and Death

1. Richard Archer, "New England Mosaic: A Demographic Analysis for the Seventeenth Century," *WMQ* 47 (Oct. 1990): 477–502; David E. Stannard, *The Puritan Way of Death: A Study in Religion, Culture, and Social Change* (New York: Oxford University Press, 1977), 54–56. John Demos suggested a much lower rate of child mortality in his study of the town of Plymouth. See Demos, *A Little Commonwealth: Family Life in Plymouth Colony* (New York: Oxford University Press, 1970), 66, 192.

2. Jeannine Hensley, ed., *The Works of Anne Bradstreet* (Cambridge, Mass.: Harvard University Press, 1967), 236.

3. See Judith S. Graham, *Puritan Family Life: The Diary of Samuel Sewall* (Boston: Northeastern University Press, 2000), 6–7 and chapter 5; Stannard, *Puritan Way of Death*, 57.

4. Bryan Rosseter to John and Joanna Cotton, 24 Sept. 1669, in Josiah Cotton memoir, 18–22, Ms. SBd-47, MHS.

5. See entries in Samuel A. Green, ed., *Diary by Increase Mather . . .* (Cambridge, Mass.: John Wilson and Son, 1900), 15–19.

6. "malignant fever" in Green, *Diary by Increase Mather*, 22. See David D. Hall, *Worlds of Wonder, Days of Judgment: Popular Religious Belief in Early New England* (Cambridge, Mass.: Harvard University Press, 1989), 231–33.

7. Steven C. Bullock and Sheila McIntyre, "The Handsome Tokens of a Funeral: Glove-Giving and the Large Funeral in Eighteenth-Century New England," *WMQ* 69 (Apr. 2012): 305–46.

8. Walley to Cotton, 16 Jan. 1676/77, *CJCJ*, 181–83; Cotton to Mather, 19 Jan. 1676/77, *CJCJ*, 183–84.

9. Mather, *Right Thoughts in Sad Hours . . .* (London: James Astwood, 1689), 49 ("surprising"), 18 ("rebellious"), 23–24 ("blasted"), 43 ("'Twas that sin").

10. Walley to Cotton, 16 and 28 Jan. 1676/77, *CJC*; Mather to Joanna Cotton, 22 Jan. 1676/77, *CJC*, 185–86.

11. Wigglesworth, *The Day of Doom . . .* (Cambridge, Mass.: Samuel Green, 1666), 15. See Peter J. Thuesen, *Predestination: The American Career of a Contentious Doctrine* (New York: Oxford University Press, 2009), chapter 2, esp. 63–64; Baird Tipson, *Hartford Puritanism: Thomas Hooker, Samuel Stone, and Their Terrifying God* (New York: Oxford University Press, 2015), chapter 6.

12. Calvin, *Institutes of the Christian Religion*, trans. Ford Lewis Battles, ed. John T. McNeill (Philadelphia: Westminster, 1960), 1:251 (book 2, chapter 1, section 8).

13. Tipson, *Hartford Puritanism*, 365; Cotton sermon of 24 Nov. 1687, in John Templestone Sermon Notebook, MS. SBd-227, MHS.

14. Baird Tipson, ed., "Stone, Samuel. Whole Body of Divinity," 248, http:// www.congregationallibrary.org/sites/all/files/Stone_Samuel_Whole _Body_of_Divinity.pdf (accessed 26 Sept. 2018); Wigglesworth, *Day of Doom*, 8.

15. Walley to Cotton, 16 and 28 Jan. 1676/77; Keith to Cotton, 29 Jan. 1676/77, *CJC*, 186–87; Mather to Cotton, 22 Jan. 1676/77, *CJC*.

16. *Magnalia*, book 6, 85.

17. Green, *Diary by Increase Mather*, 14.

18. Cotton to Mather, 24 Nov. 1676, *CJC*, 176–77.

19. Cotton to Mather, 19 Jan. 1676/77, *CJC*, 183–84; Cotton to Mather, 19 and 20 Mar. 1676/77, *CJC*, 187–89.

20. Cotton to Mather, 19 and 20 Mar. 1676/77.

21. Mather to Cotton, 23 July 1677, *CJC*, 210.

22. On the captives in Providence, see Margaret Ellen Newell, *Brethren by Nature: New England Indians, Colonists, and the Origins of American Slavery* (Ithaca, N.Y.: Cornell University Press, 2015), 170–71.

23. Entries of 24 Aug. and 23 Sept. 1676, John Hull Account Books, 2:390, 446, New England Historical and Genealogical Society Library, Boston. See the discussion of these sales in Newell, *Brethren by Nature*, 168–70.

24. "An Answer to the Several heads of Inquiry," Winslow to Lord Coventry, 1 May 1680, CO 1/44, n. 55, f. 395v, NAK, accessed via *CSP*.

25. Linford Fisher, "'Dangerous Designes': The 1676 Barbados Act to Prohibit New England Indian Slave Importation," *WMQ* 71 (Jan. 2014): 99–124.

26. Winslow certificate of 9 Aug. 1676, box 2, folder 50, Stewart Mitchell Collection, MHS; John Leverett certificate, 12 Sept. 1676, Miscellaneous Bound, MHS. See Jill Lepore, *The Name of War: King Philip's War and the Origins of American Identity* (New York: Knopf, 1998), chapter 6.

27. Church, *EP*, 38.

28. Arnold and Cotton, 7 Sept. 1676, *CJCJ*, 173.

29. Mather to Cotton, 20 Oct. 1676, printed in *CMHS*, 4th ser., 8 (1868): 689–90.

30. Keith to Cotton, 30 Oct. 1676, *CJCJ*, 175.

31. Cotton to Mather, 19 and 20 Mar. 1676/77.

32. PCR, 22 July 1676, 5:207–10.

33. PCR, 22 Sept. 1676, 5:207; PCR, 6 Mar. 1676/77, 5:223; PCR, 5 Mar. 1677/78, 5:352.

34. Peter Thacher Diary, 24 Sept. 1679, Ms. N-1649, MHS. See Edward Pierce Hamilton, "The Diary of a Colonial Clergyman: Peter Thacher of Milton," *PMHS*, 3rd ser., 71 (Oct. 1953–May 1957): 50–63.

35. Thacher Diary, 23 June 1679, 1 Feb. 1679/80 ("ready"), and 27 Feb. 1679/80.

36. Thacher Diary, 14 May and 18 Aug. 1679.

37. *RGCMB*, 24 May 1677, 5:136. See the discussion in Heather Miyano Kopelson, *Faithful Bodies: Performing Religion and Race in the Puritan Atlantic* (New York: New York University Press, 2014), 196–200.

38. Bill of sale, 9 Jan. 1677/78, in Clarence S. Brigham, ed., *The Early Records of the Town of Portsmouth* (Providence, R.I.: E.L. Freeman and Sons, 1901), 433–34.

39. Bills of sale, 27 Apr. 1677, in *The Early Records of the Town of Portsmouth*, 430–33. See Newell, *Brethren by Nature*, 172–73.

40. Job Almy inventories of 29 Feb. 1683/84 and 25 Apr. 1685, Portsmouth, Rhode Island, Town Clerk's Office. It is possible that the two Job Almy inventories are for two separate individuals. However, I have not been able to identify a second Job Almy deceased at this time. See Newell, *Brethren by Nature*, 173.

41. The list appears in a volume now bound as "Indian Deeds, Accounts, Freemen," Plymouth County Registry of Deeds, f. 29 in part 3 of that volume. The document is transcribed in PCR, 8:187, but the transcription misleadingly appends "the blackamore" to the name that appears above it, that of Abraham Pearse. See Stratton, 187.

42. PCR, 3 May 1653, 3:27; *MD* 33 (Jan. 1935): 37; inventory of 18 May 1683, Plymouth Colony Probate Records, vol. 4, part 2, p. 24, Plymouth County Probate Office, accessed via familysearch.org; "An Answer to the Several heads of Inquiry," f. 395v. On the growth of slavery in New England in the late seventeenth century, see Wendy Warren, *New England Bound: Slavery and Colonization in Early America* (New York: Liveright, 2017), 112–13 and epilogue.

43. Saffin et al. to William Welstead, 12 June 1681, Jeffries Family Papers, MHS. See Warren, *New England Bound*, 44–45.

44. Collamore inventory of 15 Jan. 1693/94, in Bangs, *Scituate*, 3:483; Williams inventory of 14 Nov. 1694, in Bangs, *Scituate*, 3:473.

45. Winslow to Charles II, 26 June 1677, CO 1/40, n. 116, f. 269r, NAK, accessed via *CSP.*

46. *Magnalia*, book 6, 56; John Cotton Jr., Journal, 22–23 July 1678, in Len Travers, ed., "The Missionary Journal of John Cotton, Jr., 1666–1678," *PMHS*, 3rd ser., 109 (1997): 101; PCR, 1 June 1680 and 7 July 1681, 6:40, 65.

47. PCR, July 1683, 6:113; Walter Clark to Edmund Andros, 2 Mar. 1687/88, MSAC, 128:71. See Ann Marie Plane, "Putting a Face on Colonization: Factionalism and Gender Politics in the Life History of Awashunkes, the 'Squaw Sachem' of Saconet," in Robert S. Grumet, ed., *Northeastern Indian Lives, 1632–1816* (Amherst: University of Massachusetts Press, 1996), 149–56.

48. Marjory Gomez O'Toole, *If Jane Should Want to Be Sold: Stories of Enslavement, Indenture and Freedom in Little Compton, Rhode Island* (Little Compton: Little Compton Historical Society, 2016), 38–39.

49. PCR, Mar. 1684/85, 6:159–60; Silverman, "The Church in New England Indian Community Life: A View from the Islands and Cape Cod," in Colin G. Calloway and Neal Salisbury, ed., *Reinterpreting New England Indians and the Colonial Experience* (Boston: Colonial Society of Massachusetts, 2003), 264–98; Rowland Cotton to Increase Mather, 27 June 1693, *Magnalia*, book 6, 61.

50. "A Conference with an Indian of New England," 1708, New England Company Manuscripts, #7957, n. 3, Guildhall Library, London (consulted on microfilm copy). On Joseph Bourne, see Daniel R. Mandell, *Behind the Frontier: Indians in Eighteenth-Century Eastern Massachusetts* (Lincoln: University of Nebraska Press, 1996), 108.

51. Simon Popmonit and Joseph Peter to Governor and Council, 31 May 1710, MSAC, 31:68. On the consolidation of Wampanoag communities and the disappearance of many enclaves, see Mandell, *Behind the Frontier*, 52–54.

52. On the role of Cape and island Wampanoags in the whaling industry, see Mark A. Nicholas, "Mashpee Wampanoags of Cape Cod, the Whalefishery, and Seafaring's Impact on Community Development," *American Indian Quarterly* 26 (Spring 2002): 165–97.

53. Petition of Simon Popmonit et al., 24 May 1700, MSAC, 30:456. See Newell, *Brethren by Nature*, 223–29; Douglas L. Winiarski, "A Question of Plain Dealing: Josiah Cotton, Native Christians, and the Quest for Security in Eighteenth-Century Plymouth County," *NEQ* 77 (Sept. 2004): 370–72, 390–93; David J. Silverman, "The Impact of Indentured Servitude on the Society and Culture of Southern New England Indians, 1680–1810," *WMQ* 74 (Dec. 2001): 622–66.

Chapter Eighteen. Bitter Cups

1. Walsham, *Charitable Hatred: Tolerance and Intolerance in England, 1500–1700* (Manchester: Manchester University Press, 2006), 4.

2. *Magnalia*, book 3, 219; Deane, *Scituate*, 181–83; Baker, Thomas Clap, and John Daman to the elders "of the Church of Christ in Scittuat at the North river," 1 Apr. 1675, in FPCN, transcription in Bangs, *Scituate*, 3:382–84. On the difference in ordination practices between the two colonies, see J. M. Bumsted, "A Well-Bounded Toleration: Church and State in the Plymouth Colony," *Journal of Church and State* 10 (Spring 1968): 268.

3. Caleb Hopkins Snow, *A History of Boston . . .* (Boston: Abel Bowen, 1825), 198; Deane, *Scituate*, 54–55, 371–73.

4. *Truth Exalted in the Writings of That Eminent and Faithful Servant of Christ, John Burnyeat* (London: Thomas Northcott, 1691), 48–49.

5. *A Memorable Account of the Christian Experiences and Living Testimonies Of that faithful Servant of Christ, Edward Perry* (1726), 63–78 (quotes on 63 and 67). There is a manuscript copy of Perry's warning in MSAC, 241:284–87.

6. Declaration printed in Meredith Baldwin Weddle, *Walking in the Way of Peace: Quaker Pacifism in the Seventeenth Century* (New York: Oxford University Press, 2001), 234–37. For context, see her chapters 2 and 3.

7. PCR, 11 Apr. 1676, 5:193; Petition of 4 June 1678, in Sandwich Monthly Meeting (Men's), Minutes, 14, NEYM.

8. Deane, *Scituate*, 33; "The Sufferings of Edward Wanton," Pembroke Monthly Meeting (Men's), Minutes, 1741–1801, f. 3, NEYM.

9. William Coddington, *A Demonstration of True Love . . .* (London: s.n., 1674), 14; PCR, 10 Mar. 1675/76, 5:190. Most sources refer to John "Rance," though he signed his surname "Raunce" in his will.

10. "The Sufferings of John Rance," Pembroke Monthly Meeting (Men's), Minutes, 1741–1801, f. 16. See Jeremiah 23; Ezekiel 34.

11. "The Sufferings of John Rance."

12. Baker to John Cotton, ca. 9 July 1677, *CJCJ*, 203–4; "The Sufferings of John Rance"; PCR, 10 July 1677, 5:240.

13. PCR, 7 June 1677, 5:233; Cotton et al. to the General Court, 12 July 1677, *CJCJ*, 205–9. See Bumsted, "A Well-Bounded Toleration."

14. PCR, 13 July 1677, 5:241–42; Shove to Thomas Hinckley, n.d., ca. 1677, HP, 23–25.

15. Remonstrance of Quakers, June 1678, HP, 18–20.

16. PCR, 5 June 1678, 263. The copy of "The Sufferings of Edward Wanton" at the Newport Historical Society (FIC.2013.39) details the property seized to satisfy his fine for the unauthorized marriage.

17. PCR, 5 Mar. 1666/67, 4:140; PCR, 2 July 1667, 4:158–59; *MD*, 3:203–16.

18. "The Sufferings of Arthur Howland," Pembroke Monthly Meeting (Men's), 1741–1801, f. 20, NEYM.

19. 11 Sept. 1682 town meeting in Marshfield, in Jeremy Dupertuis Bangs, *The Town Records of Marshfield during the Time of Plymouth Colony* (Leiden: Leiden American Pilgrim Museum, 2015), 393.

20. "The Sufferings of Arthur Howland."

21. Arnold, Cotton, and Wiswall to "Elders of the Church of Christ in Scit-tuat at the North river," Sept. 1679, in FPCN, f. 21v, in Bangs, *Scituate*, 3:381–82; record of Scituate town meeting of 24 Oct. 1679, in Bangs, *Scituate*, 3:186.

22. PCR, 1 Nov. 1679, 6:27; petition of John Bayley et al., June 1680, in HP, 38–40.

23. Town meetings of 20 June and 11 July 1676, in Bangs, *Sandwich*, 321–22.

24. Petition of 4 June 1678, 11–12.

25. Petition of William Newland, Ralph Allen, William Allen, and Edward Perry, 7 June 1681, Davis Papers, MHS.

26. See Owen Stanwood, *The Empire Reformed: English America in the Age of the Glorious Revolution* (Philadelphia: University of Pennsylvania Press, 2011), introduction and chapter 1.

27. Michael Garibaldi Hall, *Edward Randolph and the American Colonies, 1676–1703* (Chapel Hill: University of North Carolina Press, 1960), chapter 2.

28. Randolph to Lords of Trade and Plantations, 12 Oct. 1676, *ER*, 2:258 ("no slaves" and "beloved"); Randolph to Lord Coventry, 17 June 1676, *ER*, 2:207 ("stout commander"); Randolph to Charles II, 20 Sept. 1676, *ER*, 2:222–23 ("encroaching" and "reduced").

29. See "An Answer to the Several heads of Inquiry," Winslow to Lord Coventry, 1 May 1680, 1 May 1680, CO 1/44, n. 55, ff. 394v, 395v, NAK, accessed via *CSP*. Richard LeBaron Bowen estimates New Plymouth's population at five thousand in 1675 and ten thousand in 1690. Bowen, *Early Rehoboth: Documented Historical Studies of Families and Events in This Plymouth Colony Township* (Rehoboth, Mass.: n.p., 1945), 1:1–24.

30. Randolph to Winslow, 24 Feb. 1679/80, Winslow Papers, MHS; Winslow to William Blathwayt, 2 July 1680, Blathwayt Papers, vol. 6, folder 6, John D. Rockefeller Library, Williamsburg, Va.; PCR, 7 July 1680, 6:46.

31. Winslow to Blathwayt, 15 Sept. 1680, vol. 6, folder 6, Blathwayt Papers; Stephen Saunders Webb, "William Blathwayt, Imperial Fixer: From Popish Plot to Glorious Revolution," *WMQ*, 25 (Jan. 1968): 3–21.

32. M. Halsey Thomas, ed., *The Diary of Samuel Sewall, 1674–1729* (New York: Farrar, Straus and Giroux, 1973), 18 Dec. 1680, 1:47; Hinckley to Blathwayt, 24 Dec. 1680, vol. 6, folder 6, Blathwayt Papers.

33. Morton to Penelope Winslow, 28 Dec. 1680, Winslow Papers, MHS; Robinson, *Observations Divine and Morall . . .* (Amsterdam: n.p., 1625), 324.

34. Randolph to Archbishop of Canterbury William Sancroft, 27 Oct. 1686, *ER*, 4:131; Cranfield to Lords of Trade, 27 Mar. 1683, CO 1/51, n. 79, f. 222, NAK, accessed via *CSP*; *Magnalia*, book 2, 7 (emphasis in original). On Cranfield's tumultuous governorship, see Stanwood, *Empire Reformed*, 32–40. On the Hinckley family, see Robert Charles Anderson, *The Great Migration: Immigrants to New England, 1634–1635* (Boston: New England Historic Genealogical Society, 2003), 3:331–35.

35. Plymouth Colony Probate Records, vol. 4, part 2, p. 10, Plymouth County Registry of Deeds (accessed via familysearch.org); General Court to the church in Duxbury, 8 Feb. 1682/83, HP, 84–85; report of Samuel Arnold and Ephraim Morton, ca. 15 Feb. 1682/83, HP, 85–87; 50 guineas in Hinckley to Blathwayt, 18 Mar. 1682/83, vol. 6, folder 6, Blathwayt Papers.

36. Blathwayt to Hinckley, 27 Sept. 1683, HP, 91–92; "An Answer to the Several heads of Inquiry," f. 396v; Hinckley to Blathwayt, 22 Nov. 1683, HP, 94–96. See John Miller, "'A Suffering People': English Quakers and Their Neighbours, c. 1650–c. 1700," *Past & Present* 188 (Aug. 2005): 85–100; John Coffey, *Persecution and Toleration in Protestant England, 1558–1689* (Harlow, U.K.: Longman, 2000), 169–78.

37. Randolph to Hinckley, 24 Nov. 1683, HP, 96–97. See Wilfred H. Munro, *The History of Bristol, R.I. . . .* (Providence, R.I.: J. A. & R. A. Reid, 1880), 125–28.

38. Randolph to Hinckley, 24 Nov. 1683; Blathwayt to Hinckley, 27 Sept. 1683.

39. See Hall, *Edward Randolph*, chapter 4.

40. Randolph to Hinckley, 24 Nov. 1683, 97; Moodey to Hinckley, 12 Feb. 1683/84, HP, 116–21. Hinckley ignored Moodey's request to burn his letter.

Chapter Nineteen. Taxation and Representation

1. *The Book of the General Laws of the Inhabitants of the Jurisdiction of New-Plimouth . . .* (Boston: Samuel Green, 1685), 1–3 ("general fundamentals"), 19–21 (creation of counties); Scituate town meeting of 13 May 1686, Bangs, *Scituate*, 3:209–10.

2. Michael Garibaldi Hall, *Edward Randolph and the American Colonies, 1676–1703* (Chapel Hill: University of North Carolina Press, 1960), 94–97 and chapter 5; Randolph to Archbishop of Canterbury, ca. 7 July 1686, in *ER*, 4:89.

3. Randolph to Hinckley, 22 June 1686, *ER*, 4:87.

4. M. Halsey Thomas, ed., *The Diary of Samuel Sewall, 1674–1729* (New York: Farrar, Straus and Giroux, 1973), 19–20 Dec. 1686, 1:127–28; Peter Thacher Journal, 20 Dec. 1686, MHS.

5. On Andros, see Mary Lou Lustig, *The Imperial Executive in America: Sir Edmund Andros, 1637–1714* (Madison, N.J.: Fairleigh Dickinson University Press, 2002); Stephen Saunders Webb, *1676: The End of American Independence* (Syracuse, N.Y.: Syracuse University Press, 1984), 303–404.

6. Commission of 3 June 1686, in *CMHS*, 3rd ser., 7 (1838): 139–49.

7. J[ohn] C[otton], *Upon the Death of that Aged, Pious, Sincere-hearted Christian, John Alden . . .* (Boston: n.p., ca. 1687). The only known copy of this broadside is in the collections of the Boston Athenaeum.

8. Robert N. Toppan, "Andros Records," *PAAS*, n.s., 13 (1901): 240, 242.

9. See John Miller, *Popery and Politics in England, 1660–1688* (Cambridge: Cambridge University Press, 1973); John Coffey, *Persecution and Toleration in Protestant England, 1558–1689* (Harlow, U.K.: Longman, 2000), chapter 7; Scott Sowerby, *Making Toleration: The Repealers and the Glorious Revolution* (Cambridge, Mass.: Harvard University Press, 2013), esp. chapter 1.

10. Thomas, *Diary of Samuel Sewall*, 23–29 Mar. 1686/87, 1:135.

11. See Viola Florence Barnes, *The Dominion of New England: A Study in British Colonial Policy* (New Haven: Yale University Press, 1923), chapters 4 and 8; John Frederick Martin, *Profits in the Wilderness: Entrepreneurship and the Founding of New England Towns in the Seventeenth Century* (Chapel Hill: University of North Carolina Press, 1991), chapter 9.

12. Hinckley to Andros, 28 Feb. 1686/87, HP, 149–10; Toppan, "Andros Records," 259; Hinckley to Blathwayt, 28 June 1687, HP, 160–61.

13. Council order of 1 June 1687, MSAC, 11:40; town meeting of 21 May 1688, Bangs, *Scituate*, 3:216; "the suffering of Edward Wanton and Joseph Coleman," Pembroke Monthly Meeting (Men's), Minutes, 1741–1801, f. 24, NEYM.

14. Town meeting of 24 Aug. 1687, PTR, 190–91.

15. John Cotton to Rowland Cotton, 2 Sept. 1687, *CJCJ*, 348–50; *PChR*, 251, 253–54.

16. John Cotton to Rowland Cotton, 2 Sept. 1687; John Cotton to Mather, 10 and 21 Sept. 1688, *CJCJ*, 370–71.

17. Cotton to Mather, 10 and 21 Sept. 1688; Freeman to Hinckley, 20 Mar. 1684/85, HP, 132; increase noted in *CJCJ*, 399, n. 3.

18. Hinckley to Blathwayt, 28 June 1687, 154–55; Hinckley to James II, Oct. 1687, HP, 184. I am grateful to Jeremy Bangs for alerting me to the biblical allusion.

19. Affidavit of John Wise et al., 20 Dec. 1689, in *The Revolution in New-England Justified* (Boston: Joseph Brunning, 1691), 10. See Craig Yirush, *Settlers, Liberty, and Empire: The Roots of Early American Political Theory, 1675–1775* (Cambridge: Cambridge University Press, 2011), chapter 1.

20. *Revolution in New-England Justified*, 8; order of 30 Aug. 1687, MSAC, 127:59 (printed in *CMHS*, 4th ser, 7 [1838]: 190); Wilbore petition, 14 Nov. 1687, MSAC, 127:236.

21. John Insley Coddington, "The Widow Mary Ring, of Plymouth, Mass., and Her Children," *American Genealogist* 42 (Oct. 1966): 201–2.

22. PCR, 4 June and 6 July 1686, 6:190–92; Hinckley to Clarke, 5 June 1686, Pilgrim Hall, Plymouth, Mass. See Martha L. Finch, *Dissenting Bodies: Corporealities in Early New England* (New York: Columbia University Press, 2010), 197–98; Thomas A. Foster, "Deficient Husbands: Manhood, Sexual Incapacity, and Male Marital Sexuality in Seventeenth-Century New

England," *WMQ* 56 (Oct. 1999): 723–44; John Demos, *A Little Common-wealth: Family Life in Plymouth Colony* (New York: Oxford University Press, 1970), 92–97; Edmund S. Morgan, *The Puritan Family: Religion and Domestic Relations in Seventeenth-Century New England* (New York: Harper Torchbooks, 1966), 34–36.

23. PCR, 6 July and Oct. 1686, 6:190–92, 203.

24. *PChR*, 25 July 1686, 258–59.

25. Andros to Samuel Spragge [Sprague], 21 Dec. 1687, MSAC, 127:298; PTR, 23 Jan. 1687/88, 192–93.

26. Act of 17 Mar. 1687/88, in J. Hammond Trumbull, ed., *Public Records of the Colony of Connecticut* (Hartford, Conn.: Case, Lockwood, 1859), 3:427–29; Cotton to Increase Mather, 10 and 21 Sept. 1688; *PChR*, 28 Oct. 1688, 263. On the Clark's Island case, see Langdon, 219–20.

27. Deposition of Samuel Eldred, 16 Sept. 1688, MSAC, 35:129a. See Owen Stanwood, *The Empire Reformed: English America in the Age of the Glorious Revolution* (Philadelphia: University of Pennsylvania Press, 2011), 66–81.

28. On the power of antipopery and the Glorious Revolution, see Sowerby, *Making Toleration.*

29. Bradford to Hinckley, 20 Apr. 1689, HP, 190. See David S. Lovejoy, *The Glorious Revolution in America* (New York: Harper and Row, 1972), 239–45; Ian K. Steele, "Origins of Boston's Revolutionary Declaration of 18 April 1689," *NEQ* 62 (Mar. 1989): 75–81.

30. PCR, 4 June 1689, 6:208–9; Samuel Hopkins Emery, *History of Taunton, Massachusetts, From Its Settlement to the Present Time* (Syracuse, N.Y.: D. Mason, 1893), 566; PTR, 22 June 1689, 197.

31. Samuel Prince to Hinckley, 22 Apr. 1689, HP, 196; PCR, 7 June 1689, 6:207–8.

32. *PChR*, 3–7 July 1689, 265–67; Dorothy Clarke public confession in *PChR*, 25 May 1690, 269; Nathaniel Clarke membership and death in *PChR*, 206, 217.

33. William Bassitt to Hinckley, ca. 23 Sept. 1689, HP, 214–16; Steven C. Eames, "Benjamin Church," in Alan Gallay, ed., *Colonial Wars of North America, 1512–1763* (New York: Garland, 1996), 138.

34. John Wise narrative, 23 Dec. 1690, in *PMHS*, 2nd ser., 15 (1901–2): 289; anonymous narrative, 3 Jan. 1690/91, in *PMHS*, 2nd ser., 15 (1901–2): 315. See Richard R. Johnson, "Canada, New England Expedition Against (1690)," in Gallay, *Colonial Wars*, 97–99; Steven C. Eames, "John Walley," in Gallay, *Colonial Wars*, 770–71.

35. "wooden sword" in Wise narrative, 295; "consciences" in John Walley narrative, 27 Dec. 1690, in Thomas Hutchinson, *The History of the Colony of Massachusets-Bay . . .* (Boston: Thomas & John Fleet, 1764), 1:566.

36. Richard LeBaron Bowen, "The 1690 Tax Revolt of Plymouth Colony Towns," NEHGS 112 (Jan. 1958): 4–14. See also Langdon, 232–33;

H. Roger King, *Cape Cod and Plymouth Colony in the Seventeenth Century* (Lanham, Md.: University Press of America, 1994), 266–68.

37. Hinckley to Wiswall, 17 Oct. 1691, HP, 295–96.
38. Address to William III, draft in HP, 199–200; PCR, 4 June 1689, 6:209.
39. Mather to Hinckley, 12 Sept. 1689, HP, 211.
40. John Walley to Wiswall, n.d., ca. summer 1691, HP, 286; Wiswall to Hinckley, 6 July 1691, HP, 285; Cotton to Hinckley, 6 Feb. 1690/91, *CJCJ*, 404.
41. Wiswall to Hinckley, 5 Nov. 1691, HP, 299–301; Cotton Mather to Hinckley, 26 Apr. 1690, HP, 248–49.
42. "Deacon John Paine's Journal," *MD* 8 (Oct. 1906): 229. See Richard L. Bushman, *King and People in Provincial Massachusetts* (Chapel Hill: University of North Carolina Press, 1985), chapter 3.
43. McLoughlin, *New England Dissent, 1630–1833: The Baptists and the Separation of Church and State* (Cambridge, Mass.: Harvard University Press, 1971), vol. 1, part 2.
44. PTR, 3 Oct. 1692, 205; Affidavit of James Cole, 15 Sept. 1691, Pilgrim Hall; "miscarriages" in John Cotton to Rowland Cotton, 18 June 1697, *CJCJ*, 541; "breaches" in Thomas, *Diary of Samuel Sewall*, 6 Oct. 1697, 1:378. See *CJCJ*, 26–29, 539–40. See the analysis in Sheila McIntyre, "John Cotton Jr.: Wayward Puritan Minister?" in Ian K. Steele and Nancy L. Rhoden, eds., *The Human Tradition in Colonial America* (Wilmington, Del.: Scholarly Resources, 1999), esp. 131–36.
45. John Cotton to Rowland Cotton, 4 Dec. 1695, *CJCJ*, 498; John Cotton to Rowland Cotton, 12 June 1694, *CJCJ*, 441.
46. John Cotton to Rowland Cotton, 18 Feb. 1697/98, *CJCJ*, 548–49. This letter appears to have been written somewhat later than its given date.
47. Thomas, *Diary of Samuel Sewall*, 8–10 Mar. 1697/98, 1:388–89.
48. John Cotton to Joanna Cotton, 6/7 July 1698, *CJCJ*, 564–65.
49. John Cotton to Joanna Cotton, 8 July 1698, *CJCJ*, 567.
50. Rowland Cotton to John Cotton, 25 Apr. 1699, *CJCJ*, 584.

Conclusion

1. Coit to Samuel Blachley Webb, 7 Nov. 1775, in Worthington Chauncey Ford, ed., *Correspondence and Journals of Samuel Blachley Webb* (New York: Wickersham, 1893), 116–18; *Pennsylvania Journal* [Philadelphia], 29 Nov. 1775; Washington to John Hancock, 4 Dec. 1775, in Worthington Chauncey Ford, ed., *The Writings of George Washington* (New York: G. P. Putnam's Sons, 1889), 3:262.
2. Webster, *A Discourse, Delivered at Plymouth, December 22, 1820* ... (Boston: Wells and Lilly, 1821), 10, 92. On historical memory and the Pilgrims, see John Seelye, *Memory's Nation: The Place of Plymouth Rock* (Chapel Hill: University of North Carolina Press, 1998); Margaret Bendroth, *The Last*

Puritans: Mainline Protestants and the Power of the Past (Chapel Hill: University of North Carolina Press, 2015).

3. Samuel Davis, "Notes on Plymouth," *CMHS*, 2nd ser., 3 (1815): 174; James Thacher, *History of the Town of Plymouth* . . . (Boston: Marsh, Capen & Lyon, 1832), 202. On the many meanings that Americans have foisted onto Plymouth Rock and the Pilgrims, see Seelye, *Memory's Nation*.

4. John McPhee, "Travels of the Rock," *New Yorker*, 26 Feb. 1990, 108–17.

5. William Apess, *Eulogy on King Philip* . . . (Boston: s.n., 1836), 10–11.

Index

Italicized page numbers indicate illustrations.